Foucault and the Writing of History

Foucault and the Writing of History

Edited by

JAN GOLDSTEIN

BLACKWELL
Oxford UK & Cambridge USA

First published 1994

Blackwell Publishers
238 Main Street
Cambridge, Massachusetts 02142
USA

108 Cowley Road
Oxford OX4 1JF
UK

Library of Congress Cataloging-in-Publication Data

Foucault and the writing of history / edited by Jan Goldstein.
    p.   cm.
    Papers presented at a conference held at the University of
Chicago, Oct. 24–26, 1991.
    Includes index.
    ISBN 0–631–17007–3 (alk. paper). — ISBN 0–631–17008–1 (pbk.)
    1. Foucault, Michel—Congresses. 2. History—Philosophy—
Congresses. 3. Historiography—Congresses. 4. France—History—
Congresses. I. Goldstein, Jan Ellen.
B2430.F724F685 1994
194—dc20   93–39185
                                                     CIP

British Library Cataloguing in Publication Data
A CIP catalogue record for this book is available from the British Library.

Typeset in 10/12pt Ehrhardt by Photoprint, Torquay, Devon
Printed and bound in Great Britain by Hartnolls Limited, Bodmin, Cornwall

This book is printed on acid-free paper

Contents

List of Contributors

Keith Michael BAKER is J. E. Wallace Sterling Professor in the Humanities and Professor of History at Stanford University. His publications include *Condorcet: From Natural Philosophy to Social Mathematics* (Chicago: University of Chicago Press, 1975), the edited collection *The French Revolution and the Creation of Modern Political Culture*, Vol. 1: *The Political Culture of the Old Regime* (Oxford: Pergamon, 1987), and *Inventing the French Revolution* (Cambridge and New York: Cambridge University Press, 1990).

Robert CASTEL is currently Directeur d'Etudes at the Ecole des Hautes Etudes en Sciences Sociales in Paris. Two of his books on the sociology of psychiatry and psychoanalysis have been translated into English: *The Regulation of Madness: The Origins of Incarceration in France* (Cambridge: Polity Press, 1990) and *The Psychiatric Society* (with Françoise Castel and Anne Lovell; New York: Columbia University Press, 1982). He is presently working on the factors conducive to the breakdown of society and on the transformations taking place in social intervention and social policy.

Roger CHARTIER is Directeur d'Etudes at the Ecole des Hautes Etudes en Sciences Sociales in Paris, where he is presently Director of the Centre Alexandre Koyré. A specialist in cultural history, he has published in English translation *The Cultural Uses of Print in Early Modern France* (Princeton, NJ: Princeton University Press, 1987), *Cultural History: Between Practices and Representations* (Cambridge and Ithaca, NY: Polity Press and Cornell University Press, 1988), *The Cultural Origins of the French Revolution* (Durham, NC: Duke University Press, 1991), and *The Order of Books:*

Readers, Authors, and Libraries in Europe between the Fourteenth and Eighteenth Centuries (Cambridge: Polity Press, 1993).

David COHEN is Professor of Rhetoric at the University of California, Berkeley, where he specializes in ancient Greek society and law. He is the author of *Theft in Athenian Law* (Munich: Beck, 1983) and *Law, Sexuality and Society: The Enforcement of Morals in Classical Athens* (Cambridge and New York: Cambridge University Press, 1991).

Arnold I. DAVIDSON is Professor of Philosophy and a member of the Committee on Conceptual Foundations of Science at the University of Chicago, where he is also Executive Editor of *Critical Inquiry*. He has written widely on Foucault and the history of philosophy, as well as on the history of psychoanalysis, sexuality, and monsters.

François DELAPORTE is currently Professor of Philosophy at the University of Picardy (Amiens, France). A historian of medicine, he has written about the origins of the science of botany in *Nature's Second Kingdom: Explorations of Vegetality in the Eighteenth Century* (Cambridge, MA: MIT Press, 1982) and about the origins of public health in *Disease and Civilization: The Cholera in Paris, 1832* (Cambridge, MA: MIT Press, 1986) and *The History of Yellow Fever: An Essay on the Birth of Tropical Medicine* (Cambridge, MA: MIT Press, 1991).

Laura ENGELSTEIN is Professor of Russian History at Princeton University. She is the author of *Moscow, 1905: Working-Class Organization and Political Conflict* (Stanford, CA: Stanford University Press, 1982) and *The Keys to Happiness: Sex and the Search for Modernity in Fin-de-Siècle Russia* (Ithaca, NY: Cornell University Press, 1992).

Jan GOLDSTEIN is Professor of Modern European History at the University of Chicago, where she is also a member of the Committee on Conceptual Foundations of Science. She is the author of *Console and Classify: The French Psychiatric Profession in the Nineteenth Century* (Cambridge and New York: Cambridge University Press, 1987, 1990) and is currently writing a book on competing conceptions of the self and the politics of selfhood in France during the half-century following the French Revolution.

David M. HALPERIN is Professor of Literature at the Massachusetts Institute of Technology. He is the author of *Before Pastoral: Theocritus and the Ancient Tradition of Bucolic Poetry* (New Haven: Yale University Press,

1983) and *One Hundred Years of Homosexuality and Other Essays on Greek Love* (New York and London: Routledge, 1990) and a coeditor of *Before Sexuality: The Construction of Erotic Experience in the Ancient Greek World* (Princeton, NJ: Princeton University Press, 1990) and *The Lesbian and Gay Studies Reader* (New York and London: Routledge, 1993).

Carla HESSE is Associate Professor of History at the University of California, Berkeley. She is the author of *Publishing and Cultural Politics in Revolutionary Paris (1789–1810)* (Berkeley and Los Angeles: University of California Press, 1991) and a member of the editorial board of *Representations*.

Robert A. NYE is George Lynn Cross Research Professor of History at the University of Oklahoma. His most recent books are *Crime, Madness, and Politics in Modern France: The Medical Concept of National Decline* (Princeton, NJ: Princeton University Press, 1984) and *Masculinity and Male Codes of Honor in Modern France* (New York: Oxford University Press, 1993).

Giovanna PROCACCI is Researcher in Sociology at the University of Milan. She is the author of many articles and of *Gouverner la misère: La question sociale en France, 1789–1848* (Paris: Seuil, 1993). She has been a fellow at the Institute for Advanced Study in Princeton and has taught sociology at the New School for Social Research in New York.

Richard SALLER is Professor of History and Classics at the University of Chicago. His publications in the field of Roman social history include *Personal Patronage under the Early Empire* (Cambridge and New York: Cambridge University Press, 1982), *The Roman Empire: Economy, Society, and Culture* (co-authored with Peter Garnsey; Berkeley and Los Angeles: University of California Press, 1987), and *The Family in Italy from Antiquity to the Present* (coedited with David Kertzer; New Haven: Yale University Press, 1991).

John E. TOEWS is Professor of History and Director of the Program in the Comparative History of Ideas at the University of Washington in Seattle. He is author of *Hegelianism: The Path Toward Dialectical Humanism* (Cambridge and New York: Cambridge University Press, 1980) and has written on the history of psychoanalysis, contemporary historiographical theory, and cultural politics in Prussia during the 1840s.

Acknowledgments

The essays in this volume were all presented in earlier versions at a conference, "Foucault and the Writing of History Today," held at the University of Chicago on October 24–6, 1991. I would like to express my gratitude to the Florence J. Gould Foundation for its generous funding of that event and to the French Consulate in Chicago and the Division of the Social Sciences of the University of Chicago for supplying auxiliary aid. Two graduate student assistants, Stephanie Stamm and Cherilyn Lacy, provided indispensable support in a variety of chores connected with the organization of the conference and the preparation of the book manuscript. The editors at Basil Blackwell, in particular John Davey and (at an earlier stage) Virginia Murphy, contributed their sustained and sustaining enthusiasm for the book project.

Introduction

Jan Goldstein

Among the aspects of Michel Foucault that defied easy categorization was his identity as a compound philosopher-and-historian. Initially this strange admixture prompted both groups to disown him: baffled philosophers typically explained away Foucault's eccentricities by pronouncing him a historian, while historians disconcerted by his unorthodox methods conveniently wrote him off as a philosopher. Still, of these two intertwined Foucauldian identity elements, one proved more congenial to his audience than the other; and, hence, it is the philosopher who has been the more intensively studied. Foucault's early grounding in phenomenology and structuralism, his intellectual relationship to Nietzsche and to Heidegger, his philosophy of history (including such issues as the continuity or periodic rupture of the historical process and the place of the intentional actor in history), the implications of his theory for political practice – all these topics have rightly attracted a great deal of attention. An international conference held in Paris in January 1988, the first such posthumous consideration of his work, reflected this general preference for the philosophic Foucault, taking as its title "Michel Foucault philosophe."[1]

By contrast, the significance of Foucault's work for the writing of history by practicing academic historians – those quasi-official keepers of the modern collective memory – has never received extended discussion.[2] It is clear, if only from book introductions, where scholarly authors characteristically acknowledge their intellectual debts, that in the past couple of decades Foucault's ideas have influenced many historical subfields: intellectual history, the history of science and medicine, the history of penal institutions, the history of sexuality. It is furthermore clear that Foucault has been a critical force in moving certain of these subfields from the remote margins to the very center of historians' current concerns.[3] But such introductory remarks rarely specify or analyze the nature of Foucault's contribution to the historical undertaking in question, and their piecemeal nature precludes a grasp of the larger historiographical picture.[4]

This volume is the first attempt to address at length the issue of how Foucault's vision has been affecting the professional writing of history. Not all of its fourteen contributors are "professional historians" in the sense of being employed by university departments of history. But all pursue their intellectual endeavors in academic settings, and all – including the two sociologists, one classicist,[5] and one philosopher among them – are attuned to the historical dimensions, broadly construed, of their work: they study past eras, and they grapple with the issue of change, or the lack of it, over time. The contributors are predominantly Americans, but the presence of four Europeans enables the collection to shed some light on cross-cultural differences in the academic engagement with Foucault. And the group cast their net widely, together commenting on virtually all of Foucault's major works and many of his less well-known writings.

How is the relationship between Foucault's work and the so-called conventional practice of history to be characterized? If we listen to the voices of historians during the 1970s, and to that of Foucault himself, it becomes immediately obvious that the relationship can be very variously glossed. Sometimes a historian can be heard asserting the utter incompatibility of the two, as in this American comment on the epistemic ruptures that Foucault postulated in *The Order of Things*:

> The thesis is meant to shock. It is a general attack against history, against the historical mentality. Foucault refuses to conceive of intellectual history as a process of change.[6]

Sometimes the possibility of coexistence is conceded but made dependent on the strict condition that Foucault and conventional historians be placed in hermetically sealed compartments, each carrying out a personally congenial assignment in splendid isolation from the other. Thus, noting that many of the arguments of *Madness and Civilization* "fly in the face of empirical evidence," an American historian of early modern Europe proposed to his colleagues the following way of salvaging both Foucault and the historical profession:

> [R]ather than get lost in Foucault's labyrinth, we can perhaps learn to live, at least temporarily, with a double truth. Following the medieval Averroists, I would like to suggest that something may be true in philosophy but not necessarily so in history; or, to use less provocative language, that Foucault could be right about language and the human condition, but wrong about the

route by which we have arrived where we are. In this way the historian can hope to make his own peculiar contribution even if he does not reevaluate the foundations of epistemology.[7]

Not all historians were, however, so pessimistic about the prospect of forging some kind of union between Foucault's insights and the historian's craft. At the far end of the spectrum, one (perhaps not coincidentally a Frenchman) even joyfully hailed Foucault's particular philosophical medium as providing the historian with a long-craved, complete, and perfect nourishment:

> Once certain probably inevitable misconceptions are cleared away, we discover in this difficult body of thought something very simple and very new that can only gratify historians and make them feel immediately at home. It is something that they were hoping for and indeed already doing in a confused fashion. Foucault is the fully realized historian, the realization of history.[8]

Foucault himself, by contrast, neither celebrated nor damned the implications of his work for that of professional historians but offered his own distinctive slant on the matter. He distrusted the academic pursuit of both history and philosophy, regarding these as "disciplines" in the double meaning of the term: highly structured institutions for the production of particular bodies of knowledge, and instances of the typically insidious exercise of power in modern society.[9] With this *parti pris* in mind, he suggested that the adoption of a Foucauldian project would metamorphose – certainly for the better and perhaps beyond recognition – the intellectual production of both groups of academic practitioners:

> It seems to me that "historians" and "philosophers" could come together around this notion [of the relations between power and knowledge] and its possible application. The result would not, however, be an "interdisciplinary encounter" but rather a common labor of people seeking to "de-discipline" themselves.[10]

I offer these four quotations only to show the wide range of possible positions on the general issue of Foucault and history-writing, not because the quotations offer a map on which the essays in this volume can be neatly situated. While some of the contributors to the volume engage in criticism of Foucault on the grounds of factual accuracy and others tend in the direction of a celebration of Foucauldian history in the manner of Paul Veyne, most occupy intermediate, interstitial, and highly qualified positions. Nor do the essays adhere to any standard format. Rather, in ruminating on

Foucault and history-writing, the contributors have followed their own styles and intellectual inclinations: some prefer to stay on a philosophical plane, analyzing Foucault's texts in detail; others adopt a "hands on" approach, presenting themselves as historians at work and exploring the mutual (and often messy) relations between a specific piece of their own history-writing and Foucault's views; some express keen interest in the political implications of history in a Foucauldian vein; one attempts a thought-experiment in narrating a major historical event *as if* he were Foucault.

Let me then provide here a double rehearsal of the contents of the volume. In the first run-through, I will explain the order of presentation of the essays on the basis of their thematic affinities. In the second, I will discuss some of the general theoretical issues that the essays raise across the boundaries of thematic similarity.

I THE FOUR PARTS OF THE VOLUME

The volume begins with Greco-Roman antiquity, the most distant of the historical epochs that Foucault treated yet the one that he turned to latest in his career. The two essays in Part I, both focused on the multi-volume *History of Sexuality*, are related to one another as opposing sides in a debate or, at least, as an encounter of disparate sensibilities.

David M. Halperin wants to recover the radicalness of Foucault's concept of discursive sexuality, which he believes is in danger of losing its edge and being assimilated to the far more prosaic notion that cultures represent sexuality in different ways. In his view, the radical Foucauldian concept provides the undergirding for a truly "gay science" – an epistemology which would enable gay men and women to assume the authorship of their sexual experience instead of appearing as objects of the expert knowledge of moralists and physicians. Thus Halperin presents his contribution to this volume as an example of literary scholarship that, while "traditional, non-Foucauldian" in itself, can nonetheless advance a Foucauldian politics. He offers a reading of the *Erôtes*, a late antique Greek text attributed to Lucian that takes the form of a mock-philosophical dialogue on the relative merits of women and boys as vehicles of male sexual pleasure. Deftly teasing out the cultural assumptions behind the statements, Halperin seeks to show that our contemporary categories of heterosexuality and homosexuality – whether taken to denote a personal core identity or even a stable sexual orientation – were simply unthinkable to the ancient Greeks. Disclaiming any intent to idealize ancient Greek life, he marshals his analysis of the *Erôtes* to, in his words, "destabilize the binary opposition between heterosexuality and homosexuality" that obtains in our own society.

If Halperin reads in a frankly engaged mode, David Cohen and Richard Saller present themselves in a more neutral register as social historians using their professional expertise to assess the accuracy of Foucault's interpretation of certain classical texts. From this standpoint, they contest two of Foucault's claims: that Greco-Roman culture fostered the free and aesthetic self-fashioning of the individual; and that the principal arenas of such self-fashioning were homoeroticism in ancient Greece and symmetrical, companionate marriage in imperial Rome. According to Cohen and Saller, Foucault can sustain such claims only by consistently ignoring the state regulation and hierarchies of power that pervaded classical community life and political thought. In other words, looking at classical antiquity through his own rose-colored optic, Foucault neglects to point out that, while the Greeks tolerated sex between males, they regarded only the active partner in such a relation as honorable; and that, while Roman imperial authors may have praised conversation between spouses more than did their republican precedessors, they nonetheless depicted the wife's conversational repertory as limited to parroting the views of her husband. Cohen and Saller call attention not only to the historical oversights upon which Foucault's thesis of self-fashioning relies but also to the indifference to women's status and self-realization and even to the elitism (the lower classes are said to have first learned about the satisfactions of marriage from their betters) that it, wittingly or not, entails.

Part II of the volume addresses the theme of the constitution of the subject, which occupied Foucault most conspicuously in his late works but which can with little strain be read back into the early ones as well – as Foucault himself did, in one of his characteristic bouts of reappraisal.[11] Arnold Davidson takes up this theme as it appears in its *locus classicus*, the second and third volumes of the *History of Sexuality*. By situating those texts in the context of the recent French historiography of antiquity (Paul Veyne, Pierre Hadot, Jean-Pierre Vernant) – a historiography whose authors Foucault numbered among his colleagues and friends and which nurtured his own forays into this field – Davidson seeks to revise two prevailing misconceptions about Foucault's accounts of the Greco-Roman world. He argues, first, that those accounts are not primarily about sex but rather about ethics; and, second, that despite Foucault's insistence upon such motifs as an aesthetics of experience and the care of the self his ethics is neither egoistic nor a new variety of dandyism but rather features a subject constituted though philosophic *askesis*. The Foucauldian construction of ethics also, Davidson contends, opens up entirely novel possibilities for writing the history of ethics. Because Foucault distinguished four separate aspects of ethics – the part of the self regarded as the relevant domain for ethical judgment; the way in which one understands one's subordination to moral rules; the work that one performs on oneself to effect one's transformation into an ethical subject; and the telos, or mode of being at which one aims in behaving ethically – he endowed the history of ethics with unprecedented suppleness and ensured it a purview far wider than the standard history of moral codes.

Carla Hesse takes up the issue of the constitution of the modern female subject. She deliberately avoids approaching this task by applying Foucault's theories of subjectivity to primary source materials, regarding such a procedure as a borrowing from the positivistic social sciences. She finds similarly unacceptable the effort to compensate for Foucault's own lack of interest in the status of women by simply writing women into his theories. Instead, Hesse devises the more oblique strategy of comparing two texts, Foucault's 1984 essay "What is Enlightenment?" and Isabelle de Charrière's 1795 novel *Three Women*. Though the two may seem at first glance unrelated, Hesse shows that they are both in fact deliberate rewritings of texts by Immanuel Kant, that canonical modern explorer of the human subject. Foucault rewrites Kant, says Hesse, by posing as Kant's continuator and inflecting the aim of his critical philosophy so that it no longer establishes the limits of the autonomous subject, but rather discloses the radical historical contingency of those putative limits and thus points the way to their transgression. Charrière rewrites Kant by hypothetically casting the three women of her title as Kant's autonomous subjects and and then showing the utter incompatibility of that "universal" ontological status with the life situation and legal status of the late eighteenth-century European female. For Hesse, Charrière's novel thus in some manner foreshadows Foucault's essay and makes, *avant la lettre*, a Foucauldian point about the constitution of female subjectivity: that, once universal norms about the human person have been called into question, "we must," as Charrière puts it, "be content with tacking."

My own essay moves the focus of the investigation from Kant to Victor Cousin, a nineteenth-century French philosopher who, identifying himself as the continuator of Descartes but also making reference to certain affinities with Kant, placed enormous emphasis on his conceptualization of the self, or *moi*. Though derivative as a thinker, Cousin was an academic entrepreneur of genius and succeeded in establishing his brand of philosophy throughout the centralized lycée system, even adding a section called "Psychology" to the very beginning of the philosophy curriculum. As a result, all the lycée students of France received instruction about the *moi* and learned the introspective techniques needed to study it at first hand. This state-supplied inculcation in selfhood, organized along class and gender lines, thus seems to qualify as a "technology of the self" in the sense in which Foucault introduced that term in *The Use of Pleasure*. Yet Foucault explicitly excluded philosophy of mind from among those practices that he regarded as technologies of the self. Why? In seeking to answer that question, my essay also examines the shift in the vocabulary of subject-making – from *subjection* to *subjectivation* – that occurs in Foucault's writings.

John Toews rounds out the discussion of the constitution of the subject by considering Foucault's rather tortured relationship to the Freudian subject. Over the course of his career, Foucault returned repeatedly to Freud, glossing his theoretical contribution in a dazzling variety of ways, though almost always with hostile intent. Toews traces the metamorphoses that Foucault's Freud underwent from the Frenchman's earliest phenomenological works, where the influence of German philosophy upon him was strongest, through the archaeological approach in the *Histoire de la folie*, *The Order of Things*, and *The Birth of the Clinic*, and the genealogical one in the first volume of *The History of Sexuality*. Beneath the successive transformations of these three phases, Toews also discerns a persistent thematic continuity: Foucault's critique of psychoanalysis always hinged upon his contention that the apparent psychoanalytic attack on the ruling conventions of nineteenth-century culture obscured the confinement of Freud's science within those very conventions. Psychoanalysis, Foucault insisted in different registers throughout his career, remained prisoner to its failure to confront its own history. In Foucault's genealogical phase, this imprisonment entailed an inability to conceive of the subject as anything but a "natural 'given' whose 'truth' could be 'discovered,' whose essential core could be 'liberated,' and whose ultimate secrets could be elicited and scientifically retold." Toews concludes by suggesting what Foucault's long intellectual wrestling match with Freud can tell the historian who embarks on the post-Foucauldian project of writing the history of psychoanalysis.

Part III of the volume explores the history of medicine and the biomedical aspects of the history of sexuality. It begins with François Delaporte's analysis of the *The Birth of the Clinic*. Writing as an unabashed partisan of the archaeological approach to medicine that Foucault pioneered in that book, Delaporte seeks to pinpoint rigorously the features that define it. To this end, he carefully compares and contrasts archaeology with the three alternatives from which Foucault took pains to distance himself: the contemporary late eighteenth-century accounts of the advent of clinical medicine which depicted it as a simple return to the truth of the Hippocratic method after a long period of metaphysical error and obfuscation; the twentieth-century historiography of medicine which, Delaporte contends, fundamentally echoed the recurrence motif found in the contemporary rendition of the birth of the clinic; and the school of so-called epistemological history of science and medicine identified in France with the work of Foucault's teacher, Georges Canguilhem, which assessed past forms of science in terms of their role in bringing about mature forms and thus also gave implicit credence to the motif of recurrence. Delaporte stresses archaeology's antipathy to recurrence – its insistence on the novelty of each historical moment, on the nonexistence of primordial experience and on the disjunctive layers of discursive formations whose rules construct all objects relationally so that even superficially similar objects of different historical provenance (for example, the clinical method of Hippocrates and that of Xavier Bichat) must be radically different.

The point of departure for Robert Nye's essay is his research on masculinity in nineteenth-century France and, in particular the *fin-de-siècle* biology of human reproduction. What interests Nye is a persistent ambiguity in Foucault's work on a fundamental issue of scientific epistemology: did Foucault (like his teacher Canguilhem) maintain a distinction between the "noble" sciences such as physics and chemistry in which objective truth was possible, and the "dubious" human sciences such as medicine and psychiatry in which it was not; or did his later concept of discourse effectively erase such a distinction and give no domain of knowledge superior credentials over any other? Somewhat surprisingly, given the fact that it belongs to Foucault's late work, the first volume of *The History of Sexuality* reaffirms the objective/non-objective distinction in order to contrast a supposedly irreproachable nineteenth-century biology of reproduction with a highly suspect "medicine of sex" (for example, sexology, the psychiatric construct of sexual perversion, the psychoanalytic talking cure). Yet Nye's own research turned up a reproductive biology shot through with the most obvious – and sometimes comical – cultural biases, one which could even anthropomorphize the sperm and the ovum and ascribe appropriate gender traits to each. His essay demonstrates the degree to which this scientific specialty, developed during a period of highly publicized demographic crisis in France, was, *pace* Foucault, driven by the imperatives of Foucauldian bio-power.

Part IV turns to the liberal state, a topic which in this context necessitates looking not only at Foucault's book-length works but at the interviews and lectures collected in *Power/Knowledge*[12] and the lectures on governmentality that Foucault gave at the Collège de France in 1978 and 1979, shortly before his interests shifted to ancient Greece and Rome.[13] The first two essays in Part IV discuss the French Revolution, an event generally regarded as one of the points of origin of the liberal state. Since the field of French revolutionary historiography has been intensely lively in recent decades, it is hardly surprising that one of its central controversies should have spilled over into these essays; hence, by way of background, a brief word needs to be said about that historiography.

In challenging the once prevailing Marxian orthodoxy on the topic, the French historian François Furet insisted that the Revolution and its origins be interpreted not in socioeconomic terms but in political ones. Furthermore, Furet and the other historians who joined his revisionist effort gave a particular construction to the category of the political, defining it in terms of political discourse and of a new political "imaginary" set into play by the Enlightenment and the eighteenth-century quarrels between the Crown and the *parlementaires.* According to the revisionists, the revolutionaries were able to seize power not because they represented the new economic rulership of society but because a new political discourse had enabled alternatives to absolutism to be imagined and because, as events began to unfold, those who had embraced and could deploy this discourse seized the power to interpret them.

Of the two contributors of essays on the Revolution in this volume, Keith Baker has long been associated with the revisionists, while Roger Chartier is an opponent of that school (though, as he notes here, not one who favors reinstating Marxian categories of analysis). Yet Baker and Chartier both claim Foucault as a supporter of their distinctly different sides of the debate.

Chartier's wide-ranging essay brings together the many remarks on the Revolution scattered throughout Foucault's writings. Invoking Michel de Certeau as a guide to his reading of Foucault, Chartier argues that "discourse" should not be taken as an all-embracing term in Foucault's work but that "practice" should be given at least equal and possibly even top billing. Chartier carefully specifies that he considers practice neither more "real" nor more "social" than discourse. But he nonetheless insists that the two are not reducible to one another or obedient to the same kind of logic; a radical gap separates the "formality of practices" from the rules organizing the positivity of discourses. Chartier's Foucault would, then, warn us against the "intellectualist" interpretation of the Revolution advanced by the Furet school. He would, for example, characterize the Enlightenment not as a corpus of discourses but rather as the name given to a "set of multiple and intermingled practices guided by a concern for common utility which aimed at a new management of spaces and populations, whose mechanisms (intellectual, institutional, social, and so on) imposed a complete reorganization of the systems for the perception and the organization of the social world."

Baker takes a very different tack in responding to the pairing of Foucault and the French Revolution. Observing that Foucault returned again and again to the Revolution in his works without ever attempting to narrate it or to treat it as a distinct phenomenon, Baker embarks upon a spirited attempt in the subjunctive mode: to sketch the Revolution as Foucault would have done, had he been so inclined. This self-imposed assignment provides Baker with an unusual vantage point from which to analyze Foucault's approach both to the general business of history-writing and to the specific set of historical changes wrought by the Revolution. Why, he asks, did Foucault shy away from the task of treating the Revolution on its own terms? What would have been his requirements for such a treatment, if he had overcome his reluctance to undertake it? Baker stresses that the Revolution was an outright quarrel about the form of political sovereignty in France, and that one of Foucault s central theoretical contributions was to demote sovereignty from the preeminent place it was believed to hold in modern society, choosing instead to highlight and to trace the development of that newer, more covert mode of exercising power that he called surveillance or discipline. But how, then, could the Foucauldian account explain why sovereignty did not simply wither away in the nineteenth century or subsequently, why it has continued to function in tandem with discipline? Baker examines Foucault's answers to that question and finds them wanting; and by offering an alternative answer – one consonant with Foucault's ideas – he deepens and nuances the understanding of liberalism that a Foucauldian perspective can provide. Throughout his essay, he points out the affinities between his hypothetical Foucauldian French Revolution and Furet's historiography of that same event – in particular, the commitment of both to "thinking" an event of even world-shaking proportions in non-teleological, radically contingent terms.

Moving forward from the Revolution, Giovanna Procacci's essay uses Foucauldian strategies to describe how the discursive domain of "the social" was carved out in France during the period 1789–1848 and how poverty was conceptualized as the "social question" *par excellence*. Procacci notes a kind of lost opportunity in Foucault: though in the *Histoire de la folie* he spoke of poverty in the same breath as madness when discussing the breakdown of the catch-all Old Regime institution of the *hôpital général*, he never exploited this historical conjucture to undertake the theorizing of poverty as he did the theorizing of madness. Following Foucault's lead, Procacci argues that the *hôpital général* succumbed to the pressure of the new eighteenth-century science of political economy, which transformed the poor – never a "natural object" to begin with – from inexplicably blighted people requiring charity into people whose condition could be blamed upon their own lack of industry. Poverty and labor were, in other words, indissolubly joined in the discourse of liberalism. But, once the free labor market created by the French Revolution had violated the expectations of political economists by failing to provide jobs for all the poor who wanted them, such an individualistic interpretation of poverty could no longer be sustained. Procacci traces out the intricate discursive logic by which poverty then came to be construed in social terms, ascribed to "a difference in sociability or in the level of socialization" that could be removed or, in Foucauldian language, normalized through the discipline of public hygiene. Thus socially construed, poverty was, Procacci contends, effectively depoliticized. Its existence as a manifest material inequality no longer directly challenged the claims for the equality of citizens made by the liberal state, and political liberalism could thus be maintained and safeguarded. From a different angle, then, Procacci's essay explores the issue – already raised in this volume by Baker's essay – of the relationship between liberalism (as a mode of sovereignty) and what Foucault called the disciplinary apparatus.

That same issue is taken up again, and more directly, in Laura Engelstein's essay on imperial and Soviet Russia. Engelstein poses the question: can Foucault, who focused his attention on the origins of liberalism and the "small" and deceptive tyrannical mechanisms embedded within that mode of government, help us to understand "great" postliberal tyrannies, such as communist regimes? Engelstein notes that, in his treatment of Western polities, Foucault established a rough developmental progression whereby absolutist monarchies gave way to enlightened despotisms employing the administrative regulatory devices of the *Polizeistaat*, which in turn gave way to juridically liberal states making unacknowledged use of disciplinary power. But such a progression does not fit the Russian case, where all three modalities coincided during the nineteenth century. Examining key instances of the Russian–Soviet handling of homosexuality and abortion, Engelstein suggests that the long maturation of a rule-of-law state in the West as opposed to its truncated and incomplete development in Russia had important implications for the functioning of the disciplinary apparatus in each setting – implications that Foucault's own analysis, dealing exclusively with the West, occludes. And, on the basis of her integration of Foucauldian categories into a comparative perspective, she singles out the balance between law and discipline as the conceptual heart of Foucault's political theory and recasts the definition of liberalism to mean the "replace[ment of] the alliance between discipline and the administrative state with a configuration that frames the operation of discipline within the confines of the law."

Robert Castel's essay, focused on the strategy of "problematization" in Foucault, provides a fitting conclusion both to the volume as a whole and to the section on the liberal state. As a sociologist, Castel regards "problematization" – a way of conceptualizing phenomena in the present through recourse to selected historical materials – as Foucault's gift of history to the non-historian. That strategy is, in Castel's view, different from the approach conventionally taken by working historians (indeed, part of its credentials is precisely that it adds something new to the conventional historical account), but, at the same time, its validity hinges upon its compatibility with historians' accounts. Castel illustrates problematization, and its intensely problematic nature, first by reference to Foucault's *Histoire de la folie* and then by reference to his own research in progress on the economic, social, and personal precariousness of existence in western Europe in the 1980s and 1990s. In this latter capacity, he offers a Foucauldian perspective on the most recent mutation of the liberal state: the democratic welfare state in an era when longstanding expectations of continued economic growth and nearly full employment have simply failed to materialize. Under such circumstances, a new population of the perennially unemployed and of young people unable to enter the workforce defies the logic of the classic system of social protection. Because this population is capable of working it is ineligible for traditional forms of assistance, but because it has been rejected by the labor market it receives no coverage from employment-based insurance programs. It confronts society with what appears to be a wholly new problem. Yet the problem is new, Castel stresses, only against the backdrop of the social safety nets developed since the nineteenth century. It is also very old – indeed Castel suggests that a problematization *à la* Foucault would pinpoint its origin in the mid-fourteenth-century English Statute of Laborers, which condemned almsgiving to able-bodied indigents. Castel thus recommends the strategy of problematization as a way of sizing up our present situation, of locating it by reference to its elements of novelty and of continuity.

II CROSS-CUTTING THEMES

Across the substantive themes that define the four parts of the volume, the essays raise certain general questions about Foucault's work and its relation to history-writing. Some of these have already been alluded to. For example, several of our authors ask how Foucault construed his own concept of discourse and how rigorously he traced out its implications. Robert Nye is concerned with the issue of whether Foucault believed that discourses could have different degrees of truth-value and, in particular, whether a distinction between sciences and pseudosciences could be logically maintained in a Foucauldian universe. The disagreement between Keith Baker and Roger Chartier turns on another aspect of the discourse question: to what degree was discourse a kind of "master concept" for

Foucault, one which eradicated the old oppositions between theory and practice, text and context? When in 1969 Foucault described archaeology as seeking "to reveal relations between discursive formations and non-discursive domains (institutions, political events, economic practices and processes),"[14] was he mired in internal contradiction? Could there ever be, in terms of his own assumptions, a truly "non-discursive" domain – a reality that we encounter directly and whose particular objects are not themselves constituted within a discursive formation? Or did Foucault's formulations about the *non discursif* reflect not confusion but rather his own intuitive embrace of a completely coherent intellectual position, later articulated by de Certeau, which operated with the pair of categories "discourse" and "practice," emphasizing their irreducibility to one another? Foucault did, after all, speak in 1970 of a gradation (*dénivellation*) between discourses, between those casually uttered during the course of the day and disappearing in the moment of utterance and those that, through reiteration, transformation, and discussion, gave rise to new verbal acts.[15] This concept lends plausibility to the idea that he believed that analogous formal differences distinguished discourses from practices. Baker is a proponent of the first view (the internally contradictory nature of the *non discursif* in Foucault), Chartier of the second. If Chartier's Foucault is an acolyte of de Certeau, Baker's inclines toward the Derridean axiom "il n'y pas de hors-texte."

A second general theme running through the volume concerns the place in Foucault's work of the ethical project upon which he embarked in the studies of classical antiquity that form the second and third volumes of *The History of Sexuality* – and in particular its relation to the genealogical project he had earlier undertaken in *Discipline and Punish* and the first volume of *The History of Sexuality*. David Cohen and Richard Saller see a sharp break, and a turn for the worse, between the two projects. In their view, Foucault's focus on ethics entailed an abandonment of his previous commitment to situating discourse institutionally. It led him down a garden path of sorts: enamored of the self-fashioning that he believed the ancients had recommended and inattentive to the hierarchies of power that severely limited their possibilities for achieving it, he ended up, according to Cohen and Saller, producing a romantic idealization of the Greco-Roman world. My own discussion of Foucault's shift in the vocabulary of subject-making – from his grim play on the word *subjection* in the genealogical phase to his choice of the unmarked *subjectivation* in the ethical phase – tends to support at least a weak version of Cohen and Saller's claim that a new sensibility guided Foucault's ethically oriented studies.

By contrast, Arnold Davidson argues – as did Foucault himself – that the ethical project was fully consonant with its archaeological and genealogical predecessors and that together the three formed a coherent intellectual whole. And, while not addressing the problem directly, John Toews offers a formulation that resolves it by means of a Hegelian-style *Aufhebung*. Foucault's genealogical critique of psychoanalysis revealed, says Toews, that a lack of insight into the historical circumstances of its own production trapped psychoanalysis within the very conventions it pretended to destroy; the most flagrant sign of this entrapment was its unquestioned belief that the subject was a natural "given" whose "truth" could be discovered. Toews implies that Foucault's ethical project flowed dialectically from such a critique. The impasse in which psychoanalysis found itself could be surmounted by conceiving of the subject as, in Toews's words, "an aesthetically fashioned work grounded in ethical choices made in the context of knowledge of the historicity of subject-production."

Perhaps the most persistent issue to emerge in this volume, spontaneously addressed over and over in the course of the essays, is the meaning of Foucauldian genealogy – which was, after all, Foucault's "substitute" for history in its traditional guise. Almost always making their comments on genealogy in passing, the contributors have lighted upon different but compatible and, indeed, mutually enriching aspects of it. If a composite definition of genealogy were derived from this volume, it might look as follows. (1) In terms of Foucault's intellectual development, genealogy arises from the background of archaeology, a basically "vertical" conception of successive cultural forms, stacked one upon the other so as to emphasize their self-containment and radical difference from one another (Delaporte, Toews). (2) Against archaeology, genealogy accentuates the "horizontal" dimension: its hallmarks are "eventality" and narrative process (Toews, Baker). (3) Yet, while the components of a genealogy are knit together in the manner of narrative, that narrative is resolutely non-teleological: events are eruptions; outcomes are local and radically contingent, never adhering to a global necessity (Baker, Chartier). (4) Underlying the contingency of genealogy is a conceptualization of the historical field as composed of scarce and heterogeneous elements whose malleability enables unusual combinations (Procacci, Toews). (5) Genealogy, which is the first step of problematization, interrogates the past from the vantage point of the needs and perplexities of the present situation (Castel, Procacci). (6) In so doing, it is the expression of a debunking impulse: it debunks the most cherished values and institutions of present-day liberal culture by demonstrating that they originated in "mere" historical contingency and in petty or ignoble practices comically incommensurate with the loftiness usually ascribed to them (Goldstein). (7) It is also the expression of a transgressive impulse: by recovering the historical contingencies that gave rise to those supposedly timeless, metaphysical structures that stake out the limits of the human subject, it challenges us to question those limits and, ultimately, to violate them (Hesse).

III BY WAY OF CONCLUSION

In general terms, then, what does this volume tell us about the way Foucault's perspectives have been influencing the practice of history-writing? Primarily, I think, it argues for the accessibility of Foucault. By this I mean that working historians who represent a quite wide variety of epistemological, methodological, and political positions – and who have serious disagreements with Foucault on one or another point – can nonetheless connect with him intellectually and creatively assimilate his projects to their own. Foucault is not, to be sure, within the reach of every historian: those who believe that for each segment of the past there is a single, objectively true narrative that "gets it right" will find him only an annoyance. But a historian need not be, at the other extreme, a purist who embraces the most radical reading of Foucault (for example, the utter antipathy between Foucauldian scholarship and the practice of a historical "discipline" in a traditional institutional setting) in order to find him a refreshing and consistently stimulating guide to asking historical questions and conceptualizing historical phenomena. There is something in Foucault's very unsettled nature – his famous changes of mind; his alternations between an icily cold, critical eye and shows of passion, between disdain for our old, self-deceptive liberal humanism and attachment to it – that fits the unsettled world in which we write history today.

Part I

Eros and the Family in Classical Antiquity

1

Historicizing the Subject of Desire: Sexual Preferences and Erotic Identities in the Pseudo-Lucianic *Erôtes*

David M. Halperin

It is now so long that we have been accustomed to speak of "sexuality" as a "discourse" that it may be difficult to recall quite how shocking, how literally incredible that notion was when Michel Foucault originally formulated it in the first volume of his *History of Sexuality*. Our current fluency in the language of sexual discursivity, however, testifies less in my opinion to the putative success with which we have managed to transform our ways of thinking so as to accommodate Foucault's initially counter-intuitive hypothesis than it does to the slow, unconscious labor whereby we have in time assimilated that hypothesis to earlier, deeply entrenched habits of thought. If there is a tide in the affairs of men, as Shakespeare's Brutus says, there is something like an undertow or a backwash in the fortunes of critical terms and concepts. New critical vocabularies are helplessly overwhelmed and reabsorbed – or "recuperated," as we used to say, before that term lost its conceptual specificity – by older and more familiar ones, while prior epistemologies and methodologies continually resurface within the intellectual framework of even the most radical innovations.

Those of us who typically depend for our understanding of contemporary critical concepts on what Northrop Frye once called "the psychology of rumor"[1] may often find ourselves tempted to believe that we can infer the meaning of a new term from its recognizable lexical associations, from its ostensible semantic adjacency to other words with which we are already conversant. That tendency produces a kind of terminological drift whereby the vocabulary coined to articulate conceptual advances is gradually resignified until it ultimately comes to designate the very concepts it was invented to displace. The most spectacular recent casualty of such a process is of course Deconstruction, which in its current usage has come to mean very nearly the same thing as the New Criticism: common academic parlance has detached the verb *to deconstruct* from its original meaning and invested it instead with a series of progressively – or, perhaps it would be more accurate to say, regressively – normalizing significations, starting with "demystify," ranging through "dismantle," "criticize," and "analyze," and devolving finally into "unpack," "explicate," or even simply "explain." Likewise, "intertextuality" has become little more than a pretentious equivalent to "literary allusion" or "source criticism," as Julia Kristeva complained already two decades ago.[2]

In a similar fashion, Foucault's notion that sexuality is a discourse – or, to be more precise, that it is a discursive formation, the cumulative effect of multiple discourses – has been widely understood in such a way as to reconcile that notion to the non-technical, pre-theoretical meanings of both "sexuality" and "discourse," thereby preserving and even reanimating those meanings within an ostensibly Foucauldian framework of analysis. Many historians, for example, as well as many scholars working in the interdisciplinary field of lesbian/gay studies, have tended to assume that the principal achievement of Foucault's unfinished *History of Sexuality* was to have provided a precise and detailed account of how various societies *represent* sexuality *in* their discourses, as if sexuality were some ubiquitous natural reality outside of, or even prior to, discourse, and as if discourse itself were some wholly transparent cognitive or linguistic medium, rather than a highly specialized, evolved, and evolving technology for producing truths – including truths of experience. That tendency to treat Foucault's startling determination to write the history of sexuality "from the viewpoint of a history of discourses"[3] as if such a project amounted to nothing more than a banal preoccupation with the *representation* of sexuality *in* discourse has had the effect of authorizing the (re)production, under the apparent aegis of Foucauldian historicism, of an entire series of ancient positivistic distinctions between material things and mental representations, objects and words, bodies and minds, nature and culture – precisely those metaphysical dichotomies that Foucault's radical holism had in fact enabled him, and might have enabled other historians of sexuality, to evade. A second effect of attributing to Foucault such pre-Foucauldian conceptions of both "sexuality" and "discourse" has been to allow his would-be followers to resume their old habit of situating historical ruptures merely within sexual categories, rather than between sexual subjects themselves, and thus to license them to continue speaking and thinking of premodern sexual formations as "sexualities" – as quaint historical variants, that is, of a timeless and universal entity. And yet Foucault himself famously contended that what we call sexuality nowadays is in fact a distinctively modern, bourgeois production,[4] that it is not some biological or physiological reality but an unprecedented historical "apparatus" (*dispositif*)[5] for the organization of subjectivities, social relations, and knowledges – "a great surface network," as he puts it, "in which the stimulation of bodies, the intensification of pleasures, the incitement to discourse, the formation of special knowledges, the strengthening of controls and resistances, are linked to one another, in accordance with a few major strategies of knowledge and power."[6]

Foucault's attempt to refute what he calls "the repressive hypothesis" is continuous with that claim. The targets of his anti-Lacanian critique are not limited to the conventional image of the Victorian era as a period in which the discourses of sex were oppressively silenced instead of explosively produced, or to the conceptualization of power as a force of negation and prohibition instead of as a force of production and possibility. What Foucault also aims to contest by means of his attack on "the repressive hypothesis" is the common representation of sexuality as an eternal, universal presence in history, a cultural invariant whose flamboyant historical variations supposedly reflect only the differential impact on sexuality of the various mechanisms employed in different societies to *repress* it; such a representation of sexuality, as Foucault remarks in volume 2 of *The History of Sexuality*,[7] has the unfortunate effect of situating desire outside the field of human history altogether.[8] By contrast, Foucault refuses to consider sexuality or desire exterior to historical configurations of power, knowledge, and subjectivity. For him sexuality is neither "a kind of natural given which power tries to hold in check" nor "an obscure domain which knowledge tries gradually to uncover."[9] Foucault describes sexuality, rather, as "an especially dense transfer point for relations of power,"[10] indeed as "the sum of effects produced in bodies, behaviors, and social relations by a certain apparatus that derives from a complex political technology."[11] And he emphasizes, accordingly, that his own "history of sexuality" is not to be "a 'history of mentalities' that would take account of bodies only through the manner in which they have been perceived and given meaning and value; but a 'history of bodies' and [of] the manner in which what is most material and most vital in them has been invested"[12] by knowledge and power.

The history of sexuality, as Foucault conceives it, then, is *not* a history of the representations, categories, cultural articulations, or collective and individual expressions of some determinate entity called sexuality but an inquiry into the historical emergence of sexuality itself, an attempt to explain how it happened that in the eighteenth and nineteenth centuries sexuality gradually came into existence as a conjunction of strategies for ordering social relations, authorizing specialized knowledges, licensing expert interventions, intensifying bodily sensations, normalizing erotic desires, multiplying sexual perversions, policing personal behaviors, forging political resistances, motivating introspective utterances, and constructing human subjectivities. Sexuality, in the last analysis, is thus an apparatus for constituting human subjects. It is Foucault's concern with the constitution of the subject rather than with the production of sexual categories or classifications, his resolve to use the history of sexuality as a means of inquiry into the modalities of human subjectivation – as an exercise in *historicizing the subject of desire* – that imparts to his project as a whole its distinctive shape and its fundamentally radical design.[13] Such a conception still represents almost as decisive a rupture with customary modern ways of thinking about sexuality as it did when Foucault first formulated it nearly two decades ago.

To be sure, Foucault himself was not always so unambiguous about these matters as one might have liked. In the earlier and more accessible portions of volume 1 of his *History of Sexuality* he speaks freely of "the *mise en discours* of sex,"[14] of "regulating sex through useful and public discourses,"[15] and more generally of "discourse on" or "about sex" – thereby giving his incautious reader the possible impression that sex somehow preexists the discourses of sexuality. Later in the same volume, however, he goes out of his way to argue that "sex" itself, far from being a prediscursive fact – the raw material of sexuality, as it were – is a product of sexuality, an element internal to its discursive operation: "We must not situate sex on the side of reality, and sexuality on that of confused ideas and illusions; sexuality is a very real historical configuration";[16] indeed, "the apparatus of sexuality, with its different strategies, was what put in place" the very notion of "sex."[17]

Such distinctions are not simply terminological quibbles or mischievous inversions of traditional assumptions; they furnish necessary support for Foucault's attempt to displace conventional ontologies of the sexual so as to resist the preemptive claims of various modern expert knowledges, of positivist epistemologies that constitute sexuality as a (or the) real thing, an objective natural phenomenon to be known by the mind. Foucault's own discursive counter-practice seeks to remove sexuality from among the objects of knowledge and thereby to de-authorize those branches of expertise grounded in a scientific or quasi-scientific understanding of it; it also seeks to delegitimate those regulatory disciplines whose power acquires the guise of legitimate authority by basing itself on a privileged access to the "truth" of sexuality.[18] By analyzing modern knowledge practices in terms of the power relations immanent in them, and by treating "sexuality" accordingly not as a determinate thing in itself but as a *positivity* produced by those knowledge practices and situated by their epistemic operations in the place of the real, Foucault politicizes both truth and the body: he reconstitutes knowledge and sexuality as sites of contestation, thereby opening up new opportunities for both scholarly and political intervention.

Foucault's project has a special importance, resonance, and urgency for lesbians and gay men, who for too long have been the objects rather than the subjects of expert discourses of sexuality – who have been the objects, in particular, of murderously pathologizing, criminalizing, and moralizing discourses, one of whose comparatively minor effects has been to de-authorize our subjective experiences and to delegitimate our claims to be able to speak knowledgeably about our own lives.[19] Foucault holds out to us, more radically and powerfully than any other thinker I know, the possibility of a gay science without objects, of a gay self-knowing constituted by its indicative relation to a homosexuality construed not as a positive fact but as a discursive effect, and thus as a potential locus of resistance, a material for counter-practice, a source of agency.[20] Because it is based, in other words, on a notion of gay existence without a gay essence, and thus on a conception of homosexuality as a horizon of possibility instead of as an already determinate entity, the gay science which Foucault's critique makes possible offers us the prospect of devising new and empowering strategies for conjoining forms of self-knowing with modes of self-constitution.[21]

To call for such a gay science – for the emergence of a queer scholarship (in several senses of that scandalous word) – is not to call for a kinder, gentler, more objective, less prejudiced form of expertise, to be licensed presumably by non-gay-identified authorities, or by gay men accredited by straight institutions; it is not to treat homosexuality as a natural reality to be studied and understood, definitively if sympathetically, by those in a legitimate position to know. It is rather to shift homosexuality from the status of object to subject. Homosexuality, according to this vision of queer scholarship, is not something to be got right but rather an eccentric positionality to be exploited and explored[22] – and not only by lesbians and gay men but by anyone who might benefit in any way from assuming a queer subject position, especially those who feel themselves marginalized by the dominant culture because of their sexual practices or identities. It is from the eccentric positionality occupied by the queer subject that it becomes possible to envisage a variety of possibilities for restructuring the relations among sexual behaviors, erotic identities, constructions of gender, forms of knowledge, regimes of enunciation, logics of representation, modes of self-constitution, and practices of community – for reordering, that is, the relations among power, truth, and desire.[23]

It is in the interests of providing ideological support and scholarly ammunition for Foucault's discursive approach to the history of sexuality, and it is in order to demonstrate how classical scholarship (even in a traditional, non-Foucauldian form) can contribute to this enterprise, that I propose to undertake an engaged reading of a late antique Greek text. The text in question is entitled the *Erôtes*: the "Loves," the "Forms of Desire," or (as A. M. Harmon somewhat quaintly renders it) the "Affairs of the Heart"; it has been preserved in medieval manuscripts among the writings of Lucian. Stylistic considerations, however, apparently prohibit ascribing the work to the authorship of that well-known Greek satirist; the text's most recent editor and translator, M. D. Macleod, attributes it to a late antique imitator of Lucian and assigns it to the early fourth century CE, although his dating of the text has been disputed.[24] Detached at one stroke by this scholarly sleight of hand from any specific geographical, political, or cultural context, the pseudo-Lucianic *Erôtes* (as it is now dubbed) has long been relegated to the academic oblivion of Latin dissertations,[25] to the embarrassed silences of classical philologists, or to the recreational reading of bored graduate students in classics (which is how I first encountered it). Nonetheless, this anonymous little work deserves to acquire a prominent place in our emerging histories of sexuality, and in 1984 it in fact provided Foucault with the vehicle for a characteristically subtle and brilliant analysis in a late chapter of his third volume of *The History of Sexuality*.[26] Foucault's chief purpose was to contextualize the *Erôtes*, along with the opinions expressed in it, in the philosophical currents of late antiquity – the only possible historical and cultural context for it that can now be recovered. My purpose is to illustrate the interpretative opportunities for classical scholars that Foucault's historicist approach to the constitution of the desiring subject opens up, and to vindicate his claim, in the first volume of his *History of Sexuality*, that sexuality is indeed a modern discursive production.

The *Erôtes* is a notably sophisticated and elegant specimen of late antique luxury literature. Taking the form of a philosophical dialogue, but designed to mock the moral pretensions and austere postures of traditional philosophers (especially the supposedly high-minded, Platonizing advocates of boy-love[27] who by late antiquity had become stock figures of fun in the erotic literature of Greece),[28] the work features a debate between two men, Charicles and Callicratidas, over the relative merits of women and boys as vehicles of male sexual pleasure. As such, it belongs to a widely distributed genre of erotic writing which is represented in the surviving literature of the ancient world by Plutarch's *Eroticus* and by an extended passage in *Leucippe and Cleitophon*, a late Greek romance, or novel, by Achilles Tatius.[29] Similar debates can be found in medieval European and Arabic literatures,[30] in late imperial Chinese literature,[31] and in the literature of "the floating world," the luxury literature of town life in seventeenth-century Japan.[32]

In the ancient Greek context, however, the existence of such a genre raises a number of provocative issues. For one thing, most Greeks seem routinely to have assumed that most adult Greek men – whatever their particular tastes – were at least capable of being sexually aroused both by beautiful women and by beautiful boys;[33] as I have argued elsewhere, "it would be a monumental task indeed to enumerate all the ancient documents in which the alternative 'boy or woman' occurs with perfect nonchalance in an erotic context, as if the two were functionally interchangeable."[34] In fact, an instance of precisely such a nonchalant approach to matters of sexual object-choice can be found in the opening chapter of the *Erôtes*, in which one adult male speaker urges the other not to omit "mention of any of your passions, whether male or even female"(1).[35] One question it may be interesting to put to the pseudo-Lucianic text, then, is this: how do exclusive sexual preferences on the part of men get conceptualized and represented in a culture generally so indifferent to men's sexual object-choices? A second question springs immediately from the first: how can a modern interpreter of the *Erôtes* avoid reading modern sexual categories into the ancient text or manage to understand the debate contained in it as concerned with anything else besides the relative merits of "homosexual and heterosexual love"?[36] How, after all, can we – the inheritors of the Kinsey scale – conceive of exclusive preference for male or female sexual contacts except in terms of sexual orientation?[37]

It is with these questions in mind that I turn to a reading of the pseudo-Lucianic text. My reading, I must emphasize again, will be an "engaged" one and, as such, it will have a very limited scope. I am not going to attempt to provide a balanced description of the *Erôtes* as a whole or to convey much in the way of aesthetic appreciation of the work's admittedly numerous formal and stylistic perfections. Nor is it my intention – and, I trust, my reading will not produce this effect – to champion the ancients at the expense of the moderns or to promote a rhetoric of erotic self-fashioning over a rhetoric of sexuality. To belabor the obvious, it is not possible to reinstitute the ancient Greek socio-sexual system, nor, if it were, would I wish to live under it – for reasons that will emerge shortly. Finally, I am not about to undertake a critique (which it would be easy enough to do) of male sexual privilege as it permeates the world of the pseudo-Lucianic text or to analyze the operations of gendered, social power as it expresses itself in the adult male objectification of both women and boys. What I want to do, instead, is to exploit the text's cultural distance from the world of middle America in order to historicize contemporary modes of sexual subjectivation and, in particular, to problematize some twentieth-century assumptions about sexual preference, erotic identity, and the linkages often made between them. The point is not to devise a popularity contest between the ancients and the moderns but to contrast them in order to distinguish more systematically the peculiar features of their respective sexual regimes. One immediate effect of this stereoscopic – or dialectical – procedure, I hope, will be to defamiliarize current sexual behaviors and attitudes and to destabilize the binary opposition between heterosexuality and homosexuality that so decisively structures contemporary discourses of homophobia.

A number of considerations militate against interpreting the argument between Charicles and Callicratidas in the pseudo-Lucianic *Erôtes* as a dispute over the relative merits of heterosexuality and homosexuality. Chief among these factors is the dialogue's focus on pederasty to the virtual exclusion of any mention of either female or adult male homosexuality. The text contains only one mention of female homosexuality, wholly negative in intent (if subversively potent in effect), and even that does not refer to lesbianism in the modern sense of the word but rather to what the writer calls "tribadism" – that is, to the sexual penetration of women by other women.[38] "If males find intercourse with males acceptable," exclaims Charicles (the partisan of women), playing what he clearly considers to be his trump card in the argument, "henceforth let women too love one another. . . . Let them strap to themselves cunningly contrived instruments of wantonness, those mysterious monstrosities devoid of seed, and let woman lie with woman as does a man. Let wanton tribadism – that word seldom heard, which I feel ashamed even to utter – freely parade itself, and let our women's chambers . . . defile themselves with sexually indeterminate amours" (28). Needless to say, Callicratidas (the partisan of boys) does not rise to his opponent's challenge and endorse such constructive and promising proposals.

Within the realm of male eroticism, correspondingly, the *Erôtes* makes absolutely no allowance for the possibility of sexual relations among adult men – for the possibility, that is, of "homosexual" rather than merely pederastic love. Both Charicles and Callicratidas seem to agree that adult males hold not the slightest sexual appeal to other men; the terms in which they express that shared assumption are revealing, I believe, of the distance that separates the aesthetic and sexual conventions of ancient Mediterranean pederasty from the canons of modern American middle-class gay male taste. "If a man makes attempts on a boy of twenty," Charicles (the partisan of women) remarks, "he seems to me to be pursuing an equivocal love.[39]

For then the [boy's] limbs, being large and manly, are hard; the chins that once were soft are rough and covered with bristles, and the well-developed thighs are as it were sullied with hairs. And as for the parts less visible than these, I leave knowledge of them to you who have tried them" (26).[40] Each detail in this description of over-ripe boyhood is intended to evoke revulsion and disgust; it is telling that Charicles' opponent, Callicratidas, has nothing to say by way of refutation of it.

Another element in the text's representation of sexual styles that may be jarring when viewed from a twentieth-century perspective is its insistence that some same-sex desires do not weaken male gender identity but rather consolidate it. Far from being effeminized by his sexual predilection for boys, as the modem "inversion model" of homosexual desire would have it (whereby a man exclusively attracted to males has "a woman's soul in a man's body" or represents a "sexual intermediate" or member of a "third sex"[41]), Callicratidas turns out to be hypervirile: he excels, we are told, at those activities traditionally marked in Greek culture as exclusively and characteristically masculine – namely, political life, public oratory, gymnastics (9, 29), and philosophy – and he takes as his role-models the heroes and philosophers of old (46–9). Callidratidas' sexual desire for boys, then, makes him more of a man.[42] By contrast, Charicles' erotic preference for women seems to have had the corresponding effect of effeminizing him: when the reader first encounters him, for example, Charicles is described as exhibiting "a skillful use of cosmetics, so as to be attractive to women" (9); indeed, Greek women, if one is to credit the desires imputed to them by male authors, seem to have liked men who looked young[43] (no one in this world, evidently, would appear to have found adult men sexually appealing – which, to my mind, furnishes at least one good reason for not wishing to bring it back). Now cosmetic adornment is itself an indicatively feminine practice (38–41),[44] and so Charicles would seem to have been infected by femininity from his long habit of associating with women.[45] His passionate encomium of women, moreover – his defense of their claims to be loved by men and his praise of their sexual attractiveness – signals to the jaundiced eye of Callicratidas that Charicles has simply enslaved himself to the cause of women and is entirely at their beck and call: if he were a real man, the implication seems to be, he would not allow himself to be so dominated by women as to be obliged to defend their interests in public. According to the terms of Greek misogynistic discourse, there would appear to be no distinction between being the champion of women and being their slave (30). Compared to Callicratidas, then, it is Charicles who is a traitor to his gender, having been led to betray his masculine identity by the very vehemence of his sexual preference for women: he has become woman-identified. In short, the sharply polarizing tendencies of Greek sexual discourse would seem to require that excessive liking for women on the part of a man be interpreted as a sign of deviant, specifically effeminate identity. Such an identity, in fact, closely approximates to what a recent ethnographer of the American South has described as "a redneck queer," a Southern traitor to masculinity – whom she defines not as a male homosexual but, on the contrary, as "a boy from Alabama who laks girls better'n football."[46]

As the preceding account implies, neither Callicratidas nor Charicles is entirely conventional, by Greek standards, in the matter of his sexual tastes. Rather, each man is something of an extremist (5), a zealot whose fanatical attachment to his own erotic object-choice – and whose correspondingly violent revulsion against the sexual objects favored by his opponent – mark him out as peculiar and manifest themselves in his entire style of life. Each man's sexual inclination, if not exactly "written immodestly on his face and body" (as Foucault says of the nineteenth-century homosexual),[47] is at least visibly inscribed in his domestic arrangements. Callicratidas, the narrator points out, "was well provided with handsome slave-boys and all of his servants were pretty well beardless. They remained with him till the down first appeared on their faces, but, once any growth cast a shadow on their cheeks, they would be sent away to be stewards and overseers of his properties at Athens." Charicles, by contrast, "had in attendance a large band of dancing girls and singing girls and all his house was as full of women as if it were the Thesmophoria [a women's religious festival], with not the slightest trace of male presence except that here and there could be seen an infant boy or a superannuated old cook whose age could give even the jealous no cause for suspicion" (10). Callicratidas and Charicles do not represent, then, spokesmen for abnormal and normal sexualities, respectively: rather, they are both a bit queer.

Nonetheless, each man demonstrates a certain connoisseurship in speaking about the good and bad features of the sexual objects favored by his rival, a knowingness that bespeaks a broader range of erotic sympathies or a wider sexual experience than one might initially have imputed to such self-styled sexual purists. I have already cited one instance: Charicles' vivid and sensuously precise evocation of the physical attributes of a boy past his prime. Charicles' taste in boys, his ability to judge when a boy is no longer desirable, his standards for discriminating smoothness and hairiness in youthful cheeks and thighs are all confirmed in their inerrancy by the institutional arrangements of Callicratidas' household, which (according to the passage just quoted) has well-established procedures for "graduating" over-age, hirsute lads. Charicles evidently understands what Callicratidas likes and dislikes in a boy. Conversely, Callicratidas betrays an intimate knowledge of women. His violent denunciation of women's cosmetic practices (38–41) implies so extensive an acquaintance with them that one might have imagined him to be a professional beautician, were it not that his accusations come straight from the arsenal of traditional Greek misogyny.[48] Still, the very visceral nature of the terms in which he avows his disgust (he claims that "every man [who gets out of a woman's bed] is in immediate need of a bath" (42)) seems to betray at least passing personal familiarity on his part. And his acceptance, however reluctant, of the necessity of having sexual relations with women in order to beget offspring (38) demonstrates that he does not regard himself as incapable of consummating a sexual union with a woman, should the situation call for it.

On rare occasions, in fact, both Charicles and Callicratidas are able to agree about the attractiveness of a sexual object. Their desires coincide, interestingly enough, in the case of the famous statue of Aphrodite at Cnidus, by the sculptor Praxiteles. Callicratidas, of course, is initially reluctant to view this world-renowned masterpiece, because it has the form of a female figure (11), but even he is struck dumb by the sight of it, while Charicles raves over it and even kisses the statue (13). When the two men inspect the rear of the figure, however, it is Callicratidas' turn to rave, while Charicles stands transfixed with tears pouring from his eyes (14). "Heracles!" Callicratidas exclaims,

> what a well-proportioned back! What generous flanks she has! How satisfying an armful to embrace! How delicately moulded the flesh on the buttocks, neither too thin and close to the bone, nor yet revealing too great an expanse of fat! And as for those precious parts sealed in on either side by the hips, how inexpressibly sweetly they smile![49] How perfect the proportions of the thighs and the calves as they stretch down in a straight line to the feet! So that's what Ganymede looks like as he pours out the nectar in heaven for Zeus and makes it taste sweeter. For I'd never have taken the cup from Hebe if she served me. (14)

Charicles is hardly in a state to disagree. Such passages leave one with the distinct impression that what endears boys to Callicratidas and women to Charicles is not a preferred sex or gender but merely certain favorite parts of the human anatomy.

That impression is strengthened when the two men go on to discover that a discoloration of the marble they have noted on the back of the statue was caused by a young man who fell in love with it and who, having arranged to be locked up alone with the statue at night, had sex with it by stealth (15–16).[50] Charicles concludes that the feminine evokes love even when carved in stone. Callicratidas, however, observes that, although the amorous youth had the opportunity to glut his entire passion for the goddess during an uninterrupted night of love, he chose to make love to her "as if to a boy" (*paidikôs*) – that is, from the rear – in order not to be confronted by the female part of her (17). (Face-to-face intercourse would have been pretty hard to bring off, in any case, even if the lover had desired it, since Praxiteles' statue – in addition to being made of marble – was far from anatomically correct. Callicratidas' rejoinder provides one more indication of the highly sophistical tenor of the whole debate.) These passages confirm that the quarrel between Charicles and Callicratidas comes down not to a difference in sexual object-choice, to differing sexual preferences or orientations, but rather to a differential liking for particular human body parts, independent of the sex of the person who possesses them.

Furthermore, the specific arguments that the two men use in order to establish the putative superiority of their preferred sexual object display what modern middle-class readers will be apt to find not only unpersuasive but positively bizarre styles of reasoning. That is because most bourgeois Westerners nowadays tend to think of sexual object-choice as an expression of individual "sexuality," a fixed sexual disposition or orientation over which no one has much (if any) control and for which reasons cannot be given: any reasons one might give for one's sexual object-choice seem to be mere afterthoughts, adventitious rationalizations, late arrivals on the scene of sexual speciation; reasons follow the fact of one's sexual being and do not determine or constitute it. Thus, sexual preference is not something that one can be argued logically out of or into – least of all by considerations of utility or convenience. And yet those are precisely the sorts of consider-ations that Charicles invokes in order to demonstrate that women are superior vehicles of male sexual pleasure. For example, women have more sexual orifices than do boys, Charicles observes; hence, it is possible for men to make use of women "even more like boys than boys" (*paidikôteron*, i.e. by two methods of penetration instead of merely one),[51] thereby availing themselves of "twin paths to sexual pleasure," whereas "a male has no way of bestowing the pleasure a woman gives" (27). And here is yet another consideration of a practical nature: women, unlike boys, can be enjoyed for a protracted period if time. "From maidenhood to middle age, before the time when the last wrinkles of old age spread over her face, a woman is a pleasant armful for a man to embrace," Charicles points out (25), adding – a bit wishfully, perhaps – that a woman's body (unlike a boy's) remains attractively hairless as she grows older (26). Callicratidas does not dispute those assertions,[52] but counters instead with a lengthy polemic about the superiority of art to nature (33–6).

What all this evidence indicates, finally, is that the anonymous author of the pseudo-Lucianic *Erôtes* approaches the question of male sexual object-

choice not as a matter of sexual orientation but rather as a matter of taste –
the sort of thing that, as everyone knows, there's no disputing, and that
everyone just loves to dispute. (As W. H. Auden wrote in 1936, "Who can
ever praise enough / The world of his belief?"[53]) The quarrel between
Charicles and Callicratidas over the relative merits of women and boys as
vehicles of male sexual pleasure is not an argument about the relative merits
of heterosexuality and homosexuality in the modern sense but a disagreement over the respective advantages and disadvantages of different
"avenues of sexual pleasure" (cf. 27) and different stylistics of personal life.
The alternatives presented by the two disputants delineate sexual options
apparently available, in principle at least, to any free adult Greek male, such
that any man – no matter how set in his ways – might plausibly be thought
at least capable of entertaining those options, if not necessarily eager to
explore them.

To recapitulate: the text's emphasis on pederasty to the exclusion of
homosexuality (whose existence, apparently, is not even recognized); the
masculinization of the pederast and the effeminization of the lover of
women; the shared queerness of both interlocutors; the ability of each
interlocutor to put himself in the erotic subject position of the other; their
common knowingness about both women and boys; the pederast's capacity
to eroticize elements of the human anatomy independently of the sex of the
person whose anatomy is eroticized; the lover of women's utilitarian appeal
to quantitative factors as a basis for calculating relative sexual value; and,
finally, both men's treatment of sexual object-choice as a matter of taste –
the conjunction of all of those considerations (which, taken individually,
might be paralleled in modern bourgeois experience) suggests that what one
is dealing with in the *Erôtes* is something quite different from a system of
"sexuality" in the modern sense of that modern word.

In order to make sense of the quarrel between Charicles and Callicratidas
in modern terms, it may be helpful to think of it somewhat along the lines of
a passionate debate over dietary object-choice between a committed
vegetarian and an unreconstructed omnivore – or, to employ a more
ludicrous (and therefore a more exact) analogy, between someone who eats
nothing but vegetables and someone who eats nothing but meat. It is a
quarrel that springs not from fundamental differences in kind among
human beings but from the dissimilar values, ideals, and preferred styles of
life[54] which otherwise similar human beings happen (for whatever reason)
to have espoused. It is therefore a dispute about the very sorts of things that
people tend to argue about most heatedly – namely, their basic commitments. No matter how basic such commitments may be, however, they are
susceptible of being criticized or debated precisely because they derive from

what people believe and value, not from what or who they are. The probability of one disputant actually convincing the other to alter his basic commitments, and to alter the behavior that follows from them, is admittedly slim, but by citing various reasons or adducing various considerations each disputant can nurture the (no doubt foredoomed) hope that his interlocutor may come one day to look at things from the disputant's own perspective. Without the conviction that the available options admit of right choices and wrong choices, that those choices are open to everyone to make, and that one's own choice is indeed the correct one, one has little motive to get worked up over the issue – and uncommitted onlookers have little cause to find the dispute amusing or entertaining. Such is not the case with sexuality nowadays. That is why modern debates over the respective merits of the various sexual orientations, even when they take place (if they ever do) without an explicit or implicit threat of anti-gay violence, tend to be entirely different in character from the sexual debates staged by ancient Greek writers: modern sexual polemics are more like arguments about whether it is better to be a peasant or a king – matters possible to dispute in principle but impossible to alter in actual practice. The practical outcome of such arguments, in other words, is always foreclosed from the start, which makes them, at best, "forlorn / Yet pleasing," as Shelley puts it, "such as once, so poets tell, / The devils held within the dales of Hell, / Concerning God, freewill and destiny."[55]

What exactly is at stake in the quarrel between Charicles and Callicratidas may be easier to grasp if the *Erôtes* is situated in its wider generic context and compared to another text from an analogous cultural tradition, namely *The Great Mirror of Male Love* by the seventeenth-century Japanese writer Ihara Saikaku. Published in Osaka and Kyoto on New Year's Day 1687, *The Great Mirror* contains forty tales of exemplary love between men and boys. Its opening chapter justifies the choice of subject by means of twenty-three comparisons of women to boys, each of them designed to champion the latter at the expense of the former and to establish the relative advantages of boys as vehicles of male pleasure. What sets off these alternatives from the arguments of Callicratidas is that they are couched entirely in negative terms. That is, instead of purporting to demonstrate straightforwardly that the love of boys is superior to the love of women, Saikaku's comparisons show that, when affairs go badly, boy-love is on the whole less vexatious. Here is how Saikaku's argument begins:

> Which is to be preferred: A girl of eleven or twelve scrutinizing herself in a mirror, or a boy of the same age cleaning his teeth?
> Lying rejected next to a courtesan, or conversing intimately with a kabuki boy who is suffering from hemorrhoids?

Caring for a wife with tuberculosis, or keeping a youth who constantly demands spending money?

Having lightning strike the room where you are enjoying a boy actor you bought, or being handed a razor by a courtesan you hardly know who asks you to die with her?

The choice is evidently not a difficult one: "In each case above," Saikaku concludes with a partisanship so extreme as to be ludicrous and therefore self-cancelling, "even if the woman were a beauty of gentle disposition and the youth a repulsive pug-nosed fellow, it is a sacrilege to speak of female love in the same breath with boy love. . . . The only sensible choice is to dispense with women and turn instead to men."[56]

What the pseudo-Lucianic *Erôtes* shares with *The Great Mirror of Male Love*, besides its evident misogyny, is its combination of literary gamesmanship and sexual connoisseurship: it playfully explores various possibilities of sexual pleasure, presenting the (implied male) reader with specific sets of alternative options for achieving erotic enjoyment and personal satisfaction. Perhaps the final surprise that the *Erôtes* has to offer the modern historian of sexuality is its dramatization of the absurdity of the very notion of exclusive sexual object-choice, whether homo- or hetero-. It is not just that Greek males exhibited on the whole a different "sexuality" from that of modern American men of the professional classes, if one may judge solely on the basis of this one text (which, of course, it would be extremely hazardous to do in the absence of corroborating documentation).[57] Rather, they exhibited no "sexuality" at all, in the modern sense. Not only are the very notions of "sexuality" and "sexual orientation" entirely foreign to the world of this text: to the extent that the text can even accommodate such notions – to the extent that it can represent human types who roughly approximate modern hetero- and homosexual males – it treats them as outlandish and bizarre. Merely to have a fixed sexual object-choice of any kind is to be some sort of freak, apparently – a figure of fun whose foredoomed efforts at rationalizing his exclusive preference provide amusement and relaxation for one's fellow man (5, 29, 53).[58]

If my interpretation of the pseudo-Lucianic *Erôtes* proves to be persuasive, I shall have managed to provide at least some support for Foucault's proposition that sexuality is not lodged in our bodies, in our hormones, or in our genitals, but resides in our discursive and institutional practices as well as in the experiences which they construct. Bodies do not come with ready-made sexualities. Bodies are not even attracted to other bodies.[59] It is human subjects, rather, who are attracted to various objects, including bodies, and the features of bodies that render them desirable to human subjects are contingent upon the cultural codes, the social conventions, and the political institutions that structure and inform human subjectivity itself, thereby shaping our individual erotic ideals and defining for us the scope of what we find attractive. Modern cultural modes of interpellating European and American bourgeois subjects typically occlude that process of sexual subjectivation, prompting us to misrecognize it as a biophysical process – and thus to misinterpret the "sexuality effects" produced in our bodies as the collective sign of an intrinsically and irreducibly bodily event. As D. A. Miller has lately reminded us, "All the deployments of the 'bio-power' that characterizes our modernity depend on the supposition that the most effective take on the subject is rooted in its body, insinuated within this body's 'naturally given' imperatives. *Metaphorizing the body begins and ends with literalizing the meanings the body is thus made to bear.*"[60]

But just because that deployment of bio-power which we call sexuality makes use of our bodies as sites for the production of sexuality effects – in the form of literalized bodily meanings – it hardly follows that we must take sexuality itself to be a literal, or natural, reality. Rather, sexuality is a mode of human subjectivation which operates in part by figuring the body *as* the literal and by pressing the body's supposed literality into the service of a metaphorical project. As such, sexuality represents a seizure of the body by a historically unique apparatus for producing historically specific forms of subjectivity. What I have tried to do through my reading of the pseudo-Lucianic *Erôtes* is to confront the ancient discourses of erotic self-fashioning with the modern discourses of sexuality, in order to dramatize the differences between them and to make visible the historical dimensions of that supposedly ahistorical and universal entity called "the body" – to historicize that discursive space in which modern bio-power constructs "the body" as the "natural" ground of the desiring subject. One aim, and (I hope) one effect, of my interpretative strategy is to contribute, insofar as scholarship can, to the task of reconstituting the body as a potential site of cultural activism and political resistance. If the sexual body is indeed historical – if there is, as I devoutly believe, no orgasm without ideology – perhaps ongoing inquiry into the politics of pleasure will serve to deepen the pleasures, as well as to widen the possibilities, of politics.

2

Foucault on Sexuality in Greco-Roman Antiquity

David Cohen and Richard Saller

The second and third volumes of *The History of Sexuality* can be read in different ways: as a philosophical elaboration of the self-fashioning subject in cultures not yet burdened by Christian prohibitions or as socio-cultural history of classical antiquity. As philosophical elaboration, it may be suggested that these volumes should not be held to the social historian's conventional standards of presenting ancient writers' views within their social and intellectual contexts. Since *The Use of Pleasure* and *The Care of the Self* have been read as socio-cultural history – whatever Foucault's own intentions[1] – there is reason to ask whether he has properly represented the classical texts concerning the ancient experience of sexuality. In this essay we suggest that his interpretation of the Greek and Roman authors is not convincing as social or intellectual history because it ignores too many dimensions of their texts and their social contexts. Furthermore, we believe that this criticism has implications for Foucault's project of philosophical elaboration of the self-fashioning subject. By locating in some past time his self-fashioning subject, formed principally by an "aesthetics of existence," Foucault offers the reader the tantalizing possibility of recovery of such an existence in the future. But a fuller reading of the classical texts on homoeroticism and marriage reveals that Foucault's seductive myth of freedom to self-fashion is not anchored in history, insofar as it both misrepresents the classical authors' thought about the experience of sexuality and understates the powers of normalization and constraint in the Greco-Roman states.

Foucault conceives of his project not as a history of sexual practices but as a history of the experience of sexuality, "where experience is understood as the correlation between fields of knowledge, types of normativity, and forms of subjectivity in a particular culture."[2] His special interest in "forms of subjectivity" leads him to inquire into how "Western man had been brought to recognize himself as a subject of desire" through an examination of "the forms and modalities of the relation to self by which the individual constitutes and recognizes himself *qua* subject."[3] Foucault interprets the Greek and Roman authors to show that in antiquity sexuality was problematized in such a way that subjects constituted themselves through the "arts of existence" – that is, "actions by which individuals seek to transform themselves and make their life into an oeuvre that carries certain aesthetic values and meets certain stylistic criteria."[4]

Foucault's stress on individual "arts" or "aesthetics of existence" is difficult for us as social historians to reconcile with the state regulation and social hierarchies of power that pervaded classical communities and political thought. In particular, we shall argue with regard to classical Greece (1) that it is misleading to represent the societies producing the philosophical texts as largely unconstrained by a code, as Foucault does, imagining individuals unregulated and free to fashion themselves (particularly in the matter of homoeroticism); and (2) that it is wrong to represent Plato, Aristotle, and the wider philosophical discourse as concerned with self-styling subjects whose sexual experience was an individual matter, left for the most part untouched by laws. In imperial Rome of the first two centuries CE Foucault discovers an inflection in this self-fashioning subjectivity away from love of boys toward marriage experienced as a symmetrical, reciprocal relationship. Our reconsideration of the texts concerning Roman marriage suggests (1) that a more systematic examination of social relations casts doubt on the claim of a new valorization of the conjugal bond, which Foucault finds in Musonius Rufus, Plutarch, and Pliny; and (2) that, in describing the experience of marriage in imperial Rome as "relatively equal," Foucault has ignored Musonius', Plutarch's, and Pliny's insistence on the traditionally hierarchical essence of the conjugal bond.

I   CLASSICAL GREECE

Regulation of sexuality in Greek societies

At the end of the introductory section of *The Use of Pleasure* Foucault first articulates his claim that pre-Christian antiquity was not burdened by the kinds of jural and moral normalizing structures which later characterized the Christian West:

[M]oral conceptions in Greek and Greco-Roman antiquity were much more oriented towards practices of the self and the question of askesis than towards codifications of conducts and the strict definition of what is permitted and what is forbidden. . . . The accent was placed on the relation with the self that enabled a person to keep from being carried away by the appetites and pleasures, to maintain a mastery and superiority over them, to keep his senses in a state of tranquility, to remain free from interior bondage to the passions, and to achieve a mode of being that could be defined by the full enjoyment of oneself, or the perfect supremacy of oneself over oneself.[5]

This claim provides the foundation for the central thesis that Greek and Roman morality rested not on a code, but on self-fashioning according to an aesthetic ideal embodied in an "art of existence."[6]

The conceptual opposition between a fixed moral code and self-mastery strikes us as analytically inadequate. Foucault seems to assume that, because Greek city-states (*poleis*) and Rome did not have a formal and exhaustive Levitical code, the domain of morality was left to individual self-fashioning.[7] This narrow conceptualization of codification and moral constraint, and disinterest in wider normalizing powers, is expressed in a late interview: "You see, what I tried to show is that nobody is obliged in classical ethics to be truthful to their wives, to not touch boys, and so on. . . . The choice, the aesthetic choice or the political choice, for which they decide to accept this kind of existence – that's the *mode d'assujettisse-ment*. It's a choice, a personal choice."[8]

To say that it was purely a matter of personal aesthetic choice whether to be a husband, father, and head of the household (*oikos*) or a bachelor, adulterer, passive homosexual, or pander grossly underestimates the normalizing forces at work in ancient societies. These forces were most obvious in Greek *poleis* other than Athens, on which Foucault concentrates. It was a commonplace in classical political theory that different forms of constitution would produce different systems of law, and that non-democratic forms would regulate the private lives and sexual conduct of their citizens much more closely than would democracies.[9] By homogenizing "Greek thought" and taking Athens as representative of all of Greece, Foucault understates the variety of classical Greek experience, and consequently overestimates later innovations or inflections. Sparta, for example, was widely viewed in classical Greece, and in classical political theory in particular, as providing a very different model of social organization based upon a subordination of the individual to collective needs. In Spartan society there was no need for a written "code" because the rigors of socialization and the vast disciplinary authority of the ephors left very little space for self-fashioning. The Spartans may have emphasized the importance of self-mastery, but not as a way of individuals constituting themselves as moral subjects. Their famed self-mastery (*enkrateia*) was the product not of an inner freedom ordered according to an individualized "art of living," but rather of an absolute obedience to the law inculcated through a lifetime of rigorous training and relentless socialization.

For democratic Athens as well, it is doubtful that in the use of pleasure, although one had "to respect the laws and customs of the land, to keep from offending the gods, and to heed the will of nature, the moral rules to which one conformed were far removed from anything which might form a clearly defined code."[10] Now if by "a clearly defined code" Foucault means the Christian penitential, this may be right, and yet hardly illuminating, since codes of behavior less overt and less precisely defined may still exercise a powerful influence limiting individual latitude in *askesis*. The Athenians did have a law code which clearly regulated a broad range of public and private activities, though only parts have survived. Further, they conceived of a body of unwritten law which embodied the norms, particularly religious norms, of the community. Special officials were empowered to articulate these rules, though we know very little about their activities. Together, the written and unwritten law were seen as the basis of the Athenian social and political order. This is a commonplace in forensic orations given before mass juries which adjudicated competing moral claims, and it is also given systematic formulation by Aristotle, Isocrates, Plato, and Thucydides. Thus Aristotle could define injustice as "a voluntary causing of harm contrary to the law of the state or the unwritten law which appears to be recognized by all men." Among the examples he gives of such injustice are transgressions in regard to the "pleasures of the body."[11] Similarly, though Foucault places moderation and self-restraint (*sophrosune*) at the center of his notion of moral freedom to pursue an art of existence, this very self-restraint was linked to the normative force of the law.[12] Its opposite, lack of self-restraint (*akolasia*), was then defined not as excess but rather as a disposition not to obey the laws and customs of the city. Such views are found throughout the corpus of Athenian literature.

In addition to written and unwritten laws, the customs of the *polis* were viewed as possessing great normative force. Indeed, the same word is used in Greek for law and custom (*nomos*), testifying to the intimacy of their perceived relation. The fact that they did not constitute a formally recognized "code" should not be allowed to obscure their power of constraint. The Athenian orators, dramatists, and philosophers, and the historian Thucydides, portray individuals as enmeshed in restrictive matrices of religious, social, familial, legal, and political relations. For example, Pausanias, in Plato's *Symposium*, claims to describe the norms which regulated homoerotic courtship. In doing so, he uses the word *nomos* throughout his speech, and it is often difficult to discern whether in a particular passage he means law or custom, for the word can mean either.[13] More significantly, he claims to describe not a philosophically constructed ideal society but rather actual practices at Athens as governed by a complex set of *nomoi* and operating according to the politics of reputation. The whole thrust of the passage is to show the constraining force of the normative expectations of the community upon this form of sexual behavior which was viewed as being played out in the public, not the private, sphere. In the same dialogue (192b) Plato has Aristophanes claim that in contemporary Athens men who love boys have no inclination to marry, but the pressure of *nomos* directs them to do so.[14]

Foucault, principally in the chapter on homoeroticism, touches upon the crucial notions of honor, reputation, and status, yet he nowhere considers the politics of reputation as it operates in the public and private spheres to limit the freedom to fashion oneself through the panoply of norms by which judgments of honor and shame are made.[15] An agonistic society like classical Athens largely functions according to a morality which is constituted, deployed, interpreted, and manipulated to establish relations of domination, status, power, and influence. To say that it was simply a matter of "personal choice" whether to comply or not is to ignore the way in which individual aspirations and conceptions of the self were themselves a product of these institutions. Though Foucault's treatment of homoeroticism is, in our view, the most nuanced and convincing part of the book, its failure to consider fully the normalizing matrices of Athenian social relations renders its account one-sided and incomplete.

Foucault draws heavily upon Dover's *Greek Homosexuality* for his argument that the Greeks did not divide the world into homosexual and heterosexual, that homoerotic relations were governed by values of honor and shame, and that sexual activity and passivity constituted a fundamental normative axis. Building upon this, Foucault emphasizes the problematic nature of homoeroticism for the Greeks and then fits this problematization into his general scheme of ascetic self-fashioning. These latter two points are the original aspects of his work in this area and should be examined in turn.

Though one cannot speak of a "Greek" problematization of homoeroticism, this label is surely accurate for classical Athens.[16] What does Foucault mean by a problematization of the love of boys? First, he is right that our modern conceptions of "homosexuality" and "tolerance" are both out of place here. Though Athenian society is often represented as tolerant, principally because no law forbade pederasty *tout court*, the situation was more complex. Athenian values, he argues, were ambivalent: "Indeed, it seems that this practice – though it was common and accepted – was surrounded by a diversity of judgments, that it was subjected to an interplay

of positive and negative appraisals so complex as to make the ethics that
governed it difficult to decipher. And there was a clear awareness of this
complexity at the time." The only way to decipher this complexity is "to ask
how and in what form the pleasure enjoyed between men was problematic."[17] Foucault pursues this by showing how pederasty constituted a
"morally overloaded domain,"[18] governed by an intricate body of "values,
imperatives, demands, rules, advice, and exhortations that were as
numerous as they were emphatic and singular."[19] This body of rules
regulated pederastic courtship, where the honor of the boy was at stake:
"By not yielding, not submitting, remaining the strongest, triumphing over
suitors and lovers through one's resistance, one's firmness, one's moderation (*sophrosyne*) – the young man proves his excellence in the sphere of
love relations."[20]

Then, Foucault argues, through the principle of isomorphism strength
and moderation in this sphere also demonstrate the qualities necessary for
being a good citizen. Those who do not resist these problematic relations
are barred from the citizen body. Foucault identifies here a profound
contradiction in Athenian attitudes concerning the homoerotic realm, "the
antinomy of the boy." The man is permitted to pursue, provided that he
respects the laws and proprieties, but the boy must resist and prove his
strength. This explains what he calls the "oscillation . . . concerning the
natural or 'unnatural' character of that type of love."[21] This oscillation
consists in the conviction that it is natural for men to be attracted to boys,
but it is also unnatural, against nature, for a boy to be the object of sexual
desire, as Xenophon puts it, "using men as women."[22]

This problematic is at the heart of Athenian ambivalence concerning
homoeroticism.[23] Foucault rightly insists that the mere fact that no law
explicitly prohibited homoerotic relations should not be taken to indicate
that such relations were not a matter of the most intense moral and political
concern. Here his broader conceptualization of the moral and social fields
is more plausible, in our view, than in his previous analysis of marriage and
male–female relations. There he claimed that, because there was no "code"
of laws, customs, or norms in Greek society, the realm of morality in
general, and sexuality in particular, was a realm of freedom where the male
individual was left to fashion himself. His discussion of pederasty, however,
shows how far from the truth is such a view: though the laws did not
condemn pederasty, it was nonetheless "invested with values, imperatives,
demands, rules, advice, and exhortations that were as numerous as they
were emphatic and singular."[24] Pederasty was governed by rules and
constituted a "social game"[25] that operated within the moral sphere defined
by honor and shame, extending fully into the political realm. Here Foucault
found the material with which he could have studied the social and political

patterns and processes of normalization or social control, and the nexus of knowledge and power which sexuality represented.

Foucault's failure to appreciate extra-legal normalizing forces appears in his use of Xenophon's account of a homoerotic relationship to demonstrate his point about moderation and excess as a major normative axis in Greek sexual experience. Xenophon presents the case of the Spartan king Agesilaus as a moral exemplum. Agesilaus, says Foucault, "carried moderation to the point where he refused to kiss the young man he loved."[26] Thus, Foucault finds in Agesilaus confirmation that the Greeks made judgments not on the basis of whether men liked women or boys, but rather according to whether they pursued one or the other with moderation or excess.

Yet Agesilaus' concern as portrayed by Xenophon[27] is not with moderation so much as with his status and reputation and the way in which public perceptions about his sexual conduct would affect them. To avoid being slandered for homoerotic relations Agesilaus took the extreme precaution of always lodging in public places where everyone would think such doings would be impossible. Agesilaus, cognizant of the politics of reputation and the power of gossip, thus took care to justify his behavior in advance by arranging the circumstances so as to promote a particular set of inferences about his behavior. Secrecy and privacy were associated with sexual transgression, so he confined his activities to public places where he could claim, like many speakers in Athenian orations, that his behavior was open for all to see. What his actual sexual preferences were matters little. What is significant is his concern to manipulate judgments about those preferences by playing upon the normative expectations that determine reputation.

Further, Agesilaus felt that being regarded as a pederast would subject him to slander that could damage his reputation. It was not a matter of moderate or excessive pursuit of such pleasures: Agesilaus, though attracted to boys, avoided *all* behavior, whether moderate or not, that might have given rise to the rumor that he engaged in such conduct. While self-restraint is indeed prominent in the tale, it is portrayed not merely as the product of an inner self-fashioning *askesis*, but rather as part of the public/social/political realm of the politics of reputation, governed by the community's values and normative expectations associated with honor and shame.

Plato, Aristotle, and the philosophical discourse concerning sexuality

Classical political philosophy starts from the premise that, in Aristotle's famous formulation, man is a *politikon zoon*, a being whose nature is to live in a political community. Though Foucault relies heavily upon Aristotle and Plato to support his notion of the self-fashioning aesthetic, he neglects this central dimension of their political thought which views human beings as members of an *oikos* (household) and a *polis* (city-state). Thus, while he claims that *sophrosune* (moderation/self-restraint) played a crucial role in the development of the new self-fashioning subject, his interpretation of its treatment in Plato, Xenophon, and Aristotle fails to consider its political and social dimensions. The result is an account of an "art of existence" constructed around *sophrosune*, which would have us see a figure like Socrates as having "fashioned himself" according to an inner aesthetic vision. Yet Socrates, according to Plato's portrayal, claimed to be unable to live outside of the institutions in which he had been raised and he preferred to die rather than leave Athens or disobey the laws to which he accorded absolute authority.[28]

Foucault is not interested in the very different ethical views against which Plato's position on *sophrosune* was directed. He argues that the Greeks thought it was necessary to master oneself if one was to rule others, but though *sophrosune* might form *one* strand in the competitive struggle to establish social and political hierarchies it was by no means preeminent. Indeed, the meteoric rise of a figure like Alcibiades, known for his propensity for public excess, testifies to the limited significance of this criterion of judgment in the public realm. Alcibiades' career represents the realm of political practice, but alternative theoretical views of politics, ethics, and society accorded *sophrosune* a very different place than in the Platonic schema. In Plato's *Gorgias*, Callicles and Polus ridicule the self-restrained life, and it is clear from the way Plato presents the discussion that he expects most Athenians to be far more sympathetic towards such claims than towards Socratic *askesis*.

Thus, Greek ethical speculation did not center upon the ethic of moderation and self-mastery as depicted by Foucault. Polus, Callicles, and Thrasymachus all present variants of what might be called the morality of excess, a morality based upon a very different notion of moral freedom and subjectivity, as Nietzsche emphasized. On this view, the laws of the state and conventional moral values like *sophrosune* are merely instruments used by the many to restrain the naturally strong. For such men the good consists in being in a position where one can satisfy all desires to excess. Hence, moral freedom involves freedom from the artificial constraints of the laws of the many, and the life to be envied is not that of the philosopher but that of the tyrant, the man who rules by force alone with no regard for laws or institutions. This position is indeed based upon a notion of the "desiring subject," but in a very different form from that represented by Foucault as typifying "Greek thought."[29]

Foucault's appropriation of the categories of moderation and self-mastery is problematic in other ways as well. Referring to self-mastery as (*askesis*) "practical training," Foucault emphasizes that this *askesis* was not separate from other areas of civic life and virtue: "But in classical Greek thought, the 'ascetics' that enabled one to make oneself into an ethical subject was an integral part . . . of the practice of a virtuous life, which was also the life of a 'free' man in the full, positive, and political sense of the word."[30]

Now there seems to be a fundamental confusion here. Plato, who represents Foucault's best evidence for this mode of thought, repeatedly emphasizes that, as long as the world is as it is, precisely the virtue of moderation and self-mastery makes one completely unsuited for public life. The execution of Socrates is the paradigm of what happens to the man who by such standards is the ideal citizen. Indeed, not only in *Gorgias*, but later, in *The Republic* and elsewhere, Plato repeats the view that the philosophical life – that is, the life of self-restraint, justice, and virtue – requires withdrawal from the civic life of the city, from the realm of politics which is governed by different standards. This life of self-restraint characterized by Foucault as that of the life of the "free man in the full, positive, and political, sense of the word" is the life which, according to Plato, most Greeks find at best puzzling and at worst perverse. Hence, in Plato's view it is *only* in an ideal city, impossible to achieve in this world, that the most virtuous man will play the leading role, that the philosopher will be king.

Foucault's account of the politics of freedom and self-mastery largely rests upon his reading of Plato and Aristotle, who indeed taught that the good citizen is the virtuous citizen, and that *sophrosune* is a central element of this virtue. Yet Foucault minimizes a central feature of their account of the nature of such civic *sophrosune*. In *The Republic* Plato portrays a city in which a small elite will achieve self-mastery through philosophical training. It is their attainment of knowledge, not *askesis*, that will produce this result; other means are required to produce civic virtue in the rest of the population. *The Laws*, Plato's last political work, goes even further in this direction, for there Plato abandons the ideal of the philosopher ruler and develops a system where *all* the citizens fall into the latter category. Since such citizens are incapable of pursuing the philosophical education which can alone bring the true self-mastery based upon knowledge, socialization and education will be used to produce virtuous, obedient citizens. In *The Laws* virtue lies in absolute obedience to the law and customs of the city, not in Foucault's self-fashioning. Plato emphasizes that the citizens must willingly accept this system of laws which inculcates such discipline, but it is systematic socialization and education which produce the acceptance. Aristotle, in the final sections of *Politics* where he develops his own ideal *polis*, articulates a political system which is fundamentally similar in its conceptualization of civic virtue. In short, Plato's and Aristotle's political theory is founded upon a kind of self-mastery and civic virtue which bears little resemblance to the individualistic aesthetic ideal which Foucault portrays.

II IMPERIAL ROME

In the third volume of *The History of Sexuality*, *The Care of the Self*, Foucault presents a subtle reading of several authors of the early Roman empire (27 BCE to CE 235) to locate a shift in the sexual interests of the self-fashioning subject: "a closer attention, an increased anxiety concerning sexual conduct, a greater importance accorded to marriage and its demands, and less value given to the love of boys."[31] This shift, according to Foucault, was embedded in a wider social development toward the universalization of marriage as a social bond. As with Greece, Foucault's representation of the social context of the Roman discourse on sexuality and marriage is misleading in important respects, and his interpretation of the chosen imperial texts is very incomplete.

Basic to Foucault's narrative is his historicization of the marriage bond that Roman authors believed to be natural and timeless. The "greater importance accorded to marriage" takes on special significance when placed in Foucault's history of Roman social relations. In earlier, republican Rome marriage was "only a de facto condition"; it "held no interest, had no reason for being, except insofar as, although a private act, it had legal effects or at least effects relative to status: handing down a name, instituting heirs, organizing a system of alliances, joining fortunes. This meant something only to those who were capable of developing strategies in such domains."[32] All this changed under the emperors beginning with Augustus.

> The economico-political imperatives that governed marriage (making it necessary in some cases, and in others, useless) must have lost some of their importance when, in the privileged classes, status and fortune came to depend on proximity to the prince, on a civil or military "career," on success in "business," more than simply on the alliance between family groups. Less encumbered with various strategies, marriage became "freer": free in the choice of a wife; free, too, in the decision to marry and in the reasons for doing so. It could be, too, that in the underprivileged classes, marriage became – beyond the economic motives that could make it attractive – a form of tie that owed its value to the fact that it established and maintained strong personal relationships, implying the sharing of life, mutual aid, and moral support. . . . it seems that [marriage] became more accessible; the thresholds that made it "interesting" were lowered. Hence marriage appeared more and

more as a voluntary union between two partners whose inequality diminished to a certain extent but did not cease to exist.[33]

Within this social history, ethical thought about sexual relations and in particular marriage was refocused and intensified. Foucault compares Xenophon's classical Greek delineation of Ischomachus' relationship with his wife (early fourth century BCE) with Pliny's expressions of his feelings toward his wife Calpurnia (ca. CE 100). The differences between the relationships point to a relatively new way of considering married life, detached from the category of household management. The new features include: (1) an emphasis on the stylistics of the personal bond in place of household government; (2) the "valorization" of the wife as other, whose role is based on reciprocity with her husband; (3) an "art of marriage – in the form of symmetrical relationship" concentrating on conjugal sexual relations as a stimulus to love, affection, and mutual sympathy.[34] In the new stylistics marriage is: (1) dual (not just procreative but communal, as expressed in the simile of the yoke); (2) universal (not just a better alternative, but the only choice for a dutiful man); (3) singular (insofar as it surpassed all other kinship bonds, even that of parent and child).[35]

Intrinsic to the new stylistics is the art of dialogue between husband and wife: whereas Xenophon's Ischomachus gave authoritarian advice in answer to his wife's ignorant questions, Pliny and Calpurnia exchanged information and approval. The wife became "a companion to whom one opens one's soul."[36] The conclusion to the chapter, "The Marriage Tie," describes the wife as "treated as a being identical to oneself and as an element with whom one forms a substantial unity." Indeed, within this entire philosophy, "the woman as spouse is valorized as the other par excellence. . . . Compared with the traditional forms of matrimonial relations, the change was considerable."[37]

"Considerable" understates the magnitude of the changes claimed by Foucault. The Roman view of society was fundamentally hierarchical: each human being occupied a place in social hierarchies – as senator, humble citizen, or slave, male or female – to rule or to be ruled accordingly. If the new self-fashioning Roman really had come to think of his wife "as a being identical to oneself" in a "symmetrical" relationship, this would imply a revision of the most basic premise of how a Roman viewed himself in relation to others. Can such a radical shift, extending well beyond the experience of sexuality, be found in the Roman imperial texts?

The historical context and the wider discourse about marriage

For his historical account of the development of marriage, Foucault depends on the work of Paul Veyne, who claimed that in earlier Rome marriage was only a matter of legal status and property, and therefore only of interest to those with status and property; then under the emperors marriage became more widespread and based on "the law of the heart."[38] This historical claim about social practice rests on a confusion between marriage in its strict legal sense (*matrimonium iustum*) and marriage in the broader sense of a stable union between man and woman. Veyne's alleged historical shift is actually a product of a shift in his own focus from the former to the latter. *Matrimonium iustum*, with its legal implications for property inheritance, was *always* limited to a privileged subset of the population, the citizenry (though citizenship spread geographically). Marriage in its more general sense (the one of concern to Foucault) was *always* of interest to all sections of the population. Roman authors believed men's urge to marry and to cherish wife and children was natural and universal. The earliest writers provide evidence that slaves established family units as "husband" and "wife," when allowed to do so by their masters, although they had no incentives of property or status.[39] Romans did not believe, and there is no reason for us to believe, that in some early era marriage was an affectionless bond formed only by those with status and property at stake.

It is also doubtful that later under the emperors the decision to marry among the elite was freed much from traditional concerns of property and status. Social standing continued in the imperial era to depend on wealth: among the elite it remained essential for fathers or other relatives to arrange marriages with an eye to the property and status of the proposed spouse; to do otherwise would have been irresponsible in their view. Furthermore, senators and equestrians continued to see marriage bonds as political alliances between families.[40] Tacitus in the late first century CE described the marriage of his father-in-law to a woman of "splendid birth" as "an honor and a source of strength," not as an individual choice of lifestyle.[41]

The concern with property and succession explains why marriage continued to be regarded by the elite as appropriate at particular times in the life course and not at others. The respectable practice for an old widower in search of companionship remained concubinage, because any children by a concubine would not be legitimate and complicate the settlement of the estate. Foucault emphasizes that in the new stylistics sexual intercourse must be restricted to marriage for purposes of procreation, and notes that the highly ethical Marcus Aurelius abstained from sex before marriage. What Foucault does not say is that Marcus took a concubine after the death of his wife. It was a respectable choice, made by his adoptive father, Antoninus Pius, and his own grandfather, as well as other senators. The propriety of concubinage, even among the self-fashioning philosophers, shows that attitudes had not yet changed to the point that in principle the companionship of marriage was elevated above issues of succession accompanying legitimate children.[42]

To assess Foucault's claims, more important than social practice is the wider Roman discourse about marriage. The shift posited by Foucault is summed up in his contrast between Xenophon's *Oeconomicus* of the fourth century BCE and Pliny's love letters of ca. CE 100. Foucault's choice of texts is somewhat arbitrary: it is not obvious that a comparison between a treatise on household management of one period and personal letters of another should be generalized to conclude that there was a change in the subjective experience of sexuality. A more appropriate comparison could be drawn between the *Oeconomicus* and Columella's treatise on estate management from the mid-first century CE. Far from witnessing a new passionate involvement in marriage, Columella laments the *decline* in the marriage bond from ancient times, when husband and wife virtuously cooperated with a view to *concordia* and *diligentia* in the home, to his own degenerate era, when "most wives are so abandoned to luxury and idleness that they do not appear to undertake supervision of even the wool-making."[43] This is not to suggest that a comparison of Xenophon and Columella yields a truer history of sexuality and marriage, but that the selection of texts is critically important and requires reflection and justification. The male discourse about the marriage bond and the relationship to woman was many-sided and many-layered; any one strand is best understood in the context of the rest of the discourse. Full elaboration of the discourse is not possible here, but a few points may be made about the limitations of Foucault's discussion.

First, the assertion of the value of marriage on the part of Foucault's imperial moralists was part of a debate over the advantages and disadvantages of marriage – a debate going back as far as Roman literature itself. The comedies of Plautus, the earliest extant Roman literature, present male characters reflecting on how a wife would affect their style of life. The strongest statement in favor of the marriage bond in the self-representation of a senator comes from one of the earliest Latin authors, the elder Cato, who in early second century BCE "thought it more praiseworthy to be a good husband than a great senator."[44] On the other side, one of the censors of the second century BCE labelled wives a necessary nuisance.[45] That misogynistic strain continued through the imperial era, unabated by inflections. Athenaeus, in his late second-century CE *Deipnosophists*, imagined an after-dinner discussion about marriage in which the male participants in favor of wives compose a very short list of (two) good women from Greek myth and literature, and then are overwhelmed by their opponents' long list of evil women like Medea who would make dangerous wives.[46]

The fullest expression of the criticism of marriage and women was written, perhaps not coincidentally, in the same period as Foucault's moral advocates of marriage wrote. Juvenal's *Sixth Satire* presents a vicious attack on women whose unbridled sexuality and learning make them distasteful and dangerous to men.

> most serious of all is that woman, who when she begins to recline at dinner, praises Vergil, pardons the dying Dido, draws up and compares the bards, then weighs Vergil against Homer; grammarians give way, rhetoricians are vanquished, the entire crowd is silent; neither the lawyer nor herald may speak, not even another woman. . . . A philosopher, she fixes the ends of life and the honorable means. . . . Let not the matron, who reclines in company with you, have her own style of speaking; let her not twist the enthymeme curved by circular speech; let her not know all histories, and let her not understand certain things from books.[47]

This hostility toward female learning has a bearing on the interpretation of the marriage bond by Foucault's moralists, to be discussed below. The point here is that there was a centuries-long, repetitious debate among men about the value of marriage and women. The debate took the form of high philosophical argument and of ordinary abuse. Since Foucault does not attempt to sketch this debate and place his moralists within it, his claims about the increasing valorization of marriage represented in the texts of those authors are difficult to justify.[48]

Second, the varied layers of discourse about marriage enable Roman authors to discuss marriage in different terms in different contexts. The senator Pliny is held up by Foucault as the exemplar of the passionate love for wife in the new stylistics of marriage. It is true that Pliny expresses his passionate desire for his young wife Calpurnia in a few of his letters, yet in many other letters written for other purposes he repeats the most traditional attitudes toward marriage. His letters about the arrangement of marriages reveal not a freer choice of spouse based on some moral stylistic, but the most conventional social and economic values. In response to a senatorial colleague's request for suggestions of a husband for his orphaned niece, Pliny took it upon himself to recommend a candidate.[49] The letter aims to identify a man worthy to be the father of the deceased Arulenus Rusticus' grandchildren rather than a worthy or pleasurable companion for the girl. The qualities that recommend a candidate include his respectable friends, home town and family, his personal energy and modesty, his current senatorial rank (which will exempt the girl's uncle from the need to campaign on his behalf), his good looks and dignified bearing, and finally a wealthy father. To the comment about the young man's looks is appended an explanation that Pliny regards them as worthy of comment as "a sort of prize" for the "girl's chastity." The remark regarding wealth required a brief apologetic: of course, enlightened men should not be preoccupied with estate values (as were most Romans), yet for the sake of descendants of the marriage the matter could not be ignored.

This letter is valuable because it comes from the circles of the philosophically enlightened; its very existence, and the values it represents, do not present a new stylistic of marriage based on personal choice about an individual relationship. There is much in the letter about descent, public (male) virtues, and wealth; only a short reference to physical attractiveness, and not a word directly addressed to companionability. The terms of this letter are repeated elsewhere. In a letter congratulating a senior senator on his choice of a son-in-law, Pliny praises the latter's patrician descent, his erudition, and his personal characteristic of *simplicitas, comitas*, and *gravitas*. "It remains for him as quickly as possible to make you a grandfather of grandchildren similar to yourself."[50] Again, marriage is praised in terms of the relationship between two men and the prospects for posterity, without consideration of the personal relationship between husband and wife. Valorization of the conjugal relationship is difficult to discover in these criteria for arranging marriages; if there are any inflections, they are to be found in the brief apologetics regarding wealth and the stress on virtues of character. The father-in-law reveals his own value system in the choice of a son-in-law, and vice versa, as is evident in Pliny's comment on Musonius Rufus' own choice of the philosopher Artemidorus to be his son-in-law. Artemidorus possessed *sinceritas, veritas, patientia*, and *continentia*; these virtues and others won for him the competition for Musonius' seal of approval as a son-in-law. Marriage choices have not become more private and personal with the valorization of the wife so much as the terms of public prestige have changed slightly, with greater emphasis on philosophical virtues.[51]

In sum, as the historical background of practice and discourse is filled in, the inflections discovered in the texts of the proponents of the new stylistic of marriage become fainter. Advocates of the value of the marriage bond as well as detractors can be found early and late in Roman history. The attitudes toward marriage depicted by Foucault coexisted, in the same authors, with the most traditional attitudes about the purposes of marriage.

Musonius Rufus, Plutarch, and Pliny on companionship and the art of dialogue in marriage

Foucault's exploration of the nature of the new marriage bond repeatedly draws on the works of Musonius Rufus, Plutarch, and Pliny. There he finds evidence of the new stylistics emphasizing symmetry and near equality in the relationship fashioned by the husband with his wife. This representation strikes us as a very partial reading; the following pages reexamine those authors to elaborate their views of marriage with special attention to the asymmetries they envisioned.

The first point to be made is a general and fundamental one: these authors did not alter their fundamentally hierarchical view of human relationships. Musonius Rufus argued that the need for knowledge of how to rule was not limited to kings, for every man needs to rule (*archein*) "his subordinate friends, his wife and his children."[52] This is not very different from Aristotle's discussion of modes of domination in the household. So also for Plutarch it was natural for the husband to rule over (*kratein*) his wife as the mind rules over the body.[53] In his *Dialogue on Love* Plutarch looks as if he is moving away from that position in arguing that it is acceptable for an older woman to marry a younger man – something that raised eyebrows precisely because it challenged the usual pattern of domination and subordination in marriage – yet even here he returns to the basic hierarchical premise that in the marital dyad one side must command, the other must obey, and the husband must not be tainted by servility (*adouloton*).[54]

How did Pliny, Musonius, and Plutarch envision the marriage bond in particular terms? They were part of an elite culture that placed great emphasis on philosophical and literary knowledge and on rhetorical polish in the cultivation and presentation of self. The quality of the marriage bond envisioned by these authors depends in no small way on the place or standing that wives have in this culture. In elite circles it was standard practice for girls to be married in their early or mid-teens to older men. As a result, wives did not have an opportunity to acquire before marriage the education that gave their husbands standing and authority in the wider society. None of the three authors questioned the practice of early female marriage, which effectively placed wives in a position of inferiority.

Foucault touches on the education of wives only fleetingly in an explication of Pliny's letter of praise about his own wife, Calpurnia. Their relationship, in his view, illustrates the new art of dialogue between husband and wife, encompassing an exchange of information and approval. Pliny describes how Calpurnia wished to be informed of Pliny's successes in the law court. "The taste his wife has for belles-lettres is inspired by the tenderness she feels for her husband. She must be the witness and *judge* of his literary endeavors. She reads his works, listens to his speeches and receives with pleasure the compliments she may hear."[55] If this were true, if Pliny came to regard his wife as a judge of his work whose approval contributed to his self-esteem, then there would be a case for the valorization of the wife as significant other and the symmetry of conjugal companionship.

Yet Foucault has misrepresented Pliny's attitude in an essential way. To appreciate the tone of Pliny's praise, it is necessary to set the context.[56] The letter was probably written in CE 104, addressed to Calpurnia's aunt, and one of nine letters mentioning Calpurnia out of a corpus of 319. At the time Calpurnia was in her earlier teens (three years later Pliny could still attribute a miscarriage in her first pregnancy to her youthful naivety about her own body); Pliny was a senior senator, an ex-consul in his mid-forties. Pliny's praise of his wife begins with her character and descent: she is worthy of her father, her grandfather, and her aunt; she possesses the traditional virtues of managing the house frugally and maintaining her chastity. She loves Pliny, and out of her love has taken up the study of literature. What form does the study take? "She has my small works, reads them, even memorizes them." She is anxious when he goes to plead in court and happy when he is done. She sends messengers to report on the outcome and the applause he receives. When he gives a recitation, she listens from behind a screen to his praises. "She sings my poetic verses and accompanies them on the lyre, not taught by any professional but by love, which is the best master."

"Symmetry" does not describe this relationship. Calpurnia came as an unformed young girl to the house of a husband thirty years her senior and one of the leaders in Latin literature. The letter does not say that she developed a general appreciation of letters, but that she memorized and set to music her husband's compositions. To call her a "judge" of Pliny's works is to distort the relationship, since she is not represented as having the independence of mind or the education to be such. Her role is vicariously to appreciate the approval of other men, whose judgment contributed to Pliny's prestige. The new stylistic of marriage practiced by Pliny was one of traditional male domination in which the husband educated and socialized his wife, much as envisioned in Xenophon's *Oeconomicus*.

Cast in more abstract and philosophical terms, Musonius Rufus' discussion of the marital relationship directly considers the proper education of the wife. Philosophers should marry and should educate their wives and daughters, but these two prescriptions are not related in a way to suggest a new, more equal relationship. Most of the reasons given by Musonius for marriage are traditional: marriage is in accordance with nature and divine sanction, and it is a citizen's duty to reproduce the next generation. He adds that no bond is more necessary or pleasant. But the pleasure is not represented as the result of a symmetrical or near-equal bond, as is made clear by Musonius' justification of the education of women. He advocates the unconventional position of a deeper, philosophical learning for women and then grounds it in the most traditional terms. In his view, women should receive *logos* to judge good and bad; men and women possess the same senses, body parts, and the same inclination for excellence (*arete*). What excellent qualities would a woman acquire by the study of philosophy? (1) A sense of household management, including the direction of slaves; (2) a sense of chastity and self-restraint; (3) a sense of justice to make her a blameless sharer of life and a likeminded workmate; (4) a sense of love toward her children; (5) a sense of courage; (6) energetic devotion to her family, so that she would be ready to nurse her children at her own breast, "to be a servant to her husband with her own hands," "to do without hesitation things which some consider suited to slaves (*doulika*)."[57]

Musonius realizes that his assertion that a man should educate his sons and daughters in the same way will draw criticism of the sort found in Juvenal's *Sixth Satire* from those who believe that literary education and associations with philosophers teach women to be arrogant and to talk in syllogisms.[58] The typical female life course meant that advanced education remained largely the preserve of males, but the lives of the philosophers did include a few examples of learned women. One was Hipparchia, an assertive woman of learning and the wife of Crates, the Cynic philosopher named by Musonius as a successful philosopher who took a wife. Diogenes Laertius[59] reports the tradition about Hipparchia who lived in the late fourth century BCE. She is said to have fallen in love with Crates' logic and life, turning away suitors of high birth, great wealth and beauty. Hipparchia's distressed parents begged Crates to discourage her attachment to him. Crates, as an unmannered Cynic, came before her, took off his clothes and said, " 'This is the bridegroom, here are his possessions, make your choice. For there will be no union, unless you take on similar habits.' " Undeterred, Hipparchia married Crates, dressed like him, and accompanied him in public and to dinner. The tradition remembered one of the dinners when she dramatically put down one Theodorus.

Crates and Hipparchia represent as close to a symmetrical, companionate marriage as can be found in the classical world: Hipparchia used the same education to achieve a relationship with, and the same kind of reputation as, her husband. What was Musonius' attitude toward such a role for the wife? He was at pains to eschew it, assuring those men worried about uppity women that women trained in philosophy will accept their lot: "the *logos* of the philosophers summons the woman to love and to serve her husband with her own hands."[60] He affirms that both men and women need justice, men to be good citizens, women to run the household. "I do not wish to say that it is necessary for women to possess technical skill and acuteness in argument, since they will philosophize as women."[61] Musonius could have justified the education of women in terms of shared intellectual pursuits and dialogue, as exemplified by Crates and Hipparchia; instead, he advocates a gendered philosophy that reaffirms the dichotomy between public male and private female roles. In so doing, he uses the strong language of servility to describe the goal of the inculcation of the natural female role in the household. In a sense, he is answering the sort of misogynistic complaints in Juvenal's *Sixth Satire*. To the male worry that knowledge makes women forget their subordinate place, Musonius does not argue for the value of symmetry or near equality of husband and wife, but asserts that proper knowledge reinforces subordination.

Plutarch's comments on the education of the wife in his *Conjugal Precepts* are also best interpreted as part of an idealization of subordination. This tract of advice to a newly wed couple concludes with an exhortation to each. Pollianus is encouraged to study philosophy and not only for his own self-improvement. "For your wife you must collect from every source what is useful, as bees do, and carrying it within your own self impart it to her, and then discuss it with her, and make the best of these doctrines her favorite and familiar. For to her 'Thou art a father and a precious-loved mother, / and a brother as well.' No less ennobling is it for a man to hear his wife say, 'My dear husband, "You are to me" guide, philosopher, and teacher in all that is most lovely and divine.' "[62] Plutarch asserts that wives need to be taught philosophy in order to keep them away from the superstitions and unworthy thoughts that women are prone to. It is essential for the husband to do the teaching because, according to Plutarch, a wife ought to talk only to her husband.[63] For all his insights into the relation between knowledge and power and for all his interest in this tract of Plutarch, Foucault says nothing about these passages advocating the complete dependence of the wife on her husband for the knowledge that this circle of men most valued. Instead of finding the emergence of the symmetrical relationship elaborated in *The Care of the Self*, we might discover in these texts young girls being married to husbands empowered with an ethical knowledge that aimed to socialize wives to accept their subordinate, quasi-servile roles within the household.

Plutarch does advocate complete unity in the conjugal relationship, but in a way that subverts symmetry or relative equality. He proposes the metaphor of two liquids mixing and points out that in such a solution the identity of each is given up.[64] His other comments, however, make it unmistakably clear that it is the wife's identity that should be negated. The wife is to accept her husband's leadership and to conform to his character –

so much so that she is to have no independent *pathos* of her own.[65] She is to stay at home, recognizing no friends of her own, only her husband's.[66] She is to replace her natal kin with her husband's family: "it is a nice thing if the wife, in the deference she shows, is observed to incline rather toward her husband's parents than her own, and, if she is distressed over anything, to refer it to them without the knowledge of her own parents."[67] As for property, their two estates should be united and treated as the husband's, even if the wife brings more to the marriage.[68] Patently "unity" does not result in "symmetry" or "reciprocity," but in the dissolution of the wife's independent being and her absorption by her husband.

That Musonius, Plutarch, and Pliny were advocating unity in marriage is a plausible interpretation. That it involved a certain reciprocity, in the sense that the husband was to educate and to gratify as he ruled,[69] is also true. (The Romans recognized the possibility of reciprocity even in the master–slave relationship.) That the new stylistic encompassed symmetry or equality, even in some qualified sense, is very doubtful. Foucault might have considered the implications of the myth used by both Musonius and Plutarch to justify their assertion of the primacy of the marriage bond. The Alcestis myth recurs in literature and art throughout antiquity and illustrates the most profound conjugal devotion. Admetus was allowed to recruit a replacement to die in his place when the fated day arrived. His parents refused to stand in for him, but his young, beautiful wife, Alcestis, agreed to sacrifice her life. Musonius and Plutarch adduce Alcestis as the highest example of wifely loyalty, and Athenaeus includes her in his list of good women (along with one other), but it was Euripides who in his fifth-century BCE tragedy asked the ethical question: what kind of husband would ask his wife to take his place in the grave? What kind of symmetry is implicit in this mythical example?[70]

Clearly, Roman imperial authors did not advocate or imagine that they would fashion generally symmetrical relationships with their wives. However, it is true that in regard to sexual relations a certain symmetry in standards can be identified. Foucault emphasizes that Musonius sternly condemns any trace of the double standard: if the wife may not have sexual relations with slaves, then the husband should be held to no less a standard. Foucault realizes that Musonius' strictness was "no doubt exceptional."[71] Plutarch, for instance, advises the wife to tolerate her husband's peccadilloes on the grounds that he directs his lust toward humbler women out of respect for his wife, like the Persian kings.[72] Elsewhere, in advocating that the husband restrict his sexual activity to marriage, Plutarch offers the age-old reason that husbands should not make their wives jealous.[73]

How much significance should be attached to Musonius' exceptional position? As Foucault notes, the admonition to restrict sex to marriage was not new and went back to the classical Greeks. The interdiction can be found in Plato's *Laws* and Aristotle's *Politics*, but, Foucault insists, only for reasons of state.[74] Foucault may overstate the change: Musonius also refers to public interest, and Plato in passing mentions the pleasure of the couple. Furthermore, the comparisons and contrasts are, to a certain extent, arbitrary and should not be generalized without justification. One might, as Foucault does not, compare Xenophon's and Plutarch's discussions on the effects of cosmetics on spouses' sexual attraction to one another. Both authors denounce the use of cosmetics by wives, but for different reasons. For Plutarch, it is a symptom of an improper moral example from the husband: "a man fond of his personal appearance makes a wife all paint and powder."[75] In Xenophon's dialogue, Ischomachus, upon seeing his wife in cosmetics and high heels, asks her whether she would prefer to see him with a complexion made ruddy by paint.[76] The underlying premise of Xenophon's conjugal exchange exhibits greater symmetry than Plutarch's statement insofar as it gives the wife credit for independent judgment (behave as you would have me behave) and it is a symmetry in the sphere of the sexual bond. Plutarch's premise, in accord with his views about education of the wife, amounts to a trickle-down morality.

Ultimately, the difficulty with identifying inflections in the sexual and marital relations experienced by Romans of the empire is (as Foucault knew well) that neither classical Greek nor imperial Roman texts yield unified, consistent expressions. Consequently, everything depends on the choice of authors and specific texts from those authors. Suggesting that there was no sea-change, but smaller inflections, Foucault rightly hedged his claims with cautions and qualifications. Nevertheless, it is important to expand his brief qualification that inequality between spouses "did not cease to exist."[77] Whereas Foucault simply chose not to explore the issues of power and knowledge in the two-sided relationship, from our point of view any understanding of the experiences and representations of either side in such relationships is unacceptably narrow if it does not thoroughly explore the implications for the other party to the bond. As has been noted by feminists, Foucault was interested in marriage but not in women.[78] Read as a whole, the Roman authors selected by Foucault did not question the basically hierarchical view of social relations with their ideas about marriage. On the contrary, the valorization of marriage was justified by reference to the natural order, which required the subordination of wife to husband far more insistently than a symmetry or dialogue between them. Conjugal dialogue and education of the wife had the aim of teaching her to accept her subordination and even the dissolution of her independent will.

III   CONCLUSION: KNOWLEDGE AND POWER IN THE CLASSICAL EXPERIENCE OF SEXUALITY

Foucault's preoccupation with the ethic of the self-fashioning subject, this interior view of morality as the inner freedom to create, is alien to the patterns of social and political life and theory of Athens and Rome. Moreover, it also seems very much at odds with the external, political perspective articulated in *The History of Sexuality*, volume 1, *Discipline and Punish, Madness and Civilization*, and elsewhere. Without attempting a full account of this shift in focus in Foucault's work, we want to suggest some directions for further reflection.

At the beginning of *The Use of Pleasure* Foucault tries to establish the essential unity of his work, placing the last two volumes of *The History of Sexuality* in a grand unitary scheme of his major works. These volumes, however, seem distinctly different from this earlier work, including *The History of Sexuality*, volume 1. An early interview (March 1966) gives a sense of the distance travelled: "In a society, different bodies of learning, philosophical ideas, everyday opinions, but also institutions, commercial practices and police activities – all refer to a certain implicit knowledge (*savoir*) special to this society. This knowledge is profoundly different from the bodies of learning one can find in scientific books, philosophical theories and religious justifications, but it is what makes possible at a given moment the appearance of a theory, an opinion, a practice."[79] At the end of the same interview he discusses the limitations and self-referentiality of the traditional disciplines of the history of ideas, history of philosophy, and history of science because they define their field of study in relation to certain "privileged objects" in the form of a narrow canon of classical texts. From this perspective, "one cannot fail to be struck by the impossibility for our own culture to pose the problem of the history of its own thought. It's why I have tried to make . . . the history not of thought in general but of all that 'contains thought' in a culture, of all in which there is thought. For there is thought in philosophy, but also in a novel, in jurisprudence, in law, in an administrative system, in a prison."[80] These non-philosophical sources are not fully explored in the attempt in *The Use of Pleasure* to reconstruct the norms and practices, the sexual experiences of ancient Greece. There, and in *The Care of the Self* as well, Foucault examines not the strategies, tactics, and micro-physics of power, but "thought," and examines it largely in terms of the philosophical and scientific canon whose limitations he had earlier so clearly recognized.[81]

Indeed, it was precisely his disavowal of traditional intellectual history in favor of an "archaeological" methodology that enraged or inspired practitioners of many disciplines in the humanities and social sciences. In an interview in 1969 Foucault explains this method of "archaeology," setting out four questions which define such an investigation: "What are the different particular types of discursive practice that one can find in a given period? What are the relationships that one can establish between these different practices? What relationships do they have with non-discursive practices, such as political, social, or economic practices? What are the transformations of which these practices are susceptible?"[82] Although Foucault explicitly states that *The Use of Pleasure* and *The Care of the Self* deploy an archaeological method, one searches in vain for the kind of differentiation of discursive practices and their relation to institutions and power he discussed earlier. Instead we find a vaguely defined cultural/ intellectual history where a group of widely divergent texts are simply taken as given and read together as if they constitute a larger cultural "text" which can be unproblematically interpreted as "Greek thought" or "Greco-Roman society."

In discussing the first volume of *The History of Sexuality* in 1977 Foucault underscored that this investigation centrally involves a conception of power and its relation to the production of "truth."[83] He traces the beginning of this reorientation in his conception of power to the writing of *Discipline and Punish* and to the experiences of 1968. The investigation requires: "Four things: investigate what might be most hidden in power relations; anchor them in their economic infrastructures; trace them not only in their governmental forms but also in their infra-governmental or para-governmental ones; and recuperate them in their material play."[84] *The Order of Discourse* had treated power as "an essentially judicial mechanism, as that which lays down the law, which prohibits, which refuses, and which has a whole range of negative effects. . . . Now I believe that conception to be inadequate." This conception of power "not so much in terms of justice as in those of technology, tactics and strategy" provided the framework for *The History of Sexuality*, volume 1.[85] Yet it is precisely the earlier, traditional, juridical conception of sovereign power imposed from above, or lack thereof, that is central to the claims of the second and third volumes. Foucault asserts that since Greece and Rome were not "societies of the code" then they were societies of moral self-fashioning where no one imposed moral restraints upon anyone else, and where each individual was free to develop his subjectivity according to an "art of existence."[86]

The shift away from the "micro-physics" of power and institutional structures leads Foucault to reinterpret his earlier work: volumes 2 and 3 of *The History of Sexuality* "are completely similar to those I wrote on madness and punishment. In *Discipline and Punish* I didn't want to do a history of the prison as an institution. . . . Instead, I asked myself how thought about punishment has had, at the end of the 18th century and the beginning of the 19th century, a certain history. What I tried to do was a history of the relationships thought maintains with the truth."[87] Yet *Discipline and Punish* begins not with "thought about punishment", but its representation in the tortured body of Damiens and, later, in the architecture of the prison and in isomorphic institutional formations; the chapters on "Discipline" and "Delinquency" center on the institutional and material strategic matrices of power which define and enmesh the disciplinary subject.

However one reads *Discipline and Punish*, these late interviews reveal the extent to which Foucault in writing the second and third volumes of *The History of Sexuality* had moved away from the external view of the operation of the micro-physics of power upon the individual and had shifted his concern to the inner constitution of the subject. In 1984, in one of the last interviews before his death, Foucault was asked whether he had modified his view of the subject: "Your preceding works have given you the image of a thinker of inclosures and subjugated subjects who are constrained and disciplined. *The Use of Pleasure* and *The Concern for Self* offer us a completely different image of free subjects. It seems that this is an important modification of your own thought." Foucault responded that those who have taken him to claim that knowledge is a mask of power have completely misunderstood him; the relationship between power and knowledge is one neither of cause and effect nor of identity. What he wants to show is how forms of power can be linked to very different forms of knowledge and that power is not merely domination and oppression.[88] His answer does not really meet the central point of the question concerning the shift in the conception of the subject.[89]

The shift may be located between the first and the last two volumes of *The History of Sexuality*. In Foucault's words, "I changed the general project: instead of studying sexuality at the confines of knowledge (*savoir*) and power, I tried to investigate at a deeper level how the experience of sexuality as desire had been constituted for the subject himself."[90] He then describes the results of this "deeper" investigation in terms of a linear development based upon a homogenization of all of antiquity. The conception of the earlier stage in antiquity seems very much like a nineteenth century romantic notion of the freedom of men to create themselves before they were trapped in the iron cage of modernity.[91] "[I]n Antiquity the will to be a moral subject, the search for an ethics of existence, was principally an effort to affirm one's liberty and to give one's own life a certain form. . . . From Antiquity to Christianity one passes from a morality that was essentially a search for personal ethics to a morality as obedience to a system of rules."[92] In the absence of institutional and other normalizing forces, how did pre-Christian morality spread from the philosophical and scientific elite which invented it? How did it reproduce itself as a social system while remaining a morality of liberty where the powers of normalization were so minimal?[93] In Foucault's view, "at first ancient morality was addressed only to a small number of individuals.... It concerned only a small minority of the population and even among those who were free. There were several forms of liberty: the liberty of the chief of state or of the army had nothing to do with the sage." Though he believes that this morality spread in the first two centuries CE, he finds it "very difficult to know who participated in this morality in Antiquity and under the Empire."[94]

The models of historical change and social reproduction at work here are very unlike those employed in *Madness and Civilization*, volume 1 of *The History of Sexuality*, or *Discipline and Punish*. Indeed, they seem remarkably simplistic, with a small intellectual elite individually fashioning a new morality which slowly "trickles down" or mysteriously "spreads" to society at large.[95] The shallowness of this sort of account is especially noticeable in Foucault's explanation for the spread of interest in marriage to the underprivileged classes in the Roman empire: the common people, claims Foucault, only gradually became aware that marriage offered "the sharing of life, mutual aid, and moral support."[96] The simplistic elitism underlying this claim is implausible: were these advantages that ordinary Romans could not appreciate except through the intellectual guidance of their betters? In fact, the funerary commemorations of less exalted Romans celebrated just these marital values long before Foucault's imperial authors lived. Any serious analysis of the reproduction of such values would have to give attention to the whole of Greco-Roman society and to precisely those educational, military, legal, religious, cultural, and political institutions in which Foucault has no interest.

Foucault's earlier works documented change in a particularly striking manner because they were able to demonstrate the interaction of institutional developments, discursive practices, and new forms of knowledge. Having abandoned the communal, political frame of analysis for the individual, ethical – a particularly odd shift of analysis for societies conceptualizing the citizen as a *politikon zoon* – Foucault seems unable to ground this process in anything more substantial than a kind of crypto-Hegelian subjectivity slowly unfolding itself as the centuries progress. Whereas Hegel insisted upon the necessary embodiment of the Idea in institutions and practices, the model in Foucault's final work seems to be of thought itself spreading through some enigmatic process of self-generating diffusion.

Part II

The Constitution of the Subject

3

Ethics as Ascetics: Foucault, the History of Ethics, and Ancient Thought

Arnold I. Davidson

To Pierre Hadot on his seventieth birthday

In approaching the topic of Michel Foucault's significance for writing the history of ethics, I have two main goals in this chapter. First and foremost, I hope to be able to elucidate Foucault's own aims in shifting his attention, in his last writings, to what he himself called "ethics." These aims, in my opinion, have been widely misinterpreted and even more widely ignored, and the result has been a failure to come to terms with the conceptual and philosophical distinctiveness of Foucault's last works. Volumes 2 and 3 of the *The History of Sexuality* are about sex in roughly the way that *Discipline and Punish* is about the prison. As the modern prison serves as a reference point for Foucault to work out his analytics of power, so ancient sex functions as the material around which Foucault elaborates his conception of ethics. Although the history of sex is, evidently enough, sexier than the history of ethics, it is this latter history that oriented Foucault's last writings. Foucault once remarked to me, as he had to others, that "sex is so boring." He used this remark in different ways on different occasions, but one thing he meant by it was that what made sex so interesting to him had little to do with sex itself. His focus on the history of ancient sex, its interest for him, was part of his interest in the history of ancient ethics.

Whatever one's disagreements with Foucault's interpretation of specific ancient texts, his conceptualization of ethics, the framework in which he placed these interpretations, is as potentially transformative for writing the history of ethics as, to take the strongest comparison I can think of, John

Rawls's *A Theory of Justice* was, and remains, in its cultural context, for articulating the aims of political philosophy. But this transformative potential has been obscured for philosophy by a way of thinking about and writing the history of ethics that passes over the very domain that Foucault demarcated as ethics, as if whatever Foucault wrote about in these works it could not have been ethics. And this potential has been further darkened in the discussion of some classicists who, to give only a partial caricature, have been so taken up with tired and tiresome debates about whether Foucault knew enough Greek and Latin to legitimize his readings of the texts of classical and late antiquity that they have lost sight of his most basic aims. By giving an interpretation of Foucault's work that attempts to clarify these aims, and to show how they affected his readings of particular texts, I hope to reorient discussions of his last works toward what I think is genuinely at stake in them – how to conceptualize ethics and how to write its history.

My second goal, not unrelated to my first one, is to place Foucault's work in the context of writings by historians of ancient thought – Paul Veyne, Georges Dumézil, and, especially, Pierre Hadot – with whom Foucault was engaged in intense, if sometimes submerged, intellectual exchange. These writers, as well as others such as Jean-Pierre Vernant, in turn, discussed Foucault's work in terms that help us to see how it can be elaborated and criticized in philosophically fruitful ways. The reception of Foucault's last writings by French ancient historians and philosophers is so markedly disjoint from its Anglo-American reception, not, as some people seem to believe, because of the dynamics of French fads, but rather because the manner in which Foucault conceptualized issues showed clear resonances with work that had been and continues to be undertaken by the most significant historians of ancient thought in France. Setting the proper intellectual context will help us to understand better the contours and emplacement of Foucault's own writing on ancient thought, and thus help us to see how his conceptualization of ethics relates to, derives from, and modifies a set of considerations that were not his alone.

One of my ultimate interests in Foucault's interpretation of ethics stems from the way in which I think it can be used to transform our understanding of texts and historical periods that he himself did not discuss. In other parts of this project to reassess Foucault's history of ethics, I try to show how his *conceptualization* of ethics provides a compelling interpretative framework for understanding the genre of early Christian virginity treatises. Less predictably, I also argue that Old Testament texts on abominations can be rethought, and certain longstanding problems resolved, by sifting these texts through the specific conception of ethics rooted in Foucault's work. But this interest in using Foucault requires a positioning of his thought centered around the history of ethics, and it is to this philosophical positioning, its concepts, its sources, and its consequences, that I shall restrict myself here.

The first volume of Michel Foucault's *The History of Sexuality* was published in 1976. The back cover of that volume announced the titles of the five forthcoming volumes that would complete Foucault's project. Volume 2 was to be called *The Flesh and the Body*, and would concern the prehistory of our modern experience of sexuality, concentrating on the problematization of sex in early Christianity. Volumes 3 through 5 were to focus on some of the major figures (of the eighteenth and nineteenth centuries) around which problems, themes, and questions of sex had come to circle. Volume 3, *The Children's Crusade*, would discuss the sexuality of children, especially the problem of childhood masturbation; volume 4, *Woman, Mother, Hysteric*, would discuss the specific ways in which sexuality had been invested in the female body; volume 5, *Perverts*, was planned to investigate exactly what the title named, the person of the pervert, an ever-present target of nineteenth-century thought. Finally, volume 6, *Population and Races*, was to examine the way in which treatises, both theoretical and practical, on the topics of population and race were linked to the history of what Foucault had called "biopolitics."[1]

In 1984, when volumes 2 and 3 of *The History of Sexuality* were finally published, some years after they had been expected, many of Foucault's readers must have been, to say the least, bewildered by their content. This bewilderment was occasioned, most immediately, by the profound chrono-logical reorientation of these two volumes. Volume 2, *The Use of Pleasure*, studied problems of sex in classical Greek thought, while volume 3, *The Care of the Self*, analyzed these problems as they appeared in Greek and Latin texts of the first and second centuries AD. Moreover, in the introduction to volume 2, which served as an introduction to his new project, Foucault reconceptualized the entire aim of his history of sexuality, introducing a set of concepts that had been absent from volume 1. The most significant philosophical consequence of this reorientation was Foucault's conceptualization of ethics, his theoretical elaboration of ethics as a framework for interpreting these Greek and Roman problematizations of sex. I shall leave aside here many of the general features of Foucault's conceptualization of ethics, since I have discussed them at length elsewhere.[2] But, given the way this chapter will proceed, I should at least remind readers that Foucault thought of ethics as that component of morality that concerns the self's relationship to itself. Foucault argued that our histories of morality should not be so exclusively focused on the history of codes of moral behavior, but that we must also pay careful attention to the history of the forms of moral subjectivation, to how we constitute ourselves as moral subjects of our own actions. Foucault thought of ethics proper, of the self's relationship to itself, as having four main aspects: the ethical substance, that part of oneself that is taken to be the relevant domain for ethical judgment; the mode of subjection, the way in which the individual establishes his or her relation to moral obligations and rules; the self-forming activity or ethical work that one performs on oneself in order to transform oneself into an ethical subject; and, finally, the telos, the mode of being at which one aims in behaving ethically.[3]

Another way of understanding Foucault's new concern with the self's relationship to itself is to think of it, as Foucault himself explicitly did in 1980–1, as at the intersection of two themes that he had previously treated, namely a history of subjectivity and an analysis of the forms of governmentality. Foucault claimed that he had undertaken to study the history of subjectivity by studying the divisions carried out in society in the name of madness, illness, and delinquency, and by studying the effects of these divisions on the constitution of the subject. In addition, his history of subjectivity attempted to locate the "modes of objectivation" of the subject in scientific knowledge, for example knowledge concerning language (linguistics), work (economics), and life (biology). As for the analysis of forms of "governmentality," a crucial concept for Foucault's work beginning around 1977, this analysis responded to a "double objective." On the one hand, Foucault wanted to criticize current conceptions of power which, in one way or another, thought of power as a unitary system, a critique undertaken most thoroughly in *Discipline and Punish* and volume 1 of *The History of Sexuality*. On the other hand, Foucault wanted to analyze power as a domain of strategic relations between individuals and groups, relations whose strategies were to govern the conduct of these individuals.[4] Thus Foucault's new concern with the self would be

> a way of doing the history of subjectivity: no longer, however, by way of the divisions between the mad and those who are not mad, the ill and those who are not ill, delinquents and those who are not delinquents; no longer by way of the constitution of the field of scientific objectivity giving rise to the living, speaking, working subject. But rather by the putting into place and the transformations, in our culture, of the "relations to oneself," with their technical armature and their effects of knowledge. And one could thus take up, under another aspect, the question of "governmentality": the government of the self by the self in its articulation with relations to others (as one finds it in pedagogy, advice for conduct, spiritual direction, the prescription of models of life, etc.).[5]

As I would interpret Foucault, ethics, or the self's relation to itself, is therefore part of both the history of subjectivity and the history of governmentality. Our "technologies of the self,"[6] the ways in which we relate ourselves to ourselves, contribute to the forms in which our subjectivity is constituted and so experienced as well as to the forms in which we govern our thought and conduct. We relate to ourselves as specific kinds of subjects who govern themselves in particular ways. In response to the questions "What kinds of subjects should we be?" and "How should we govern ourselves?" Foucault offered his history of ethics.

As has received frequent commentary, beside the concepts I have already mentioned, Foucault's last works introduced other related notions, most prominently that of the aesthetics of existence and styles of existence. These notions are, in my opinion, far more complex and multilayered than most commentators have acknowledged, but I shall not now undertake the detailed exegetical work that would be necessary to disentangle all of these layers. Certainly one central aspect of these notions has been lucidly described by Paul Veyne:

> The idea of styles of existence played a major role in Foucault's conversations and doubtless in his inner life during the final months of a life that only he knew to be in danger. *Style* does not mean distinction here; the word is to be taken in the sense of the Greeks, for whom an artist was first of all an artisan and a work of art was first of all a work. Greek ethics is quite dead and Foucault judged it as undesirable as it would be impossible to resuscitate this ethics; but he considered one of its elements, namely, the idea of a work of the self on the self, to be capable of reacquiring a contemporary meaning, in the manner of one of those pagan temple columns that one occasionally sees reutilized in more recent structures. We can guess at what might emerge from this diagnosis: the self, taking itself as a work to be accomplished, could sustain an ethics that is no longer supported by either tradition or reason; as an artist of itself, the self would enjoy that autonomy that modernity can no longer do without. "Everything has disappeared," said Medea, "but I have one thing left: myself."[7]

This aspect of Foucault's idea of the aesthetics of existence reaches its apogee in *The Care of the Self*, especially in the chapter entitled "The Cultivation of the Self." In this chapter, Foucault argues that in the texts of the first two centuries AD with which he is concerned there is an "insistence on the attention that must be brought to bear on oneself," and that the added emphasis on sexual austerity in these texts should not be interpreted in terms of a tightening of the moral code and its prohibitions, but rather in terms of "an intensification of the relation to oneself by which one constituted oneself as the subject of one's acts."[8] More specifically, he argues that the practices of the self in late antiquity are characterized by the general principle of conversion to self – *epistrophé eis heauton*.[9] This conversion to self requires that one change one's activities and shift one's attention so as to constantly take care of oneself. One result of this conversion, claims Foucault, is the "experience of a pleasure that one takes in oneself. The individual who has finally succeeded in gaining access to himself is, for himself, an object of pleasure."[10] And Foucault quotes Seneca:

> "*Disce gaudere*, learn how to feel joy," says Seneca to Lucilius: "I do not wish you ever to be deprived of gladness. I would have it born in your house; and it is born there, if only it is inside of you . . . for it will never fail you when once you have found its source . . . look toward the true good, and rejoice only in that which comes from your own store [*de tuo*]. But what do I mean by 'your own store'? I mean your very self and the best part of you."[11]

These texts certainly appear to advocate an aesthetics of existence, a cultivation of the self, which culminates, to quote Veyne's words again, in "that autonomy that modernity cannot do without," and which is symbolized by the pleasure that one takes in oneself, a pleasure of which one cannot be deprived. But, as Pierre Hadot has convincingly argued, Seneca opposes pleasure and joy – *voluptas* and *gaudium* – and it is misleading for Foucault to speak of the joy described by Seneca as "a form of pleasure."[12] More importantly, as Hadot indicates, Seneca finds his joy not in his self *per se*, but in that "best part of the self" that Seneca identifies with perfect reason and, ultimately, with divine reason:

> The "best part" of oneself, then, is ultimately a transcendent self. Seneca does not find his joy in "Seneca", but by transcending Seneca; by discovering that he has in him a reason that is part of universal Reason, that is within all human beings and within the cosmos itself.[13]

Hadot has argued that an essential element of the psychic content of the spiritual exercises of ancient philosophy is "the feeling of belonging to a Whole," what he often describes as a cosmic consciousness, a consciousness of being part of the cosmic whole.[14] This consciousness is summarized in Seneca's four words: "Toti se inserens mundo" ("Plunging oneself into the totality of the world").[15] So adjacent to the cultivation of the self, that movement of interiorization in which "one seeks to be master of oneself, to possess oneself, to find one's happiness in freedom and inner independence," emphasized by Foucault, there is "another movement, in which one raises oneself to a higher psychic level . . . which consists in becoming aware of oneself as part of Nature, as a portion of universal Reason."[16]

Indeed, I would claim, following Hadot, that one of the most distinctive features of that care of the self studied by Foucault in volume 3 of *The History of Sexuality* is its indissociable link with this cosmic consciousness; one philosophical aim of this care of the self is to transform oneself so that one places oneself in the perspective of the cosmic Whole. The care of the self receives its distinctive philosophical tint in late antiquity through those practices that raise the self to a universal level, that place the self within a cosmic dimension that at the same time transforms the self, even to the point, as Hadot writes, of surpassing the self:

> In Platonism, but in Epicureanism and Stoicism as well, freedom from anxiety is thus achieved by a movement in which one passes from individual and impassioned subjectivity to the objectivity of the universal perspective. It is a question, not of a construction of a self as a work of art, but, on the contrary, of a surpassing of the self, or, at the least, of an exercise by which the self situates itself in the totality and experiences itself as part of this totality.[17]

As Foucault himself made clear in his 1981–2 course at the Collège de France, the care of the self has a very long history.[18] In trying to recapture the different forms in which the care of the self has appeared, it is essential to understand not only the ways in which the self became an object of concern, but also the ways in which one went beyond oneself, relating the self to something grander than itself. The spiritual exercises of ancient philosophy, that philosophical *askesis* so central to Foucault's last works, could, at one and the same time, result in an intense preoccupation with the self and in a sort of dilation of the self that realized the true magnitude of the soul.[19] Hadot is concerned that by focusing too exclusively on the cultivation of the self – and by linking his ethical model too closely to an aesthetics of existence – Foucault was suggesting "a culture of the self that is too purely aesthetic."[20] In other words, writes Hadot, "I fear a new form of dandyism, a version for the end of the twentieth century."[21] Without taking up Foucault's discussion – in his essay "What is Enlightenment?" – of dandyism in Baudelaire,[22] I do think that there is a use of the concept of styles of existence to be found in Foucault's last works that can and ought to be preserved; one, moreover, that aligns Foucault's writings more closely with Hadot's own interpretation of ancient thought. Although I believe that Foucault's interpretation of the culture of the self in late antiquity is sometimes too narrow and therefore misleading, I think that this a *defect of interpretation, not of conceptualization.*[23]

Foucault's conceptualization of ethics as the self's relationship to itself provides us with a framework of enormous depth and subtlety, and it is this framework – of ethical substance, mode of subjection, self-forming activity and telos – that allows us to grasp aspects of ancient thought which would otherwise remain occluded. I have argued elsewhere that Foucault's conception of ethics is, in fact, indebted to Hadot's work in *Exercices spirituels et philosophie antique*, to Hadot's history of ancient philosophy as a history of spiritual exercises.[24] Nevertheless, by giving detailed conceptual content to the idea of the self's relationship to itself, by analyzing this relationship in terms of four distinct components, Foucault makes it possible for us to see precisely how to write a history of ethics that will not collapse into a history of moral codes. Furthermore, his conceptualization allows us to examine the connections, the kinds of dependence and independence, among these four aspects of ethics, thus showing us the various ways in which continuities, modifications, and ruptures can occur in one or more of these four dimensions of our relation to ourselves. In some historical periods, for example, the ethical substance may remain constant, while the mode of subjection gradually alters; or the telos may stay continuous, while the self-forming activity is modified. In other periods, the ethical substance, mode of subjection, self-forming activity, and telos may be so inextricably intertwined that they undergo change together, thereby resulting in an entirely new form of the self's relationship to itself.

Pierre Hadot has brilliantly shown that one of the fundamental aspects of philosophy in the Greek, Hellenistic, and Roman eras is that philosophy "is a way of life, which does not mean only that it is a certain moral conduct . . . but that it is a way of existing in the world, which should be practiced at each instant and which should transform all of life."[25] A sense of philosophy as a way of life is also expressed by Foucault when he explains his own motivation in writing the second and third volumes of *The History of Sexuality*. After claiming that for him philosophical activity consists in "the endeavor to know how and to what extent it might be possible to think differently,"[26] Foucault writes:

> The "essay" – which should be understood as the assay or test by which, in the game of truth, one undergoes changes, and not as the simplistic appropriation of others for the purpose of communication – is the living substance of philosophy, at least if we assume that philosophy is still what it was in times past, i.e., an ascesis, *askésis*, an exercise of oneself in the activity of thought.[27]

For Foucault himself philosophy was a spiritual exercise, an exercise of oneself in which one submitted oneself to modifications and tests, underwent changes, in order to learn to think differently. This idea of philosophy as a way of life and, I shall argue, of ethics as proposing styles of life is one of the most forceful and provocative directions of Foucault's later thought.

In approaching these ideas, I want first to distinguish between the notions of a way of life and a style of life.[28] In the ancient world *philosophy itself* was a way of life, a way of life that was distinct from everyday life, and that was perceived as strange and even dangerous. In conveying this fact about philosophy, I can do no better here than to quote Hadot's marvelous description:

> to be a philosopher implies a rupture with what the skeptics called *bios*, that is, daily life. . . .
>
> This very rupture between the philosopher and the conduct of everyday life is strongly felt by nonphilosophers . . . philosophers are strange, a race apart. Strange indeed are those Epicureans, who lead a frugal life, practicing a total equality between the men and the women inside their philosophical circle – and even between married women and courtesans; strange, too, those Roman Stoics who disinterestedly administer the provinces of the Empire entrusted to them and are the only ones to take seriously the laws promulgated against excess; strange as well this Roman Platonist, the Senator Rogatianus, a disciple of Plotinus, who on the very day he is to assume his functions as praetor gives up his possessions, frees his slaves, and eats only every other day. Strange indeed all those philosophers whose behavior, without being inspired by religion, nonetheless completely breaks with the customs and habits of most mortals.
>
> By the time of the Platonic dialogues Socrates was called *atopos*, that is, "unclassifiable." What makes him *atopos* is precisely the fact that he is a "philo-sopher" in the etymological sense of the word; that is, he is in love with wisdom. For wisdom, says Diotima in Plato's *Symposium*, is not a human state, it is a state of perfection of being and knowledge that can only be divine. It is the love of this wisdom, which is foreign to the world, that makes the philosopher a stranger in it.[29]

Stoics, Epicureans, Platonists, Cynics, and even Skeptics each embodied the philosophical *way of life*, a way of life whose peculiarity, whatever its particular guises, was everywhere recognized. And early Christianity, itself conceived of as a way of life, namely living in conformity with the divine Logos, was also presented as a philosophy.[30] Socrates attempted to convert his interlocutors from the unexamined way of life to the philosophical way of life. It was this experience of philosophy as a way of life, and not simply as a theoretical doctrine, that brought Socrates into deadly conflict with the authorities.

Given this basic characteristic of philosophy itself as a way of life, there were, of course, different philosophies, what I shall call different *styles of life*, different styles of living philosophically. Each philosophical school –

Stoic, Epicurean, Platonist, and so on – represented a style of life that had a corresponding fundamental inner attitude.[31] As Hadot says, "In this period, to philosophize is to choose a school, convert to its way of life, and accept its dogmas."[32] I propose that we take each particular conceptual combination of ethical substance, mode of subjection, self-forming activity, and telos as representing a style of life. One's style of life, as specified by a determinate content and mesh of each of these four components, gives expression to the self's relationship to itself. To indicate what part of oneself one judges, how one relates oneself to moral obligations, what one does to transform oneself into an ethical subject, and what mode of being one aims to realize is to indicate how one lives, to characterize one's style of life. Although Foucault does not explicitly use the notion of style of life in exactly this way, this usage is, I believe, consistent with his interpretation of ancient philosophy. Reading the last volumes of *The History of Sexuality*, it is evident that the idea of the care of the self is part of a broader conceptual matrix, and that a history of the care of the self must be written in terms of a history of ethics.[33] In every historical period the care of the self is expressed in particular relationships of the self to itself, particular styles of life. As the self's relationship to itself undergoes modification, as the way in which one cares for oneself changes, one's style of life will change. And when Foucault says that the problem of an ethics is the problem of "a form" (I would say "style" here) "to be given to one's conduct and one's life" he does in fact link the notions of ethics and style of life in a conceptually intimate way.[34]

Some of Foucault's most suggestive, and philosophically revealing, invocations of the notions of *askesis* and style of life can be found in his discussions of his own attitude to homosexuality. Foucault claims that one goal of homosexuality today is "to advance into a homosexual *askesis* that would make us work on ourselves and invent, I do not say discover, a manner of being that is still improbable."[35] Let me underline, in this quotation, the connection between *askesis* and manner of being, a connection that is, so I would claim, also to be uncovered in Foucault's discussion of ancient male/male sexual practices. He insists that the notion of a homosexual mode or style of life, with its new forms of relationship, is what is most significant about contemporary gay practices:

> Is it possible to create a homosexual mode of life? This notion of mode of life seems important to me. . . . It seems to me that a way of life can yield a culture and an ethics. To be "gay," I think, is not to identify with the psychological traits and the visible marks of the homosexual, but to try to define and develop a way of life.[36]

Just as Foucault argued that ancient thought was not primarily concerned with the morphology of the sexual act,[37] so he too was interested not in the nature of the sexual act itself, its morphology or shape, but in the style of life, and the corresponding art of life, of which these sexual acts are part.[38] Even in his most explicit discussion of gay male sexual practices – "les pratiques physiques de type fist-fucking" – Foucault insists on relating these practices to a style of life that expresses a new sense of masculinity, a sense that is devirilized, even desexualized ("devirilisées, voire dé-sexuées").[39] So it is these "new forms of relationship, new forms of love, new forms of creation" that most captured Foucault's attention and interest.[40] Foucault believed that "what most bothers those who are not gay about gayness is the gay lifestyle, not sex acts themselves."[41] As strange as it may sound at first, Foucault pointed to homosexuality as one resource for answering the question of how to practice spiritual exercises in the twentieth century. Ultimately, for Foucault, one link between the ancient practices of self-mastery and contemporary homosexuality is that both require an ethics or ascetics of the self tied to a particular, and particularly threatening, way of life. I know it would have given Foucault genuine pleasure to think that the threat to everyday life posed by ancient philosophy had a contemporary analogue in the fears and disturbances that derive from the self-formation and style of life of being gay.[42]

Although Foucault's famous declaration that he is interested in writing the history of the present[43] must certainly be acknowledged as at play in his interpretation of ancient texts, and in the linkages that can be found in his emphases on ancient philosophical *askesis* and contemporary homosexual *askesis*, such a concern with the history of the present, which I share with Foucault, need not, and should not, lead us to transform the ancient intensification of the relation to the self into the modern aestheticization of the self. The ancient experience of the self ought to retain its distinctive-ness, not simply for reasons of historical accuracy, but especially if it is to provide a philosophical standpoint from which we can begin to learn how to think differently. In "The Individual within the City-State" Jean-Pierre Vernant has reminded us how conceptually specific is the ancient notion of *psuché*, and how distinct it is from the modern intimacy of the self. Vernant makes analytically useful distinctions between the individual, the subject, and the ego. The history of the individual, in the strict sense, concerns "his place and role in his group or groups; the value accorded him; the margin of movement left to him; his relative autonomy with respect to his institutional framework."[44] Vernant marks out the subject as "when the individual uses the first person to express himself and, speaking in his own name, enunciates certain features that make him a unique being."[45] Finally, the ego is the ensemble of psychological practices and attitudes that give an interior dimension and a sense of wholeness to the subject. These practices and attitudes constitute him within himself as a unique being, real and original, whose authentic nature resides entirely in the secrecy of his interior life. It resides at the very heart of an intimacy to which no one except him can have access because it is defined as self-consciousness.[46]

Vernant compares these three levels to three literary genres – the individual corresponds to biography, a genre based on the life of a single character, in contrast to epic or historical narrative; the subject corresponds to autobiography or memoirs, where the individual tells his own life story; and the ego corresponds to confessions or a diary "in which the inner life, the unique subject of a private life – in all its psychological complexity and richness, and its relative opacity or incommunicability – provides the material for what is written."[47] Following Arnaldo Momigliano and others, Vernant also stresses that, although the Greeks produced some forms of biography and autobiography, both the classical and Hellenistic periods lacked confessions and diaries; moreover, "the characterization of the individual in Greek autobiography allows no 'intimacy of the self.'"[48]

After charting the evolution from the Homeric to Platonic conceptions of *psuché*, a transformation that takes us from the soul as "a ghostly double of the body" to the body "as a ghostly reflection of the soul,"[49] Vernant insists on the importance of the fact that the Platonic *psuché* is "a *daimón* in us, a divine being, a supernatural force whose place and function in the universe goes beyond our single person."[50] This *psuché*, as impersonal or super-personal force, is "*the* soul in me and not *my* soul."[51] Thus Vernant claims that the Greek experience of the self could not have given rise to a *cogito ergo sum*, since my *psuché* is not my psychological ego. Citing Bernard Groethuysen's formula, he maintains that the ancient consciousness of self consists in the apprehension of the self in a *he*, and not yet in an *I*. There is no Cartesian, or even Augustinian, self-consciousness in the ancient preoccupation with the self.[52]

Can we reconcile Foucault's emphasis on the ancient care of the self with Vernant's historically nuanced argument that this *psuché* is a *superpersonal* force? How is the Greek and Roman "intensity of the relations to self" to be placed alongside the fact that this self is but a "simulacrum of the divine?"[53] The philosophical ideal that allows us to put together the care of the self and the *psuché* as *daimón* is the figure of the sage or wise man. The figure of the sage is notably absent from Foucault's writings on ancient philosophy, and it is precisely this absence that sometimes permits him to pass too smoothly from ancient to modern experiences of the self. By anchoring the ideal of the sage at the basis of ancient ethics, we can better see the abyss that separates *psuché* from any possible aestheticization of the self.

The figure of the wise man, although described in different terms in different philosophical schools, was, according to Hadot, the "transcendent model that inspired all of philosophy" and that, moreover, was the basis for constructing the two other regulative models of ancient thought, the figure of the ideal king and the idea of God.[54] Of the many aspects of this figure that were crucial to ancient thought, I want to focus on what Hadot, in his brilliant essay "La Figure du sage dans l'Antiquité gréco-latine," describes as a

> fundamental theme . . . wisdom is the state in which man is at the same time essentially man and beyond man, as if the essence of man consisted in being beyond himself.[55]

Or, as Paul Veyne puts a similar, if more specific, claim, in his introduction to the French translation of Seneca's *De tranquillitate animi*, Stoic eudemonism is an "ethics of the ideal" that aims to imitate the figure of the sage, "a dream situated beyond human capacities."[56] Jules Michelet differently stressed this aspect of the ideal in his formulation, "Greek religion culminated with its true God: the sage."[57]

Despite their contrasting concrete ideals of wisdom, all of the ancient philosophical schools conceived of philosophy and the philosopher as oriented towards this "transcendent and almost inaccessible ideal."[58] Even if, as Cicero claimed, the true sage is born perhaps once every five hundred years, nevertheless the philosopher can attain at least a certain relative perfection; he can hope to become, if not the ideal and divine sage, "a sage among men, conscious of the distance that separates him from the gods," a relative sage.[59] But this achievement can only be attained through the arduous path of spiritual exercises that require nothing less than a transformation of one's way of life. It is this self-transforming, life-transforming *askesis* that makes Socrates, and every other true philosopher, *atopos*.

In his interpretation of Seneca, Hadot draws out a series of equivalences that takes one from the true good to the best part of the self to perfect or divine reason. Thus on this reading, as I have already indicated, Seneca's true good, which is the best part of his self, is also a transcendent self; it is the sage or *daimón* in Seneca.[60] So in letter 23, when Seneca urges the turning of one's attention toward the true good, he is urging a conversion to self that is at the same time a conversion to the *deus* in each one of us.[61] To be a philosopher, a lover of wisdom, is to exert a constant care of the self that, proceeding by way of spiritual exercises, culminates in the surpassing of the self, brings one to an identification with universal Reason, the god, the sage that both is and is beyond one's self. The joy obtained when one achieves this identification requires struggle and combat with oneself, since we are "too readily satisfied with ourselves," substituting pleasurable delights for real joy.[62] Real joy, writes Seneca, "is a stern matter" ("verum gaudium severa est"), and it demands that we go "deep below the surface" in order to take up the perspective of the god that is within us.[63] We can acquire this real joy from within ourselves, provided that we surpass ourselves, so transforming ourselves. The ancient spiritual progress that aims at wisdom, the life of the sage, confronts the apparent paradox, as formulated again by Hadot, that "man appears, in that which is most his own, as something that is more than man, or, to speak more precisely, the true self of each individual transcends each individual."[64]

Foucault is absolutely correct to emphasize the ancient care of the self, for conversion to self is a precondition of the spiritual transformation that constitutes philosophy. Such a conversion is, however, not to be confused with the kind of psychologization or aestheticization that shrinks the world to the size of oneself. Rather, this conversion, dilating the self beyond itself, brings about that cosmic consciousness in which one sees the human world "from above."[65] The care of the self does not take the form of a pose or posture, of the fashioning of oneself into a dramatic character. To invoke Plotinus' formulation, it is, instead, the sculpting of oneself as a statue, the scraping away of what is superfluous and extraneous to oneself. The art of living required by the realization of the self is not compared, by Plotinus, to painting, which was considered an art of addition, but rather to sculpture, an art of taking away. Since the statue already exists in the block of marble, it is sufficient to take away what is superfluous in order to make the statue appear. So when Plotinus tells us that if we do not yet see our own beauty we should sculpt our own beautiful statue of ourselves, far from urging any aestheticization of the self, he is enjoining a purification, an exercise that liberates us from our passions and that returns us to our self, ultimately identified by Plotinus with the One.[66] The beauty of this sculpting is not independent from the reality of the Good;[67] it is not an aestheticization of morality, but a spiritual transfiguration in which we scrape away at ourselves, identifying with the Good beyond ourselves so that we can see our own beauty, that is, so that the "divine glory of virtue" will shine upon us.[68] So, as Plotinus maintains, "it is right to say that the soul's becoming something good and beautiful is its being made like to God."[69]

Although underlining the cosmic consciousness of the ancient sage, Hadot does acknowledge that the figure of the sage in ancient thought corresponds to a more acute consciousness of the self, the personality, of interiority.[70] But the internal freedom recognized by all the philosophical schools, "this inexpungeable core of the personality," is located in the faculty of judgment, not in some psychologically thick form of introspection.[71] When Epictetus or Marcus Aurelius distinguish between the things themselves and the judgments we form of those things, they are insisting on the fundamental distinction between that which depends on us (our judgments) and that which does not depend on us (the things themselves) in order to make us conscious of the power we have to be independent, to choose the judgments and representations we will have of things, and not to be concerned with the things themselves.[72] Internal freedom of judgment leads to *autarkeia*, self-sufficiency, that assures the sage *ataraxia*, tranquillity of the soul. The dimension of interiority in ancient thought, constituted by vigilance and attention to the self, by self-examination, and exertions of the will, memory, imagination, and reason, is in service of a freedom to judge that will guarantee one the independence of wisdom.[73] It is an internal life ultimately concentrated around the sage or *daimón* in one, therefore allowing the philosopher to separate himself from passions and desires that do not depend on him. This is a kind of interiorization that aims at transcendence, and, if Foucault's interpretation of ancient ethics seems sometimes to border on an aestheticization of the self, Hadot's interpretation insists on the divinization of the self.

This is not the occasion on which to sketch further the history of ethics as the history of the self's relationship to itself, the history of ethics as ascetics. Foucault has pointed to homosexual *askesis* and the homosexual style of life as exemplifications of this history. Hadot has himself indicated that certain experiences of the modern artist partake of the cosmic consciousness of the ancient sage; as Paul Klee wrote, "His progress in the observation and the vision of nature makes him accede little by little to a philosophical vision of the universe that allows him freely to create abstract forms. . . . The artist thus creates works, or participates in the creation of works that are in the image of the work of God."[74] If most of modern moral philosophy finds the idea of ethics as a spiritual exercise strange, to say the least, still it would be false to conclude that these ethical problematizations disappear from the history of philosophy after the ancients. The thematics that Stanley Cavell identifies as moral perfectionism constitutes one continuation of this history of ethics. When Cavell portrays Emersonian self-reliance as "the mode of the self's relation to itself"[75] or when he describes Wittgenstein's *Philosophical Investigations* as exhibiting, "as purely as any work I know, philosophizing as a spiritual struggle,"[76] he is working towards a conceptualization of ethics that shares with Foucault and Hadot the idea that what is at issue is not only a code of good conduct but a way of being that involves every aspect of one's soul.[77] And as Cavell follows out Emerson's remark in "History" – "So all that is said of the wise man by stoic or oriental or modern essayist, describes to each man his own idea, describes his unattained but attainable self" – he is pursuing the ancient conception of the sage or *daimón* in us, that self-reliance both within and beyond one's self.[78]

Paul Veyne has described the Nietzschean *Übermensch* as the modernized version of the ancient sage.[79] If the *Übermensch* is such a modernized version, then, obviously enough, it is not identical with the ancient figure. But there are points of comparison so startling that it would be perverse to overlook them. Hadot's interpretation of ancient philosophy lays great emphasis on the representation of philosophy as an exercise and training for death, and as a meditation upon death.[80] In his 1981–2 course at the Collège de France, Foucault devoted detailed descriptions to those ancient "exercises of thought" known as *praemeditatio malorum*, meditation on future evils, and *melete thanatou*, meditation on or exercise for death.[81] He interprets the latter as "a way of rendering death present in life," an exercise by which the sage effects spiritual transformation.[82] Such a dimension seems to me to capture precisely the force of Nietzsche's introduction of the idea of the eternal recurrence in section 341 of *The Gay Science*. I quote this section in full:

> What if some day or night a demon were to steal after you into your loneliest loneliness and say to you: "This life as you now live it and have lived it, you will have to live once more and innumerable times more; and there will be nothing new in it, but every pain and every joy and every thought and sigh and everything unutterably small or great in your life will have to return to you, all in the same succession and sequence – even this spider and this moonlight between the trees, and even this moment and I myself. The eternal hourglass of existence is turned upside down again and again, and you with it, speck of dust!"
>
> Would you not throw yourself down and gnash your teeth and curse the demon who spoke thus? Or have you once experienced a tremendous moment when you would have answered him: "You are a god and never have I heard anything more divine." If this thought gained possession of you, it would change you as you are or perhaps crush you. The question in each and every thing, "Do you desire this once more and innumerable times more?" would lie upon your actions as the greatest weight. Or how well disposed would you have to become to yourself and to life to *crave nothing more fervently* than this ultimate eternal confirmation and seal?[83]

How could one fail to see that this is a modern meditation that effects spiritual transformation; that it problematizes one's way of life through a series of questions with ancient reverberations? This is from Seneca's 59th letter:

I shall now show you how you may know that you are not wise. The wise man is joyful, happy and calm, unshaken; he lives on a plane with the gods. Now go, question yourself; if you are never downcast, if your mind is not harassed by any apprehension, through anticipations of what is to come, if day and night your soul keeps on its even and unswerving course, upright and content with itself, then you have attained to the greatest good that mortals can possess.[84]

If this thought gained possession of you, so Seneca believed, it would change you as you are.

In concentrating on questions of interpretation of ancient texts, I hope to have shown, first, that Foucault's conceptualization of ethics as the self's relation to itself does *not depend on* any modern understanding of subjectivity. Writing this history of ethics is part of writing a history of the self. Second, Foucault's conceptualization does not entail a narrowing of the domain of ethics, as if this history were threatened with a collapse into a history of the varieties of egoism. The demarcation of the self's relation to itself as the central arena of ethical problematization is inextricably tied to the theme of the proper way of life. The self's relation to itself manifests one's style of life, and the philosophical way of life forces a transformed relation to oneself.

In his extraordinary interpretation of the *Apology*, *Crito*, and *Phaedo* in his last lectures at the Collège de France, as well as in his 1983 seminar at the University of California at Berkeley, Foucault argued that Socratic *parrhésia*, the Socratic practice of truth-telling, is a specifically ethical practice, and is distinguished from other kinds of truth-telling, and especially from political truth-telling, by its objective – to incite each person to occupy himself with himself. Thus the essential theme of ethical *parrhésia* is the care of the self.[85] It is evident in listening to these lectures that Foucault wanted to link the theme of the care of the self to that of the peculiarly philosophical way of life, a link that, although perhaps not explicit, is present in his discussion of Socrates' last words in the *Phaedo*. Taking up Georges Dumézil's remarkable "Divertissement sur les dernières paroles de Socrate," Foucault follows Dumézil in arguing that one cannot interpret Socrates' last words – "Crito, we owe a cock to Asclepius" – as acknowledging a debt to Asclepius (the god to whom the Greeks offered a sacrifice when a cure was at issue) for having cured Socrates of the illness that is life.[86] Despite this traditional and often repeated interpretation, Dumézil and Foucault attempt to show that it is completely at odds with Socratic teaching to impute to Socrates the claim that life is an illness and that death thus cures us of life. But Asclepius is the god one thanks for a cure, and so, following a complicated philological and philosophical path that I will not attempt to reconstruct here, Dumézil and Foucault argue that the illness that Socrates is cured of is that corruption of the soul which results from following the general, ordinary opinion of mankind. Socrates is not concerned with the opinion of the masses, appealed to in the *Crito* in an attempt to convince him to escape from prison; he is rather concerned with himself and with his own relation to truth, and he has courageously learned to free himself from the soul-sickness of common opinion.[87] Socrates' ethical *parrhésia*, divorced from the opinion of the public, is his style of life. It is this style of life which he ceaselessly presents to others, for which others put him to death. Foucault says that it is the principle of concerning oneself with oneself that Socrates bequeaths to others;[88] he might have equally underscored the figure of Socrates that endures for us as a constantly irritating and inspiring reminder of the philosophical way of life. Socrates reminds us of nothing less than the fact that, for the practitioners of ancient philosophy, philosophy itself was a way of life.[89] Ethical problems were not resolved by producing a list of required, permitted, and forbidden actions, but were centered around one's attitude to oneself, and so to others and the world – one's style of living.

In his last writings Foucault expressed concern that the ancient principle "Know thyself" had obscured, at least for us moderns, the similarly ancient requirement that we occupy ourselves with ourselves, that we care for ourselves. He insisted that we not forget that the demand to know oneself was "regularly associated with the theme of the care of the self."[90] It is in this spirit that I have urged that the care of the self must itself be placed in the context of a style of life, that in order to make sense of the care of the self we must widen our vision to include the style of life that gives form and direction to the self's relation to itself. Classical Greek, Hellenistic, and Roman thought, early Christianity, and even the Old Testament[91] all prescribe the care of the self, but the styles of life in which this care is embedded are so different that it affects the notion of care, the notion of the self, and the notions of how and why we are to bear this relation of care to ourselves. One of the great virtues of ancient thought is that knowledge of oneself, care of oneself, and one's style of life are everywhere so woven together that one cannot, without distortion, isolate any of these issues from the entire philosophical thematics of which they form part. If we ignore these dimensions of the moral life, we shall be able to do justice to neither history nor philosophy. And, without doubt worse, we shall not be able to take account of ourselves, of who we have become, of how we might become different.

4

Kant, Foucault, and *Three Women*

Carla Hesse

[W]e have to give up hope of ever acceding to a point of view that could give us access to any complete and definitive knowledge of what may constitute our historical limits.

Michel Foucault, "What is Enlightenment?"

The task of this essay is to explore the relationship between the writings of Michel Foucault and current practices in writing the history of women.[1] From the very outset it seems necessary to pose the following question: how did it become meaningful to pair "Foucault" and "women" as potential interlocutors in contemporary historiographic debate? One possible formulation of an answer to this question has been elaborated over the past decade by feminist historians, most notably in France and the United States, who have been closely linked to what in the United States is now referred to as the "gender-turn" in feminist historiography, and in France as a shift from the "history of women" to the "history of sexual difference."[2] In contrast to an earlier generation of historians who had assumed "women" to be a self-evident subject of historical inquiry, this later historiography followed Foucault in his basic insight that power in modern societies is constituted and deployed, above all, through the very process of constructing social and political identities, and the concomitant notions of agency which are attributed to them. Over the past decade these historians have produced a detailed account of the history of normative discourses on women and gender difference and their repeated reformulations within the (male-dominated) modern disciplines. And as a kind of corollary to this history of norms, we have witnessed, as well, the renewal of the writing of histories of resistance to, or transgressions of, these norms. In other words, the social history of women has been rewritten as a meta-history of social categories.[3]

This work has played an important role in assessing the limits and possibilities for political action available within modern political culture by disclosing the normative character of categories once assumed to be neutrally descriptive. Yet it seems to me worth observing that this post-Foucauldian historiography has nonetheless remained wedded to a series of assumptions about the relationship between theory and history, more generally, that bear further scrutiny. To be more precise, appropriations of Foucault's work by historians of women have for the most part occurred within a model of the relationship between theory and history established by the positive social sciences. Within this model, theories are applied to and tested by facts which they organize and, in so doing, explain. Thus Foucault's theories have been viewed less as an object of historical scrutiny and study by these historians than as a set of research tools, a set of questions and methods, that could be applied, more or less systematically, to their field of study. Of course one of the reasons for this is that, like earlier theories, Foucault's theory of "power/knowledge" evolved with near-total indifference to the intensive feminist research into the history of sex/gender systems.[4] The posture of women's history in relation to Foucault's theory thus became one of writing women/gender into the picture. In this formulation Foucault has stood for "theory" and women/gender for "history," that is, another set of variables to be considered within its frame. The theory and its author under these circumstances risk becoming precisely that transcendent Archimedean point of historical delimitation that Foucault so consistently resisted. One important consequence of this mode of relating to Foucault's theories is that women have succeeded in writing themselves into a history of the disciplines, but they have not succeeded through this writing in arriving at a historical vantage point from which they can point to a possible way out of the vise of those norms they have successfully described. The kind of history that might open the possibility of a way out of normative discourses, by exposing their contingency, I would like to suggest, will require a reformulation of precisely the terms of this historiographic relationship between women's history and the writings of Michel Foucault.

This essay is an attempt at such a reformulation. It sets out to reverse the terms of the positivist formulation of the relationship between history and theory that has unwittingly structured the current historiographic uses of "Foucault" in the writing of the "history of women." Rather than viewing theory (in this case, Foucault's theories of subjectivity) as something that can be applied to the facts (in this case, the discursive formations which maintain the parameters of gender categories) and in so doing organize them into an explanatory frame (a pattern of domination and resistance) it will set out to examine Foucault's own textual practices as a *historical* problem of interest to women's history. It will attempt to show that careful attention to the genealogy of the philosophical practices Foucault himself employs can perhaps get closer to an answer to the important historical question of how, in contemporary historiographic discussion, this odd and asymmetrical couple, "Foucault and women's history," have come to be paired.

I FOUCAULT'S KANT

In 1984 Michel Foucault chose to rewrite Immanuel Kant's famous essay "What is Enlightenment?" two hundred years after its initial publication in the *Berlinische Monatschrift* in 1784.[5] Indeed, Foucault begins his essay with a historical reflection upon the context of Kant's publication: he was responding to the newspaper's open question to its readers. And Kant was not the only philosopher to respond to the paper's inquiry. Unbeknownst to Kant at the time of his writing, the newspaper had already published a response by the philosopher Moses Mendelssohn a few months earlier. Foucault identifies the moment of Kant's response as marking the advent of modern philosophy, not because of the answer that Kant offered, but because of the persistence from that moment forward of the philosophical project of responding to this question. He writes, "What is modern philosophy? . . . modern philosophy is the philosophy that is attempting to answer the question raised so imprudently two centuries ago: Was ist Aufklärung?" For Foucault, this advent of a new mode of philosophical inquiry was instanced by the unwitting, yet shared impulse of both Kant and Mendelssohn to respond to the newspaper's question. In his view, the unintended confluence of two distinct philosophical traditions (the German *Aufklärung* and the Jewish *Haskala*) toward the same aim established, without willing it, a new common ground for philosophy.[6]

It would be possible to read Foucault's essay as yet another response, like those of Kant and Mendelssohn, to the question posed by the *Berlinische Monatschrift*, and indeed Foucault invites his readers to "imagine that the *Berlinische Monatschrift* still exists." However, I would like to suggest that reading this essay as a simple parallel gesture is inadequate, for reasons which Foucault himself is aware of at the outset. First, if the significance of the question has persisted for the past two hundred years, the *context* of this questioning, the forum of the public newspaper, no longer exists. As Foucault writes: "Today when a periodical asks its readers a question, it does so in order to collect opinions on some subject about which everyone has an opinion already; there is not much likelihood of learning anything new. In the eighteenth century, editors preferred to question the public on problems that did not yet have solutions."[7] Thus, despite Foucault's suggestion that his reader imagine that the *Berlinische Monatschrift* is still asking readers its famous question, Foucault's own essay was in fact written as a seminar paper that he intended to deliver at the University of California, Berkeley, in 1984. It was only published posthumously. This historical shift in the locus of philosophical inquiry from the public newspaper to the academic seminar room is not without significance, and it will receive further attention shortly. Let us simply remark here that it marks an important discontinuity between Foucault's essay and Kant's.

A second and equally significant discontinuity between Foucault's response and that of his eighteenth-century counterparts is that, while Kant and Mendelssohn both unwittingly responded to the same anonymously posed question, in responding to the same question two hundred years later Foucault cannot help responding at the same time to Kant (and Mendelssohn) as well. That is, Foucault's mode of philosophical inquiry cannot help being not only critical but also genealogical in its practice. Indeed, this is precisely Foucault's purpose in writing the essay: a reformulation of the Kantian critical philosophical project of self-constitution as a historical project of investigating the formation of modern notions of subjectivity and, more specifically in this case, modern philosophical subjectivity.

For Foucault, the great novelty in Kant's formulation of the problem of enlightenment is to be found in his new posture toward time, "a new mode of relating to contemporary reality." By this he means Kant's abandonment of both totality and immanence as a means of understanding the present in favor of a negative (critical) formulation: the present is no longer of interest because it may contain a sign of eternal truth, but rather because it offers "a way out" or "an exit" from "immaturity," Kant's word for tutelage or tradition. With Kant, the possibility of enlightenment is now rooted in "the difference today introduces." This "consciousness of discontinuity," however, is more than mere "sensitivity to the fleeting present"; it is the will to "heroize" the present, in the face of this consciousness. Such heroics, insofar as they contain an awareness of their contingency, are inevitably ironic. Thus, for Foucault, the muse of the modern philosopher (Kant) is the poet (Baudelaire), "not the man who goes off to discover himself ... he is the man who invents himself," the autonomous self-constituting subject.[8]

Philosophical inquiry, since Kant, has thus become a critical process of "analyzing and reflecting upon limits," the limits that constitute this autonomous subject. But while identifying himself with the mode of inquiry that he calls Kant's "limit-attitude" Foucault also announces a difference, between Kant's project and the needs of philosophy today:

If the Kantian question was that of knowing the limits knowledge has to renounce transgressing, it seems to me that the critical question today has to be turned back into a positive one: in what is given to us as universal, necessary, obligatory, what place is occupied by whatever is singular, contingent, and the product of arbitrary constraint? The point, in brief, is to transform the critique conducted in the form of necessary limitation into a practical critique that takes the form of possible transgression ... that criticism is no longer going to be practiced in the search for formal structures with universal value, but rather as historical investigation into the events that have led us to constitute ourselves and to recognize ourselves as subjects of what we are doing, thinking, saying. In that sense, this criticism is not transcendental, and its goal is not making metaphysics possible: it is genealogical in its design and archeological in its method.[9]

In this essay, then, Foucault at once writes himself into the genealogy of the Enlightenment, but does so in such a way (by rewriting Kant) that he at the same time also inflects the aim of that critical project toward a new end: genealogy rather than metaphysics. The Kantian task of delimitation now becomes one of transgressing limits, of assessing what limits are no longer necessary to our self-constitution.

For these reasons it seems clear that a careful contextualization of Foucault's essay would locate it within a more subterranean trajectory of modern philosophical inquiry, a trajectory that departs not from the common impulse to respond to the question "What is enlightenment?" but, rather, from the impulse to rewrite Kant. And it is here that the question of women's history reenters the picture. It reenters because, while Kant had many eighteenth-century interlocutors, to my knowledge the first person to consciously define her philosophical project as a *rewriting* of Kant was Isabelle de Charrière Belle Van Zuylen (1740–1805). I would thus like to suggest that if the unintended, yet shared impulse of Kant and Mendelssohn to answer the question "What is enlightenment?" established a common threshold for modern philosophical inquiry, so too Charrière and Foucault's unwittingly shared impulse to rewrite Kant marks the appearance of a new mode of inquiry, one that is not only critical but also genealogical in form. Charrière's encounter with Kant offers a particularly valuable context within which to read and interpret Foucault's own essay on Kant and the Enlightenment because it allows us to situate Foucault within the history of the French reception of Kant; and, moreover, because it allows us to examine the part played by sexual difference in the fabrication of the post-Kantian philosophical subject.

II CHARRIÈRE'S KANT

In the winter of 1794–5 the novelist Isabelle de Charrière read Kant's essay "On the Proverb: That May be True in Theory But is of No Practical Use," and this encounter resulted in the composition and pseudonymous publication in 1795 of her novel entitled *Trois femmes*.[10] Charrière's novel was one of the earliest critical public responses to Kant in the French language. It was also a powerful voice of resistance to the efforts of French revolutionary government officials to reshape the Enlightenment project along Kantian lines after Thermidor (1794–5). Yet, despite the recent renewal of interest in the writings of Isabelle de Charrière among literary critics, surprisingly little critical attention has been devoted to the novel *Trois femmes*, or, for that matter, to Charrière's post-revolutionary writings as a whole.[11] Historians of philosophy have been even more categorical in their neglect of Charrière's role in the early Francophone reception of Kant. With near unanimity commentators depict her as an enthusiastic, but philosophically naive, critic of Kant.[12]

This lack of serious scholarly attention to the philosophical dimension of Charrière's work is no mere oversight. Rather, it is the by-product of a series of generic distinctions between academic and commercial culture, between philosophy and literature, and between men and women's writing, that were emerging at precisely the moment in which the two authors in question were writing. The encounter between Charrière and Kant has never been fully explored because historians of philosophy have not read, and have had little inclination to read, Charrière's novel. Nor, reciprocally, have literary historians and critics taken the time to read seriously the particular texts of Kant that were in question for Charrière. Transgressing this generic boundary, by reading across it, may permit us to interpret Charrière's "misunderstanding" of Kant as a symptom of something more than a personal failing or, as several critics have claimed, a weakness of her sex. Indeed, the appearance of this generic impasse between philosophy and fiction, between analysis and narrative, is where our story must begin.

French interest in Kant's writings was directly linked to a series of major initiatives by the government to revive and reinstitutionalize cultural life during the Thermidorian period that followed the fall of Robespierre and brought an end to the Terror (1794–5). From at least the spring of 1794 the national government's Committees of Public Safety and Public Instruction had been receiving reports deploring the state of French intellectual culture.[13] In the view of these distressed officials, the declaration of freedom of the press and freedom of commerce, along with the collapse of the royal academies and other forms of official cultural patronage between 1789 and 1791, had left the fate of French literary culture exclusively in the hands of the uneducated consumer and the profit-oriented publisher. As a consequence, far from unleashing the forces of reason, virtue, and public utility, the Revolution had, on the contrary, led to an explosion of decadent literary publications that preyed upon the private passions and desires of citizens. Of central concern to republican cultural elites was the seemingly insatiable demand for prose fiction.

These concerns were translated into legislative action by the key cultural luminary of the National Convention, Henri Grégoire, in a major report to the Convention in October of 1794.[14] Grégoire's report announced nothing short of a cultural Thermidor. The government, he declaimed, must repudiate Rousseau's anti-representationalism in the cultural as well as the political sphere. Just as representative government was to eclipse direct democracy with the promulgation of the new constitution of the Year III, so too official representatives of republican culture should be designated. Active government patronage of selected authors and publishing ventures would thus replace the laissez-faire policies that the government had implemented after 1789 in a misguided attempt to institute the Rousseauvian cultural ideal of transparent and unmediated intellectual exchange among citizens themselves. Upon hearing Grégoire's report, the National Convention enthusiastically voted to distribute huge sums to "encourage and reward" select men of letters, scholars, and artists.

Significantly, the guidelines for dispensing government patronage outlined by Grégoire recast the cultural world within the pre-revolutionary classical academic categories of "arts and sciences," though the content of these categories was now to be thoroughly republican in character. Grégoire's report thus recontextualized the practice of Enlightenment philosophy within the agenda of a republicanized academic classicism: culture in the service of public order and civic virtue. This revival of academic intellectual culture culminated in the founding of the Institute, a year later, in the fall of 1795.

Thermidorian cultural policies thus effected a series of crucial reorientations in the French revolutionary government's relationship to cultural life. First, they represented an attempt to reassert the power of an officially sponsored academic culture over that produced through the mechanism of the commercial marketplace. More importantly, they also marked a self-conscious attempt to reshape the practice of Enlightenment philosophy by transforming it from a cultural movement wedded to market modes of dissemination into an academic discipline supported by state patronage.[15] The pre-revolutionary commercial public sphere that made possible the mode of philosophical inquiry exemplified by the open-ended questions to readers in the *Berlinische Monatschrift* was thus to be eclipsed by the officially subsidized academic journal. Equally significant, the new academic philosophical practices encouraged by the government, in sharp contrast to the pre-revolutionary underground philosophical movement, privileged analytic over narrative modes of philosophical inquiry and exposition.

Second, government patronage increasingly took the form of stipends to particular authors, rather than subsidies for particular publications. This favoring of the author over the text as a governing principle of patronage culminated in the creation of the Institute – a corporation of officially subsidized writers.

Third, the key motive behind these developments was the desire to temper the erotic passions inflamed by market-driven literary culture. Official academic culture would encourage the inculcation of the cooler virtues of reason and self-discipline in the service of public utility rather than the satisfaction of personal desire. In generic terms this meant encouraging the production and publication of science and analytic philosophy as an antidote to prose fiction and especially novels. One crucial effect of these policies was to encourage cultural institutions and genres that were nearly exclusively male, and to privilege men within those forms, such as prose fiction, where women had played a significant role.[16]

These broader cultural developments are absolutely critical to understanding the motivations behind, and the significance of, the introduction of Kant's writings into France, and of Isabelle de Charrière's response to them. Indeed, the links between the cultural policies of the Thermidorian government, Kant's publication in France, and Charrière's novel are quite direct. Within weeks of his speech to the Convention concerning literary patronage, Henri Grégoire began making inquiries among German-speaking republican intellectuals about Kant's work, hoping to find in it a secular moral philosophy powerful enough to respond to the post-Thermidorian Christian revival on the one hand, and to the spread of atheistic materialism on the other.[17] News of French government interest in Kant spread quickly. Thus the German-born and -educated journalist-translator Louis-Ferdinand Huber (1764–1804) wrote to his former mentor, Friedrich Schiller, on January 31, 1795:

> I made a first attempt to introduce a selection of Kantian philosophy in France by translating and offering long excerpts of Kant's article in the *Berlinische Monatschrift* on Theory and Practice and I sent it to a friend in Paris. Grégoire of the Committee of Public Instruction seems to have taken great pleasure in it and I think that a more complete essay on Kantian philosophy would be well received in a place where the end to the oppression

of Robespierre has provoked a lively movement toward more serious scientific learning.[18]

He was not wrong. The government found in Kant's political writings a powerful idiom for legitimating and internationalizing its faith in a secular republicanism rooted in the fraternal discourse of universal reason. In March, Huber thus reported that plans were under way for a French translation of Kant's *Perpetual Peace*.[19] Then in April a notice on Kant written by Huber appeared in the *Moniteur*, celebrating him as a German genius "capable of giving philosophy a new life" in France.[20] In 1796 the first French translation of the *Perpetual Peace* was published in Paris by Henri Jansen, with a government subsidy.[21]

Kant thus became in the eyes of French government officials the Thermidorian philosopher *par excellence*. The academic, the university man who stood apart from the men of the world and advocated conformity to philosophical principles rooted in abstract reason rather than religious faith or historical materialism, he could offer the moral stability critical to the success of the universalizing republicanism of the Directory. Significantly, while Kant, in his essay on enlightenment, had conceived of the modern philosophical subject as comprising two distinctive modes of reasoning (critical "public" reasoning as a citizen, and instrumental "private" reasoning as an obedient servant of the state), the French Thermidorian's conception of the model Kantian philosopher laid heavy stress on the role of the philosopher as an official servant (albeit of a republican state) rather than that of the critical citizen. Thus, in face of the intense political pressures to legitimate and consolidate the fledgling republic, the Thermidorian government wedded the figure of Kant to the regime and produced a version of the Kantian philosophical subject reduced to the statist (or in Kantian terms "private") half of itself.

III   CHARRIÈRE'S *TROIS FEMMES*

Louis-Ferdinand Huber was not working alone when he began translating and synthesizing Kant's work for the French. In the summer of 1794 he had installed himself in Neuchâtel.[22] There, in the continuous company of Charrière, already a noted novelist, and the soon-to-be-noted novelist-politician Benjamin Constant, he spent the fall studying Kant's moral philosophy and began work on the translation of the essay on *Theory and Practice* that he was to send to Grégoire.[23] In these same months, as Huber strategically courted the patronage of the Committee of Public Instruction, his friend and collaborator, Isabelle de Charrière, worked simultaneously on a response both to the new cultural policies of the Thermidorian regime and to Kant's essay itself: her novel *Trois femmes*.[24]

Charrière's *Trois femmes*, published under the pseudonym of the "Abbé de la Tour," is a divided into two parts. Part 1 is a tale recounted by its pseudonymous author/narrator, describing the moral dilemmas of three women of his acquaintance. Part 2 shifts into the epistolary mode and comprises a series of letters written principally by one of the three women to the "Abbé." The novel was at every level a searing *cri de coeur* against the emerging cultural vision of the Committee of Public Instruction in Paris. In response to the post-revolutionary cult of the philosopher as officially sanctioned public servant – be that philosopher Voltaire, Rousseau, or Kant – Charrière offered the pseudonymous and generic figure of the cosmopolitan, freethinking "Abbé de la Tour." The ironic reference to the ex-abbé, Henri Grégoire, was no doubt intentional. Indeed, the second part of the novel, a series of letters addressed by a female character to the said "Abbé" in Paris, is in fact a quite explicit satirical critique of the educational and cultural reforms of the Thermidorian regime. Here Charrière overtly expressed her misgivings about the sanitized literary culture to be offered in the new republican textbooks, public libraries, and curriculum of the *école normale*, and even more adamantly denounced the emergence of a state-sponsored author-cult: "The philosophical clergy," she writes, "is as much a clergy as any other, and it was not worth the trouble to drive the *curé* from Saint-Sulpice in order to ordain the priests of the Pantheon."[25]

She further expressed her dissent from the Thermidorian cultural regime through her choice of genre. In response to the official privileging of the analytic philosophical essay or treatise, Charrière revived the popular pre-revolutionary genre of the *conte philosophique*, the philosophical tale. Indeed, the opening of the novel is an explicit pastiche of Voltaire's *Candide*.[26] And by naming her principal female protagonist Emilie she added yet another layer of allusion to the pre-revolutionary tradition of the philosophical narrative, this time to Rousseau's *Emile*.

Finally, while the publication of Kant's essays in France was made possible through government subsidy, Charrière's novel was financed by raising private subscriptions, with any profits from its sale to go to a female friend in financial distress.[27] Charrière's novel thus represented the persistence of the textual practices and modes of production characteristic of the oppositional enlightenment of the Old Regime, rather than the official enlightenment of the new one.

In light of these observations it would be possible to characterize Charrière's textual practices as vestigial, as a post-revolutionary after-shock of pre-revolutionary cultural life. I would like to suggest, however, that her resistance to the Thermidorian reshaping of the Enlightenment project along Kantian lines was not simply a residual expression of resistance, but rather a constitutive act that articulated a distinctively feminist relationship to the problem of modern subjectivity as it was presented by Kant in the essay on *Theory and Practice*. Rather than reading her novel as a Thermidorian echo of the old cultural regime, Charrière's response to Kant, for reasons which will become apparent shortly, can only be adequately interpreted as an attempt to come to terms with the part played by sexual difference in the fabrication of the post-revolutionary (which is to say modern) moral subject, and in the elaboration of a critique of that mode of subjectivity as well.

The preface to *Trois femmes* opens in a salon with a group of friends discussing the meaning of duty. The Abbé de la Tour suggests to his hostess that the complexities of Kant's theory of the categorical moral imperative can perhaps be illuminated by the stories of three women of his acquaintance. In the tale that constitutes Part 1 of the novel the Abbé recounts the dilemmas of three women, each of whom finds herself caught in a moral compromise in which she sacrifices absolute virtue for the sake of happiness – both her own, and that of those she loves.

Charrière's tale of the three women has been interpreted as a titillating, yet philosophically derivative exposition of the consequentialist critique of Kantian morality that was being elaborated at that very moment by numerous contemporaries and, in particular, her then companion Benjamin Constant.[28] By this reading, the moral of Charrière's novel is simply that consideration of consequences may justify a compromise in absolute principles. However, when *Trois femmes* is read carefully against Kant's "On the Proverb: That May Be True in Theory But is of No Practical Use" it becomes apparent that the novel is a systematic rewriting of Kant's essay from a woman's point of view. Read as a feminist rather than a con-sequentialist response, the novel reveals that it is the question of autonomy rather than contingency that lay at the heart of her critique of the Kantian moral system.

Kant's essay, it is true, was intended as a refutation of his consequential-ist critics. In it he illustrates the three maxims of the categorical imperative in the form of a response to *three men*: "the man of affairs," represented by the German philosopher of practical morality Christian Garves (1742–98); "the statesman," represented by Thomas Hobbes; and the "man of the world," represented by Moses Mendelssohn.[29] His purpose is to demon-strate that the a priori categorical imperative can and should be sustained not only in theory but also in practice by men in the real world. In a critical passage of the essay, however, Kant explicitly excludes two categories of individuals from full participation in the "originating contract" among citizens that is a precondition for the functioning of the three maxims of the categorical imperative – women and servants.[30] Women and servants, Kant writes, by nature, do not have the capacity for maturity, that is, autonomous self-determination.

Charrière's "three women" take on a different significance in this light. They serve as three counter-examples, who by the fact of sexual difference are put in a different and unequal relationship to both moral and juridical law. In fact, it could be argued that Kant's distinction between virtue and duty is only relevant for those who have the capacity for self-government. Charrière's examples thus pose a somewhat different question to the Kantian ethical model than the one raised by consequentialists. They raised the question whether the categorical imperative can function in relation to moral actors who do not have equal standing under the law.[31]

Let us consider her three stories a bit more closely. Like Kant's men, Charrière's women represented three juridically distinct spheres: the private sphere of the household, the civil sphere constituted through marriage, and the cosmopolitan sphere of multinational business. The first story concerns Josephine, faithful servant to the young orphaned Emilie. Josephine's understanding of her categorical duty as a servant is to sacrifice everything – including her honor if need be – for her mistress. Thus she succumbs to the seductions of the manservant at the nearby château, in part because she likes him, and in part because she expects benefits for her mistress. Josephine is in fact doubly excluded from participation in the Kantian self-regulating moral community on the basis of her sex and her social status. If by nature she is incapable of self-rule, how can she therefore be held accountable for her actions? Thus Josephine points out that the blame for her lapse in virtue should lie with her mistress, because it was *she* who failed in her duty as mistress to effectively regulate her servant's moral conduct.[32]

But did the *female* mistress herself have the ultimate authority to lay down the law in the home? In fact the story of Josephine was taken from Charrière's experience. Her own chambermaid and companion, Henriette Monachon, had a second illegitimate child in 1795 and refused to marry the father. As a consequence, the Council of State of the Principality of Neuchâtel found her guilty of moral depravity and expelled her from the principality, *despite* the petitions and pleas of her mistress, Charrière.[33] Deprived in reality of the power to regulate the morals of her own household, in the fictional version Charrière imagined a recourse beyond the law: the young mistress, Emilie, permits herself to lie in order to manipulate the two servants into a marriage, thus preserving, legally at least, the honor and employment of the faithful and devoted servant girl. Charrière thus raises the following question: when both servant and mistress have no say in making the rules, do they have a duty to abide by them?

The second story is that of the young mistress Emilie herself. She is the sole orphan of a French noble émigré, and thus deprived of her fortune by no act of her own will. Emilie falls in love with the heir to the local seigneurie, Théobald d'Altendorf. Deprived of the social and financial resources to earn the approval of his socially conservative parents, does Emilie have a categorical duty to forgo her love? Or might she elope with the young man without dishonor? Her moral situation is further compli- cated by the fact that if she marries the German baron she will by law lose her French citizenship. Is love of country a higher duty than private love? Here again it becomes clear that the line between moral virtue and civic duty cannot be drawn absolutely. Emilie's dilemma was not circumstantial, it was categorical: all French women who married foreigners by law lost their native citizenship and were literally assimilated into the husband's legal identity.[34] Again, the generic fact of Emilie's sexual status as a woman pitted her private desire for self-determination at moral odds with her civic identity and duty. Emilie chooses to follow her desire, but at the loss of her legal citizenship and her autonomous legal identity as an unwed woman in her majority. The disgrace and disinheritance risked by the attempted elopement of the young couple is narrowly averted by the intervention of Emilie's friend and mentor Constance, who rallies Théobald's parents to their marriage before the couple's flight becomes public. The moral disgrace of their attempt is thus concealed.

Charrière's third woman, her "woman of the world," is named Constance. A French-born widow, she is the sole heiress to a great fortune made unscrupulously in the French colonies and now secured in investments throughout Europe.[35] Though acquired by immoral means, her claim to the fortune is, she reports, legally secure. Moreover, there are no retrievable traces of the private persons from whom the fortune had been extracted by her husband's ancestors. In the face of these circumstances did she have a moral obligation to restore the fortune? If so, to whom? Constance is literally a woman of the world in the sense that, through marriage, then widowhood, and then emigration, her lineage (both familial and national) has been obliterated. Perhaps, Emilie suggests, she has an obligation at least to restore the fortune to the various states in which it was made? But her fortune is now dispersed throughout the globe. Therefore to which nation should it be restored? To what nation does she owe allegiance? That of her birth? Of her dead father? Or of her dead husband? What moral obligation does she have to amend for crimes she did not commit, or to benefit nations she did not choose? Finding herself beyond the laws of any nation, Constance decides that she is free to make use of her fortune as best she can for the good of those around her.[36]

As these stories make apparent, Charrière's central criticism of Kant's essay on *Theory and Practice* did not reside in the problem of contingency – that is, in the distinction between theory and practice. Rather, it resided in the question of autonomy – in the distinctions between man and woman and between servant and master. The Kantian model, Charrière revealed, left the problem of female moral autonomy *categorically* contingent on women's relationships to men and their laws. Moral contingency, in the case of women, was a symptom of their being categorically denied the right of autonomous self-constitution. Her critique of Kant's examples, then, was not from the consequentialist perspective, but from perspective of those who remained categorically outside the law.

Charrière's three women, like Kant's modern men, were post-revolutionary actors, who, freed from their lineages through political upheaval, confronted the possibility of self-governance. Each of the three women in fact inhabited a legal twilight zone. They were all adult women, between or beyond father and husband, and between or beyond nations. But that post-revolutionary world did not offer women the Kantian possibility of reconstituting themselves as independent subjects of the law, that is as its authors. In this context, the significance of Charrière's own textual practices – her use of a generic pseudonym to offer a novel entitled *Three Women* – at last becomes apparent. Identities constituted as categorically beyond the law cannot be constituted as authors, that is as self-constituting subjects of the law, but rather only as generic objects of it: as "three women."

In the end, Charrière's story becomes a story of how these three women constitute their ethical life beyond the laws of men. *Trois femmes*, as scandalized readers recognized at the time, was the story of a band of outlaws; a story of the ethical life of women beyond the laws of propertied men.[37] Charrière's three women band together through self-election and form an outlaw community based upon the ethical principle of total sacrifice to one another, and a reservation of the right to bend rules that they had no part in creating. This female outlaw bond is symbolically instituted by the gift of a ring from Constance to Emilie, bearing the interlocking first initials of the two women on the eve of Emilie's marriage to Théobald. This scene, the gift of the ring from one woman to the other, ends Part 1 of the book, by sealing the outlaw bond between the women *before* the legal bond between man and wife.[38]

But perhaps Kant was simply wrong. Could women become subjects of the law? Were women and servants capable of self-critical maturity? The second part of the novel addresses these questions through a series of pedagogical experiments. Emilie's young husband Théobald decides to devote himself to the Kantian pedagogical project of bringing talented men in the community to critical maturity through an enlightened education. Like Grégoire and the Committee of Public Instruction in Paris, he builds a school and a library in the local village and supervises its progress. Simultaneously, Constance embarks on two parallel experiments. Two baby boys – one of noble, the other of plebeian origin – are accidentally mixed up at birth. Constance sees in this accident the occasion to raise the two boys in absolute equality. It will then be possible to determine whether traits of nobility are biologically or socially transmitted.

A second invitation to experiment presents itself when twins, one male and one female, are born to a single woman who dies in childbirth. Constance decides to adopt and to raise them with inverted gender roles: the boy is to be named Charlotte and the girl Charles, and they are to be taught tasks appropriate to the opposite sexes. She writes: "This ought to suffice, and it should prove to everyone that there is nothing in the nature of man and women that determines anything whatsoever relating to our intellectual capabilities."[39] Constance's experiments offered a possible response to Kant's categorical exceptions of women and servants to the rights of citizenship by fact of nature.[40] They opened up the possibility of assimilation into the male social compact.

Interestingly, however, Charrière left the outcome of these pedagogical experiments hanging. This resistance to definitively determining the nature of sexual difference, and consequently the capacity of her three women as moral agents, emerges in the second part of novel as a central thematic preoccupation. Thus Constance's confident assertion that her pedagogical experiment with the twins will irrefutably determine the intellectual equality of the sexes is immediately followed by a long meditation upon the limited efficacy of definitive proof. She observes that, even though the equal capacities of women have been demonstrated convincingly time and again, human beings need, and will ever need, to see things proved over and over again. She then offers what can only be read as a proverbial rejoinder to Kant's own proverbial point of departure for his essay. She writes to the Abbé, "The proverb that says, 'Two certainties are worth more than one,' has it not greater wisdom and does it not better suit the imperfections of human faculties?"[41] Moral truth, then, like the epistemological truth about sexual difference upon which it stands, she suggests, is only meaningful through its enactment. There can, in this sense, be no end to the story of sexual difference, nor of its consequence for moral conduct, it will always be in need of further determination.

This ultimate indeterminacy of the moral subject is dramatically enacted through the narrative strategy of the second part of the novel. In effect, the narrative structure works in a riptide-like relationship to its thematic content. Thematically, the first part of the novel offers three diagnostic case studies of women at the moral crossroads between a traditional world bounded by lineage and a modern one rooted in self-determination. The second part of the novel presents their efforts to construct a new, post-revolutionary order through a series of pedagogical experiments and reforms. But it immediately becomes apparent that the very textual basis for establishing this new order can never be firmly grounded. With Part 2 the narrative structure of the novel shifts from a third-person account of the stories of the three women recounted in the past tense by the Abbé de la Tour, to a series of letters written in the first-person present tense, primarily by Constance, to the Abbé de la Tour in Paris reporting on the pedagogical reforms that she, Théobald, and Emilie are undertaking in Altendorf. The shift to the epistolary form thus sets the pedagogical problem temporally into the open-ended present.

Moreover, though a certain degree of unity in the narrative voice is sustained in the second part through Constance's role as principal correspondent with the Abbé de la Tour, Constance's letters are never entirely her own: frequently Théobald interrupts her as she writes, inserting his own, often conflicting account of the subject at hand, or adding an ironic postscript. Thus the differences of opinion between the reformers in Altendorf, and most notably between Théobald and Constance on the question of sexual equality, are not simply reported in the letters, they are enacted through their very composition. There is only one set of letters to the Abbé, but these letters are many-voiced and embody conflicting and constantly shifting viewpoints.[42] It is thus the recipient, rather than the sender(s) of the letters, the reader rather than the author(s), who comes to form the only stable point of reference for the narrative. Ultimately, the authorial position is not merely destabilized but disrupted entirely by the appearance in Altendorf of British troops. Both Constance and Emilie fear that they shall be identified as French women and consequently delivered by the English to their distant relatives in France. They thus determine to flee into further obscurity along the borders of the Rhine. This disruption of the narrative by the flight of two of its (female) authors is literalized in a final letter comprising a series of discontinuous and fragmentary passages, punctuated by long elisions, in which Constance informs the Abbé that in order to remain anonymous they will no longer be able to send or receive letters.[43] Thus the story of the three women does not end. Rather, its protagonists move on.

Instead of opting for the liberal feminist solution of demanding entrance for women into the male legal compact as self-authoring subjects, Charrière held on to the separate and contingent relation of women to the law. Emilie may have become *legally* German in marrying Théobald, but she reserved her right *to act* like a French woman. Rather than a demand to enter into the law, Charrière offered a reworking of post-revolutionary philosophical subjectivity as the figure of the outlaw. She sought to expose the limits of Kant's moral system from the outside. In so doing she drew from the French pre-revolutionary traditions of the underground Enlightenment, its pseudonymous and contingent relationship to the law, and its use of narrative to undermine and expose.

In her refusal to write an end to the story of gender, however, she resisted the temptation of placing women within the genealogical binary constituted through the debate between the consequentialists and Kant. That is, she refused to determine where women should stand, ultimately, in relation to the law. Through her refusal to close, a gesture common to many of Charrière's works, she ended her novel by celebrating the power of narrativity itself.[44] Thus, in reply to Théobald's impatience to institute a new order rooted in moral perfection, Constance retorts, "Il faut se contenter de louvoyer" ("We must be content with tacking, improvising").[45]

Charrière thus constituted post-revolutionary moral subjectivity as contingent to, but not independent of, the law. Like the pseudonymous authorial identity, the Charrièrian moral subject emerges only in relation to the text in question – in the service of its text. *Trois femmes* thus elaborated an alternative textual ethics to that advanced by the Thermidorian regime. In response to its encouragement of authorial self-constitution in the service of the state, Charrière offered an outlaw ethics of writing for the other, of contingent self-constitution in relation to both inlaws and the outlaw band. This conception of the self as ever-fleeting, moving always on the margins, marked a rupture not only from Kant but from Voltaire as well. Unlike her pre-revolutionary predecessor, ultimately, Charrière did not seek entry into the law; rather she sought to move, like Constance and Emilie, always along and across its borders.

IV   FOUCAULT AND *TROIS FEMMES*

In closing I would like to return to Foucault and his re-authoring of Kant's essay "What is Enlightenment?" Foucault's last essay can in many respects be interpreted as an unwitting reprisal of Charrière's project of exposing the limits of the Kantian ethical model by recovering its historical contingency. More interestingly, like Charrière, Foucault translates the critical project of self-constitution into a textual strategy of ironic substitution. In the case of Foucault, the irony lay in the heroic substitution of one author for another – himself for Kant – rather than in a generic inversion of the object of knowledge – the pseudonymous offering of *Three Women* in place of Garves, Hobbes, and Mendelssohn. These two variants of the gesture of self-constitution through ironic substitution – heroic re-authorization and generic inversion – disclose the gendered nature of the constitution of post-Kantian philosophical subjectivity in relation to the law. Foucault and feminism stand, as it were, in a relationship constituted through this lens of the law. On the one side, the ironic author, and on the other, the generic outlaw. The dialogue between women and Foucault thus emerges as a dialogue between the confined and the expelled, or, to put it in positive terms, between the worm and the bird, one boring the apple from its core, the other pecking at its skin, and each taking nourishment from the very law whose limits it contests.

5

Foucault and the Post-Revolutionary Self: The Uses of Cousinian Pedagogy in Nineteenth-Century France

Jan Goldstein

In the 1980–1 annual report of the Collège de France, Foucault supplied the obligatory résumé of his course for that year, the series of lectures entitled "Subjectivity and Truth," in which he sketched out the plan for what would later become volumes 2 and 3 of his *History of Sexuality*. "I have begun an inquiry," he wrote,

> into the modes of self-knowledge that have been put into use and their history: How has the subject been established at different moments and in different institutional contexts as an object of knowledge that is possible, desirable, or even indispensable? How has the experience that one can have of oneself, as well as the knowledge that one can form from that experience, been organized by certain schemas? How have those schemas been defined, valorized, recommended, imposed?

Foucault went on to say that he would take as the "guiding thread" (*fil directeur*) of this inquiry something he called "technologies of the self." By this he meant "the procedures, which have doubtless existed in all civilizations, that are proposed or prescribed to individuals in order to fix, maintain, or transform their identities with particular ends in view" and which operate by means of either "a mastery of the self by the self or a knowledge of the self by the self." What interests me particularly about this passage are the other candidates for "guiding thread" that Foucault mentioned, and pointedly rejected, just before announcing his heuristically valuable new category of "technologies of the self." "It is clear," he observed in the immediately preceding sentence, "that neither recourse to an originary experience nor the study of philosophical theories of the mind (*âme*), passions, or body can serve as the principal axis of such research."[1]

I certainly have no quarrel with Foucault over his discarding, in this quest for a locus of the constitution of the subject, "recourse to an originary experience." If Foucault has taught us anything, it is surely the illusory nature of what is sometimes appealed to as unmediated, originary experience; he has insisted, powerfully and persuasively, on the historical specificity and hence the continual malleability of those objects that we have tended to take for granted as given, timeless, and natural. But, while I agree that it is futile to look for the locus of the constitution of the subject in some alleged originary experience, I wonder about Foucault's blanket dismissal of philosophical theory as playing a significant role.

My doubts stem from the historical research in which I am presently engaged, research which I did not initially conceive in explicitly Foucauldian terms but which should probably be called Foucauldian in its general spirit and which also intersects at several points with Foucault's own work. Hence I would like to use the occasion provided by this paper to explore more systematically than I am wont to do the relationship between my findings, as a historian pursuing a specific and delimited research project, and Foucault's global propositions about the constitution of the subject. I should make clear that I do not regard such an exploration as a cut-and-dried positivist exercise which can confirm or disconfirm Foucault's propositions by reference to some theory-neutral "facts." Rather I see my detailed historical material as providing a practical, concrete standpoint from which to interrogate Foucault's propositions and, I hope, to arrive at a fuller and more critical understanding of them. My discussion will focus on *Discipline and Punish* and the first two volumes of *The History of Sexuality*.

I   A THREE-WAY COMPETITION OF PSYCHOLOGIES

In order to carry out such an exploration, I have first to outline my current research project. It begins with the hypothesis that, through its destruction of the guilds and the other corporate bodies that had formed the matrix of individual life under the Old Regime, the French Revolution problematized the nature of the self. Already in 1776, Turgot's attempted abolition of the guilds had raised the psychological question, prompting the Paris glove-makers to assert in their handwritten protest against the reform measure that "Each person has an existence only through the corporate body (*corps*) to which he is attached."[2] But, if the Revolution lent urgency to the problem of knowing just who the individual removed from the corporate setting was, it also furnished tools for a solution to that same problem. By ratifying the epistemology of the Enlightenment, it gave warrant and impetus to the development of a "science" of psychology which would, contemporaries believed, provide objective knowledge about the human mental apparatus and hence firm conceptual grounding for the freestanding individual.

In fact, not one such "objective" science but three emerged and competed in the half-century following the Revolution: *idéologie*, which was the updated version of the sensationalist psychology of Locke and Condillac; eclecticism, the name generally given to the rational spiritualist psychology of the philosopher Victor Cousin; and phrenology. None of these three psychologies remained confined to the rarefied academic or scientific milieux which had given rise to them. On the contrary, their proponents actively sought their popularization and did not shrink from enmeshing them in the most intense political conflicts of the day. Each of the three thus acquired a clear political affiliation – hardly a surprising outcome if one takes seriously my claim that the psychological question was, from the first, bound up with the social and political upheavals of the Revolution. Each also functioned much like Freudian psychoanalysis in twentieth-century America, furnishing appropriately acculturated individuals with a set of categories on which they routinely drew to make sense of their own and other people's inner lives.

Sensationalism, which depicted the mind as a blank slate inscribed by sensory experience, was the psychological doctrine associated with the Revolution itself: it was regularly invoked by the revolutionaries, and its insistence on human plasticity was consonant with their call for radical social and political change. Thus a wide variety of new cultural practices inaugurated during the revolutionary decade – the revolutionary festivals, the new calendar, the renaming of Paris streets – were publicly justified in the language of sensationalism. On the floor of the legislature, their supporters cited the expected sensory impact of such practices on the "imaginations" of the individuals comprising the national collectivity and the increase in civic spirit that would thereby accrue.[3] By the end of the eighteenth century, the French proponents of sensationalism had elaborated its byword "sensory experience" with new research into the physiology of the nervous system, thus enhancing the scientific character of the doctrine and accentuating its biological roots.

Its challenger, eclecticism, was the psychological doctrine of the *juste milieu*, the cautious and conservative form of liberalism that became orthodoxy under the July Monarchy (1830–48) and that sought a middle way in politics between the abstract egalitarian ideals of the Revolution and the traditions of the Old Regime. Articulated by Victor Cousin, eclecticism represented an analogous middle way in psychology: it combined a limited reliance on sensationalism with a priori belief in a self, or *moi*, a repository of self-initiated mental activity and free will known through introspection and serving, as Cousin liked to say, as the "vestibule" to metaphysics.[4] Siding with traditional practice, eclectics opposed the conversion of psychology into a branch of biology, resolutely defending the linkage between metaphysics and any investigation of the human mind. But they nonetheless evinced a characteristically modern attitude toward knowledge in their use of the language of science. Their philosophical psychology was, they maintained, a fully fledged scientific endeavor, grounded in observation and differing from physics only as a function of its more elusive subject matter.

Finally phrenology, brought to France around 1808 by its Viennese founder Franz Joseph Gall, lodged all intellectual and affective traits in discrete brain organs whose relative size in any given individual was revealed in the contours, or bumps, of that individual's cranium. Entering the scientific mainstream under the July Monarchy, phrenology affiliated politically in two directions – either with a brand of liberalism to the left of the *juste milieu*, or with the nascent socialist movement.

Thus, of the three psychologies, two had biological roots and situated themselves on the left of the political spectrum, the other self-consciously eschewed biological roots and just as self-consciously located itself at the political center. This non-biologistic, politically centrist psychology – Cousinian eclecticism – also seized the offensive in the struggle among the three.

Eclectics designated the unity of the self as the most important criterion in the construction of a psychological science. As Cousin observed, "character is unity!" Modern men, in contrast to the men of antiquity, were filled with "anxiety because they have not made for themselves a self which persists. They are not themselves," but are rather dissipated in "everything that surrounds them."[5] Having indicated the primacy of the unitary self, eclectics went on to charge that neither of their competitors could provide theoretical grounding for it. The sensationalists could not because they built up mind from the raw material of atomistic sensations and provided no means for it to overcome its fragmentary origins. The phrenologists could not because they dispersed mental attributes among a series of discrete brain organs and, like the sensationalists, failed to account for a unifying force or locus of personal identity. Herein, said the eclectics, lay their own obvious superiority. By deemphasizing the material (and hence divisible) substratum of mind, and taking instead the high road of metaphysics, they affirmed the unity of the self a priori, making it incontrovertible.

The state educational system, tentatively established during the Revolution and subsequently given its canonical form by Napoleon, provided the principal arena in which the competition among the three psychologies was played out. The sensationalists set the pattern when they "captured" the central schools, founded under the Directory in 1795 as an experiment in republican secondary education, and installed by legislative decree a curriculum based upon the tenets of *idéologie*. The centerpiece of this curriculum was a course in general grammar – not grammar as ordinarily construed but the principles by which linguistic signs could be affixed to sense impressions in order to produce, from the bottom up, an utterly transparent system of ideas that would correspond with complete accuracy to the contours of external reality. Cleansed of traditional prejudices, popular errors, and all other forms of mental sloppiness, such a system of ideas was expected to be eminently suited to the new republican order. Preparatory to general grammar, more basic courses in drawing and natural history aimed at strengthening the students' visual acuity and powers of observation and thus at improving the quality of the sensory input from which all mental processes were supposed to derive. In the case of natural history, a discipline centered on the taxonomy of the plant and animal kingdoms, the student would also learn rudimentary skills connected to the great epistemological principle: the correct assignment of words to things.[6] Cousin probably had in mind the popularity of pedagogical regimens constructed along these lines when he complained that modern men had lost themselves through the dissipation of their attention "in everything that surrounds them."

While thoroughgoing, the *déologue* capture of secondary education proved notably short-lived: the central schools fell with the Directory in 1799, to be replaced by lycées under Napoleon. The career of phrenology in the state educational system was similarly checkered. Banned by the Restoration government as subversive, Gall's science was rehabilitated by the July Monarchy and reached the zenith of its educational establishment in 1836, when it was briefly added to the course offerings of the Paris Faculty of Medicine. But in general phrenologists eager to propagate their doctrine – and most agreed with the colleague who asserted that "Phrenology consists wholly of its practical application"[7] – retreated to less formal channels, especially public courses for adults taught outside the state educational system.

Only eclecticism secured lasting institutionalization. Indeed, through the control that Cousin gained over the educational bureaucracy, his intellectual creation achieved something like hegemony over French academic philosophy until the closing decades of the nineteenth century. A "philosophical regiment" trained by him at the Ecole Normale Supérieure and at the Sorbonne obtained academic employment and carried his message ("our cause") throughout the provinces; in this loyal band, historians have discerned the beginnings of the professionalization of philosophy in France.[8] At the insistence of Cousin, a subject called "psychology" was added to the standard lycée course in philosophy and made its first substantive section – a curricular innovation voted in 1832 by the Royal Council of Public Instruction (of which Cousin was a member).[9] Henceforth the youth of France, or more precisely the male bourgeois youth who alone attended the lycées, would be instructed about the holistic *moi* and taught the meticulous introspective techniques required to explore it directly. A pedagogical manual published in 1838 by one of Cousin's disciples bears witness to the centrality in the philosophy classroom of this training in introspection, enumerating the difficulties the teacher might encounter in his efforts to lead his young charges to grasp the "interior reality" (*fait intérieur*).[10] The Cousinian canon emphasized the ability to verbalize the interior life: students, says the 1832 decree, should be able to "*describe* the phenomenon of the will and the conditions surrounding and affecting it."[11] For these initiates into eclectic philosophy "self" became a keyword in a way that it had not been for previous generations of French students, leading one contemporary to remark:

> This word [*moi*], which in the past belonged only to the domain of grammar and which was nothing more than the most notable of pronouns, has become, after the word "God," the substantive noun *par excellence*.[12]

It seems safe to conclude that Cousinian psychology functioned in nineteenth-century France as a structure of power/knowledge in Foucault's sense. It was, in the first place, officially prescribed as a form of pedagogy throughout the state system of secondary education and also given maximum impact by its strategic location in that part of the lycée curriculum regarded as its summit or crown: the *classe de philosophie* of the third and last year.[13] Second, as an emanation of bureaucratic power – and in keeping with the precise meaning that Foucault gave to power – Cousinian pedagogy both created and constrained its recipients.[14] It conferred a literal gift of selfhood: the knowledge that one was the possessor of a *moi* – a source of will and willed activity in the world that could be known and talked about. But at the same time it exacted assent to a set of allegedly fixed, immutable principles about "the true, the beautiful, and the good."[15] Designed to promote socio-political consensus and stability, these principles were, according to Cousin, the self-evident results of the very metaphysical speculation that the students' prior passage through the "vestibule" of psychology had equipped them to undertake.

Though creative up to a point, Cousinian introspection thus had a predetermined outcome. Encouraging students to make contact with a principle of efficacy within themselves, it was nonetheless anything but open-ended.

Third and finally, by conferring its gift of selfhood only on the elite segment of the population which attended the lycées, Cousinian psychology implicated itself still more deeply in power relations. Cousin was quite clear that everyone had a *moi* in principle, but he tempered this stance of psychological democracy by his unquestioned assumption that in the majority of people the *moi* would remain more or less fused in a "primitive synthesis" of the elements of consciousness, rather than becoming detached, scrutinized, and appropriated through reflection.[16] He even went so far as to specify that the degree to which these originally fused elements of consciousness were subsequently disaggregated and made known formed the sole basis of the difference between people.[17] Thus, like instruction in Greek and Latin, but more intimately tied to an individual's sense of self, instruction in eclectic psychology became a marker, a criterion for distinguishing socially dominant from marginal groups. Bourgeois males learned psychology, but workers did not and women did not. The significance of these exclusions was underscored by their longevity. For example, even after the Third Republic founded lycées for girls in the 1880s, women still did not learn psychology. Republican educators omitted it from the female curriculum in all but the most watered-down form at the very same moment that they were retaining it full strength in the newly overhauled philosophy curriculum of the boys' lycées.[18]

Perhaps the most dramatic indication that eclectic psychology functioned as a structure of power/knowledge was its surprising prominence in a long debate over a bill on secondary education that took place in the French Chamber of Peers in 1844. The subject of the bill was private secondary instruction – that is, the terms under which agencies other than the state, and in particular the church, might open and maintain secondary schools. Hence the passions that the bill brought forth in the Chamber derived most obviously from clerical and anticlerical sentiment, from the fear that the post-1806 state monopoly on secondary education was producing a generation of godless youth or, conversely, that the reintroduction of unsupervised clerical secondary education would revive the benighted mental habits of the Old Regime. But the clerical–anticlerical polarity is in itself insufficient to explain the attention that the Chamber of Peers lavished on the teaching of Cousinian philosophy.

The word "philosophy" figured only once in the text of the bill – in the brief first article, which defined secondary education by listing the various subject matters it comprised. Yet this seemingly innocuous reference immediately provoked heated discussion about whether philosophy ought to be part of the secondary curriculum at all or relegated to the sheltered preserve of the university where far fewer students would encounter it. That the French lycée taught more philosophy than any of its European counterparts was cited as an argument both for and against the continuation of the practice: routinely teaching philosophy to sixteen-year-olds was, depending upon the speaker, either a mark of the French national genius, or a sort of pedagogical recklessness that needlessly agitated young people and contributed to French political instability.

In this context, the Cousinian psychology that had been institutionalized in the school system for the past dozen years was exposed to sustained political scrutiny. It was broached through its filial relationship to the more traditional philosophy of Descartes. Though far from unqualified admirers of Descartes, the Cousinians had always identified him as their forebear, especially insofar as he had made the observation of the self by itself the starting point of all metaphysical inquiry. He had even introduced one of their favorite words into the French philosophical vocabulary, renaming "soul" as "self." At the same time, Descartes's "self," a relatively early arrival on the historical scene, was not quite the *moi* of the Cousinians, as they were at pains to point out:

> [Descartes] does intentionally say "me" (*moi*) instead of saying "my soul"; but he does not say "the self" (*le moi*) to designate the soul or the mind in general. It is only in the German school that we encounter the latter formula for the first time and thus arrive at a degree of abstraction that cannot be authorized by the psychological or experiential method of Descartes. "The self" in the system of Kant is not the soul or the human person but, less inclusively, consciousness, thought insofar as it reflects on itself.[19]

Given its intimate ties with Cartesianism, Cousinianism was already implicitly involved in the legislative debate when the *rapporteur* for the commission appointed to study the bill on secondary education observed that the Cartesianism "taught by preference in France . . . not only because it is of French origin but because it is in fact the true and sound philosophy" had certain generally unrecognized drawbacks. Firm and mature minds could, he said, weather without difficulty the period of provisional doubt counselled by Descartes, but that same suspension of belief was likely to "imperil" delicate young minds and rob them of their natural "serenity." Hence the *rapporteur* recommended that secondary schools purvey only the safer branches of philosophy, those that did not overstimulate young minds but instead allowed them to "exercise their vigor under the yoke of a salutary discipline."

What he called "elementary psychology" met these specifications. "There is nothing dangerous about the study of psychology," he told his fellow legislators, "*as long as* it remains confined within its proper boundaries, limits itself to the analysis of the faculties of the mind . . . and does not trespass upon the domain of metaphysics."[20] Put differently, the ontological status of the Cousinian *moi* and its role as antechamber to metaphysics – features unabashedly Cartesian in inspiration[21] – disqualified it for adolescent consumption. But the Minister of Public Instruction, apparently more sanguine about the long-term consequences of metaphysical flight, refused to support the *rapporteur*'s interdiction. Everyone knew, he said, that the Cousinian psychology taught under the July Monarchy had thoroughly "purged [and] transformed" the *really* worrisome psychology of Condillac, accused of "reducing human intelligence to sensation."[22] Indeed, educators had rightly dropped psychology from the secondary school curriculum in 1814, when that discipline was equivalent to sensationalism. But they had later just as rightly restored it because it could, in its Cousinian variant, be certified as both "innocent" and "invaluable."[23]

Thus, as improbable as it might seem, the precise pathways for gleaning psychological knowledge became a matter for debate among the politicians of the July Monarchy. Nothing could better illustrate the conflation of power and knowledge in this area than the political urgency of determining in 1844 whether those pathways ran from brute sensation up to the higher reaches of intelligence or, alternatively, inward to a sanctum of subjectivity and then outward to apprehend a universe whose timeless structure framed and supported that same subjectivity. Even entertained by the legislators was the surprising proposition that psychological understanding ought not, for political reasons, be widely sought and disseminated at all.

II   COUSINIAN *MOI* AND FOUCAULDIAN SUBJECT

We can now return to the passage from Foucault which opened this paper and begin to look at my historical material through its prism and at the prism itself from the vantage point of my material. Does the three-way competition of psychologies, and the decisive victory achieved by eclecticism, tell us little or nothing about the constitution of the modern subject because it took place, in large part, in the domain of "philosophical theories of the mind, passions or body"? Are Foucault's propositions internally consistent on this point? How, at various points in his career, did Foucault construe the relationship between the regime of power/knowledge (of which Cousinian psychology was a part) and the constitution of subjectivity? And what might have been at stake for him in his exclusion of philosophy from a shaping role in the constitution of the subject?

Foucault discussed the constitution of the subject, (or something closely approximating that theme) in three books, each time from a different perspective. Moving from *Discipline and Punish*, to the first volume of *The History of Sexuality*, and on to *The Use of Pleasure*, he made successive additions to the density of his account; but not until the third book did he take stock of what he had done and, announcing a fundamental reorientation, attempt to assess how the fruits of his earlier projects might relate to the goals of his new one. This procedure is of course vintage Foucault: the auto-criticism, backtracking, and shifting of direction are typical of his approach to writing. But by the time of *The Use of Pleasure* the mocking, postmodern refusal to be pinned down that had characterized his earlier work ("Do not ask who I am and do not ask me to remain the same: leave it to our bureaucrats and our police to see that our papers are in order"[24]) had lost some of its hard, unsentimental edge and become almost tinged with a Romantic's quest for sincerity ("There are times in life when the question of knowing if one can think differently than one thinks, and perceive differently than one sees, is absolutely necessary if one is to go on looking and reflecting at all. People will say, perhaps, that these games with oneself would better be left backstage"[25]). Indeed, as I shall argue, this tacit change in Foucault's *self*-representation paralleled a somewhat more explicit change in his abstract conceptualization of the self.

In tracing the thread of Foucault's thinking about the constitution of the subject, a useful starting point is the strong characterization of Hubert Dreyfus and Paul Rabinow. Writing in 1982, they ascribed a neat division of labor to *Discipline and Punish* and the first volume of *The History of Sexuality*: the former provided a "genealogy of the modern individual as object," the latter a "genealogy of the modern individual as subject."[26] There is certainly textual evidence in each of the books in question to support this characterization. In a stunning denouement in *Discipline and Punish*, Foucault announced that the disciplinary examination and the assiduous compilation of data-filled dossiers that accompanied it made possible "the everyday individuality of everybody," which he glossed as "the constitution of the individual as a describable, analysable *object*."[27] In *The History of Sexuality*, by contrast, he depicted confession in its religious and scientific guises as "an immense labor to which the West has submitted generations in order to produce . . . men's subjection (*assujettissement*): their constitution as *subjects* in both senses of the word."[28] Both books depicted the individual as an effect of power, brought into being either by the observations and written notations of the disciplinary expert or by the provocations and definitive interpretations of the confessional expert. Yet if, in Foucault's play on words, subjection to sexual confession produces a subject, the disciplinary examination, he tells us, "functions as a procedure of *objectivation* and subjection."[29]

Why the difference? A plausible answer, backed up by Foucault's choice of figurative language, might be that the disciplinary apparatus is ocular and its confessional counterpart auditory: the disciplinary expert views a docile body; the confessor-scientist hears a speaking subject, albeit in a highly constrained speech situation. Thus the central images of *Discipline and Punish* are the gaze, the eye of power, and the Benthamite Panopticon. *The History of Sexuality* is larded instead with oscillations between speech and silence and, in one of its many comic moments, uses the trope of synecdoche to refer to Freud as "the most famous ears of our time."[30] In sum, ocular instruments of power would seem to move around the contours of corporeal externality, thus producing individuals as objects; auditory ones would seem to penetrate into interior spaces where they can conjure up desires and other secrets, thus producing individuals as subjects.

Whatever its validity and usefulness, this distinction is, I think, too neat. In the first place, the two books have a partially overlapping cast of characters; many of the *savoirs* that appear as the disciplines of the earlier book reappear as the confessional sciences of the second book – clinical medicine, psychiatry, to some extent pedagogy.[31] It is furthermore clear that virtually all the Foucauldian disciplines relied for their data not only on the spatial location and enhanced visibility of bodies but also on the spoken reports (descriptions of symptoms, recitations of lessons, narrations of crimes) of incarcerated persons.

I have a second reason for refusing to press this distinction too far, one that is less empirical than methodological. Isn't there, after all, a significant connection between the way authoritative scientific experts construct us from the outside as objects, and what (the same or different) authoritative scientific experts can elicit from inside us in the medium of speech as the content of our subjectivity? It is, after all, our *internalization* of the objective knowledge about us that lends this knowledge much of its practical force and serves as one measure of the authority of those who pronounce it. Though Foucault never spelled out such a line of argument, his formulations do, I think, basically if elliptically concur with it. In particular, his notion of punishing "the soul" through the gentle bodily training prescribed by the disciplines, rather than punishing the body directly by the gory tortures of the Old Regime,[32] seems to refer to a mechanism by which we internalize, literally take to heart, the judgments made about us by others. This mechanism of internalization – of converting the outsider's expert knowledge about us into that subjective interiority that we perpetually carry around with us – can, after all, be adduced as an explanation of the enhanced efficiency and ease of large-scale operation that Foucault attributed to discipline as a mode of power.[33] In any case, by the early 1980s, Foucault had homogenized his vocabulary and adopted the term "subject" to refer to *both* those individuals produced by disciplinary procedures and those produced by confessional ones.[34]

In *The Use of Pleasure*, where Foucault highlights the problem of the subject and grapples with it more deliberately than ever before, he also attempts a schematic integration of the approaches to the historical constitution of the subject dispersed throughout his earlier work. Although *The Use of Pleasure* is the second volume of *The History of Sexuality*, Foucault's intellectual interest in sexuality had, by the time he wrote it, waned appreciably;[35] and for purposes of volume 2 he demoted it to the subordinate role of case study. It commands our attention because it is one domain, presumably one among several or even many, in which "the individual constitutes and recognizes himself *qua* subject." Foucault now viewed the historical specificity of human experience at any given moment as constructed along three axes: "the sciences (*savoirs*) that refer to it; the systems of power that regulate its practice; the forms within which individuals are able, are obliged, to recognize themselves as subjects." Analysis of the first two, *savoir* and *pouvoir*, had of course comprised the bulk of his earlier work; analysis of the forms of subjectivity would occupy him in his current project.[36]

Unfortunately, Foucault never spelled out the implications of this tripartite mapping.[37] In particular, he never indicated what, if anything, the structures of power/knowledge (the first two axes and the factors he had once held directly and exclusively responsible for the genesis of the individual) had to do with the various historical experiences of subjectivity (the third axis). His vocabulary in *The Use of Pleasure* sometimes echoed the arresting double entendre on "subject" that had figured in and indeed epitomized his earlier work. He spoke of the "mode of subjection" (*mode d'assujettissement*) to the moral code as an aspect of the formation of the subject,[38] thus suggesting that subjects remained for him the power-effects that they had been in *Discipline and Punish* and the first volume of *The History of Sexuality*. But he now also employed a new term, "subjectivation" (*subjectivation* in the French), which, by virtue of its sudden insertion in his prose, suggested that Foucault might no longer simply equate subject-making with subjection. In fact, in *The Use of Pleasure* "subjectivation" functions as the governing rubric in Foucault's system of classification: the "mode of subjection" to the moral code is subsumed under it as one of its four possible types.[39]

But Foucault left the freight carried by the term "subjectivation" unpacked; especially tantalizing is the possibility that the term contains a hint of human agency that Foucault's earlier work had categorically rejected. A comment he made in a 1983 interview reinforces this hint. Foucault insisted that the forms of human self-recognition as subject, the domain that he idiosyncratically labeled ethics, enjoyed relative autonomy from macro-structures of political, social, and economic power.[40] But Foucault also supplied clues that point in the opposite direction. For example, a contemporary American work that he cited as a rare example of the history of subjectivation, Stephen Greenblatt's *Renaissance Self-Fashioning*, specifies that the "increased [sixteenth-century] self-consciousness about the fashioning of human identity as a manipulable, artful process" was correlated not with a widening of the sphere of human autonomy, but on the contrary with a new capability of "the family, state and religious institutions [to] impose a more rigid and far-reaching discipline upon their middle-class and aristocratic subjects."[41]

If its implications for human agency remain elusive, it is nonetheless clear that subjectivation is subject-making in the reflexive mode: its special domain is the relationship that the self establishes to the self (be it "self-reflection, self-knowledge, self-examination, [or] the transformations that one seeks to accomplish with oneself as object"[42]), and its privileged modus operandi is the so-called technology of the self. What is unclear is the place of power/knowledge in subjectivation – necessary, peripheral, or incompatible. If, for example, we take the psychoanalytic confession as a mode of subject-making through subjection (this is Foucault's claim in the first volume of *The History of Sexuality*), does it follow that it is *not* a mode of subjectivation because it requires the mediation of the powerful/knowledgeable figure of the psychoanalytic expert? Or does it perhaps become a mode of subjectivation only after it has been thoroughly habituated so that an individual continues to perform its rituals of self-decipherment in solitude as well as in the presence of the Freudian doctor? I pose these questions because the relationship Foucault postulates, or fails to postulate, between structures of power/knowledge and technologies of the self is relevant to the historical significance of Cousinian psychology and to the question whether, as a "philosophical theory of mind," that psychology can be assigned a role in the business of Foucauldian subject-making.

We have already seen that Cousinian psychology qualifies as a structure of power/knowledge. Hence it is definitely a candidate for the constitution of the subject as that concept is understood in *Discipline and Punish* and the first volume of *The History of Sexuality*; whatever Foucault might have us believe, its nature as a philosophical theory would not be grounds for exclusion. Indeed, in its selective application and consequent function as a marker of social class, it follows rather closely the pattern set by Foucault himself in the first volume of the *History of Sexuality*, where sexuality is presented as the single, privileged locus of the constitution of the modern subject. Just as well-articulated knowledge of oneself as possessing a Cousinian *moi* was the exclusive prerogative of the male bourgeoisie in the nineteenth century, so Foucault indicates that the "deployment of sexuality [did] not operate in symmetrical fashion with respect to the social classes." The eighteenth-century (male) bourgeoisie "endowed itself, in an arrogant political affirmation, with a garrulous sexuality" and was for a long time "unwilling to acknowledge that other classes had a body and a sex."[43]

But even if we follow the trend of Foucault's last work and relegate power/knowledge to merely incidental status in the process of subject formation, even if we focus solely on the "technologies of the self" that Foucault associated with subjectivation in *The Use of Pleasure*, Cousinian psychology still retains its credentials for inclusion. The introspection it featured and taught to lycée students bears all the marks of a technology of the self, as some passages from Cousin's celebrated 1828 lectures will show:

> What is psychological analysis? It is the slow, patient, and meticulous observation, with the aid of consciousness, of phenomena hidden in the depths of human nature. These phenomena are complicated, fleeting, obscure, rendered almost imperceptible by their very closeness. The consciousness which applies itself to them is an instrument of extreme delicacy.[44]

> There is, Gentlemen, a psychological art, for reflection is, so to speak, against nature, and this art is not learned in a day. One does not fold back upon oneself easily without long practice, sustained habit, and a laborious apprenticeship.[45]

Why, then, the stricture in the 1980–1 annual report of the Collège de France? Why Foucault's insistence that philosophy of mind was fundamentally irrelevant to the constitution of the subject? It is possible that Foucault was thinking of such philosophy as confined to a narrow, bookish coterie and hence as incapable of doing the large-scale work of, say, sexuality in constructing a kind of everyday subjectivity for everybody. It is possible that he was unaware of, or had momentarily forgotten about, the wide institutional dissemination of *idéologie* and especially of eclecticism, that he failed to register the nineteenth-century professionalization of philosophy and hence the emergence of a cadre of "philosophical pedagogues" who joined the ranks of the growing disciplinary apparatus.[46] It is, in other words, possible, that he overlooked some of the "facts" and thus arrived at an erroneous generalization. But, since it has long been my belief that Foucault usually knew as many "facts" as historians do, I would like to suggest that something else was at issue.

The dismissal of philosophy of mind in the annual report of the Collège de France was not an entirely isolated remark. More complicated versions of it can be found both in *Discipline and Punish* and in the first volume of *The History of Sexuality*. Thus, discussing the shift from public torture to penal leniency, Foucault emphasized the displacement of the point of application of punishment: from the body to the so-called soul.[47] He then pondered "this entry of the soul on to the scene of penal justice."[48] The soul in question had undergone a historical mutation; it was no longer "the soul represented by Christian theology, ... born in sin and subject to punishment," but an entirely new-model soul, "born rather *out of* methods of punishment, supervision, and constraint." He continued:

> This real, non-corporal soul is not a substance; it is the element in which are articulated the effects of a certain type of power and the reference of a certain type of knowledge. ... On this reality-reference, various concepts have been constructed and domains of analysis carved out: psyche, subjectivity, personality, consciousness, etc.

"Psyche, subjectivity, personality, consciousness" – these keywords of the discourse of nineteenth-century philosophy of mind have undergone a Foucauldian defamiliarization. Instead of appearing in their usual guise as high-flown objects of intrinsic interest which would sooner or later have to engage the ruminations of serious Western thinkers, they are reduced to accidental by-products, the "present correlative of a certain technology of power."[49]

A comparable defamiliarization of the same discourse takes place in *The History of Sexuality*. In one of the wonderfully mock-heroic passages that typify this text, Foucault has just noted of nineteenth-century psychiatry that "It was enough to make one's voice tremble, for an improbable thing was then taking shape: a confessional science, a science which relied on a many-sided extortion, and took for its object what was unmentionable but admitted to nonetheless." The entrance into scientific discourse of such lowly, unpedigreed elements scandalized and repelled many members of the educated community; it also engendered

> a theoretical and methodological paradox: the long discussions concerning the possibility of constituting a science of the subject, the validity of introspection, lived experience as evidence, or the presence of consciousness

to itself were *responses to this problem* that is inherent in the functioning of truth in our society: can one articulate the production of truth according to the old juridico-religious model of confession, and the extortion of confidential evidence according to the rules of scientific discourse?[50]

Here again the discourse of philosophy of mind undergoes a surprising transformation at Foucault's hands. No longer a self-evidently important endeavor of high intellectual seriousness, it becomes instead a mere surface effect of power – this time of the bio-power that must impress on modern individuals their fundamental identity as sexual beings and to this end invents a scientific version of the confessional, a strange and awkward hybrid whose very "improbability" in turn raises "theoretical and methodological" problems that crave solution. In short, in both books Foucault presents, in passing, a genealogy of philosophy of mind.

With its Nietzschean overtones, Foucauldian genealogy is a polemical use of the past designed to debunk the most cherished values and institutions of liberal culture by showing that they originated in mere historical contingency and in petty or ignoble practices which present a comic contrast to the loftiness usually ascribed to them. Thus *Discipline and Punish* performs its genealogical magic on the ideal of enlightened humanitarianism, on the inductive scientific method, on the constitutional state.[51] The first volume of *The History of Sexuality* provides a genealogy of Freudian psychoanalysis, turning it from a system of emancipatory ideas to the handmaiden of a largely repressive power. But while the humanitarian ideal, the scientific method, the constitutional state, and the heroic myth of psychoanalysis all seem obvious choices as "sacred cows" appropriate for genealogical debunking, philosophy of mind seems far less obvious, even a bit odd, in this capacity. Its present sway over our society is, after all, negligible. In addition, Foucault's genealogical account of it is, I think, particularly demeaning. Unlike the other discourses for which Foucault provided a genealogy, philosophy of mind is, in Foucault's account of it, not merely of ignoble provenance but also bereft of a directly functional role in power relations. It is almost completely useless and purposeless, a kind of highly elaborated discursive scratch for an intellectual itch generated by new mechanisms of power.

We are left, then, with something of a paradox. Foucault's genealogies of philosophy of mind implicitly deny the latter efficacy as a mechanism of power, much like his comments in the annual report of the Collège de France explicitly deny it efficacy as a technology of the self. Both denials seem at odds with the case of Cousinian psychology in nineteenth-century France. But, while Foucault seems to *under*estimate the historical importance of philosophy of mind in the constitution of the subject, he seems to *over*estimate its present-day importance, as seen in his providing it with a genealogy. These contradictory positions seem in turn to betray a deep ambivalence toward philosophy of mind on Foucault's part – an ambivalence that may well have grown out of the very salience of philosophy of mind in the French educational system that formed him intellectually and certified him as a professor. Foucault's *thèse d'état* was, after all, technically in the field of philosophy, even if his work on the history of madness in the classical age stretched that rubric practically beyond recognition and prompted his philosopher-mentor Jean Hyppolite to suggest that the historian of science Georges Canguilhem would be more qualified to preside over the dissertation defense.[52] Torn between contrary evaluations, Foucault seems to give credence to the traditional self-interpretation of French academic philosophy – the crown of education, the mark of general culture – even as he attempts to expose such philosophy as largely unnecessary surface noise. These internal contradictions and ambivalence do not, in some simple fashion, discredit Foucault's account of things. But they do suggest that his work may be in more than one place subtly marked by a French cultural bias to which we, in turn, should be attuned when we attempt to assess the validity of that work and its relevance to our own situation.

6

Foucault and the Freudian Subject: Archaeology, Genealogy, and the Historicization of Psychoanalysis

John E. Toews

Throughout the thirty-year period spanning Michel Foucault's first significant publications in 1954 and the multi-volume project left unfinished at his death in 1984, the theory and practice of psychoanalysis played a prominent role in the formulation and reformulation of his project of historicizing cultural criticism. The persistence of this concern was sustained in part by a negative animus. Psychoanalysis continually reappeared in Foucault's writing as the cultural epitome or the pivotal intersection of the sets of cultural practices, systems of thought, and forms of experience which were the object of his interpretive analysis and historical critique. Although occasionally perceived as pushing against and questioning the boundaries of the ordering categories and constitutive practices of the existing cultural formations in the "West," it was ultimately judged as reaffirming those limits. Unlike Heidegger, Kant, and especially Nietzsche, who provided positive stimulus and guidance in the formulation of Foucault's historical projects[1] – or literary figures like Hölderlin, Roussel, and Bataille, whose writings intimated possibilities of alternative forms of experience, transgressing the limits of contemporary culture – Freud, and psychoanalytic discourse more generally, persistently retained the role of the "other" against which Foucault's own projects were defined.

This continuity in the privileged position occupied by psychoanalysis as a primary object of Foucauldian cultural critique was clearly connected to

Foucault's belief that psychoanalytic theory and practice straddled the central problematic of modern culture – the experience of human existence as both constituted and constituting individual subjectivity. In each of the three major domains – systematic, "scientific" knowledge of human beings; action with, over, and against others in the networks of power; and reflexive self-knowledge and ethical self-determination – in which Foucault pursued his project of writing "a history of the different modes in which, in our culture, human beings are made subjects,"[2] psychoanalysis was an imposing cultural presence, epitomizing generalized positions, organizing a heterogeneity of practices and discourses, staking out influential claims. Foucault's critique of contemporary culture was thus deeply entangled in his interpretive analysis and reconstruction of the historical conditions of the possibility of psychoanalysis; in Foucauldian terms the archaeology and genealogy of the modern subject could virtually be reformulated as the archaeology and genealogy of psychoanalysis.[3]

"Archaeology" and "genealogy" are Foucauldian terms describing the structural and narrative dimensions of the procedures of historicization. But it would be misleading simply to translate Foucault's terms into the conventional academic historical practice of cultural and temporal contextualization. Foucault's historicizing activity repudiated and undermined those historically constructed boundaries that protect the disciplinary production of specialized historical knowledge from the combat of contemporary cultural conflicts and the anxieties of self-reflective theoretical analysis. And Foucault clearly relegated conventional forms of historiography and definitions of historicization to the confining limits of the cultural worlds that were the object of his own procedures of historicization, and thus judged them incapable of grappling with the historical conditions which made those worlds possible. Foucault is significant for contemporary historians of psychoanalysis not only because he has broadened and revised the research program for contextualizing Freudian theory and practice, but also and primarily because he has illuminated the assumptions and implications of such historicizing practices, the contextual limits of conventional historical contextualizing.

I FOUCAULT'S STARTING POINT: EXISTENTIAL ANALYSIS VERSUS FREUDIAN PSYCHOLOGY

Before examining the archaeological and genealogical approaches through which Foucault historicized psychoanalysis in his writings of the 1960s and 1970s, it is useful and illuminating to remind ourselves that Foucault's intellectual point of departure was a conceptualization of psychoanalysis as a theory of subjectivity whose limitations were most clearly revealed when it was inserted into the philosophical context of its relations to Husserlian and Heideggerian phenomenology. The extended and detailed comments on Freudian texts (more extended and detailed than anything Foucault wrote subsequently) in Foucault's first two published works – a lengthy introduction to a translation of Ludwig Binswangers *Traum und Existenz* (1954) and a critical, synoptic overview of the perspectives of current psychiatry: *Maladie mentale et personnalité* (1954) – develop the general perspective of a phenomenological and existentialist critique of psychoanalysis, with a specific commitment to the Heideggerian interpretive construction of the forms of being-in-the-world as the governing structures of human existence.

In the introduction to the Binswanger essay, Foucault elaborated a multi-layered philosophical critique of the Freudian conception of human subjectivity.[4] First, he developed the claim that the Freudian subject was actually a composite constructed from two ultimately unreconciled approaches to the interpretation of human experience. Freud's metapsychological conceptualization of libido as an ultimate "presence" from which all human expressions derived their meaning was criticized as a mystifying, "theological" objectification of the meaning-creating subject which conformed to the reductive perspectives of psychological positivism. This aspect of the Freudian subject had been developed by Melanie Klein and her followers. However, a contrasting conception of human subjectivity as constructed individual identity, formed within structures of language that could never fully articulate the unconscious identity of the subject of desire, was developed in Freud's clinical interpretations and case studies. This side of Freud was developed by Lacan and his disciples. But the unity between these two dimensions – between "a psychology of the image which demarcates the field of presence, and a psychology of meaning which defines the field of linguistic potentialities" – could not be found within the framework of psychoanalytic thinking. For Foucault this unreconciled division was clearly a "fault" or a "limitation." Psychoanalysis could not grasp the unity of human experience as a subjectivity lived in the world but continually dissolved the unity of "personality" into the opposing "determinisms" of nature and culture. Husserlian phenomenology provided a general and abstract analysis of selfhood as expressive intentionality articulated in a world, but could not connect its categories to the concrete materiality and historicity of lived existence. It was only with Heidegger's interpretations of the modalities of human being-in-the-world that a way had been found to resolve the problematic "posed by the twofold tradition of phenomenology and psychoanalysis" and grasp human subjectivity in both its concrete finite reality and its constitutive forms.

In Foucault's view, psychoanalysis, because of its self-divided, doubly reductive conception of human subjectivity, could not finally provide insight into the universal structures of experience as modalities of self–world relations grounded in an "original movement" of "radical freedom" in which human subjectivity emerged as a transcending act that "projects itself toward a world which constitutes itself as the setting of its history." Psychoanalysis was blind to experiences of primal subject/object identity, of encounters with the "point of origin from which freedom makes itself world," and thus hapless before expressions like dreams, imaginary literature, and even the fantasies of "mad" individuals in which such originary experiences from the "abysses of the soul" were articulated. What was at stake here was a failure to grasp the origin and essence of human subjectivity as an act of radical, self-constituting freedom, and thus also an inability to see the core of human inauthenticity and discontent in the subject's self-alienating subordination to the mystified, petrified forms of culture. With its assumption of a subjectivity resolutely private and individual and yet determined by the anonymous "external" worlds of instinct and history, nature and culture, psychoanalysis presupposed the conditions of the pathologies it hoped to cure. A cure could only be found if this framework, this self–world orientation, itself became the object of interpretation and etiological analysis. By "losing its temporality," Foucault wrote, the subject alienated itself from "that existence in the world in which his freedom bursts forth; being unable to possess its meaning, he abandons himself to events; in this fragmented, futureless time, in that incoherent space, one sees the mark of a disintegration that abandons the subject to the world as to an external fate."[5]

The existential critique of Freud in Foucault's first writings made possible a further contextualizing move. As a form of the alienation of existence from authentic freedom and unity, psychoanalysis was inserted into the context of collective social history as the psychological pathology derived from the social pathology of the contradictions of capitalism. The truth of psychoanalysis, Foucault claimed, would finally be revealed in its historical fate as an epiphenomenal expression of capitalist/bourgeois society. The totalizing and universalizing assumptions in Foucault's judgment of the limits of psychoanalysis from the standpoint of Heidegger's insight into the authentic structures of human experience were thus matched by his historicization of psychoanalysis from the standpoint of the totalizing social dialectics and historical teleology of a Marxist social history.

The attempt to join together an existentialist or phenomenological description of human existence as alienated constituent subjectivity with a Marxist analysis of the dialectics of the capitalist epoch in world history was not, of course, unique to Foucault. In Germany such attempts can be traced back to the philosophical neo-Marxism of the 1920s (Adorno, Fromm), and it mirrored a central problematic of thinkers like Sartre and Merleau-Ponty in Foucault's immediate environment in the 1950s. The historicization of the Freudian subject as a product and mirror of the contradictions of bourgeois/capitalist social experience was an integral part of this leftist intellectual perspective.

Within a few years, however, Foucault had lost confidence in the foundations of both ends of his analysis – the universal structures of subjectivity presupposed in phenomenology and existentialism, as well as the temporal and structural totalism of Marxian historical dialectics. Over time they became less guides for analyzing the contemporary forms of experience than exemplars and components of those forms. They tended to merge with, rather than oppose, psychoanalysis as integral components of the social/cultural formation whose inner structures and historical conditions of possibility needed to be described. By the time of the publication of *Histoire de la folie* in 1961 Foucault was convinced that a critique of the culture-bound historical limitations of psychoanalysis could not be defined in terms like inauthenticity, self-contradiction, or self-alienation, which assumed both an essentialist conception of the subject as integral personality and a totalizing conception of history as a dialectical teleology. During the 1960s his insistence that the phenomenological subject and Marxist historical dialectics were part of the Old Testament rather than the New was one of his more publicly provocative positions.

But some very fundamental elements of Foucault's original historico-philosophical construction and critique of psychoanalysis survived this disillusionment and transformation. He remained convinced that psychoanalysis represented a form of thinking and an organization of experience which extended far beyond the confines of a particular specialized discipline and addressed the most fundamental structures of the human experience of self-identity and difference; that it was a major, unavoidable interlocutor in the universalizing critical discourse traditionally defined as "philosophical." Second, Foucault maintained his belief that the psychoanalytic mode of describing and thinking existence was connected in obscure but fundamental ways to the emergence of a general social/cultural formation (akin to, if not synonymous with, Marxian capitalism or Weberian rationalism) that characterized the unique historical reality of the modern Western world, a social/cultural formation that cut across specific state, ethnic, national, class, and gender lines, and provided the contextual "field" in which other conflicts were defined and played out. By the early 1960s he had formulated the outlines of what he felt was a non-essentializing, non-teleological, non-totalizing conception of the governing forms within which particular social and cultural experiences were historically constructed. Almost inadvertently, it seemed, he referred to his new historicizing perspective in 1961 as an "archaeology" that reconstructed the structures of "constant verticality" in historical cultures.[6]

II THE ARCHAEOLOGICAL HISTORICIZATION OF THE FREUDIAN SUBJECT

In each of Foucault's three major historicizing archaeological studies of the 1960s psychoanalysis emerges near or at the conclusion as both an exemplary epitomization and a problematic self-reflection of major components of the "modern" (historical/anthropological/individualizing) cultural formation which displaced the constituent forms of "classical" western European culture at the end of the eighteenth and beginning of the nineteenth centuries. The thematic focus in these works displays a clearly recognizable continuity with Foucault's conceptions of the historical limitations of psychoanalysis in his pre-archaeological writings, and his critical judgments mirror his former view of psychoanalysis as a cultural practice whose apparent demystification and dismantling of the ruling conventions of nineteenth-century culture obscured its ultimate confinement within those boundaries. The problem for Foucault was to articulate the nature of these limiting forms in a way that avoided recourse to totalizing and essentializing conceptions of subjectivity and historical development.

The thematic continuity between pre-archaeological and archaeological historicizations was most obvious in *Histoire de la folie*, where psychoanalysis is prominently featured as an articulation of the characteristic ways in which nineteenth-century European culture managed or exorcised the experience of the radical contingency of its own ordering categories and limiting boundaries. In the question of the cultural containment of madness, the Heideggerian question of the contingency and "radical freedom" of self-definition reappeared in new form. Madness defined the limits of cultural order; to confront, to listen to, to experience madness was to encounter the radical contingency of order, to face its constructed nature. (To construct order with full knowledge of such madness was to create order as an aesthetic "work.") In order to ground, to center, to stabilize the rules of their own cultural formations, to perceive or impose them as universal and absolute, cultures developed various procedures for controlling this experience.

Unlike the classical cultural formation which silenced, excluded, confined, and dominated the "other" as the irrational which threatened a self-defining, monologic rational order from the "outside," nineteenth-century culture defined the otherness of madness in subjective, psychologizing, "interiorized" terms, as a form of cultural and moral immaturity that was amenable, through the organization of internal guilt rather than external punishment, to pedagogical discipline, moral management, and therapeutic intervention.[7] Just as the West colonized foreign, alien cultures in order to assimilate and appropriate them as subordinate, controlled elements of its own identity, so it colonized its internal otherness.[8] Nineteenth-century culture psychologized madness and subjected it to therapeutic management – thus the centrality of psychology and psychoanalysis in its self-sustaining, reproductive procedures. Psychoanalysis brought the psychologizing management of madness to a fulfillment that seemed in some ways to actually break out of the self-relating monologue of the paternalistic, psychologizing expert and confront, and engage in dialogue with, the voices that articulated the "outside" of its own internal sameness. In psychoanalytic therapy the external restraints and interventions of asylum treatment were removed; madness was allowed to speak without being externally censored, manipulated, judged, or punished. Yet Foucault saw these changes as immanent transformations within the existing structure of paternalistic control and condescension. All of nineteenth–century psychiatry converged on Freud, Foucault averred, because he accepted its essential principles with absolute seriousness, giving quasi-divine status to the paternalistic medical expert, focusing all of the powers previously distributed throughout the "collective existence of the asylum" on this single presence.[9]

Foucault saw this focused concentration of the principle of order and authority in the relation between a benign father figure, eliciting confessions of transgression from, but not engaging in symmetrical dialogue with, a series of individualized minors and dependants, as a correlate of the focus of social authority in the paternalistic bourgeois family, and increasingly in the socializing institutions of the welfare or "police" state, although these correlations and connections were seen as specific relationships of autonomous "systems," not expressions of a single totality or derivations from a common center. The existence of madness in modern culture was "enveloped . . . in a 'parental complex.' It was this 'historical sedimentation' which psychoanalysis would later bring to light, according it through a new myth the meaning of destiny that supposedly marked all of Western culture and perhaps all civilization, whereas it had been slowly deposited by it and only solidified quite recently at the turn of the century."[10] The experience of madness was reduced to a subjective psychological resistance to, or transgression of, paternally defined order, and expressed in individual guilt.[11]

In an essay published soon after *Histoire de la folie*, Foucault expanded this paternalistic theme to nineteenth-century European culture's general response to the death of God and the problem of grounding the particularity of its cultural order on some absolute center. The Freudian obsession with the father and the father's position as the organizing center of cultural/ethical order, which was forcefully revealed in the oedipal theory, was thus seen as an example of self-mystifying cultural and social practices aimed at concealing the absence of the father and the radical contingency of all cultural order. Psychoanalysis could only deal convincingly and effectively with neuroses – limited irregularities within this paternalistic structure – but was hapless before the true madness of the psychoses in which the father's authority, the center of all law and signification, collapsed.[12] Thus psychoanalysis, as Foucault had already stated in 1954, was ultimately unable to grasp its own contingency, to historicize itself, to engage in a direct confrontation and reciprocal dialogue with madness, to experience its "outside" and thus gain insight into the "tragic" nature of encultured human experience.[13]

As at once a therapeutic institution, a set of procedures for managing the interiorized personality, and a systematic "scientific" interpretation of human existence, psychoanalysis operated within the limited, contingent, historically constructed framework of a cultural system that had emerged around 1800. Foucault's historicizing, archaeological activity aimed at reconstructing the systems or governing networks of thought and practices that made this historical construction possible, at describing the contextual field in which the forms of experience of that culture could appear. The enabling condition for a historicization of psychoanalysis was an experiential and intellectual transcendence of its historical field or framework. Without the limiting frameworks of a universal philosophical anthropology or a dialectical historical teleology Foucault was left only with those "lightning-like" confrontations with radical otherness articulated in art, especially literature. The autonomy of art, as a radically free construction of worlds and orders with languages disconnected from any representational or expressive function, articulated for Foucault the immanent form of seeing the present from the perspective of its possible impossibility, of transgressing the limits of culturally ordered worlds, of encountering nothingness, madness, and death. Foucault's "literary" appreciations of Raymond Roussel, Georges Bataille, Friedrich Hölderlin, Maurice Blanchot, Pierre Klossowski, and others, which accompanied his archaeological writings in the 1960s, articulated the precondition of any perspective that could transcend the forms of contemporary culture and thus define them as an object of analysis.[14] But experiences of the transgression of cultural limits, encounters with the "outside" of the world in which the forms of experience were defined in a particular culture, also entered into his archaeological writings as their essential problematic. In *Histoire de la folie* the issue was the ways in which the formation of various cultural practices succeeded in controlling experiences of otherness, closing off possible openings into the abysses of radical historicity and thus affirming their own solidity, universality, permanence. The peculiar problem of modern culture was the task of constructing and maintaining an order in the face of a collapse of collective belief in both transcendent religious authority and metaphysical cosmic order, that is, on purely immanent grounds. The question was how finite human existence – "man" – came to serve as the god-term for a cultural order; the task to investigate the construction of this center of modern Western culture's historical preconditions, this ultimate referent that controlled the play of language.

In the conclusion of *The Birth of the Clinic* (1963) Freud and "Freudian man" were simply mentioned as exemplars of the dependence of Western discourse regarding human existence on the experiences of finitude and individuality which defined the possibility of modern clinical medicine as a "positive" science.[15] In *The Order of Things*, Foucault expanded the scope of his inquiry to an archaeology or "vertical" cultural analysis of some of the networks of relations that constructed human existence as both objective and subjective finitude, as "empirical and transcendental" being. The broadening of scope, however, was accompanied by a narrowing of focus to the level of linguistically articulated knowledges or sciences, of systems of representation. The institutional and non-linguistic, "social," components of cultural construction, still much in evidence in *The Birth of the Clinic*, were replaced by a synoptic analysis of the a priori determinants of the discursive construction of the knowledge of "man" in the sciences devoted to systematic "truthful" knowledge in three major dimensions of experience – biological life, economic production and social relations, and cultural/linguistic meaning. In this analysis, psychoanalytic "science," the Freudian construction of human existence, played an ambivalent role.

On the one hand, Foucault reasserted his already familiar claim that psychoanalysis brought into a clarifying focus the underlying assumptions of the dominant modern Western knowledge of human existence. The models for the study of man as both determined empirical objectivity and originary, creative subjectivity, developed in the analysis of life, labor, and language, came together and found a pivotal point in the work of Freud but "without, for all that, leaving [their] fundamental arrangement."[16] But Foucault also delineated a different, more exalted place for psychoanalysis among the sciences of man in modern culture – as one of the "counter-sciences" (along with ethnology and linguistics) which reflected critically on the foundations of the human sciences, and began to interrogate and unveil the conditions of their possibility. Psychoanalysis thus seemed to function as both a maker and an unmaker of modern man, a soporific and an alarm clock for the great "anthropological sleep."

The critical function of psychoanalysis was displayed in its attempt to address directly the organizing categories and founding assumptions of modern humanist Western culture. It did not simply assume the reality of "man" as finite subject/object constructed in relation to death, desire, and law *per se*, but advanced directly at these "figures" which defined the boundaries of "man." Psychoanalysis, Foucault claimed, "leaps over" the organizing representations of human existence to the experience of the very possibility of the existence of these representations. For thinkers operating within the confines or implicit governing regulations of the modern anthropological episteme, the objects of psychoanalysis must seem mythical or transcendent, but, claimed Foucault, they constituted "the very forms of finitude." Death is that which makes all positive knowledge of man's mode of being within finitude possible; desire functions similarly as the unconscious presupposition of action; and the figuration of law/language in the father's "no" is the presupposition of all order and meaning. But the confrontation with these figures was also a confrontation with "madness in its modern form," that is an encounter with the radical historicity of existence, with the possible dissolution of the finite human subject through a "liberated" immersion in death, desire, and language. The encounter with these figures thus presented a vision not of a different world but of the instability and radical contingency of our own; it revealed the "finitude on the basis of which we are." The meaning of these figures were revealed to the analyst, in a savagely illuminating but ultimately non-conceptualizable and non-verbalizable fashion, claims Foucault, most clearly in the psychoses and especially in schizophrenia.[17]

Because psychoanalysis could not ultimately integrate into rational or empirical discourse the objects of its investigation, the goals of its quest, it could not produce a general theory of man. It was left instead with the interminable interpretation of the practices in which the construction of individual subjective identity takes place in the face of death, desire, and language. Foucault seems to be saying that there is implicit in psychoanalytic practice an encounter with the madness of death, desire, and language that cannot be articulated in a general theory, but only approached in the endless renewals of clinical interpretation. In an essay written about the same time, this position is clarified somewhat. The psychoanalytic practice of interpretation is seen as an interminable process which contains no referents or ultimate organizing realities that could stop the endless play of language with language, of interpretation with interpretation. The "absolute point" in interpretation could only be the point where the interpreter would disappear or dissolve into the self-mirroring fluidity of language: the experience that at bottom there is only interpretation, no thing to be interpreted – the void of "madness." Foucault claimed that, unlike Nietzsche, Freud resisted and struggled against this experience.[18] Yet for a brief period in the late 1960s Foucault seemed uncertain as to whether or not Freud should be grouped with Nietzsche as a "transdiscursive figure" who initiated a new discourse that was at least in some ways, or perhaps potentially, a transgression of the episteme centered on "man."[19] Increasingly during the 1960s Freud appeared to Foucault as a Nietzsche controlled, or domesticated. In a sense psychoanalysis tried to incorporate Nietzsche's transgression of the limits of the anthropological episteme within the confines of the discourse of "man."[20]

Connected to Foucault's continuing uncertainty about the appropriate positioning of psychoanalytic discourse within the vertical network of discursive formations constituting the forms of experience of modern Western culture, and its immanent temporal transformations, was his difficulty in resolving the problem of defining the temporal and spatial boundaries of the cultural formation in which Freud was to be situated. Although he continued to use very general terms like "Modern," "Western," and "European" to name the formation that was the object of his interpretive analysis, his work persistently emphasized the need to clarify discontinuity and difference in relation to conventional usages of such terms, and he resisted the claim that his reconstruction of a network of discursive correlations among certain human sciences implied the existence of some essential identity that could ground a concept of cultural totality. If the network of a priori determinants of the structuring of experience in psychoanalytic discourse was simply one of many possible such contextual networks in modern Western culture, was it possible to imagine psychoanalysis in constant interaction with other, heterogeneous discursive formations? But what would transgression mean under these circumstances?

During the 1960s Foucault's historicization of the present clearly focused on the need to reveal the cultural discontinuities that determined the historical specificity and thus contingency of the cultural relations that defined the experience of self and world in the modern period (post-1800) in Western societies. This aim required a delineation of the specific level – between the general and formal determinants of language and thought and the conceptually articulated interpretations of ideologies, world-views, and philosophies – in which both the contingency *and* the systematicity of the defining preconditions of historical experience were embedded. The apparent continuities of forms and contents that extended beyond these a priori determinants, or the differences that seemed to constitute fundamental oppositions within them, were viewed as elements redefined by the systematic relations of epistemes, archives, or discourses. Thus positivism and hermeneutics were elements in the same world, operating within the same contextual field, while the classical analysis of wealth and the nineteenth-century analysis of production were not segments of the same "economic" discourse, but participants in discursive formations separated by a radical historical break in contextual field.

After 1970, however, Foucault's emphasis shifted significantly away from the systematic reconstruction of such "vertical" contextual determinants of the construction of experience to the horizontal processes, the narratives of contingent events, in which these determining contextual fields were produced. That is, his primary focus seemed to shift from the simple demonstration of difference between cultural orderings of experience to ways in which these cultural orderings were organized out of heterogeneous elements in a contingent temporal sequence of events. In one of his last works he noted that, from a genealogical perspective, discursive formations were not universal structures but "historical events."[21] The archaeological analysis of the systematic organizing regularities of experience was not abandoned, but placed into the historical problematic of how such governing orders defining the experience of self and world came into being, how the apparently anonymous networks within which individual human subjects were produced were themselves produced in contingent historical processes. This shift, moreover, was correlated with a renewed emphasis on the sphere of non-discursive social relations (power) which existed in correlative and interactive relations with discursive relations (knowledge). The construction of the modern "subject," Foucault claimed in 1975, must be regarded as an effect of the combined work of the human sciences and the disciplinary organization of new modes of technical control over the bodies and the consciousness of human beings.[22]

The implications for the historicization of psychoanalysis in Foucault's shift in emphasis from archaeological descriptions of discursive systematic-ities to genealogical accounts of the organization of such systematicities within the play of power/knowledge relations became evident in the mid-1970s. In *Discipline and Punish* (1975) Foucault provided an extensive analysis of how the technologies of power in disciplinary society provided the historical conditions for the knowledge of human beings as individual subjects, docile bodies with manipulable "souls." That the psyche of psychoanalysis was not just a contingent appearance within a discursive formation but also the historical product of specific relations of power was hinted at, but not developed. It was only with the first volume of the *History of Sexuality* (1976) that the significance of Foucault's shift in critical approach and cultural focus for his historical critique of psychoanalysis became more obvious.

III PSYCHOANALYSIS AND THE GENEALOGY OF THE SEXUAL SUBJECT

The elements of continuity in Foucault's historicizations of psychoanalysis in the 1960s and 1970s should not be ignored. In 1976 as in 1966, Foucault perceived psychoanalytic therapeutic practice and its scientific discourse as a complex formation that stood at the crossroads where most of the important genealogies of the modern subject met and interacted. It also functioned as a kind of epitome of structural similarities in the techniques and discourses that produced the modern sexual subject as well as of an unreflective scientific perspective that denied the historicity of its know-ledge. But in 1976 this epitomizing or pivotal function did not seem to be matched by any historically transcending or redeeming possibilities.[23] For Foucault such transcending possibilities – insights into the abyss of contingency or into the ultimate historicity of all order – were no longer tied to apocalyptic encounters with the figures of death, desire, and the primal father's law that marked human finitude. They were now, rather, the result of dogged erudition in pursuing the lowly "descents" or genealogies of all "higher" truths, all essences, totalities, and necessities. He now insisted that all transcending experiences were situated within particular contexts of competing and multiple discourses and thus were discrete historical openings into new possibilities within an endlessly specific work of freedom. Foucault seemed to have no great confidence that the resources and perspective for an investigation of the contingent "descent" of psychoana-lytic "truth," and for reflective self-awareness of the ethical and aesthetic dimensions of self-definition or self-making, were available within psycho-analytic theory and practice. It was the fashioned rather than self-fashioning subject that Foucault identified with psychoanalysis.

The primary context deployed by Foucault in his new historicization of psychoanalysis was the heterogeneous conglomerate of proliferating discip-linary practices and discourses that constituted the "apparatus" (*dispositif*) of sexuality in the modern period of Western history. It was within the relations of this network that human existence was constructed as psycho-sexual subjectivity, as the individually organized expression of sexual desire, the unique embodiment of an essential, "deep" (unconscious) intention-ality. This sexual apparatus was, in turn, intimately entangled in the two major dimensions of the constitution of modern disciplinary society – the positive harnessing of productive and reproductive individual energies for social purposes through processes of psychic identification induced in (or extorted from) individuals, and the manipulation and administrative supervision of populations as resources of power. Psychoanalysis was exceptional not only in the extent of its relations within this complex network, but also in the exemplary fashion in which its particular practices and knowledge correlated with the forms of experience in both the sexual apparatus and the disciplinary society of manipulated, psychic normalization more generally.

Psychoanalysis was situated first of all in the position of a culminating synoptic articulation of a regime of truth, a proliferating network of systematizing scientific discourses whose genealogy could be traced back to the eighteenth century. Psychoanalysis did not "discover" the repressed, hidden, censored, prohibited "truth" of the sexual etiology of the basic forms of human behavior and consciousness, and thus the sexual essence of subjective identity, but merely carried forward what was already a massive positive construction (*scientia sexualis*) of the truth of human existence as fundamentally defined and shaped by sexual desire, a construction which was itself a complex transformation of discourses constructing the identity of the desiring human subject within the categories of flesh and spirit, or passions and reason in earlier periods. In a number of critical areas in which psychoanalysis claimed originality – the origins of subjective identity in the formation of childhood sexuality within the familial matrix, the sexual basis for the conflicts of feminine self-identity, the sexual foundations of problems of deviance and normalization in society – Foucault pointed out its derivative and episodic nature within an established discursive and therapeutic network which had been producing sexuality as the foundation of individual human action, signification, and self-identity since the beginning of the nineteenth century. Those who saw Freud as a discoverer of the sexual foundations of subjective identity had "gotten their dates wrong."[24]

Second, Foucault inserted psychoanalysis as therapeutic practice within a network of technologies for the reconstruction and redefinition of the body and its pleasures. The confession/interpretation model of the psychoanalytic patient–doctor relation constituted a late synoptic form of the established cultural ritual of individuation, psychologization, and subjection in a disciplinary, normalizing society. The patient was constructed as a malleable and dependent subject, seduced into finding the truth of its identity as sexual subject in the deciphering interpretations of the observant "scientific" expert.[25]

Foucault also attempted to formulate a historical account of the unwillingness or inability of psychoanalysis to recognize or acknowledge its "own history" and thus its participation in the anonymous collective apparatus of sexuality in which its object and its truth were constructed and controlled. The historical peculiarity of psychoanalysis within the contextual field of the sexual apparatus, and a source of the tension in its theory and practice, was its particular compromising or composite character, in which constructivist theories of truth and practices of power were assimilated into and used to reinforce a concept of scientific truth grounded in the assumption of essential forms of experience which could be uncovered or discovered, and a conception of power as submission to a general law emanating from a sovereign authority. But even in this aspect psycho-analysis was not particularly original and reproduced within its own structures the "paradox of a society, which from the eighteenth century to the present, has created so many technologies of power that are foreign to the concept of law" that it feared "the effects and proliferations of those technologies," and attempted "to recode them in forms of law."[26] It was this ability to harness the constructivist implications of the sexual apparatus that explained the "enormous consumption of analysis" in modern Western societies.[27] Within Freud's own temporal context, Foucault admitted, there had been a certain defensive legitimacy, and an oppositional quality to the "retreat" into the forms of a liberal, juridical model in response to the racial theories and power technologies of fascism. But the "progressive" or "subversive" uses of the repressive hypothesis, the juridical model of power, and scientific pretensions regarding the "will to truth," were in the "last analysis a historical retro-version." In the context of the normalizing powers of a disciplinary society it was high time to "conceptualize the deployment of sexuality on the basis of the techniques of power that are contemporary with it."[28]

Foucault's genealogy of the sexual apparatus thus reconstituted his old critique of psychoanalysis in a new form. Psychoanalysis was historically delimited by its failure to confront its own history. Foucault's archaeology and genealogy of the sexual apparatus were directed toward the never completed tasks of establishing "how it was possible for psychoanalysis to take the form it did at the time it did," and of making psychoanalysis face "the question of its own history."[29] Foucault's final writings made clear that the failure of psychoanalysis to confront its own history entailed an inability to conceive of the subject not as a natural "given" whose "truth" could be "discovered," whose essential core could be "liberated," and whose ultimate secrets could be elicited and scientifically retold, but as an aesthetically fashioned work grounded in ethical choices made in the context of knowledge of the historicity of subject-production. The real object of his historicization, like Nietzsche's, was the "will to truth," which repetitively transformed historically organized and politically imposed constructions into universal essences to which human freedom should "subject" itself. The genealogy of psychoanalysis within the field of the sexual apparatus thus opened up the dimensions of a contemporary task: the ethical task of constructing ourselves as works of art, to turn subjection into subjectivation, "a work carried out by ourselves upon ourselves as free beings."[30]

IV CONCLUSION: WRITING THE HISTORY OF PSYCHOANALYSIS IN THE CONTEXT OF FOUCAULT

Foucault does not provide a history of psychoanalysis or even a model or outline for such a history. What he does provide is a context for writing a history of psychoanalysis, a perspective for relating the components of the conglomeration of research projects reconstructing the contingencies of the descent of the Freudian texts within various relational networks, and for grasping the significance of those components and networks in terms of the issues of self-definition and cultural construction in the present. This context can be divided into four dimensions:

1 From the Foucauldian perspective the Freudian corpus and the psychoanalytic discourse that it initiates must be inserted into the scientific disciplinary discourses or other systems of representation that preceded and accompanied it.[31] The issue here is to avoid a stylized reduction of psychoanalysis to a single closed position among competing positions (positivist, hermeneutic) and to investigate the correlations within the network of those inherited discourses and the ways in which that network was reorganized within the psychoanalytic discourse. Foucault was less interested in what distinguished Freud from his contemporaries or generally his contemporaries from each other than in the contours of shared limits and categories whose shape is just beginning to emerge for us because we no longer live entirely within them. Foucault's focus on the problem of subject construction within the discourses of the human sciences and science of sexuality has proven enormously illuminating in situating psychoanalysis within its own time and culture, but it does operate at a very high level of abstraction, and there is a danger in that. The self-reflective and critical dimensions of psychoanalytic texts are often lost, or perhaps denied, in this reduction to discursive regularities. Highlighting the extent to which the construction of subjectivity and sexual identity is a problematic issue, a matter for

conflicted, critical self-reflection in psychoanalytic, especially Freudian texts, would reveal historically transcending qualities that might provide insight into the ways in which psychoanalytic discourse (e.g. of the Lacanian feminists) remains contemporary with Foucault's writing and thus a vital element in the history of the present.

2 Foucault situates psychoanalytic theory and therapy within the context of the institutions and social practices of a modern disciplinary, normalizing society, and the apparatus that constructs individuals whose subjectivity is defined by their sexuality. This aspect of the Foucauldian historicization does not dissolve the validity of studies that connect the formation and reception of psychoanalysis to political and juridical liberalism, bourgeois social practices and behaviors, or the processes of ethnic and gender identification and differentiation.[32] But it has complicated and contextualized these various existing forms of contextualization. First, it has opened up the issue of the selective and "constructed" nature of all social and cultural contextualizations, which always define themselves in terms of present concerns. Second, Foucault's own successive and variant contextualizations all focus thematically on the issue of the construction of modern subjectivity, on the cultural conditions of self-fashioning, and provide a way of integrating, or at least drawing into a single network, previously isolated and diverse contextual interpretations.

3 Third, Foucault presents us with an approach that avoids (in principle) essentializing and reductive hierarchical relations both among the various discursive and non-discursive contexts and more generally between the discursive and the non-discursive, between linguistic and non-linguistic practices. To borrow and bend a phrase from Lévi-Strauss, there are no inherently privileged contexts. As Foucault's own changing constructions of psychoanalysis make obvious, contextualization not only follows interpretation but is a part of interpretation. Within the practice of historicizing interpretation, the contingency of both the components of "context" and the specific relations among such components must be assumed.

4 Finally, Foucault places a question mark before historical procedures and self-representations that isolate the process of historicizing psychoanalysis from a critical confrontation with the "truth" claims of psychoanalysis. Theoretical reflection, cultural critique, and historical scholarship merge in Foucauldian historicization. To write a history of Freud's discovery of "truth," his insight into "human" reality, his cure for "human" suffering, is not to take the historicity of psychoanalysis seriously, and is thus to evade the question of the historical investigator's own historicity and its theoretical and ethical implications. As Foucault noted in *The Use of Pleasure*, although his works were historical "by

reason of the domain they deal with" they were inherently "philosoph-ical" in their attempt to "think one's history" and thus learn the extent to which one "can free thought from what it silently thinks, and so enable it to think differently."[33]

The great lack in Foucault's historicization of psychoanalysis lies in its failure to provide a clear view of ways in which these larger issues work themselves into the reading of specific Freudian texts, and particularly how the assimilation and reproduction of the inherited "apparatus" of power/ knowledge relations was actually "problematized" and reconstructed in the thinking and writing of the processes of textualization. Because of his constant struggle to integrate psychoanalysis as a scientific discourse and a set of institutionalized practices into the confines of a world that could now be mapped from the outside, Foucault paid little attention to the particular differences through which the Freudian texts established their own discursive reality, and thus to the cultural formation of psychoanalysis as a critical reflection and transcending, transformative action in relation to its own various contexts. In one of his last interviews (May 1984), however, Foucault himself hinted at the direction one must go in historicizing psychoanalysis "beyond" or "after" Foucault, moving from the archaeology and genealogy of representations and behaviors to the history of "thought" as critical reflection on these formations, processes, and events:

> For a long time I have been trying to see if it would be possible to describe the history of thought as distinct both from the history of ideas – by which I mean the analysis of systems of representation – and from the history of mentalities – by which I mean the analysis of attitudes and types of action (*schemas de comportement*). It seemed to me there was one element that was capable of describing the history of thought: this was what one could call the element of problems or, more exactly, problemizations. What distinguishes thought is that it is something quite different from the set of representations that underlies a certain behavior; it is also something quite different from the domain of attitudes that can determine this behavior. Thought is not what inhabits a certain conduct and gives it its meaning; rather, it is what allows one to step back from this way of acting or reacting, to present it to oneself as an object of thought and question its meaning, its conditions, and its goals. Thought is freedom in relation to what one does, the motion by which one detaches oneself from it, establishes it as an object, and reflects on it as a problem.[34]

This perspective, and the late Foucauldian practices connected with it, seemed in some ways to mark a return to conventional modes of intellectual history as a textual exegesis and narrative of textualized thinking. This was a method of research and writing appropriate to the task of examining historical forms of "subjectivation," of the conditions and techniques of self-fashioning as an ethical and aesthetic activity. But Foucault's "return" was a return with a difference and was indelibly marked by its passage through the laborious procedures of archaeology and genealogy. Historicizing psychoanalysis "after Foucault" must also take such labors, and their risks and obligations, upon itself in order to integrate a critical self-consciousness into its present reconstructions of, and engagements with, textualized psychoanalytic "thought," in order to make the history of psychoanalysis an act of thinking "one's own history" and liberating one's own thought "from what it silently thinks."

Part III

The Life Sciences and Modern Sexuality

7

The History of Medicine according to Foucault

François Delaporte

The Birth of the Clinic is interesting not only because of its content but also because of its overall orientation and its relation to other, similar works. More than just a contribution to the history of medicine, the book breathes new life into the subject. *The Archaeology of Knowledge*, by contrast, is more an account of the methodology that went into the making of this new history. As such, the *Archaeology* can be read as the work of a historian reflecting on the practice of his discipline. In order to understand the first work properly, it is sometimes necessary to borrow from the second. But, in order to see the ways in which *The Birth of the Clinic* marks a break with other histories of medicine, that work must be compared to its predecessors.

When he wrote *The Birth of the Clinic* some 180 years after the period the book describes, Foucault obviously did not intend to respond to historians who had written in the late eighteenth and early nineteenth centuries, contemporaneously with the events he treats.[1] Nevertheless, we find in their writings the full range of positions that Foucault sets out to attack. The reason is that modern historians of medicine continued to defend these earlier views: their works rest on the same foundations. Hence it was enough to demolish the old edifice to undermine the new one as well. While offering some discussion of the so-called contemporaries, I shall nevertheless concentrate my remarks on the accounts given to us by modern historians of medicine such as Erwin H. Ackerknecht, Jacques Léonard, Henri Ey, and Jean-Charles Sournia. But I shall also dwell on epistemological history,[2] which Foucault partly accepts and partly rejects. My purpose here is thus not to assist at the birth of a new way of thinking but to situate its place of origin. I shall begin by showing why Foucault chose to keep his distance from contemporary, modern, and epistemological histories of the clinic alike. Building on this analysis, I shall then attempt to delve more deeply into the guiding themes of his "archaeology of the medical gaze."

I HISTORIES OF THE CLINIC CONTEMPORANEOUS WITH ITS BIRTH

Let us begin with contemporaries, who saw the birth of the clinic as a major, indeed crucial, event in humanity's self-understanding: the concrete individual was at last apprehended by the language of rationality. But contemporaries soon chose to describe this change in terms of a simple, direct confrontation between a gaze and a body. In other words, they once again invoked the timeless principle according to which medical knowledge comes into being at the patient's bedside. It was as if the theme of the clinic had been dredged up out of antiquity, where it originated. But why, then, did this not happen until the end of the eighteenth century? A series of obstacles had supposedly stood in the way of the fundamental empirical observations. For contemporaries, the experience of the patient's bedside was a constant, but one that idle theories had allegedly obscured. Clinical experience was invariant, but medical systems were in constant flux. Thus the clinic "was supposed to promote positive accumulation. . . . In the invariant of the clinic, medicine is supposed to have brought truth together with time."[3]

How did Foucault criticize this contemporary history of the clinic? For one thing, he alleged that contemporaries were wrong to take the kind of experience on which the clinic was founded and graft onto it a primary experience drawn from the supposed history of medicine: the cost of doing so was a negation of innovation and a concealment of differences. In other words, a metaphysical idea has been used to negate history, which is thereby reduced to a search for a hidden meaning. But Foucault also rejected the search for an ontological foundation that would somehow ground medical discourse. The assumption behind such a search is that the precise essence of the being itself can somehow be brought to light: the origin is presumably the locus of truth. This clinical "empiricism" is not based on a rediscovery of the absolute value of the visible or on a repudiation of medical systems. It is an epistemological myth. Foucault does not accept the medical profession's explanation. If it were true that the clinic had simply been rediscovered, then the idea of the clinic would have to be invariant. The clinic would no longer be a fit subject for historical study; the only possible history of the clinic would be the history of all that masked, obscured, or repressed this supposedly invariant idea.

Foucault's thought is in a sense the antithesis of this contemporary notion. Hence he refused to base his argument on contemporary discourse, "on the repetition," as he put it, "of what they were able to say in another era."[4] And he rejected certain themes, such as the origins, the continuity, and the simplicity of the "clinical" object. Attending to history rather than metaphysics led Foucault to show that the clinic was based on metaphors quite different from those of which it would in turn become the foundation. The clinic does not refer back to some fundamental, age-old experience. It is historically dated. No proposition can pass itself off as the product of a millennial continuum, and the word "medicine" applies to different realities at different times. If the clinic had recently bestowed certain privileges on observation, they were more numerous than, and of a different nature from, the privileges it was traditionally allowed: the gaze, no longer wedded to the immediate, now came equipped with a whole technical and conceptual armature.

Thus the problem is not one of an enduring foundation. It is not a matter of reconstituting what the clinic might have been in itself, as if in some primordial experience prior to being organized by discourse. Rather than attempt to assume the vantage point of "prediscursive experience," rather than seek to penetrate the enigma of "things" prior to discourse, we should instead focus on the rules governing the formation of objects that take shape only within discourse. In other words, we must try to write the history of "discursive" objects. To do this, we must treat discourses as practices that shape the objects of which they speak; we must analyze the rules governing the formation of such objects.

This means granting primacy to discontinuity. Discontinuity comes from history itself: it is necessary to explain not how something that always existed was somehow hidden but rather to account for innovation. If Foucault speaks of the "birth" of the clinic, it is because what preceded the clinic has died. The names of diseases and the grouping of symptoms were no longer the same. Also different were the perceptual codes that one applied to the patient's body, the field of objects subjected to observation, the surfaces and depths that the gaze traversed. In short, to describe the rules that shape the formation of discourse is to establish the diversity and disparity of the discourses to which those rules give rise.

II MODERN HISTORIES OF THE CLINIC

Why have I insisted from the outset on the history of the clinic according to contemporaries? In part, as we have just seen, because Foucault criticized their discourse and proposed replacing the search for origins with a search for beginnings, the given with the constructed, the continuous with the discontinuous. And in part, as we shall see in a moment, because later historians of medicine often rely on these early accounts. Indeed, later historians have revived themes that have about them some of the flavor of both founding myths and history of the most traditional kind. People believe, even today, in Hippocratic medicine as the eternal source of all medicine. People believe, even today, in continuities, anticipations, and rudimentary precursors. What is more, modern historians have revived contemporary explanations of why the clinic was at long last rediscovered: existing medical doctrines, they say, were called into question, and observation once again took precedence over theory.[5]

But historians of medicine have added analyses of their own. Roughly speaking, one can adduce two independent lines of research: one structural, the other genetic. Consider structure first. The birth of the clinic is an event, some historians say, that must be placed in its proper context. Medicine, according to Léonard, is "the medicine of a cultural context," indeed, "the medicine of a socio-economic milieu." To write the history of the clinic is to do a synchronic analysis: one makes a vertical slice through time in order to isolate a moment whose coherence is based on such notions as "mentality," "spirit," "climate," and "cultural ambiance." Using these notions it is possible to establish a commonality of meaning and seemingly causal links between simultaneous or successive phenomena belonging to a given period of study. Now consider genetics: it will come as no surprise to discover that the genetic account of the same phenomena is based on such notions as "development," "evolution," and "maturation." More than that, the notion of "influence" furnishes a magical explanation of transmission and communication. Across time and distance influence is the element that binds together entities variously characterized as individuals, works, ideas, or theories.[6]

Let us turn now to Foucault's critiques of modern historians of medicine. He argues, to begin with, that their history is based on empiricism. Focusing their attention on individuals, works, and themes, historians expound generalities and report anecdotes. Second, this traditional history has a basis in humanism, summed up by the image of Pinel freeing lunatics from their chains – an image with which Foucault dealt at some length in *Madness and Civilization*. The idea of progress is the guiding light of medical history. Finally, the historian pretends to take on the function of memory. Note, in passing, that the myth of total history implies a faith that history is a great, anonymous work. The historian's false humility ill conceals a pretension that is at once naive and silly: naive, because it pretends to reconstitute "reality," and silly, because its nattering about this so-called reality is in fact just a discourse about appearances.

Here once again, Foucault's thought is in a sense the antithesis of this historian's notion. Where historians see boundaries or cracks that must one way or another be filled in by restoring continuities, the archaeologist sees ruptures and differences to be explored in depth. There is no continuity between the proto-clinic and the clinic: the "clinical" function exists only in the practice of "teaching and discovery," which is very different from the "teaching" function in the proto-clinic. In other words, the proto-clinic is to the clinic as the scene of a theatrical experience is to the place where a "manner of teaching and *saying* becomes a way of learning and *seeing*."[7] So the clinical ideal, in its most general formulation, is perhaps the same in Hermann Boerhaave, the early eighteenth-century Dutch physician credited with inaugurating the method of teaching medical students at the patient's bedside, and Xavier Bichat, the late eighteenth-century French physiologist and founder of pathological anatomy; but in fact what makes it possible and coherent is not at all of the same order in both cases. As for the alleged paradoxes of the French Revolution noted by Ackerknecht ("This revolution, which wanted to abolish hospitals, improved them and made them the center of medicine"[8]), Foucault prefers to show how the economists' themes briefly coincided with those of the medical classifiers: a gaze that takes in a species and a compensatory assistance given at home. This new idea of "natural" assistance and "natural" illness, each unfolding in unobstructed fashion in its own milieu, gave rise to the idea of eliminating the hospital. But that latter idea would not prevent the inversion of this thematic structure on the basis of a new institutional spatialization of disease. In other words, the same logic that argued for the suppression of the hospital could – and did in fact – argue for the renovation of the hospital, for turning it into a rationalized domain where all diseases were collected and then grouped by type so as, in effect, to restore the originary distribution of their essences.[9] In sum, Foucault shows how a passage occurred between the idea of the abolition of the hospital and the idea of the hospital as a necessary space for the production of scientific knowledge and the provision of health care. His non-paradoxical account takes us far from Ackerknecht, whose paradox explains nothing.

One might say that before *The Birth of the Clinic* the history of the clinic did not exist, because nothing could disappear. History had to be detached from the image of a millennial, collective memory that recovered the past with the aid of documents. *The Birth of the Clinic*: the book's very title indicates an opening for thought, a history that is a history of the constitution of knowledge and that takes for granted the transformation of "documents" into "monuments." Documents do not enable us to reconstitute the past. The mass of documents must itself be searched for unifying structures, series, and relations.

In contrast to history as memory, Foucault offers "archaeology." This is no misnomer: the archaeologist does not lay bare an edifice; he rather invents and constructs one. This accounts for the importance of propositions that are events at once hidden and visible. They are hidden because they are not given at the outset (what is given is the mass of documents). They become visible the moment they are granted the status of rectifying statements by and through theories. But, make no mistake, the archaeologist does not concoct a fiction: he constructs his object in an ideal space-time, but that space-time is neither imagined nor invented. Foucault does not propose to represent things as they happened but to constitute the unities underlying the visible diversity of things by dismembering discourse, fragmenting it into distinct parcels in such a way as to reveal relationships that would otherwise have remained invisible.

In sum, Foucault subjects to theoretical elaboration what historians of medicine accept without prior examination. He problematizes what had seemed self-evident. That is why he investigates how objects emerge, objects such as organic lesions, deep foci, tissue changes, anatomo-clinical signs and correlations; that is why he studies the emergence of techniques for making observations, detecting pathological foci, and keeping records; and that is why he studies how new concepts such as disease, life, and death are constructed and how old categories such as nosological species, fever, and medical constitution disappear.

III   EPISTEMOLOGICAL HISTORY

I now turn to historical epistemology. This discipline has several features in common with archaeology. Epistemologists are critical of contemporary accounts, which they take not as avenues to be explored but as versions of history whose veracity is to be challenged. They are also critical of the historians' history: the history of medicine, they say, is not the explanation of a cultural phenomenon in terms of its conditioning by the global cultural environment. Third, historical epistemology has little affinity with history-as-memory, which pretends to give an account of things "as they really happened." Finally, the discipline gets on without "words and things." It can do without "things" because it focuses on "discursive objects": the objects of science are not the objects of nature. And it can do without "words" because the object of historical discourse is not scientific discourse as such but the historicity of scientific discourse.

For Canguilhem, the problem is to conceive of the past and present of a discipline as being at once intertwined and distinct. Using the concept of "scientific ideology," he was able to provide a foundation for combining the themes of continuity and discontinuity in the history of medicine. In effect, this concept designates the models of operational medicine and underlies their ambiguity. On the one hand, a scientific ideology must be linked to the present of science, for it may constitute an epistemologically necessary stage for the emergence of a medical science capable of achieving its ends. To cite just one example, nothing remains today of Broussais's physiological medicine. Yet this system had its subversive effects, which led to the disappearance of medical ontology and essentialist nosology. On the other hand, if the promises of ideology are kept, it is "not in the areas where the ideology thought they would be, nor . . . in the manner predicted by the ideology."[10] Thus a scientific ideology also emerges at a point of rupture, and that is why it must be distinguished from authentic knowledge. To show that it disappears as "pseudoscience" is to describe the vanishing of an illusion expressive of a desire to base a therapeutics on a theory. That illusion, moreover, is a failure to recognize the methodological requirements and operational possibilities of the science that will come to occupy ideology's place. As Canguilhem shows, it took a revolution in chemistry and a Pasteurian detour through crystallography for chemotherapy to fulfill the promise of its ideology.

This example should help to clarify Foucault's position with respect to historical epistemology and, in particular, help us to understand why, in *The Birth of the Clinic*, he did "not want to rely on the actual consciousness of clinicians."[11] Archaeological description does not coincide with epistemological analysis. Recall that, for Foucault, archaeology consists in analyzing the transformation of fields of knowledge, or, in other words, studying changes in the rules by which objects, concepts, and theories are formed. The birth of the clinic, Foucault argued, cannot be identified with an emerging science or with figures that remotely anticipate sciences of the future or, conversely, with forms of knowledge that immediately rule out scientificity of any kind. Foucault therefore described transformations without prejudging the future, yet he did not on that account write a history encumbered by the indeterminacy of infinite possibility. Foucault wrote the history not of a medicine in search of scientificity but of practices as they existed in different periods: "Broussais had said the last word for his time on the *manner of seeing*. Since 1816 the physician's eye knew how to look at a sick organism. The historical and concrete *a priori* of the modern medical gaze was now fully constituted."[12]

What distinguishes archaeology from epistemological analysis should now be clear. Foucault describes discursive formations, which are neither "pseudosciences" nor "sciences in a prehistoric state" nor "scientific ideologies." In other words, Foucault does not ask retrospective questions. *The Birth of the Clinic* therefore does not contain the program or project of a rational medicine whose successive approximations might be analyzed by examining the interplay of dead ends and comparatively successful ventures. By contrast, for Canguilhem, the form of the solution that a doctrine such as Broussais's might offer to the problem of etiology remains incomparable, in its field and concepts, to the problematic of bacteriology. Physiological medicine and the concept of inflammation are seen as profoundly alien to Pasteurian medicine and its postulates. In essence, the recurrence method is the only one capable of clarifying whether or not one is dealing with a science. Despite the effort to retain the positive function of physiologism, the search for the condition of impossibility takes precedence. It guarantees separation; it eliminates and limits. In short, it circumscribes scientific ideologies.[13]

In closing, I would like to discuss certain issues of historical method that are, I think, central to Foucault's thinking.

(1) Consider first the question of discontinuity and the use of the recurrence method. For contemporaries, the birth of the clinic represented only an apparent break with the past because in reality it was a return to the ancient clinic. For historians, the discontinuity was not so much an epistemological dividing line as a more or less logical pretext for defining a period to be exhaustively explored. Finally, for epistemologists, the recurrence method is a technique for exploring the past of a relatively recent branch of science. It is not incorrect to say that Foucault accepts the traditional periodization, according to which modern medicine begins at the turn of the nineteenth century. But the important point is the way in which he identifies the break. By studying this point certain inadequate characterizations of his work can be rectified:

(a) It is sometimes alleged that Foucault's discovery of a discontinuity in the history of medicine implies a critique of modern medicine's claims of objectivity. According to Henri Ey, the logical culmination of such a critique would be some form of "anti-medicine." At the beginning of his book Foucault quotes Pierre Pomme, but it does not follow from this that he intends a critique of present-day medicine. In fact, the Pomme quotation, dating from the 1760s, takes on its full meaning only in relation to the one from A.-L.-J. Bayle, produced some six decades later. By juxtaposing the two, Foucault simply wants to point out what the nature of the break is. It is clear that, *for us*, Pomme speaks a strange language while Bayle's is still intelligible. This is because Bayle's text belongs to a medicine that is familiar to us but on the verge of vanishing. What made the archaeology of the clinic possible was the old age of clinical medicine coupled with the beginnings, in the 1960s, of a reorganization of medical knowledge. Epistemology, by pointing to the terms in which a certain medicine expressed itself in its final stages, also established the criteria for deciding which was the correct break. Foucault thus relied on modern medicine in two ways. Knowledge of the present-day clinic justified going back in time all the way to Bayle. A modern medical discourse exerted its epistemological control on Foucault, who refers to "a new experience of disease just now being born, an experience which gives us a historical and critical grasp on that which it is relegating to the past."[14]

(b)   This discontinuity, it is sometimes said, proves that Foucault subscribed to some form of the principles of structuralist analysis. Hence *The Birth of the Clinic* describes the replacement of an archaic structure by a modern one. In fact, Foucault's method is that of an epistemologist. To see this, look once again at the quotation from Pomme, which represents archaic medicine. The language in terms of which it becomes possible to write the history of this medicine is taken from the present. In this there is no anachronism, because the point is to revive a language that is unequivocally dead. The important point is that the medicine of species has vanished without a trace because it was denied the means of survival. But how can it be made intelligible? In search of the object of archaic medicine, Foucault speaks of space and language. Using the method of historical recurrence, he adopts the language of natural history rather than that of modern medicine. There are two advantages to this procedure: it avoids making an archaic scientific idiom seem fantastic or stilted, and it avoids viewing the archaic science from the vantage of modern medicine. Archaic medicine was botany. The method, though archaeological, is still in part Bachelardian.[15]

(c)   Finally, it is sometimes alleged, in my view incorrectly, that Foucault was a historical relativist. If Foucault used the recurrence method, it was to pinpoint the moment when what he calls a "new medical spirit" emerged. As is well known, Bachelard somewhat earlier referred to what he called a "new scientific spirit." Both men thus refused to think in terms of continuity. But Foucault differs from Bachelard in that his aim is not to distinguish between obsolete science and approved science: "The new medical spirit," Foucault writes, "is not to be numbered among the psychological and epistemological purifications."[16] Thus he eschewed the kind of history for which vulgar and scientific knowledge were definitively distinct. Does this mean that he thought in terms of a succession of arbitrary structures? Look at the terms Foucault uses: his purpose, he says, is to describe an "epistemological reorganization," to identify "redistributions" and "displacements." In other words, he is analyzing an "epistemological transformation." This is the expression he prefers to "scientific revolution" because it indicates that the goal is to describe the constitution of rules governing the formation of objects.

(2) Let us turn next to the problem that Foucault sets himself. The discontinuity in question is a sign of a complex process at the conclusion of which the medical gaze is at last capable of focusing on a sick organism. At first sight the idea of looking for the causes of disease by examining individual bodies seems an obvious one, but Foucault believes that it is less obvious than it appears.

The clinic's contemporaries soon saw a connection between the new medical spirit and the discovery of pathological anatomy. In their eyes, however, medicine was able to establish itself on a firm scientific basis only after it had overcome obstacles that morality, religion, and prejudice placed in the way of opening cadavers. Historians of medicine also point to certain filiations: Morgagni–Bichat and Auenbrugger–Corvisart. They also stress the cooperation of physicians and surgeons and treat pathological anatomy as an extension of clinical observation. Finally, epistemologists often argue that the idea of "life" as constituting a distinct phenomenal order or normative activity came from Bichat, thanks to whom biology was founded on the opposition between the natural (as telos rather than determinism) and the pathological. Thus they regarded Bichat's "vitalism" as defining an important scheme for interpreting healthy or morbid organic phenomena.

Foucault criticized all these versions of history. In the first place, the reconstruction by contemporaries was simply wrong: there were no obstacles to performing autopsies. Contemporaries merely invented, as retrospective justification of the clinic, a version of history according to which scientists first demanded to open up bodies and then proceeded to the observation of disease. Second, the historians are wrong when they argue that pathological anatomy was a direct extension of observational medicine. This account is based on the assumption that the distance between the subject and the object of knowledge is steadily diminished. This is not the place to criticize the axioms implicit in this theory of knowledge. It is enough to point out their consequences: the belief that pathological anatomy answered the same need as observational medicine, coupled with the belief in the alleged role of surgery. Finally, the epistemologists are not really wrong in thinking that Bichat associated the uniqueness of living things with their susceptibility to disease: a physical body cannot deviate from its natural type. But for Foucault vitalism as a concept was incapable of accounting for the discovery of pathological anatomy. According to him, Bichat began with an experiment in which only death could give life to a positive truth. Hence "the irreducibility of the living to the mechanical or chemical is secondary to the fundamental connection between life and death. Vitalism appears against this background of 'mortalism.' "[17]

Foucault's version of history is distinguished from the foregoing by the way in which he identifies, describes, and fits together the various elements that together enable him to solve the problem of how the clinic was constituted. Clinical thinking, which is wrongly credited with anatomical curiosity, was in fact what prevented people from grasping the lessons of Morgagni and Auenbrugger. Anatomy and the clinic were contrasting figures of knowledge. What changes made it possible to link one with the other? In pathological anatomy, first of all, it was the perception of real analyses.[18] Paradoxically, progress began with a problem of classification. Bichat discovered not Morgagni but "analysis" in the body itself. Bichat thus built on work done in clinical analysis (membranes and surface examination). This led him to pose new questions to pathological anatomy, which was seen as the foundation of a new nosology. The first of these questions involved the relation between the interpretation of symptoms and anatomical perception. Morgagni was now rediscovered: an organic space emerged as a double of the natural space of nosology. The second question concerned death and its relation to life and disease. On these points Bichat's analyses marked a break in the history of Western medicine. Everything else flows from this: the return to Auenbrugger can be explained in terms of the return to Morgagni. There is no justification for percussion (or for pathological anatomy) if disease is nothing but a series of symptoms. It becomes necessary, however, if the patient is a "volume."

Thus we see that to understand the emergence of pathological anatomy is to describe a transformation that involved both the object of knowledge and the type of perception that caused the object to appear. Solutions to the problem lie in both what preceded the moment in question and what changed at that moment. Morgagni and Auenbrugger both have their place in this history, as we have just seen, but it is not the place generally attributed to them.

(3) Finally, let us consider the constitution of the object of research. Discontinuity makes it possible to establish a field. Within that field one then had to establish the system of relations that allowed the

configuration space of the disease to be superimposed upon a localization space.

For contemporaries, the clinic had always been present. For historians, this object has no specificity: it is given in the multiplicity of discourses on disease and the diseased. Their goal is therefore to revive the past as the totality of individual (or social) experiences. For epistemologists, the description of "scientific ideologies" can be accomplished only against a background of proven scientific discourse.

Foucault holds that the clinic's contemporaries are wrong to search for the form of truth in a novel style of discourse. The historians of medicine, for their part, fail to see that the object posited as the correlate of various medical assertions is not identical to the object that emerges in different periods. "Discourse concerning disease" is therefore discredited, because its unity is irrelevant. For Foucault, the unity of a discourse is achieved not through the permanence and singularity of an object but through the space in which various objects emerge and undergo transformation. It is achieved through the rules that enable objects to appear in a given period and that define the transformation of those objects.

More precisely, the task is to show not how different practices determine the structure of knowledge but how, and by what right, those practices figure among knowledge's conditions of emergence. Several levels of analysis are pertinent. Take the example of the clinical medicine that preceded the anatomo-clinical medicine just described. Different factors are relevant: socio-political, economic, institutional, pedagogical, conceptual. But these various factors are heterogeneous and independent. Within medical discourse, however, the relations among them allowed the formation of a whole range of objects. Foucault shows how these analogical structures of experience culminate in the identity of a unitary perception. These diverse experiences gradually came together in the person of the hospital physician: "Eye that knows and decides, eye that rules."[19]

It is clear that the object of the history of the clinic does not belong to any of the disciplines formed at the turn of the nineteenth century. The natural place of the clinic is not in any one of the discursive (or non-discursive) practices where one might expect to find it. Is not the history of the clinic precisely the history of its *constitution*? Hence the theoretical locus of the "clinic" object need not be sought outside the analysis that produced its history. The history of the clinic consists in the description of a set of relations. But – and this is the inevitable difficulty – these relations are not given in either things or words. Paul Veyne saw the point clearly: "*The Birth of the Clinic* already linked the transformation of medical discourse to institutions, to political practice, to the hospital. ... To explain history and to make it explicit is to ... relate seemingly natural objects to a small number of datable practices and to explain those practices ... in terms of other, similar practices with which they are associated. This painterly method yields strange portraits, in which relations replace objects."[20]

My conclusion will be brief. In 1986, Erwin H. Ackerknecht was still looking forward to the time when "M. Foucault's 'archaeological' exercises will be forgotten."[21] Of this determination to forget Foucault, which is an attack on seriousness, one might say what Nietzsche said about "seriousness for truth." To wit: "And does not every thing that we take *seriously* betray us? It always shows what has weight for us and what does not."[22]

Translated by Arthur Goldhammer

8

Love and Reproductive Biology in *Fin-de-Siècle* France: A Foucauldian Lacuna?

Robert A. Nye

Like carrion-eaters, we historians are notorious for picking over the works of philosophers in order to extract what is useful for our own purposes, while paying scant attention in the process to the epistemological consequences of our intellectual foraging. Since they deal with the "past," the writings of Michel Foucault have proved to be particularly attractive to my opportunistic discipline, chiefly, I would argue, because in his work Foucault constitutes for us wholly new objects of historical study or tells us how old ones are linked together in surprising ways. But as we convert his bold assertions into the cautious, massively documented studies that are the coin of our trade, many of us are grateful that Foucault himself served, and in a sense continues to serve, as a lightning rod for draining off the sort of methodological and epistemological criticism that might complicate our cautious labors. It has often seemed prudent to us to stand just the right distance from Foucault to avoid the barbs of those whose blood boils at the thought of the latest Gallic intellectual heresy, while staying close enough to him to share in the *cachet* of Parisian style.

I had become so accustomed to his fearless speculations that I was brought up short when, in a recent rereading, I encountered a philosophical scruple in the introductory volume to *The History of Sexuality* which seemed to suggest that I ought not to have done what I had just finished doing in my present study of masculinity in France. The passage in question appears near the opening of the chapter on "scientia sexualis," where Foucault shows how a late nineteenth-century discourse of sexuality incorporated medical and hygienic concepts into an economy of boundaries and norms. In his words,

> When we compare these discourses on human sexuality with what was known at the time about the physiology of animal and plant reproduction, we are struck by the incongruity. Their feeble content from the standpoint of elementary rationality, not to mention scientificity, earns them a place apart in the history of knowledge. They form a strangely muddled zone. Throughout the nineteenth century, sex seems to have been incorporated into two very distinct orders of knowledge: a biology of reproduction, which developed continuously according to a general scientific normativity, and a medicine of sex conforming to quite different rules of formation. From one to the other, there was no real exchange, no reciprocal structuration; the role of the first with respect to the second was scarcely more than as a distant and quite fictitious guarantee: a blanket guarantee under cover of which moral obstacles, economic or political options and traditional fears could be recast in a scientific-sounding vocabulary. . . . A disparity of this sort would indicate that the aim of such a discourse was not to state the truth but to prevent its very emergence. Underlying the difference between the physiology of reproduction and the medical theories of sexuality, we would have to see something other and something more than an uneven scientific development or a disparity in the forms of rationality; the one would partake of that immense will to knowledge which has sustained the establishment of scientific discourse in the West, whereas the other would derive from a stubborn will to nonknowledge.[1]

Now, while some of Foucault's commentators have attempted to show that in both his archaeological and genealogical writings he has maintained a distinction between the "noble" sciences of physics and chemistry, and the "dubious" human sciences, including medicine and psychiatry, others have argued that, in converting the world into discourse, Foucault has abandoned objective science by giving no domain of knowledge an advantage over any other.[2] One may find apparent proof for each contention easily at hand. In an interview from 1982 Foucault says, "You know the difference between a real science and a pseudoscience? A real science recognizes and accepts its own history without feeling attacked."[3] But he elsewhere speaks of the "games of truth" each science plays in constituting its boundaries and its proper objects of study, and in the interview "Truth and Power" he dismisses the usual distinction between "truth" and "ideology" by arguing we must study the "truth effects" that "are produced within discourses [of truth] which in themselves are neither true nor false."[4]

To complicate issues still further, biology, it would appear, is a special

case, falling somewhere between these two discursive domains, and it is by
no means clear that Foucault decided where it belonged. With his teacher
Georges Canguilhem, he appears to recognize the distinction between the
sciences of life and other sciences, but, also like Canguilhem, he contrasts
self-regulating organic systems with human societies that think about
themselves with the help of biological models.[5] Yet elsewhere he assimilates
biology to the human sciences with their notorious epistemological
sensitivity to the discontinuities and upheavals of political and social
history.[6] The paragraph I have cited above from *La Volonté de savoir* by no
means clears up this problem, because Foucault speaks both about the
"biology of reproduction" and also, more pointedly, about the "physiology
of *animal* and plant reproduction." Are we to suppose that Foucault
believed the scientific discourse of *human* reproduction was penetrated
more thoroughly by the "background practices" and needs of the
administrative and political domain than the discourse concerning plants
and animals?[7] We get little help from Foucault's own "historical" studies on
the politics of health in the Old Regime, where he considers the "various
measures of incitement to marriage and procreation" produced by the
mercantile state, but does not directly assess the role of contemporary
theories of human (or animal) reproduction in the strategies of *bio-pouvoir*
(bio-power) that governed the demographic outlook of the old monarchy.[8]

Perhaps our work here will clarify Foucault's conception of the place of
the history of biology in the history of science and the epistemological
differences between the sciences (if any) which distinguish their respective
histories or – to use Foucault's phrase – endow them with different "truth
effects." Meanwhile, I would like to present in this paper a historical
account of the biology of sex and reproduction in *fin-de-siècle* France that
dares to go where Foucault himself seems to have been reluctant to tread –
for whatever reason – using approaches that I think are compatible with
those Foucault has himself employed in his analyses of medicine and the
human sciences. Though, as I have mentioned, Foucault has occasionally
discounted the utility of the distinction between valid science and ideology,
his notion that both science and ideology arise in similar if not identical
discursive contexts suggests that in his view the gap between even a
"serious" science and its ideological and rhetorical elaborations might not
be as great as the traditional view would appear to hold.[9] We might find
evidence, in other words, of a politics of reproductive science embedded in
the structure and logic of science itself, in addition to the more predictable
influence one might expect to find in the rhetoric and representations in
which scientific conclusions were announced to the general public. In short,
I find abundant evidence that there was not only a considerable amount of
"exchange" and "reciprocal structuration" between biology and medicine

in this era, which Foucault specifically denies, but clear indications that laboratory scientists were just as driven by the search for "relevant" solutions to the demographic crisis of their nation as their less insulated and more frankly political colleagues in the medical hygiene establishment.

As is still true nowadays, "reproductive biology" was a general research area made up of various disciplines, not a scientific discipline as such. In France, embryologists, histologists, cytologists, physiologists, and botanists all made contributions to this area which were based on laboratory microscopy, sometimes combined with traditional fieldwork, especially in marine biology.[10] However, biological generalists who specialized in inheritance theory, demographers, and even animal behaviorists also made contributions to understanding the processes and implications of reproduction, reading one another's findings and incorporating them into their own work. When I mention "reproductive biology" in this essay, therefore, it is usually in reference to work in one of these scientific specialties or to a vulgarization of it.

The context for this history was a massive demographic crisis that gave France the lowest marital fertility rate in the industrialized West, raising widespread fears of the "depopulation" of the fatherland and the fall of France from great power status. Though her European neighbors enjoyed buoyant population growth until 1900 or so, the French population virtually ceased to reproduce its own numbers in the last years of the nineteenth century; in several years before World War I, deaths actually exceeded births.[11] Concerns about this problem helped generate an array of voluntary movements and an official state policy of pronatalism, but neither legal reforms nor direct economic aid to families had any appreciable effect.[12]

The problem of depopulation appeared at about the same time as an articulate feminist movement and a female challenge of the historic gender lines in the professions, education, and several traditionally male occupations, but because of the prevailing concern about the birth rate these developments did not succeed in provoking either the legal or the practical changes that occurred elsewhere.[13] Rather, there seems to have been a considerable surge of support for a strengthening of a procreative "family order," which placed a high premium on marital love, heterosexuality, and the sanctity of the domestic regime.[14] In deference to well-established cultural and bio-medical beliefs, French repopulationists attempted to reinforce the doctrines of sexual difference and complementarity on which they believed marital fertility depended. This was the social and cultural context in which a scientific discourse on reproduction was produced.

In general, the favored explanation for the crisis of reproduction was that it was somehow related to physical exhaustion or a deficit in the energy levels required for healthy and prolific fertility.[15] Part of the reason for this lies in the assumption of the native Lamarckian tradition – updated in the second half of the century as "neo-Lamarckism" – that heredity was a *force* of reproduction based on the strength and distribution of energy in an organism's economy; likewise, in degeneration theory, insufficient energy was both a cause and a consequence of syndromes of biological decline. In contradistinction to that position, the German embryologist August Weismann was arguing by the mid-1880s that scientists should assume the existence of an unbridgeable gap between the "germ" (sexual) cells and the "soma" (body) cells, the former being the unique and independent carriers of hereditary information. This assumption was later incorporated into Mendelian and neo-Darwinian inheritance theory, which triumphed virtually everywhere after 1900 except in France.[16]

French embryologists, for their part, were inclined to resist this bifurcation of the organism between germ and soma cells in favor of explanations of epigenetic influence and concepts of vital equilibria, which had served native physiology since the mid-eighteenth century. The presence of these theories encouraged the retention of the formative role of environmental adaptation and the corollary idea of acquired characters, which were together, for French life scientists, the sources of most variation in nature. Thus, while Weismann and his heirs could speak of the "immortality" of an organism that managed to pass on its germ plasm, French scientists like Armand Sabatier problematized the continuity of the soma, which could perish in maladaptive variations or in the depletion of the energy the organism required for reproduction.[17]

Fertilization and reproduction, Sabatier held, were two separate things, or, rather, fertilization was but a moment in a reproductive *process*, which shaped the new organism from a stage well before conception until birth.[18] French embryologists continued to favor this *epigenetic* tradition well past the time it was abandoned elsewhere in favor of neo-Mendelian genetics, which held, to the contrary, that the hereditary information contained in the chromosomes of the parents could not be influenced in any way by the intrauterine environment.[19] The French persisted in exposing embryos and fertilized eggs of various animal species to different physical influences such as temperature and nutrition to see if they could influence the rate or outcome of the developmental process or the sex ratios of new organisms.[20] With respect to the population problem, this deeply rooted scientific outlook encouraged French demographers and biologists to regard the decline in the birth rate as a matter of organic weakness, in keeping with the pessimistic determinism of degeneration theory. In his review of the vast scientific literature on depopulation in 1938, Joseph Spengler concluded that among the most popular of the "involuntary" causes of *dénatalité* was the assumption of an enfeeblement of the "genetic instinct" of the "race."[21]

In the scientific and popular thinking of the era, most of the responsibility for procreative debility fell on males.[22] If one isolates the common assumptions, it emerges that males, more often than not, were the weak link in the generative equation, with respect to both the general problem of low fertility and the specific one of a deficiency of male births in the whole population, another of the scientific concerns of the *fin de siècle*.[23] There existed a strong commitment to the notion that, in the earliest stages of embryological development, it was the male "element" that formed the "ectoderm" of the embryo where the nervous system and circulation were located, while the egg shaped the dark and passive regions of the interior.[24] Thus, since males were the source of the "active" parts of the embryonic economy, it was their generative material that was held responsible for a couple's failure to produce viable offspring.[25] Thus the population crisis of France was also a crisis of a nation wounded in its virility.[26]

These concerns about the "strengths" and "weaknesses" in male progenitors coincided with a major reorientation in theories about sexual reproduction and the evolution of sex. Until 1880 or so, researchers who looked at the vast array of reproductive mechanisms employed by living forms believed that sexual reproduction was a minority phenomenon in nature, far less important than fission, budding, or asexual spore production.[27] In the late 1870s the first convincing observations were made of a sperm fertilizing an egg, and later work showed that the egg began to develop only after nuclear material from the sperm and egg had joined together.[28] It was soon apparent that sexual reproduction was more widespread in nature than previously realized, and that its "rediscovery" solved the knotty problem that had perplexed Darwin about the source of the variations that were the raw material of evolution.

When this development was linked together with the idea of organic evolution and the "perfection" of a division of labor in organisms and societies, it produced a powerful new combination. The physiologist Henri Milne-Edwards had suggested much earlier in the century that there was a natural hierarchy in nature which distinguished structurally simple and undifferentiated organisms from those where specialization of function had produced more complex and thus "higher" forms.[29] Herbert Spencer later cast the division of labor in an evolutionary framework, insisting that evolutionary processes progressed from states of "homogeneity to heterogeneity," thus making complex organisms (and societies) superior *by nature* to simpler forms. As is well known, this kind of reasoning was taken up generally by evolutionary theorists in the late nineteenth century, whether of the Darwinian or neo-Lamarckian variety, where it often served as the scientific underpinning for social Darwinist, colonialist, and nationalist ideologies.

There were also implications in this combination of ideas for sex, and French thinkers were quick to take them up. They concluded that asexual forms of reproduction were the earliest, and therefore the most primitive kinds. Reproduction itself, scientists argued, had evolved from simple fission through hermaphroditic varieties of self-fertilization, concluding with sexual reproduction, where the males and the females of the species were separate beings characterized by a high degree of physical dimorphism. This was true not only phylogenetically (in terms of evolutionary development), but ontogentically as well (in terms of the present hierarchy of species). Thus, as Armand Sabatier put it in 1886, "In the measure that one descends toward the inferior animals that constitute present-day fauna, one will see the sexual differences between individuals disappear and their reproductive elements become increasingly uniform and capable of sufficing by themselves for reproduction."[30]

In terms of French evolutionary theories, this meant that *ascendant* evolution was promoted by increasing differentiation, since, as Alfred Fouillée wrote, "In simple fission, As will produce As and Bs will produce Bs. But without a *marriage* of letters, one would never have obtained the *Iliad* or the *Odyssey*."[31] Any organism that gradually specialized its internal functions, including those of reproduction, was able to use its energy more efficiently for purposes of adaptation and the "struggle for life."[32] Just as an organism's need for nourishment drove it to perfect its digestive system, the sex drive stimulated it to economic refinements of specialization in reproduction.[33]

In his authoritative review of the literature on the evolution of sex in 1893, Alfred Fouillée explained the implications of this division of reproductive labor for species. Among humans and in most other advanced species, a salutary saving in energy had been obtained by the evolution of two distinctly different kinds of gametes in each sex. The spherical and passive female ovum represents the ultimate realization of the principle of the conservation of energy, which Fouillée called the "anabolic" principle, following the usage of Patrick Geddes and J. A. Thomson.[34] The sperm, on the other hand, represents the "catabolic" principle of *expenditure* of energy, as seen by its constant motion, agility, and hardiness. Fouillée was not shy about anthropomorphizing this distinction. As he wrote, "The egg, voluminous, well nourished, and passive, is the cellular expression of the characteristic temperament of the mother; the lesser volume, less-nourished aspect, and preponderance of activity of the father sum up the masculine element."[35]

Partly because of such language, and because in most species legions of spermatozoa competed to fertilize a few eggs, it became common to speak about the egg as the "conservative" element in sexual reproduction, and the sperm as the "progressive" source of variation and change, or, as Fouillée contrasted them, "tradition" and "personal innovation."[36] These kinds of descriptions of the male and female gametes were repeated in technical and popular scientific works and in several disciplines from the 1870s through the first decade of the twentieth century.[37]

The evolutionary forces that had produced these disparate male and female gametes worked also to differentiate the bodies and minds of men and women. There were several standard arguments based on selection mechanisms that attempted to explain aspects of male and female difference in the second half of the nineteenth century.[38] Yet, as had been true of the "form and function" argument of the late eighteenth century, in the end a women's reproductive function was again the principal evidentiary basis for her "inferiority" to men. But in the new evolutionary paradigm it was not the simple fact of her childbearing, which had been the source of Michelet's earlier sentimental effusions on women, but her role in the evolution of sexual reproduction that was decisive.[39]

Charles Darwin's theory of sexual selection, which he advanced in 1871 as an appendix to his *Descent of Man*, offered one explanation of how dimorphism drove "progressive" evolution. Within the general mechanism of natural selection, sexual selection explained how in some species the "fittest" males were able to pass on their hereditary material by overawing male rivals and sexually monopolizing females.[40] On descriptive grounds alone, this explanation was appealing to French naturalists as evidence for the "courage" or "hardiness" of the male sex.[41] But, in its focus on how sexual selection determined *male* qualities in species already characterized by physical dimorphism, Darwin's theory did not convincingly address the general problem of the evolution of sexual reproduction, or the evolutionary logic behind the qualities of females.[42] Alfred Fouillée summed up the objections of French evolutionary theorists in revealing language. Sexual selection, he wrote, "is an incomplete explanation. Force and agility are not simply an ulterior adaptation; they are a *primordial* characteristic of masculine activity. It is an internal, not an external determinism that has produced a division of functions between the sexes and the 'primary' characteristics of male and female, for the benefit and perpetuation of life and the species."[43]

There was something too instrumental and secondary about Darwin's evolutionary explanation of sex difference to satisfy most French biologists. They resisted sexual selection for the same reason that they opposed the Weismannian/neo-Mendelian notion that the determination of sex was made by germ cells isolated from the rest of the organism. Neither provided a sufficiently holistic account of the links between reproduction, the orientation of the sex instinct, and the sex of the organism. Darwin's theory slighted the complementarity of sexual identities, and Weismann's "mosaic" theory of inheritance separated sex from other inherited characters. After passing the whole of the literature on sexual dexerminism under review in 1913, the evolutionary biologist Maurice Caullery concluded that "If sexuality is an aspect of the entire organism, impregnated within it, so to speak, its seat is not only in the genital glands [in the hereditary codes of the gametes, as Weismann would have it], but may be read in every one of its organs, in an infinite number of signs distributed throughout the organism."[44] Most French scientists and doctors who commented on this issue preferred to believe that individuals were literally *saturated* with their sex.

The French were not alone in having contingent motives for understanding the laws of human reproduction. Class and ethnic tensions encouraged scientists and intellectuals in all industrializing countries to search for eugenical solutions to their social problems, including "dysgenic" controls on the multiplication of undesirable populations. The general demographic dilemma of the French, however, encouraged their scientific and political elites to study reproduction as a way of increasing the quantity and quality of the whole population.[45] This situation favored the production of biological norms whose cultural and social meanings were unequivocally clear and which operated in the way Canguilhem and Foucault have described, that is as a "positive conception, which insists ... on its biological function of inclusion and regulation, in the sense not of a regimentation but of a regularization, by reference to the distinction alleged by the human sciences between the normal and the pathological."[46]

Among the most practical of these "positive" incitements was the principal finding that all of nature obeyed iron laws of sexual attraction, the origin of which could be traced back through the mists of evolutionary time to an era when a division of sexual labor gave a competitive advantage to species organized to exploit it. The adaptive value of the impulse lay in its implementation of procreation; because mutual attraction promoted the survival of the species, the aim to fertilize was assumed to be inherent within it. Since physical dimorphism was the sign and the trigger for this natural drive, it seemed logical to conclude that a species which had evolved more distinctive forms of sexual dimorphism would enjoy a competitive advantage over those which were less marked because it would breed more effectively and prolifically. An excellent maxim, therefore, for a society that wished to promote a politics of procreation would be: *vive la différence.*

Such a politics could not expect to be effective by repeating the outmoded formulas of P.-J. Proudhon and Michelet about the virtues of keeping the "weaker" sex shut up at home. Some allowance had to be made for the modern bourgeois woman who made forays outside the home, who had more input on courtship and marriage arrangements, and who might by the late 1880s have an education that was "separate but equal" to that of her husband or brothers. In order to be practical as well as *être de son temps*, a procreative discourse needed to take note of contemporary feminist concerns, but nonetheless find some way to square the new findings about the universality of sexual affinity with an updated version of the doctrine of the separate spheres. A thorough review of the vast literature and iconography advocating these views between 1880 and 1914 would alone produce a book-length study; I must be content with a brief review of the principal arguments.

One of the first books to articulate the new discourse of procreation was Dr Henri Thulié's *La Femme: Essai de sociologie physiologique* (1885). Thulié was a well-known medical activist who served in the Paris municipal council and edited the influential public hygiene journal *Revue philanthropique*. As a militant republican anticleric, Thulié believed that the new republic could mobilize citizens to improve the birth rate more effectively than the church had ever done. By proclaiming "La République doit-être la fécondité," a chivalrous state could help liberate women from the legal constraints that forced them into unproductive, loveless marriages, eliminate the economic hardships that forced many women into a sterile prostitution, and repress the vices and "marital frauds" (contraceptive practices) that distracted them and discouraged motherhood.[47]

But if Thulié was a legal reformer, demanding equal financial and social rights for women, abolition of the dowry system, paternity searches, and state support for maternity, he was not a believer in either full political equality or in the equality of the sexes. On the contrary, it was a premise of his brand of feminism that men and women were profoundly different as sexual beings, and that their mutual attraction and fecundity depended on maintaining this difference. How, he asked, "can we confuse force with grace, will with tenderness, logic with finesse, anger with calm, a burning and vainglorious bravery with a tenacious courage free from preoccupation with glory? Man is struggle, woman is love."[48] The "shame" of France will be expunged and the honor of both sexes restored when marriage is restored to its primacy and a woman is "able to freely choose her sire" (*géniteur*).[49] The freedom of marital choice, Thulié warned, must never be confounded with either vulgar promiscuity or a utopian legal equality. Let us consider, he asks, the monstrousness of life in a world of perfect sexual equality, where a society of hermaphroditic beings can fertilize one another, and themselves, all of whom enjoy the same aspirations, pleasures, responsibilities, and aptitudes. Ordinary human lasciviousness would be doubled, sexual exhaustion would be the rule, and for any work to be done at all we would have to castrate some of our number, like the bees, to make a worker class.[50]

Such a nightmare of sexual homogenization, sterility, and exhaustion fueled much of the serious research on human fertilization, encouraging the search for the laws of sexual attraction that governed the chain of being from micro-organisms to mammals, from the sperm and egg to the sexed adult. In 1888 the French microscopist François Maupas published the results of an experiment purporting to show that single-celled ciliates could "revitalize" themselves and increase their rate of reproduction by exchanging nuclear material in a side-by-side "conjugation." This primitive form of sexual reproduction allowed them to avoid the fate of a control group of similar creatures which were kept in isolation from one another, and which eventually died out after diminishing in size and vitality.[51]

Summing up a decade of research in cytology, the experimental psychologist Alfred Binet found a host of references in French scientific *mémoires* to the love life of "sexed" single-celled organisms. As he coyly put it: "The female pursued by the male seems to be moved by two contrary desires, one to receive the male, and the other to escape him. This refusal, which is never more than temporary, and more apparent than real, has the effect of exciting the male to deploy ever greater means to charm her."[52] Armand Sabatier was moved by similar considerations to write about the sperm and the egg as "sexed" cells, driven together by their respective "active" and "passive" natures.[53] After observing sperm cells in his microscope, G. Balbiani wrote in a *mémoire* of 1878, "I do not think, for my part, that the spermatozoa move blindly, but that they obey a sort of internal impulsion, a will that directs them to a determined end."[54] When these willful sperm reached the neighborhood of the egg, claimed Henri Beaunis, the egg bulges out in their direction, sending out tiny wands of protoplasm to make contact and ensure penetration.[55]

There thus was a general agreement among French theorists that sexual reproduction had thrived precisely because evolution selected for difference and made reproduction dependent upon it. The principal argument was that evolution "develops in each sex the qualities appreciated by the other ... it is thus a great advantage for the conservation of the species that the sexual elements arise, not only on different individuals, but in particular on individuals who are distinguished from one another by the very characters that affirm their sexuality."[56] As we have seen already, these references to the "sexual elements" did not refer to the sex glands alone, but to "a sort of total polarization of the sexed individual by means of the sexual element."[57]

Another line of argument portrayed the organic drives underlying sexual dimorphism as useful collective adaptations. This view was first espoused by Alfred Espinas, who based much of his sociology on entomological research on insect societies. Employing the popular device of treating communities of insects as stand-ins for human ones, Espinas argued that in the course of evolutionary development agglomerations of individuals begin to interact in such a way that selection operates on them as a unit, and selects for group characteristics, of which individuals are only the exemplars. Bees, ants, termites, and human societies are the most notable examples of this kind of evolution. Highly specialized and unique reproductive mechanisms had evolved in all of them.

Espinas's idealism inclined him against the doctrine that the laws of sexual attraction were simply organic drives implanted in individuals; he preferred to think of them as social "representations" which had evolved to ensure reproduction and group survival. Thus the collective representation shared by the two sexes instructed each to see the other as "its virtual half which propels it toward that second part by means of an organic drive. Each is drawn to the other as to the absolute condition of its specific existence, better still, as to the condition which is its complete present existence." Despite the metaphysical language he preferred, it is quite clear that Espinas's sociology also treated sex as a thing that permeated individual biology. Thus male pursuit, female coquetry, the whole panoply of the symbolic discourse of love, is engraved in the female's mind,

> in order to determine for her, in the measure that the effects of that representation descend into the depths of her organism, the physiological modifications necessary for fertilization. Thus the [courtship] phenomena we have just considered are symbols, but on the other hand are also biological phenomena. For what is beauty if not organization made tangible, form breathed into life![58]

However one chose to represent the attraction of the "opposite" sexes – as a sublimation of lower instinct or as the organic expression of collective ideals – the same problematic seems to have inspired all commentators on the subject. In the words of the biologist Jacques Delboeuf, "How, at the risk of zoomorphism, do individuals of healthy and robust nations marry?" If otherwise unconstrained, they go in search of mates:

> They walk together in the streets, crowd together in salons, entwine with one another at balls, but in all these contacts that chance provides, one alone succeeds in inflaming them. Why? What are sympathy and antipathy? What is it that leads this young woman to attract that young man and precipitates her toward him? ... they are each unknowingly obeying the will of a sperm and an egg. But let us be certain about this, this is not random in either the sperm

or the egg. . . . They both know what they need and what they are looking for. To that end they give their orders to their respective brains through the intermediary of the heart, and the brain obeys without knowing why. . . . A society whose customs and laws hinder intelligent choices dictated by the sperm and the egg is doomed to depopulation and death.[59]

In the thirty years or so before 1914, a consensus of opinion emerged in France on the relation of sex to the population problem that cut across most other ideological differences. Thus, while one might expect feminists to deplore the social and legal conventions that worked to inhibit the "natural" procreative drives in men and women, anti-feminists also applauded the return of divorce, worked to further liberalize it, and demanded an end to the system of marriage and dowry contracts that constrained men and women alike in the free choice of a mate.[60] Even the bitterest opponents of female political and legal emancipation believed that allowing greater reproductive choice would promote more "variations," "associations," and "renewals," and lead to a greater number of offspring.[61]

A similar convergence marked a related debate about the merits of the scientific effort to dissect the noble sentiment of love into its component instincts, obsessions, or chemical tropisms. Catholic or neo-Kantian commentators deplored the popularity of naturalistic "physiologies of love," which reduced the noble sentiment of love to a "genital act."[62] Their materialistic opponents mocked the hypocrisy and bad faith of religious and moral teachings on love and marriage, arguing they produced misery, not happiness, and did not correspond to the passions and drives of ordinary humans.[63] However, neither camp minimized the importance of sexual attraction to love, and both were in remarkable agreement that the aim of marriage was to procreate. Thus Léon Blum, pilloried for his suggestion that women should have affairs before marriage, should be read as arguing that the traditional matrimonial system produced not only unhappy marriages, but infertile ones. There was, in his words, an ominous gap between "the function [of marriage] and the organ."[64] An old man exhausted by sexual adventures forced upon a young and inexperienced girl was a recipe for anger, sexual disorder, and divorce.[65] But, where the attraction was mutual, a marriage between equals in age and sexual experience would be far more stable and fertile than the monstrous arranged affairs of yesteryear.[66]

All commentators, even the most progressive feminists, were worried about the malign effects on sexual dimorphism from rapid social and economic progress, which might doom the French to sterility and national suicide. Some worried about masculine women. The feminist Jean Finot hoped that the "variability" that would appear in women who entered the male workforce would be countered by "the compensatory instinct of dimorphism," which alone allows the "race to survive."[67] Opponents of feminism like Rémy de Gourmont were less sanguine. He worried about the masculinizing effects of education and sport, and mused about the dangers to the "race" of destabilizing women's natural "maternal laziness" by allowing them to assume male roles in the economy. "The duty," he wrote, "of each being is to persevere in his being [*être*] and even to augment the characteristics special to him. The duty of woman is to preserve and accentuate both her aesthetic and her physical dimorphism."[68]

And what of men? Were there special dangers to them from a selection "against the grain"? If women were regarded as the stable and conserving influence in inheritance, males provided the element of variability necessary for progress. With respect to the evolution of sexual dimorphism, this meant that men were believed to vary more frequently and more radically from one another, while women were believed to cleave more closely to "type." There was a risk that a greater number of "feminine" men would be produced through the normal mechanism of evolutionary advance, and that their relatively greater proportion of intellect to instinct might crowd out their instinctive urge to breed.[69] But French commentators hoped that French women might serve as a prophylactic against this eventuality. Thus, Edouard Toulouse did not think homosexuality would make headway in the French armies because French women were so naturally feline and coquettish that their charm "will preserve us from such sentimental aberrations," a formulation that suggests something less than burning confidence in the manliness of French men.[70]

In the weakened demographic and geo-political situation of the nation, it is not surprising that, when an "ideal" or "typical" sexual identity was invoked, those features were stressed that could contribute best to the national welfare. There is no shortage of such descriptions in the scientific literature, just as there is a widespread affirmation of the need to revitalize the family as the cadre within which the next generation of warriors and wives would be nurtured.[71] Alfred Fouillée captured the spirit of this discourse of familial regeneration perfectly when he referred in 1893 to the "human trinity" of man, woman, and child, and spoke of the "equivalence in the *blood tax* demanded of men for the external defense of the nation and from maternity for the conservation and education of the race."[72]

The extraordinary alignment of these biological discourses on love, human reproduction, sex difference, the evolution of sex, and the "romance" of the egg and the sperm bear witness to the close connection in this era between the language of the embryological laboratory and the language of national revival and regeneration. Did Michel Foucault miss a chance to extend his analysis of *fin-de-siècle* discourses on sexual knowledge and power further into the domain of biology? Did he eschew consideration of reproductive biology because of some disciplinary line he believed divided biological science from medical practice? I hope I have provided here an answer to the first of these questions; the second I leave to the epistemologists.

Part IV

The Liberal State:
Origins and Elaborations

9

The Chimera of the Origin: Archaeology, Cultural History, and the French Revolution

Roger Chartier

I

In this essay I would like to take Michel Foucault's work as a starting point, and to propose an interpretation of the French Revolution that will relate the origins of that event not only to the new political discourses that appeared in France after the mid-eighteenth century but also (and more fundamentally) to the connections between discursive practices and other practices – ones that were deployed in registers different from and irreducible to the order of discourse. The work of Foucault was so permeated with references to the French Revolution that it appears to furnish a solid framework for such a perspective. One preliminary question cannot be eluded, however: is it so easy to enlist Foucault's work in the service of a historian's investigation that aims at rendering intelligible the motivations that, in the late eighteenth century, made a radical and sudden rupture with the Old Regime thinkable, and hence possible?

In fact, Foucault's work does not readily lend itself to practical application by historians. Such a project supposes that a certain number of texts (books, articles, lectures, interviews, etc.) are to be considered as forming a body of works ("Foucault's work"); that such a body of works can be assigned to an "author" whose proper name ("Foucault") refers to a specific individual endowed with a unique life history, and that, on the basis of the reading of this primary text ("Foucault's work"), it is legitimate to produce another discourse in the form of commentary. According to Foucault, however, those three operations are not as evident or as unmediated as they long seemed in the "traditional history of ideas."[1]

To begin with, Foucault removed the supposed universality of these operations by restoring their variability. Thus, by specifying the particular historical conditions (juridical and political) that made the proper name a fundamental category in the classification of works (he calls this the "author-function"), he invites consideration of the reasons behind and the results of such an operation, which are: to guarantee the unity of a body of works by ascribing it to one sole font of expression; to resolve the eventual contradictions between the texts of a same "author," explained by changes undergone as his or her life evolved; to establish a relationship between the works and the social world by setting the author, as an individual, in his or her time.

Moreover, for Foucault, all the operations that designate and assign works must always be considered as operations of selection and exclusion. How can a work be extracted from "the millions of traces left by an individual after his death"? The answer to this question required a decision to separate (following criteria with neither stability nor universality) the texts constituting the work ("Foucault's work") from other texts, written or spoken, "without quality," thus not assignable to the "author-function."

Finally, for Foucault, those various operations – delimiting the works, attributing them to an author, and producing a commentary – are not neutral operations; they are borne along by the same function, a restrictive and constraining function that aims at controlling discourses by classifying them, ordering them, and distributing them.

Foucault's first and formidable challenge to his readers is to undermine the foundations of the intelligibility and the interpretation of any works (including Foucault's own) in our configuration of knowledge. This creates a dizzying and unique tension in which any reading of a text of Foucault's is always – simultaneously and necessarily – a questioning of that reading and of the ordinary concepts ("author," "work" (*oeuvre*), "commentary") that govern relations with texts in our society. In a remark in "The Discourse on Language" in which he may perhaps be confessing something about himself, Foucault does not exempt the author from subjection to the categories governing the regime of discourse production at a particular historical moment. He says:

> I think that, for some time, at least, the individual who sits down to write a text, at the edge of which lurks a possible *oeuvre*, resumes the functions of the author. What he writes and does not write, what he sketches out, even preliminary sketches for the work, and what he drops as simple mundane remarks, all this interplay of differences is prescribed by the author-function. It is from his new position, as an author, that he will fashion – from all he might have said, from all he says daily, at any time – the still shaky profile of his *oeuvre*.[2]

The author's assimilation of those categories that account for works in the common order of discourse is what makes possible the articulation between writing, understood as a free, fecund, and contingent practice, and the procedures that aim at controlling, organizing, and selecting discourses. Still, the fact that the interpreter and the author both accept the conventions that command the mode of assignment and classification of works does not mean that those conventions can be considered neutral or universal.

Foucault adds a second challenge. His entire project for critical and historical analysis of discourses is founded on an explicit objection to the concepts used in the "traditional history of ideas," the most immediately mobilizable resource for understanding or aiding others to understand a text, a body of works, or an author. For Foucault, the postulate of the unity and the coherence of a body of works, the attempt to show creative originality, and the inscription of meaning into discourse are all categories that must be countered by the construction of a different and indeed contrary approach attentive to the discontinuities and the regularities that constrain the production of discourses. Understanding a set of statements thus supposes recourse to principles of intelligibility that challenge the old notions (which have hardly been spruced up in recent years) of the history of ideas.

This raises a difficult question: under what conditions is it possible to produce a "Foucauldian" reading of Foucault? That is, how can we read his works on the basis of that "slender wedge" (as he writes ironically) that "consists not in dealing with meanings possibly lying behind this or that discourse, but with discourse as regular series and distinct events" and that permits "the introduction, into the very roots of thought, of notions of *chance*, *discontinuity*, and *materiality*." Must we oppose Foucault to Foucault and place his efforts in the very categories that he considered as powerless to render an adequate account of discourses? Or should we submit his works to the procedures of critical and genealogical analysis that they proposed and, by that token, annul what permits us to delimit their uniqueness and singularity? Foucault was undoubtedly delighted to have fabricated this "tiny (odious, too, perhaps) device" that insinuates a vexing doubt into the very heart of commentary that claims to pronounce on the meaning or the truth of his works. We can almost hear the metallic and lightning-swift laughter of Michel Foucault in this good joke on all – and they have been and will continue to be many – who attempt to read him.[3]

II

That laughter has an even more caustic resonance to the historian who hopes to make the origins of the French Revolution (or any other phenomenon) intelligible. In one of his few texts explicitly devoted to the works of Nietzsche, probably his fundamental philosophical reference, Foucault presents a devastating critique of the very notion of origin as historians are accustomed to using the term.[4] Because it justifies an endless quest for beginnings, and because it annuls the originality of the event, which is supposed to be already present even before it occurs, the category of "origins" masks both the radical discontinuity of "emergences" (irreducible to any prefiguration) and the discordances separating different series of discourse or practice. When history succumbs to "chimeras of the origin," it purveys several presuppositions (without always being aware of doing so): that every historical moment is a homogeneous totality endowed with an ideal and unique significance present in each of its manifestations; that historical development (*devenir*) is organized like a necessary continuity; that events are linked together, the one engendering the other in an uninterrupted flow that permits decreeing one the "cause" or the "origin" of the other.

For Foucault, "genealogy" must part company with precisely these classic notions (totality, continuity, causality) if it strives for an adequate comprehension of ruptures and divergences. The first of the "particular traits of historical meaning, as Nietzsche understood it – the sense which opposes 'wirkliche Historie' to traditional history" is thus to transpose "the relationship ordinarily established between the eruption of an event and necessary continuity. An entire historical tradition (theological or rationalistic) aims at dissolving the singular event into an ideal continuity – as a teleological movement or a natural process. 'Effective' history, however, deals with events in terms of their most unique characteristics, their most acute manifestations."

With a radicality permitted by the form he has chosen – a "commentary" on texts of Nietzsche's – Foucault gives a totally paradoxical definition of the event, paradoxical because it situates the contingent not among the accidents of the course of history or the choices of individuals, but in transformations in relations of domination, which is what seems to historians the most determined aspect of events and the one least open to chance. As Foucault says:

> An event . . . is not a decision, a treaty, a reign, or a battle, but the reversal of
> a relationship of forces, the usurpation of power, the appropriation of a
> vocabulary turned against those who had once used it, a feeble domination

that poisons itself as it grows lax, the entry of a masked "other." The forces operating in history are not controlled by destiny or regulative mechanisms but respond to *haphazard conflicts*. They do not manifest the successive forms of a primordial intention and their attraction is not that of a conclusion, for they always appear through *the singular randomness of events*. (my emphases)

Teeming facts, multiple intentions, interlocking actions thus cannot be ascribed to any system of determinations capable of giving a rational interpretation of them – that is, of pronouncing on their meaning and their causes. Only by accepting this renunciation will "the historical sense free itself from the demands of a suprahistorical history." For traditional historians, the price to be paid is not small, since it is the abandonment of all claim to universality – a universality they hold as the condition of possibility and the very object of historical comprehension. Foucault says, commenting on Nietzsche:

"Effective" history differs from traditional history in being without constants. Nothing in man – not even his body – is sufficiently stable to serve as the basis for self-recognition or for understanding other men. The traditional devices for constructing a comprehensive view of history and for retracing the past as a patient and continuous development must be systematically dismantled. Necessarily, we must dismiss those tendencies that encourage the consoling play of recognitions.

III

On the ruins of what Foucault calls the "history no one does any more" (nor should do), what is to be constructed? In several texts published between 1968 and 1970, at a turning point in his intellectual development, Foucault often refers to the practice of historians, an essential characteristic of which ("a certain use of discontinuity for the analysis of temporal series") could be used to shore up intellectually his own project of a critical and genealogical description of discourse and legitimize its strategy. The essence of "the effective work of historians" lies not in the invention of new objects but in a "systematic putting into play of the discontinuous" that breaks in fundamental ways with the sort of history imagined or consecrated by philosophy, which was a recital of continuities and an affirmation of the sovereignty of consciousness. Foucault says:

Attempting to make historical analysis the discourse of the continuous and to make the human consciousness the original subject of all knowledge and all practice are two aspects of the same system of thought. Time is conceived in terms of totalization, and revolution is never anything but reaching awareness.[5]

Contrary to this "system of thought," the history that Foucault calls "history as it is practiced today" – the history of economic conjunctures, demographic shifts, and social change that dominated the historical scene in the 1960s, following the leads of Fernand Braudel and Ernest Labrousse – considers multiple and articulated series each commanded by a specific principle of regularity, each tied to its own conditions of possibility. Contrary to what historians think they are doing (or say they are doing), this approach does not in any way banish the event, any more than its preference for the long time-span implies the identification of immobile structures. Quite the contrary: it is by the construction of homogeneous and distinct series that discontinuities can be identified and emergences situated. At a certain distance from both "philosophical history" and structural analysis, the history that deals in the serial treatment of massive archival materials (in "The Discourse on Language" Foucault mentions "official price-lists [*mercuriales*], title deeds, parish registers, . . . harbor archives") is neither the ongoing narration of ideal history, nor history in the Hegelian or Marxist manner, nor a structural description without events:

> History has long since abandoned its attempts to understand events in terms of cause and effect in the formless unity of some great evolutionary process, whether vaguely homogeneous or rigidly hierarchized. It did not do this in order to seek out structures anterior to, alien or hostile to the event. It was rather to establish those diverse converging, and sometimes divergent, but never autonomous series that enable us to circumscribe the "locus" of an event, the limits to its fluidity and the conditions of its emergence.[6]

One can thus imagine a connection between the contingent singularity of emergences, as designated by "effective history," and the regularities that govern temporal series, discursive or non-discursive, that are the object of the empirical work of the historians.

This leads Foucault to a dual conclusion – paradoxical in the light of the naively anti-eventalized definition of *Annales* history – associating the series and the event and detaching the latter from any reference to a philosophy of the subject. Foucault states:

> The fundamental notions now imposed upon us are no longer those of consciousness and continuity (with their correlative problems of liberty and causality), nor are they those of sign and structure. They are notions, rather, of events and of series, with the group of notions linked to these; it is around

such an ensemble that this analysis of discourse I am thinking of is articulated, certainly not upon those traditional themes which the philosophers of the past took for "living" history, but on the effective work of historians.[7]

IV

Often Foucault opposed, term by term, his analysis aimed at discerning "discursive formations" and the history of ideas, that "old patch of ground cultivated to the point of exhaustion."[8] To counter the traditional criteria for the classification and identification of discourses ("author," "text," "work," "discipline"), archaeological description relies on other and less immediately visible principles of delimitation. To quote from the "Réponse au Cercle d'épistémologie": "When, in a group of statements, one can discern and describe *one* system of dispersion, *one* type of enunciative distance, *one* theoretical network, *one* field of strategic possibilities, one can be sure that they belong to what might be called a *discursive formation*."[9] We need to be on guard here for the differences between these notions and the apparently closely related or identical notions that seem appropriate for individualizing groups of utterances. The *référentiel* – principle of dispersion – of a series of discourses is not the stable, unique, and exterior "object" that is its supposed aim. It is defined by the rules of formation and transformation of the mobile and multiple objects that those discourses construct and posit as their referents. The *écart énonciatif* – enunciative distance – does not designate one unique and codified form of enunciation considered inherent to a set of discourses but rather a *régime d'énonciation* – an enunciative pattern – that displays dispersed and heterogeneous statements related to one another by a similar discursive practice. The *réseau théorique* – theoretical network – operates in the same fashion on the conceptual level, aiming at the rules of formation of notions (including their possible contradictions) rather than the presence of a system of permanent and coherent concepts. Finally, the *champ des possibilités stratégiques* – field of strategic possibilities – challenges any individualization of discourses based on the nature of their themes or their opinions. What it designates is a similarity of theoretical choices, which can quite easily express contrary opinions or, inversely, differences in those choices short of a common set of themes.

I have two reasons for recalling these four notions, which Foucault presents as fundamental to his archaeological description of discourses in 1968 and in 1969, although they no longer figure explicitly in either "The Discourse on Language" or in later works. First, just when he was inaugurating a new way of working, Foucault used these various stages of analysis to give retrospective coherence to his past works. He characterizes each of his previous books as the exploration, through the study of a particular discursive formation, of one specific problem in archaeological analysis: "the emergence of a whole group of highly complex, interwoven objects" in his *Histoire de la folie* (1961); the forms of enunciation of discourse in *The Birth of the Clinic* (1963); "the networks of concepts and their rules of formation" in *The Order of Things* (1966).[10] Admittedly, in this reading Foucault describes his own labors with the aid of criteria (unity, coherence, meaning) that belong more to the history of ideas than to the archaeology he proposes. Nonetheless, it designates a fundamental departure from traditional approaches by considering discourses as practices that obey rules of formation and operation.

Hence – and this is a second reason for paying heed to the notions opposed to the classical concepts of intellectual history – the need to consider how discursive practices are articulated with other practices of a different nature. This theme, which was to become central in Foucault's work after *Discipline and Punish*, is sketched on several occasions in *The Archaeology of Knowledge*. Unlike direct and reductive causality, but also unlike the postulate of the "sovereign, sole independence of discourse,"

> archaeology . . . reveals relations between discursive formations and non-discursive domains (institutions, political events, economic practices and processes). These *rapprochements* are not intended to uncover great cultural continuities, nor to isolate mechanisms of causality. Before a set of enunciative facts, archaeology does not ask what could have motivated them (the search for contexts of formulation) nor does it seek to rediscover what is expressed in them (the task of hermeneutics); it tries to determine how the rules of formation that govern it – and which characterize the positivity to which it belongs – may be linked to non-discursive systems: it seeks to define specific forms of articulation.[11]

This projected archaeology has a particular pertinence to reflection on the French Revolution and its origins. It maintains the exteriority and the specificity of practices that are not in themselves of a discursive nature in relation to the discourses that, in many ways, are articulated on the basis of those practices. Recognizing that access to such non-discursive practices is possible only by deciphering the texts that describe them, prescribe them, prohibit them, and so on, does not in itself imply equating the logic that commands them or the "rationality" that informs them with the practices governing the production of discourses. Discursive practice is thus a specific practice (Foucault calls it "strange") that does not reduce all other "rules of practice" to its own strategies, regularities, and reasons. In this sense, I must take issue with the current positions that assimilate social realities to discursive practices (for example, by considering that the "claims to delimit the field of discourse in relation to nondiscursive social realities that lie beyond it invariably point to a domain of action that is itself discursively constituted . . . [and] distinguish, in effect, between different discursive practices – different language games – rather than between discursive and nondiscursive phenomena"[12]). Such positions annul – wrongly, in my opinion – the radical difference separating "the formality of practices" (to cite a category of Michel de Certeau's) and the rules organizing the positivity of discourses.

Maintaining the irreducibility of that gap leads us to question two ideas that recur throughout all strictly political history of the French Revolution: first, that it is possible to deduce the practices from the discourses that serve as their foundation and justification; second, that it is possible to translate the latent meaning of social operations into the terms of an explicit ideology. The first operation, classic in all the literature devoted to the connections between the Enlightenment and the Revolution, credits the diffusion of "philosophical" ideas with the acts of rupture from the established authorities, thus supposing a direct, automatic, and transparent engendering of actions by thoughts. The second leads to the conclusion that the sociability of the voluntary associations (clubs, literary societies, Masonic lodges) that proliferated during the eighteenth century was implicitly Jacobin, or that political practice during the first months of the Revolution already arose out of a terrorist ideology.

Against these two operations of deduction and translation, a different articulation between sets of discourses and patterns of practice must and can be proposed. There is neither continuity nor necessity between the one and the other. If they are connected, it is not through causality or equivalence but through difference; through the gap that exists between the singular specificity of discursive practices and all other practices. Thus, with respect to the eighteenth century, we should stress the gap between the (competing) discourses that, in representing the social world, proposed to refound it and the (multiple) practices that, as they came into being, were inventing new ways of dividing things up.

This perspective can easily lead to characterizing the Enlightenment somewhat differently. Instead of accepting the classic definition of the Enlightenment as a corpus of specific statements or a set of clear and distinct ideas, should we not rather see that term as covering a set of multiple and intermingled practices guided by a concern for common utility which aimed at a new management of spaces and populations, whose mechanisms (intellectual, institutional, social, and so on) imposed a complete reorganization of the systems for the perception and the organization of the social world? Accepting this view leads to a profound reevaluation of the relationship between the Enlightenment and the monarchy, since the latter, the target *par excellence* of philosophic discourse, was doubtless the most vigorous source of practices instituting reforms. Tocqueville clearly states this notion in book 3, chapter 6 of *The Ancien Régime and the Revolution*, which he entitles "How certain *practices* [my emphasis] of the central power completed the revolutionary education of the masses." Thinking of the Enlightenment as a sheaf of practices without discourse (or outside of discourse) – in any event, of practices irreducible to the ideological affirmations intended to justify them – is perhaps the surest way to avoid teleological readings of the French eighteenth century (which are more persistent than one might think) that view it from the standpoint of its necessary end-point – the Revolution – and retain in it only what led to that supposedly necessary outcome: the Enlightenment.

V

To establish a firm distinction between discursive practices and non-discursive practices is not to consider only the latter as belonging to "reality" or to the "social." Against those (historians, in particular) who have "a very impoverished notion of the real," Foucault states:

> We have to demystify the global instance of *the* real as a totality to be restored. There is no such thing as "the" real that can be reached by speaking about everything, or about certain things that are more "real" than others and that one would fail to grasp, to the profit of inconsistent abstractions, if one kept to showing other elements and other relations. One must perhaps also ask about the principle, often admitted implicitly, that the only *reality* to which history should lay claim is *society* itself. A type of rationality, a way of thinking, a program, a technology, a set of rational and coordinated efforts, of definite and actively pursued objectives, instruments to attain this goal, etc. – all that is of reality, even if it does not claim to be "reality" itself or the whole of "society."[13]

Thus Foucault annuls the division, long held to be fundamental to historical practice, between living experience, institutions, and relations of domination, on the one hand, and, on the other, texts, representations, and intellectual constructs. The real weighs equally on either side: all such elements constitute "fragments of reality" whose arrangement we must grasp in order to "see the interplay and the development of diverse realities that articulate with one another: a program, the connection that explains it, the law that gives it constraining force, etc., are just as much realities (although in another mode) as the institutions that give it body or the comportments added to it more or less faithfully."[14]

VI

"What is the status of the reality that rationality represents in modern Western societies?"[15] Foucault's question helps us to understand why he gives the Enlightenment central importance, and also why his historical analysis of the formation and the functions of rationality is not a critique of reason. To recognize the contradiction between the emancipating philosophy of the Enlightenment and the dispositions, reliant on Enlightenment ideas, that multiplied constraints and controls is not a denunciation of the rationalist ideology as the matrix of the repressive practices characteristic of contemporary societies. As Foucault puts it, "What reader will I surprise by stating that analysis of the disciplinary practices of the eighteenth century is not a way of making Beccaria responsible for the Gulag?"[16] Establishing such a connection would be doubly mistaken: first, by constituting ideology as the determining instance of social operations, whereas all regimes of practices are endowed with a regularity, logic, and reason of their own, irreducible to the discourses that justify them; second, by ascribing the mobile and problematic figures of the division between the true and the false to a referential, original rationality, given, once and for all, as "the" rationality. Ten years before the bicentennial of the French Revolution, Foucault wrote (perhaps imprudently) : "As for the *Aufklärung*, I know no one among those who do historical analyses who sees it as *the* factor responsible for totalitarianism. I think, what is more, that posing the problem in such a fashion would not be of any interest."[17] His warning seems to me another way of stressing the oversimplification of any analysis of the Revolution that plays the game of retrospective dovetailing to inscribe 1793 in 1789, Jacobinism in the decisions of the National Assembly, and terrorist violence in the theory of the general will.

VII

The French Revolution is present in all of Foucault's major books from the *Histoire de la folie* to *Discipline and Punish*. In none of them, however, is it considered as a time of a total and global rupture reorganizing all intellectual disciplines, discourses, and practices. What is essential lies elsewhere, in the disparities that run throughout the Revolution and in the continuities that place it within longer time-spans. When, in *The Archaeology of Knowledge*, Foucault sums up the analysis of the discursive formations identified in his earlier books, he stresses disparities:

> The idea of a single break suddenly, at a given moment, dividing all discursive formations, interrupting them in a single moment and reconstituting them in accordance with the same rules – such an idea cannot be sustained. . . . Thus the French Revolution – since up to now all archaeological analyses have been centred on it – does not play the role of an event exterior to discourse, whose divisive effect one is under some kind of obligation to discover in all discourses; it functions as a complex, articulated, describable group of transformations that left a number of positivities intact, fixed for a number of others rules that are still with us, and also established positivities that have recently disappeared or are still disappearing before our eyes.[18]

"Let the friends of the *Weltanschauung* be disappointed" by this removal of the event from all possibility for a non-contradictory totalization.

Unlike the certitude of a radical accession to power or an absolute inauguration, which suffuses the words and the decisions of the actors in the event, Foucault's insistence on the discordances that separate the various discursive series (the ones that were invented or transformed with the Revolution, or the ones in no way affected by it) recalls forcefully that the reflective and voluntary portion of human action does not necessarily provide the meaning of historical processes. Tocqueville and Cochin – the two authors usually hailed by the historians who plead most forcefully for a return to the primacy of politics, of the idea, and of consciousness – demonstrate this point by stressing that, in reality, the men of the Revolution did the opposite of what they said and thought they were doing. The revolutionaries proclaimed an absolute rupture with the Old Regime, but they strengthened and completed its work of centralization. The enlightened elites claimed to contribute to the common good within peaceful *sociétés de pensée* loyal to their king, but they invented the terrorist mechanisms of Jacobin democracy. The point here is not whether or not these two analyses are accurate but that they refuse to conceive of the Revolution according to its own categories – beginning with the proclamation of a radical discontinuity between the new political era and the old society. The intelligibility of the event supposes, to the contrary, a gap between it and the awareness that its actors had of it. That the revolutionaries believed in the absolute efficacy of politics, invested with the dual task of refounding the body social and regenerating the individual, does not oblige us to share their illusion. That the Revolution can be characterized, above all, as "a political phenomenon, a profound transformation of political discourse involving powerful new forms of political symbolization, experientially elaborated in radically novel modes of political action that were as unprecedented as they were unanticipated,"[19] does not imply that the history of the event need be written in its own language.

With *Discipline and Punish* and the texts that prepared or surrounded it, analysis seems to encroach on the Revolution. In no way does Foucault consider its chronological stages or the succession of political events as pertinent to resolving the question he poses, which is, "Why did the physical exercise of punishment (which is not torture) replace, with the prison that is its institutional support, the social play of the signs of punishment and the prolix festival that circulated them?"[20] An attempt to understand why incarceration was placed at the center of the modern punitive system (the aim of *Discipline and Punish*) leads Foucault to determine a specific domain of objects and to construct a temporality of his own that bears little resemblance to the usual periodizations. Indeed, he situates the formation of the "disciplinary society" that invented the technologies of subjection and the methods of surveillance that the prison both inherits and exemplifies between the age of French classicism and the mid-nineteenth century.

As Foucault's analysis advances, he establishes a number of temporal divisions: from the late eighteenth century to the early nineteenth for the shift to a penal policy of detention; the decades from 1760 to 1840 for the reduction of torture and the transformation of the economy of illegalism; the period from the latter half of the seventeenth century to the nineteenth century for perfecting disciplinary techniques in military, medical, and educational institutions and manufacturing concerns. He assigns to the "conjuncture" of the eighteenth century the fundamental fact of the universalization of disciplines made necessary by an enormous population increase, the growth of the mechanisms (and not only the economic mechanisms) of production, and the domination of the bourgeoisie. For Foucault, in fact, modes of discipline and liberties, "everyday panopticisms" and juridical norms, are indissociable mechanisms that assured and perpetuated a new and socially designated hegemony. He states:

> Historically, the process by which the bourgeoisie became in the course of the eighteenth century the politically dominant class was masked by the establishment of an explicit, coded, and formally egalitarian juridical framework, made possible by the organization of a parliamentary, representative regime. But the development and the generalization of disciplinary mechanisms constituted the other, dark side of these processes. . . . The real, corporal disciplines constituted the foundation of the formal, juridical liberties.[21]

Foucault's analysis, which he repeats elsewhere,[22] seems surprising today for its borrowings from the most rudimentary sort of Marxism of the unified concept of a bourgeoisie, the category of formal liberties, and a model of historical development that substitutes one dominant class for another. What interests me here is not those highly debatable interpretations but the fact that Foucault inscribes the revolutionary period, as he does the periodizations organizing his demonstration, within a longer time-span, hence eliminating its singularity.

Thus Foucault traces a perspective for historical comprehension that uncouples the significance of the event and the consciousness of individuals. This makes it possible to consider the Revolution and the Enlightenment as belonging – together – to a long-term process that embraces them and reaches beyond them and to see them both, although with different modalities, as tending toward the same ends and inhabited by similar expectations. Alphonse Dupront expressed this notion forcefully (but without sociological oversimplification):

> The world of the Enlightenment and the French Revolution stand like two manifestations (or epiphenomena) of a greater process – that of the definition of a society of independent men without myths or religions (in the traditional sense of the term); a "modern" society; a society with no past and no traditions; [a society] of the present, wholly open toward the future. The true connections of cause and effect between the one and the other are those of this common dependence on a broader and more whole historical phenomenon than their own.[23]

The "veritable Revolution," as Dupront writes, is not the complex of events that the actors – and often the historians – have designated as such, but "a broader historical development . . . that is essentially the passage from a traditional mythology (a mythology of religion, of sacralities, of religious and political authority), to a new mythology, or renewed common faith, one of whose most vehement affirmations is that it does not care to be or know itself to be mythical."[24]

VIII

The relationship between the Revolution and the Enlightenment is central to Foucault's commentary, in 1983, on two texts of Kant's, "What is Enlightenment?" (1784) and the second dissertation of *The Conflict of the Faculties* (1798).[25] In his analysis of the latter text, Foucault follows Kant's demonstration step by step as Kant attempts to show how the French

Revolution constituted an indisputable "historical sign" of the existence of a permanent cause guaranteeing the constant progress of the human race. In order to do so, Kant distinguishes between the Revolution as a grandiose event and a voluntary enterprise, and the Revolution as producing among all peoples "a wishful participation that borders closely on enthusiasm." As a historical process, the Revolution, which accumulated miseries and atrocities, could just as easily have failed as succeeded and, in any event, its price was so high that it dissuaded imitations for ever. Thus it cannot be held as a demonstration of the ineluctable progress of the human race – one might say, quite the contrary. On the other hand, the welcome given to that event attests to the force of the "moral tendency of the human race," which urges men to give themselves a freely chosen constitution in harmony with natural law ("one, namely, in which the citizens obedient to the law, besides being united, ought also to be legislative") and "created in such a way as to avoid, by its very nature, principles permitting offensive war." The Revolution, or, more accurately, the reactions that it set loose, revealed a "predisposition" in human nature that "permits people to hope for progress" more fundamental than the hazards of the event in which it is manifest. Hence Kant states: "Now I claim to be able to predict to the human race – even without prophetic insight – according to the aspects and omens of our day, the attainment of this goal. That is, I predict its progress toward the better which, from now on, turns out to be no longer completely regressive." In themselves, neither the course nor the outcome of the Revolution counts; its importance lies in its giving a spectacular visibility to the virtualities underlying both the *Aufklärung* and the philosophers' task:

> Enlightenment of the masses is the public instruction of the people in its duties and rights vis-à-vis the state to which they belong. Since only natural rights and rights arising out of the common human understanding are concerned here, then the natural heralds and expositors of these among the people are not officially appointed by the state but are free professors of law, that is philosophers who, precisely because this freedom is allowed to them, are objectionable to the state, which always desires to rule alone; and they are decried, under the name of enlighteners, as persons dangerous to the state.[26]

With the commentary on these texts that opened his course at the Collège de France in 1983–4, Foucault intended to show that Kant not only originated the philosophical tradition that holds as central the question of the conditions of possibility of true knowledge (which Foucault calls an "analytic of the truth") but was also the first to constitute the present as an object of philosophical interrogation. In both of Kant's texts (1784 and 1798), "discourse has to return to a consideration of its actuality, first, in order to find its own place in it, second, in order to say what it means, finally, in order to specify the mode of action that it is capable of exerting within that actuality."[27] This reference to the basis of a critical tradition that considers "the question of the present as a philosophical event to which the philosopher who speaks of it belongs" seems to me to characterize the work of Foucault even better than the formula that is so often cited: "My books aren't treatises in philosophy or studies of history: at most, they are philosophical fragments put to work in a historical field of problems."

IX

> In the last years of the eighteenth century, European culture outlined a structure that has not yet been unraveled; we are only just beginning to disentangle a few of the threads, which are still so unknown to us that we immediately assume them to be either marvelously new or absolutely archaic, whereas for two hundred years (no less, yet not much more) they have constituted the dark, but firm web of our experience.[28]

In *The Birth of the Clinic* as later in *Discipline and Punish*, Foucault situates the constitution of the discourses and the practices that provided the basis for "modernity" in the half-century (roughly speaking) from 1770/80 to 1830/40 that included the Revolution.

Foucault's characterization of that decisive period has often been badly misunderstood. Although it was indeed the moment in which disciplinary procedures, the technologies of surveillance, and panoptical mechanisms were constituted as the essential methods for the organization and the control of the social space, that does not mean that they actually gridded, policed, and disciplined the social world. Their proliferation shows their weakness, not their efficacy: "When I speak of a 'disciplinary' society, that does not imply a 'disciplined society.' When I speak of the diffusion of discipline, it is not to assert that 'the French are obedient'! In the analysis of the procedures put into effect for instituting norms there is no 'thesis of a normalization.' As if, precisely, all those developments were not on the scale of a perpetual insuccess."[29] There is thus an "obverse" to the history of disciplinary measures – an obverse of interwoven resistances, deviations, and illegalisms. To combat oversimplified readings of his work, Foucault recalls the force of rebellious practices that respond, in various ways, to the microtechniques of constraint:

> Resistances to the Panopticon will have to be analysed in tactical and strategic terms, positing that each offensive from the one side serves as leverage for a

counter-offensive from the other. The analysis of power-mechanisms has no built-in tendency to show power as being at once anonymous and always victorious. It is a matter rather of establishing the positions occupied and modes of action used by each of the forces at work, the possibilities of resistance and counter-attack on either side.[30]

"Strategy," "tactics," "offensive," "counter-offensive," "positions," "counter-attack": the military vocabulary indicates that, even if it is not equal, the battle between the procedures of subjection and the comportment of the "subjected" always takes the form of a confrontation, not that of an enslavement. It is in that confrontation that "we must hear the distant roar of battle."[31]

The late eighteenth and early nineteenth centuries were fundamental also because they constructed a new figure of power, anonymous, autonomous, and operating through practices that are not accompanied or legitimated by any discourse. That conception of power, which inhabits all the measures that aim at rendering it both constraining and hidden, widely disseminated and coherent, managed and automatic, must by no means by confused with Foucault's concept of power. Here again, Foucault reacts vigorously to a misinterpretation frequently committed by the critics (and the adepts) of *Discipline and Punish*. He says:

> The automaticity of power, the mechanical nature of the devices in which it takes shape, is absolutely not the *thesis* of the book. It is rather the idea in the eighteenth century that such a power would be possible and desirable; it is the theoretical and practical search for such mechanisms; it is the desire, ceaselessly manifested at the time, to organize such devices that constitutes the *object* of analysis. Studying the way in which people attempted to rationalize power – for which a new "economy" of the relations of power was conceived in the eighteenth century – and showing the important role that the themes of the machine, of the gaze, of surveillance, of transparency, etc., played in them, is not to say either that power is a machine or that an idea of the sort was born mechanically.[32]

Confusion between the "thesis" and the "object" has been one of the major and recurrent reasons for misunderstanding Foucault's work. It marked the readings given to the famous lecture "Qu'est-ce qu'un auteur?" that Foucault gave on February 22, 1969 to the Société Française de Philosophie, which have often (and wrongly) equated the question posed (the conditions of the emergence and distribution of the "author-function," defined as the mode of classification of discourses that assigns them to a proper name) and the theme of the "death of the author," which bases the meaning of works on the impersonal and automatic functioning of language.[33] Foucault corrects just such a mistaken view of the intentions of his work in his reply to Lucien Goldmann's objections during the debate that followed his lecture. Foucault says:

> The death of man is a theme that allows light to be shed on the way in which the concept of man has functioned in knowledge. . . . It is not a matter of affirming that man is dead; it is a matter of seeing, on the basis of the theme – which is not of my invention [and] which has been repeated incessantly since the late nineteenth century – that man is dead (or that he is about to disappear, or that he will be replaced by the superman), in what manner and according to what rules the concept of man has been formed and has functioned. I have done the same thing with the notion of the author. Let us hold back our tears.[34]

X

When Foucault distinguishes, as in *The Archaeology of Knowledge*, between discursive formations and practices that "are not themselves of a discursive nature", when he shows, as in *Discipline and Punish*, how practices without discourse come to contradict, annul, or "vampirize" (the word is Michel de Certeau's[35]) the proclamations of ideology, Foucault's work retains all its critical pertinence today, both regarding the "semiological challenge" and the "return to politics."

We all know of the "linguistic turn" proposed to historians of texts and practices: to hold language as a closed system of signs that produce meaning merely by the way their relations function; to think of social reality as being constituted by language, independent of any objective reference.[36] In contrast to these formulations, Foucault (perhaps paradoxically for those who made a structuralist of him, a label that he always vehemently rejected[37]) helps us to recall that one cannot reduce the practices that make up the social world to the "rationality" that governs discourses. The logic commanding the operations that construct institutions, dominations, and relations is not the same hermeneutic, logocentric, scriptural logic that produces discourses. That practices, articulated with but not homologous to discourses, are irreducible to discourses can be considered the fundamental partitioning principle in all cultural history, which is, by that token, invited to avoid unguarded use of the category of "text," too often used to designate practices whose procedures in no way obey the "order of discourse."

The theme of the "return to politics" often (although not always, as Keith Baker's work proves) figures as the inverse of the "linguistic turn."

Far from postulating that the production of meaning is automatic, it stresses the liberty of the subject, the part of reflection in action, and the autonomy of decisions. Hence it rejects all initiatives that aim at establishing determinations of which individuals are not conscious, while it affirms the primacy of the political, held to be the most comprehensive and most significant level in all societies.[38] Here, too, Foucault helps to define a perspective opposed, term by term, to that proposition – first, by considering the individual not in the supposed liberty of his or her own, separate "I" but as constructed by the configurations, discursive or social, that determine its historical figures; and, second, by postulating not the absolute autonomy of politics but, at each particular historical moment, its dependence on the balance of tensions that both fashions its devices and results from its efficacy.

XI

Foucault revolutionized history in two ways. First, after him, it has become impossible to consider the objects of which the historian claims to write the history as "natural objects," as universal categories whose historical variations (be they madness, medicine, state, or sexuality) the historian simply notes. Behind the lazy convenience of vocabulary, what we need to recognize are singular demarcations, specific distributions, and particular "positivities" produced by differentiated practices that construct figures (of knowledge or of power) irreducible to one another. As Paul Veyne has written:

> Foucault's philosophy is not a philosophy of the "discourse," but a philosophy of relation. For "relation" is the name of what some have designated as "structure." Instead of a world made of subjects or of objects or of their dialectic, of a world in which consciousness knows its objects in advance or is itself what the objects make of it, we have a world in which relation is primary: it is structures that give their objective faces to matter. In this world, we do not play chess with eternal figures like the king and the fool [i.e. the bishop]; the figures are what the successive configurations on the playing-board make of them.[39]

Thus there are no historical objects that preexist the relations that constitute them; no field of discourse or of reality delimited in a stable and unmediated fashion: "Things are only the objectivations of determinate practices, the determinants of which must be brought to light, since consciousness does not conceive them."[40] Thus it is by identifying the demarcations and the exclusions constituting the objects history gives itself that history can conceive of them not as the circumstantial expressions of a universal category but, quite the contrary, as "individual and even singular constellations."[41]

To transform the definition of the object of history is necessarily to modify the forms of writing. In his commentary on *Discipline and Punish*, Michel de Certeau stressed the rhetorical displacement (and the perils) implied by a history of practices without discourses that constructs these "panoptical fictions":

> When, instead of being a discourse on other discourses that preceded it, theory ventures into the non-verbal or pre-verbal domains in which only practices without accompanying discourses are found, certain problems arise. There is a sudden change, and the foundation offered by language, ordinarily so sure, fails. The theoretical operation suddenly finds itself at the limit of its normal terrain, like a car arriving at the edge of a cliff. Beyond there is nothing but the sea. Foucault works at the edge of the cliff, attempting to invent a discourse to treat non-discursive practices.[42]

Hence, in *Discipline and Punish*, there is a contradictory *écriture* that organizes the discourse on knowledge on the basis of the very procedures that are its object and, at the same time, constructs "panoptical fictions" to exhibit and subvert the foundations of the punitive rationality established at the end of the eighteenth century. As de Certeau says, "On a first level, Foucault's theoretical text is still organized by the panoptical processes that it elucidates, but on a second level this panoptical discourse is only a scene or a narrative trick that inverts our triumphant panoptical epistemology."[43]

XII

"At the edge of the cliff." The image is a vivid expression of the disquietude appropriate to any history that attempts the operation, at the limit of the possible, of accounting, within the order of discourse, for the "reason" for practices – both the dominant practices that organize norms and institutions and the scattered and minor practices that make up the fabric of daily experience or introduce illegalities.

But there is help for all who draw close to the edge of that cliff: there is the work and the thought that was always "situated at the point where an archaeology of problematizations and a genealogy of practices . . . intersect."[44]

Translated by Lydia G. Cochrane

10

A Foucauldian French Revolution?

Keith Michael Baker

Could there be a Foucauldian account of the French Revolution? What might it look like? An acquaintance with more wit than sympathy for these questions compared them to asking: "If Foucault had been a painter, what colors would he have used?" The skepticism is warranted. I certainly have no fully developed "Foucauldian account of the French Revolution" to offer in what follows. Nonetheless I find it intriguing, as a historian interested in the Revolution whose approach to history has also been shaped by reading Foucault, to ask how Foucault himself might have thought about it. Nor can I resist this opportunity to try out a few ideas and speculations about how one might indeed bring some of his ideas and perspectives to an exploration of the topic.

In large part, then, what follows is offered as a *jeu d'esprit* – a thought-experiment to see what might now be said about the French Revolution and its origins in a Foucauldian voice. But the impersonation is only partial and sometimes breaks down. My interest in Foucault's writings, and their obvious relevance to much recent work on the French Revolution, derive principally from his emphasis on the power of discourse to constitute the domains of experience that count as real and legitimate in any given situation. While imagining how some of his ideas and arguments might advance a discursive analysis of the Revolution, I have also stepped aside to criticize them at points where they seem to be inconsistent or underdeveloped in relation to that project.

Foucault may not have been a historian of the French Revolution any more than he was a painter. But the Revolution nevertheless lay at the heart of his researches. "Up to now," he admitted in *The Archaeology of Knowledge*, "all archaeological analyses have been centred upon it."[1] Many of his books – particularly such powerful earlier works as *Madness and Civilization, The*

Birth of the Clinic, *The Order of Things*, and *Discipline and Punish* – were devoted to a critical reconsideration of profound transformations in European culture traditionally interpreted as the historical work accomplished by the Revolution as it liberated humanity in the name of Enlightenment. Moreover, the arguments in those books frequently depended upon quite specific references to legislation enacted by successive revolutionary assemblies and to the practices and innovations of other revolutionary institutions.

Yet, although the revolutionary period served as a key location for so many of Foucault's investigations, he nowhere offered anything that might reasonably be called a sustained interpretation of the French Revolution as a phenomenon in itself. Nor need one look hard to find reasons in his thinking for this lack of interest in its specific character. Understood as a phenomenon of events and actions compressed into an extremely short time period, the Revolution held little charm for a Foucault who began by sharing the structuralist and *Annaliste* tendency to dismiss the significance of events and minimize the importance of the acting subject. This minimization of the significance of action and events also served one of his principal intellectual agendas, which was to unmask the emancipatory claims of enlightened, humanitarian reason. To the extent that the Revolution presented itself, and has traditionally been seen, as the conscious implementation of the emancipatory logic of the Enlightenment, it was at once primary as a site of Foucault's concerns and secondary as a surface effect of more general processes of subjectivization and discipliniza-tion – that subjection in the guise of liberation – that remained his fundamental intellectual concern.

Such an approach would not necessarily have precluded an interpretation of the French Revolution as a critical moment in long-term transforma-tions, and Foucault does seem to think of the entire revolutionary period, in a general way, in those terms. At the same time, his willingness to conceptualize the Revolution as a period of European consciousness, rather than as a specific political phenomenon, was constrained – at least after *The Archaeology of Knowledge* – by his critique of the entire notion of periodization. "Archaeology disarticulates the synchrony of breaks, just as it destroyed the abstract unity of change and event. The *period* is neither its basic unity, nor its object: if it speaks of these things it is always in terms of particular discursive practices, and as a result of its analyses," he argued in the passage of *The Archaeology of Knowledge* to which I have already referred.

> Thus the French Revolution – since up to now all archaeological analyses have been centred on it – does not play the role of an event exterior to discourse, whose divisive effect one is under some kind of obligation to

discover in all discourses: it functions as a complex, articulated, describable group of transformations that left a number of positivities intact, fixed for a number of others rules that are still with us, and also established positivities that have recently disappeared or are still disappearing before our eyes.[2]

In this analysis, the "French Revolution" could indeed be usefully retained as a conventional general term to describe a particular set of discursive transformations. But the term had no analytical force in itself; it could neither provide a global characterization of an entire age nor offer a more general explanation of the particular transformations it was used to identify.

Foucault's critique of the assumptions of traditional historiography therefore directed his attention away from the French Revolution, at least as it was customarily understood either as period or event. But how could a philosopher-historian who ultimately identified the workings of power as his fundamental object of study have failed to find fascinating the political dynamic the Revolution so explicitly offered? It was, after all, a struggle for and about power, a struggle in which power itself took on new forms and articulations. But it was also a struggle for and about power explicitly conceived in terms of sovereignty – the form of power in which Foucault claimed to be least interested. His early works sought principally to reveal the constitution of power underlying the discourse of truth (i.e. to discover the power in that which presented itself as the very antithesis of power). His later works sought precisely to repudiate the identification of power with sovereignty, understood as the title and capacity to repress, and to develop an alternative conception of power as productive rather than repressive: power, that is, as the force inherent in the production of all human relations. Neither of these agendas required (indeed, each militated against) the development of a specific interpretation of the French Revolution.

Foucault's relative silence on the subject of the character of the French Revolution as a specific phenomenon was thus scarcely accidental. Indeed, this very silence spoke loudly, particularly in France, against a traditional historiography (whether non-Marxist or Marxist) that had made the Revolution central – as period or event – to historical understanding. But his silence need not be ours. We can persist, at least for a while, in asking what a Foucauldian account of the French Revolution might look like.

I   SOME ELEMENTS OF A FOUCAULDIAN HISTORY

A Foucauldian approach to the French Revolution would doubtless have been expected to look somewhat different at varying points of his career.

After the publication of *The Order of Things*, one might reasonably have looked (despite its author's subsequent denials that he was ever a structuralist of any kind) for ways of characterizing the Revolution as the effect of a structural mutation in the episteme producing an entirely different kind of politics (or perhaps introducing what we know as politics for the first time). After the appearance of *The Archaeology of Knowledge*, that approach would have given way to an attempt to understand the Revolution as the effect of a new political hierarchization of competing discourses.[3] After *Discipline and Punish*, in turn, the emphasis would have shifted towards identifying the Revolution as the effect of a specific technology of power. It is important, then, to allow for chronological variations of this kind, recognizing that Foucault himself acknowledged the existence of a number of false starts or partial formulations in his work. I would nevertheless suggest that there would be at least two essential requirements of a Foucauldian account of the French Revolution: first, an identification of a specific technology of power; second, a genealogical or "eventalized" analysis of the appearance of that phenomenon.

As for the first of these requirements, a Foucauldian approach to the French Revolution would surely be a disenchanted one, seeking to reveal the mechanisms of power within the discourse of emancipation. It would be unlikely, for example, to draw a critical distinction between the emancipatory moment of 1789 and the repressive moment of 1793. More particularly, it would seek to derive the phenomena of the Revolution from the operation of a specific technology of power. Foucault and Foucauldians have not themselves done this. But we have learned a great deal in recent years, from François Furet and those who have followed his lead, about the specifically political mechanisms and dynamic of the Revolution.[4] Drawing on that work and giving it a somewhat more Foucauldian cast, we might describe the revolutionary technology of power, first, as a technology of *dedifferentiation*, involving a simultaneous individualization of human subjects and universalization of their relations.[5] Apart from the fact that the term is ugly enough to be a Foucauldian neologism, *dedifferentiation* has the virtue of suggesting a procedure that can be continued indefinitely through the production of new differences to be removed. The process of dedifferentiation required the abolition of an existing legal apparatus that distinguished between subjects on the basis of their status within a corporate social order (as on the Night of the Fourth of August and subsequent legislation deriving from it). It also required the creation of successive new legal apparatuses (first, the legislation that became summarized in the constitution of 1791; later, the legal institutions of the Terror). But it also required more than a legal apparatus.

It required, second, what might be called a technology of *transparison*, or

making transparent. To achieve the total individualization and universalization of the subject, social and political life had to be made entirely
transparent. Each had to be open to all. Hence the critical importance in
the Revolution of such instruments of transparison as the press and the
popular societies. But these instruments of transparison continuously
produced new obscurities to be dispelled – in the same way as the
disciplines of penality, in Foucault's analysis, continuously produced
criminals to be reformed. "If all hearts are not changed," Robespierre
insisted, "how many countenances are masked!"[6]

Dedifferentiation also involved a technology of *politicization*, which is to
say the production of political subjectivity, or the subjectivization of politics.
Each individual was now to be seen as a political actor; all actions were to
be understood as political actions; every phenomenon was to be revealed as
the expression of a political will. This subjectivization of politics was also its
moralization. "Within the scheme of the French revolution, that which is
immoral is impolitic, that which is corrupting is counter-revolutionary,"
Robespierre explained.[7] Hence the need for tactics of *denunciation*, methods
of identifying and eliminating individuals whose obscure, devious, immoral
wills blocked the circuit between individualization and universalization.
Denunciation individualized the political criminal even as it condemned
him or her in the name of the universal. It proclaimed that the fate of the
entire nation, indeed of all humanity, was being betrayed in the conduct,
the speech, even the thoughts of the individual denounced. Denunciation
was the corollary of political subjectivity.

All of this depended, too, upon a discourse of *rupture* that placed the
Revolution within the regime of the "true" (which is to say the "natural"
and "moral") as opposed to an unnatural, corrupt, despotic, perverse Old
Regime. Within this discourse, politics had to become the domain of truth;
sovereign will had to recapitulate the voice of reason; human institution had
to restore the order of nature. The discourse of a radical break with the past
drove the revolutionary dynamic and legitimated the revolutionary technologies of power by constantly producing new continuities with the past to be
destroyed, new contaminations of the Revolution by the lingering corruption of the Old Regime.

It would not be enough, though, for a Foucauldian account of the French
Revolution, to identify and analyze the operation of a specific technology of
power. It would also be necessary to provide a "genealogy," or "eventalized" analysis of its appearance. "Eventalization" is a term adopted by
Foucault after the publication of *Discipline and Punish* to describe an
analytical procedure emphasizing the radical historicity of the phenomenon
being studied.[8] This approach posits the singularity of the phenomenon, its
radical contingency, the possibility that it could have been otherwise. It

places in question the self-evidence of the phenomenon, its givenness or naturalness as a feature of the world. Eventalization, then, is a procedure of radical historicization.

It is worth emphasizing that the fundamental methodological assumption of "eventality" – the basic postulate of the contingency of historical phenomena – is not as different as one might initially imagine from the assumptions of much recent historical work on the French Revolution. Indeed, the need for an analysis of the French Revolution that allowed for the contingency of its political invention, rather than simply deriving its character from the logic of presumed social necessities, was precisely the point at which Cobban, Furet, and other revisionist historians parted from the Marxian interpretation. The illusion of inevitability was one of the first assumptions Furet condemned in the Marxist catechism of the French Revolution. "The postulate that 'what actually happened' did so of necessity," he argued, "is a classic retrospective illusion of historical consciousness, which sees the past as a field of possibilities within which 'what actually happened' appears *ex post facto* as the only future for that past."[9]

What, then, would an eventalized account of the Revolution entail? It would certainly involve identification of the Revolution's *conditions of possibility*. Since an eventalized account would be premised on contingency, it could not proceed by reference to causal necessity. It could only identify conditions making the Revolution possible without absolutely determining its occurrence or necessitating its specific character. Analysis of these conditions, in turn, would be expected to comprise a *heterogeneity of elements*. This also seems to be a logical implication of the Foucauldian stress on contingency, which denies the possibility of any global cause or ultimate ground of explanation.

But there is a more radical implication of the argument for eventality, both generally and in relationship to recent debates over the social interpretation of the French Revolution. It precludes recourse to that totalized ground of explanation that has seemed firmest to historians since the eighteenth century: the ground of "society." Foucault distinguished his project from the normal activity of historians at precisely this point. Historians, he argued,

> take "society" as the general horizon of their analysis, the instance relative to which they set out to situate this or that particular object ("society, economy, civilization," as the *Annales* have it). My general theme isn't society but the discourse of true and false, by which I mean the correlative formation of domains and objects and of the verifiable, falsifiable discourses that bear on them; and it's not just their formation that interests me, but the effects in the real to which they are linked.[10]

Society, considered from this perspective, becomes not an ultimate cause but a positive effect of the discourses and practices by which it is constructed or produced. "Rather than making the state–society distinction a historical and political universal by means of which we can investigate all concrete systems," Foucault argues, "one can try to see it as a form of schematization appropriate to a particular technology of government."[11] It follows from this deconstruction of the social as a global ground of explanation that a Foucauldian account of the French Revolution would place it in the context of a heterogeneity of discourses overlapping and/or competing in their constitution of a world, and of a political struggle over the hierarchization of these discourses.

This, finally, would require something that Foucault came frequently to talk about, but seems never to have really integrated into his analyses: namely, a close attention to the *tactics of production* of the phenomenon being analyzed. Tactics require tacticians, which is to say human actors. So the more a Foucauldian analysis moves in the direction of emphasizing heterogeneity, contingency, and eventality, the more it must find a place for (historically constituted) individuals and groups as agents (conscious or unconscious) of a political transformation that could have been otherwise. While this appears to be the least "Foucauldian" (or should I say the most "un-Foucauldian"?) of the propositions I am suggesting here, it seems to me to be a necessary implication of the previous ones. Nor is it as much at odds with Foucault's thinking as might at first appear. For, while Foucault denied the existence of "Man" as a kind of transcendent subject prior to history, he did not deny the existence of "men" (or "women") as individual agents engaged in political struggles. Indeed, it was precisely the historically conditioned character of these agents, and the form of the struggles in which they engaged, that he sought to elucidate.

Rather than simply assuming the existence of the acting subject, Foucault argued, we should try to account historically for his/her/its/their production and character. One can allow that the subject position occupied by any individual (or shared by any group of individuals) is the consequence of a particular discursive formation. But this is also to say that discourse is articulated and acted out as a form of practice in human lives – individually and in the aggregate. In positing that there will be a heterogeneity of discourses in any given situation, then, one must also allow that individuals become the site of the heterogeneous subject positions constituted by these competing discourses. The resulting tensions, expressing themselves both within and among individuals and groups, may also at times become so intense as to propel these latter into conscious action to resolve them through a politics of rehierarchization, recodification, or transformation of discourses. Something like this seems to have happened in 1789.

II "SOVEREIGNTY" AND "SURVEILLANCE"

"I believe the great fantasy is the idea of a social body constituted by the universality of wills." The language could be François Furet speaking of the political imaginary that drove the dynamic of the French Revolution. In fact, it is Foucault speaking of the nineteenth century.[12] I find the remark suggestive, because it implies the possibility that a Foucauldian account of the French Revolution might also seek to explain it in terms of a fusion between two incompatible forms of power, which for the moment I will simply call *sovereignty* and (for want of a better word) *surveillance*.[13]

Much of Foucault's later writing revolved around the problem of "cutting off the king's head."[14] This meant the effort to displace a conventional conception of power deriving from the juridical notion of sovereignty: a conception of power as the exercise of a political will that is unitary, repressive, external to the subject. Foucault's aim, of course, was to substitute an alternative conception of power as the key to his analysis of modern society. The elements of this alternative conception varied somewhat over the course of his writings (a fact that makes *surveillance* less than an entirely satisfactory term to designate it). But they included emphases on power as constituted by regimes of truth rather than by the exercise of political will, as polymorphous and pervasive rather than unitary, as productive rather than repressive, as internal rather than external to the subject, as subjectivizing rather than subjecting.

Sovereignty and *surveillance* are not just distinct conceptions of power in Foucault's analysis. They are also distinct – and antithetical – modes of power coexisting in modern society. Thus in one of the lectures collected in *Power/Knowledge* Foucault spoke of "the emergence, or rather the invention," in the seventeenth and eighteenth centuries, of "a new mechanism of power possessed of highly specific procedural techniques, completely novel instruments, quite different apparatuses, and which is also, I believe, absolutely incompatible with the relations of sovereignty." This type of power, he argued, is "in every aspect the antithesis of that mechanism of power which the theory of sovereignty described or sought to transcribe." It "ought by rights to have led to the disappearance of the grand juridical edifice created by that theory. But in reality, the theory of sovereignty has continued not only to exist as an ideology of right, but also to provide the organising principle of the legal codes which Europe acquired in the nineteenth century, beginning with the Napoleonic Code."[15]

Why did the relations of sovereignty not disappear? Foucault offered two answers to this question: first, the theory of sovereignty, particularly in its democratized form, served as an "instrument of criticism of all the obstacles that can thwart the development of disciplinary society," presumably beginning with those corporate legal institutions of the Old Regime that stood in the way of greater individualization of subjects. Second, it "allowed a system of right to be superimposed upon the mechanisms of discipline in such a way as to conceal its actual procedures."[16] This strikes me as an unconvincing reworking of the Marxist conception of the juridical state as superstructural, with the infrastructure simply redefined as mechanisms of disciplinary coercion rather than capitalist modes and relations of production. Why, after all, do disciplinary mechanisms need to be masked by the juridical theory of sovereignty when they possess their own legitimation as regimes of truth? But the discussion points to the possibility of analyzing the specific character of the French Revolution as an intense fusion of these two different modes of power, and of understanding its historical outcome as structuring the possibilities of their subsequent relationship in modern society. I shall return to this latter point below.

III   CONDITIONS OF POSSIBILITY

The appeal of Foucault's notion of eventality is that it frees the historian to look anywhere for the conditions of possibility of the phenomenon under consideration. Its drawback is that it offers no way of determining in advance where one should look, or of closing off the number of places in which one might do so. No list of conditions of possibility can therefore be considered logically complete. I can therefore only offer several that seem to me to be both worth exploring and "Foucauldian" – the latter in the sense that they have a particular resonance in relation to Foucault's own thinking.

The first, and perhaps the most general, condition of possibility of the French Revolution would seem to me to be the invention of society as the metaphysical ground of collective human existence. To the extent that the Revolution entailed an effort to absorb sovereignty into the body of society, it could not occur without a prior invention of society as the entity into which sovereignty was to be absorbed. Following the lead of Marcel Gauchet and Brian Singer, I would say that the conception of society as an ultimate and autonomous ground of human existence was unthinkable within a religious imaginary that saw the entirety of order and existence – metaphysical and physical, natural and human – as emanating from the Divinity.[17] Society could only appear as a representation of collective human existence once the ontological link between the Creator and the created was broken, which is to say when collective human existence seemed no longer to depend (as in the world best described by Loyseau, who stated very clearly the metaphysical basis for the traditional claims of monarchical absolutism) upon the maintenance of a divinely ordained and instituted order of relations among beings, a complex, differentiated, and hierarchical order upheld in the realm of the human by the king acting as lieutenant of God.

"Secularization" is, to my mind, too weak and gradualizing a term for the breaking of this link: it serves to naturalize by transforming into a long-term process ("secular" in the other sense of the term) the consequences of a more abrupt and dramatic shift in the religious mentality of western Europe. I would be tempted to relate this shift to a kind of Augustinian mutation in the religious imaginary – perhaps not global, but at least relatively general. Augustinianism was the religious nightmare of the eclipse of God, the severing of humanity from its ontological foundations in the Divinity. It was the intimation that the Fall had severed humanity and nature so radically from God that humankind could neither strive for grace nor approach by human means the spiritual reality informing the universe. It was the appearance of subjective individualism in its negative, Christian guise: the individualism of the sinner cut off from a now hidden God, and hence from true communion with his or her fellows; the individualism of the sinner necessarily flawed in his or her reason and morality. It was the delegitimation of authority and the dissolution of social order: the terror of the choice between anarchy and absolute, even arbitrary, power.

"Society" emerges, in consequence of this metaphysical shift, as the ontological horizon of human life, the only possible realm of existence of a humanity that finds itself cut off from God. In religious terms, it became the locus of the Calvinist investment in human action that made success in this world an indirect sign of grace; or, conversely, it was revealed by the Jansenist logic of the livable to be a merely (and irremediably) human order in which individual sinners acting out of self-love produced (without their knowledge or intent) the same effects as if they had acted out of Christian charity. (The migration of Nicole's analysis of self-love into economic theory, by way of Mandeville's *Fable of the Bees*, is well known.[18]) In epistemological terms, it became the zone of the probabilities of everyday life that offered all the knowledge remaining to a human mind denied rational access to the essence of the universe. In political terms, it emerged as a middle ground between civil war and absolute rule (the alternatives so dramatically posed by Hobbes), an autonomous domain of individualism without anarchy, order without arbitrary power.[19]

The invention of society also entailed the production of the social body. What happens to power as it ceases to be that natural justice sustaining the relations of order instituted by the Divinity in human affairs? It can be all the more emphatically divinized – and simultaneously fragilized – as in Bossuet; it can be rethought as artificial and self-referring, as in the doctrine of "reason of state." Or it can be instrumentalized to find its new justification in acting upon "society" and in the production of the social. Foucault sketched some aspects of this latter process in one of his late lectures, on "Governmentality," published in English in a recent volume, *The Foucault Effect.*[20] There are many problems with this lecture, to my mind, but it is also particularly suggestive in that it is one of the few places in which Foucault actually turns to the nature of the state and its history.

He does so by distinguishing three successive forms of the state. The first he calls "the state of justice, born in the feudal type of territorial regime which corresponds to a society of laws – either customs or written laws – involving a whole reciprocal play of obligation and litigation."[21] Juridical sovereignty emerged in this context as the ultimate instance, or final earthly court of appeal, adjudicating the play of obligation and litigation in a particularistic order. But it is important to emphasize that this sovereignty, while unitary (as the last instance), was also limited by that which it functioned to uphold; it was not the totalizing Leviathan Foucault generally invokes in his references to sovereignty as a mode of power.

Movement toward the totalization of power seems more closely associated with the second form of the state Foucault identifies, "the administrative state, born in the territoriality of national boundaries in the fifteenth and sixteenth centuries and corresponding to a society of regulation and discipline."[22] Historians would recognize this as the early modern form of the nation-state, the form in which new mechanisms of civil and military administration are devised and implemented to control territories, expand social resources, and mobilize them for the purposes of continuing warfare.

The chronology here is somewhat suspect. I, for one, would want to place the appearance of this administrative state in the seventeenth century, where it found its most immediate justification as a response to the problems of maintaining order and meeting the expanding needs of war in conditions of economic decline and social unrest. But this is not a crucial feature of Foucault's categorization. The more basic point lies in his discussion of the slide – which I would place in the eighteenth century – from an administrative state to a third form of state, which he calls a "governmental state, essentially defined no longer in terms of its territoriality . . . but in terms of the mass of its population with its volume and density."[23] The essence of the "governmental state," in this analysis, is that it operates in relationship to a domain (*civil society*) assumed to possess its own regularities, autonomous life, and independent existence. By fostering these autonomous processes and regulating them only as seems necessary for their optimal functioning, governmentality aims to achieve maximum results by minimum application of power.

It might be pointed out, by way of digression, that much of Foucault's discussion of governmentality revolves around the question of managing the welfare of a growing population, which he seems to treat here, as elsewhere, as a kind of external variable to which the administrative state is obliged to respond. To my mind, a more rigorous Foucauldian analysis would need to focus on the extent to which the problem of population was itself produced by the administrative state, both conceptually (by way of the link between taxation and taxability) and empirically (as a consequence of greater order and discipline within society). "Population" is not some extra- or non-discursive phenomenon that somehow intrudes upon the discourse of the administrative state. To the contrary, it is a problem and a positivity produced by the very practice of that state.

To put the point more generally, the domain of the social was not simply discovered by the state and its administrators; it was created by the action of the administrative state through its regulations and disciplines; it appeared at the point at which order and discipline had been fully enough incorporated into human existence that it could now appear as possessing its own autonomy and regularity. This is to say that the domain of the social has been produced, not discovered: controls have produced the regularities of the market, just as disciplines have produced the effect of subjectivity.

It is not difficult to see the beginnings of a shift from the discourse of the administrative state to the discourse of the governmental state in the decades preceding the French Revolution. Such a shift seems evident, for example, in the language of Turgot's celebrated *Mémoire sur les municipalités* of 1775, which proposed the transformation of government from a vehicle of sovereign power into the instrument of a public reason emanating from, and operating upon, the independent existence of an autonomous social order. It is no less evident in the speech with which Calonne opened the Assembly of Notables in 1787, declaring as he did that the old slogan of royal power, "as the king wills, so wills the law," would henceforth yield to the new slogan, "as the people's happiness wills, so wills the king." The Notables were unconvinced!

This brings me to a third aspect of what I would take to be a Foucauldian approach to the French Revolution, which is that it would entail the analysis of a *conflict of discourses*. The three modes of political power that Foucault sketches in his lecture on "Governmentality" did not simply succeed one another. They also coexisted in time. Foucault remains rather vague regarding the consequences of their coexistence, but I would want to suggest that it produced increasingly radical contradictions in French political life on the eve of the French Revolution, which exhibited themselves in an increasingly intense conflict among competing discourses of power.[24]

At the heart of this conflict were the fundamental tensions between the judicial and the administrative agents of the monarchy. Against the administrative state, the agents of the traditional state of justice asserted a discourse of justice that sought to sustain the juridical constraints on sovereignty and restrain the "despotic" action of governmental power within the traditional legal forms of a historically constituted society of orders and Estates. Against the juridical state, the agents of administrative/ governmental power asserted a discourse of reason that sought, in the name of modernity and the growth of civil society, to transform rule into reason, justice into the rational government of the social, law into education, and representation into a mechanism for the auto-administration of society. But against both the discourse of justice and the discourse of reason there also emerged a political discourse of will. Whereas the judicial discourse opposed justice to will, as the lawful and constituted *vis-à-vis* the arbitrary and contingent, the political discourse opposed will to will, which is to say liberty (the active expression of a general political will) *vis-à-vis* despotism (the exercise of any will that is individual or particular, rather than national or general). And whereas the administrative discourse dissolved sovereignty into the rule of reason – thus transforming government into the enlightened management of the autonomous mechanisms of individual choice and collective decision that comprise society – the political discourse reclaimed sovereignty in the name of the collectivity of the nation as a whole.

As I have tried to suggest elsewhere, the tension among these discourses drove the political struggles of the Old Regime that culminated in the great crisis of 1788 and 1789. The Revolution, one might say, became the way in which these tensions were resolved (and others were created) by a political rehierarchization and recombination of elements within those discourses. The discourse of justice was transformed into the rights of the individual subjects produced by the administrative state, just as the administrative discourse of reason was combined with the political discourse of will. *Surveillance* was fused with *sovereignty* to produce the logic of *transparence*.

From this perspective, the emergence of "public opinion" as a new form of authority, which I have also discussed in another context,[25] might take on a new significance. After mid-century, the tribunal of public opinion became the instance of last resort in the new oppositional politics that came to characterize the Old Regime in its last decades. But, if public opinion was invoked by all the actors in these constitutional conflicts, it is notable that its most systematic theorists appeared on the ministerial side. Necker's discussion of the concept in his *De l'administration des finances de la France*, taken up and elaborated by Peuchet in his dictionary of *Police* for the *Encyclopédie méthodique*, conferred upon the force of public opinion all the essential features of a rationalized absolutist authority. Public opinion now cast the new light in which the actions of all estates and conditions, rulers and ruled, were to be judged. Given its universality, objectivity, rationality, tranquillity, and transparence, all would be revealed in an apolitical politics where the shadows of arbitrary will would necessarily be dispersed by the power of truth. Perhaps it does not stretch the imagination too far to see in this notion of public opinion a political version of the principles of panopticism analyzed by Foucault in *Discipline and Punish* and elsewhere. It is certainly remarkable that, when the Revolution came, the practice of political denunciation – when it became a patriotic duty – was closely linked to the theory of public opinion.[26] The denouncer had the right, and obligation, to expose the obscure treacheries of each and every individual to the light of the new political panopticon. Denunciation, one might even say, was the democratization of surveillance.

Among the issues referred to the tribunal of public opinion in the last decades of the Old Regime none were more dramatic than the celebrated court cases that became the *causes célèbres* of the pre-revolutionary period. These trials suggest another condition of possibility that might loom large in any Foucauldian account of the French Revolution: the appearance, at the end of the Old Regime, of a phenomenon that might be called *political subjectivity*. Part of this phenomenon obviously involves notions of individual citizenship as a subject position that came into play as a monarchical government seeking to extend the reach of its tax policies found opponents increasingly determined to resist them. The conditions for the transformation of subjects into citizens became the central issue in the extended conflict over taxation and representation that led up to the events of 1789. The Revolution resolved that issue dramatically, but within the context of an intense moralization and personalization of politics. In this context, a universalized conflict of values was symbolically represented and collectively experienced at the level of the individual personality. Good and evil were subjectivized and given an individual human face in the form of violated personal virtue and monstrous personal vice. These are the features of the revolutionary political morality that I wish to highlight in using the term *political subjectivity*.

Several expressions of this subjectivization of politics can already be identified on the eve of the Revolution. The most obvious might be the increasingly radical and explicit personal defamations of individual members of the royal family and other members of the court. The pre-revolutionary attacks upon Marie-Antoinette immediately spring to mind in this context.[27] Less well known, but no less telling, are the increasingly virulent denunciations of royal ministers. Maupeou and Calonne, for example, became the targets of campaigns of vilification that were striking in their violence. In the case of Maupeou, that very personification of ministerial despotism in the 1770s, the minister also became the imagined victim of fantasies of physical violence in which he was ripped apart by an avenging crowd and the remnants of his body were cast to the dogs.[28] A discourse of expiatory popular violence was already spreading in the political culture of the Old Regime, well before it was acted out, at the time of the Fall of the Bastille, in the massacre of such agents of "despotism" as Flesselles, Foulon, and Bertier de Sauvigny. Barnave gave revolutionary legitimation to Old Regime impulses in his celebrated question regarding these deaths: "This blood, was it so pure?"

The Fall of the Bastille suggests yet another aspect of the appearance of a discourse of political subjectivity in the decades preceding the Revolution. Well before 1789, as the researches of Reichardt and Lüsebrink have made clear, the fortress of the Bastille had already come to epitomize the crushing weight of royal despotism, as had the inhabitants of its dungeons the fate of those unhappy souls who fell victim to the evil of arbitrary and corrupt power pervading an entire social order.[29] It makes little difference that so few of these archetypical political victims were actually to be found when the dungeons were thrown open in July 1789. Within the oppositional political culture of the Old Regime, the Bastille had arisen, and was now to fall, as the ultimate instrument of political victimization. The discursive production of victims – Foucault might have called it the *Bastille effect* – became one of the most remarkable features of the subjectivization of politics at the end of the Old Regime.

Why this dramatic personalization of politics? Several possible explanations might be imagined. The first might point to relatively traditional elements in the situation: the fact that personal attacks upon a ruler or those closely surrounding him might be expected to provide the vehicle for opposition within a political system where public power was literally embodied in the person of a monarch; the fact that at least some of the clandestine political literature of the period sought to continue the personal maneuvering of court factions by other means. But it nevertheless seems to be the case that the politics of personal vilification became more intense and widespread in the last decades of the Old Regime, perhaps paradoxically in response to the progressive depersonalization of royal power that occurred with administrative centralization. As the king's mystical body was progressively dissolved into an administrative system separate from his natural body, the personal passions imputed to this (merely) natural body could be exploited within a discourse of political opposition. Similarly, the more thoroughly power was refashioned in the name of reason, the more critical became the insistence that this *bureaucratie* was at bottom profoundly, and viciously, personal – the expression simply of the compounded arbitrariness of a thousand petty despots exercising their wills in the name of the king. The demonization of power in the persons of the ministers and their agents thus became a strategy of opposition to the rationalization and expansion of the institutions of the administrative state.

If the demonization of the agents of power was one aspect of the subjectivization of politics in the last decades of the Old Regime, then the beatification of its victims was another. To understand this phenomenon more fully, we must return to the fact that the most potent machine for the production of the discourse of victimization became the judicial system and the publicity surrounding its most notorious cases. The importance of these *causes célèbres* in pre-revolutionary political culture has been made progressively clearer in recent years by the research of Sarah Maza.[30] Their existence depended upon the fact that written trial-briefs presented by barristers on behalf of their clients had long been considered privileged speech under the legal system of the Old Regime and could therefore be printed and circulated, legally and rapidly, without prior censorship. But their celebrity derived from the manner in which the authors of these judicial *mémoires* used them to portray a continuing social melodrama in which hapless victims fell prey to evil predators, virtue fell prey to vice, innocence to corruption, liberty to despotism, bourgeois modesty to aristocratic pride. This novel forensic rhetoric drew directly, as Maza clearly demonstrates, upon the new theory and practice of the melodrama to moralize, subjectivize, and intensify the politics of everyday life. It condensed the evils of the Old Regime into a new kind of political morality tale, a Manichean drama in which an aristo-despotic monster violated the rights, and the virtue, of an outraged humanity.

Voltaire and Beaumarchais were among the writers to demonstrate the political potential of this new literary form. But most judicial *mémoires* were written not by playwrights but by barristers, the court lawyers who spent much of the eighteenth century attempting (as the recent work of David Bell has shown[31]) to free the practice of the bar from the control of the parlementary magistrates and to redefine their status as professional men of the law. In this situation, the discourse of victimization served a key function. The production of victims, one might say, was part of a professionalizing strategy in which barristers presented themselves no longer as servants of the court, but as public spokesmen for violated humanity. As the barristers became the defenders of universal justice before the bar of public opinion, so they reconstituted their clientele as victims, personalizing the effects of evil in a corrupt social order. Seen from this perspective, victims were the product of the professionalizing barristers, just as criminals became the product of the professionalizing criminologists. Victims were not "normalized" subjects in the Foucauldian sense; instead, they were "denormalized" subjects, virtuous citizens who had become the objects of arbitrary political will and social oppression. They were the afflicted form of the new political subject, personalized proof of the need for an entire regeneration of the social body.

The invention of society; the production of the social body; conflicting discourses of power; the panopticism of "public opinion"; the appearance of political subjectivity: these, then, would seem to offer some of the conditions of possibility that a Foucauldian account of the French Revolution might identify. It would still be necessary in such an account to show how these conditions of possibility were transformed into the particular technologies of power that came to characterize the Revolution as a political phenomenon. But that would involve an analysis of the strategies and tactics that created the revolutionary moment in 1789: the strategies that defined the frontiers of political conflict, the tactics that defined, and redefined, the subject positions brought into play. It would require us, in the last analysis, to return to the level of actors and events.

IV A HISTORY OF THE PRESENT?

A Foucauldian account of the French Revolution, finally, would also be a "history of the present." It would need to seek in the historical phenomenon of the Revolution the genealogy of specific features of contemporary life. To the extent that the account were cast in terms of the opposition between sovereignty and surveillance, it might therefore conclude by asking whether (and how) the Revolution fixed the relationship between these two forms of power still operational in modern society. More specifically, it might ask what (if anything) in the Revolution contributed to the manner in which sovereignty continues to coexist with that other form of power that "ought by rights" to have led to its disappearance. In the language suggested by Laura Engelstein in chapter 12, this is to inquire into why, at least in Foucault's France, discipline remained "framed by law."

Why, in any case, did Foucault believe that the appearance of the techniques of power he associated with surveillance should logically have led to the disappearance of those he associated with sovereignty? The answer is built into the technological metaphor itself. As Foucault presents the argument in *Discipline and Punish*, the techniques of surveillance are simply more efficient than the techniques of sovereignty: they can achieve more at less cost. Surveillance (or *discipline*, the term Foucault uses more frequently in this text) can do more by invisibly "fabricating" individuals for an enlightened modern society than can sovereignty by visibly constraining subjects within a traditional one. It can reach further into the density of human existence, aggregating individuals into greater social masses, moving them with less force. Thus a new " 'technological' threshold," of efficiency is crossed in the eighteenth century when it becomes possible to "substitute for a power that is manifested through the brilliance of those who exercise it, a power that insidiously objectifies those on whom it is applied; to form a body of knowledge about these individuals, rather than to deploy the ostentatious signs of sovereignty."[32] And since more efficient technologies, once invented, must necessarily drive out the less efficient, sovereignty must necessarily be replaced (or colonized from within) by surveillance.

One might indeed argue that the process Foucault outlined in *Discipline and Punish* was already quite evident within the French monarchy of the eighteenth century. Certainly, many of the techniques of surveillance appeared under the aegis of monarchical power, emanating as they did from its institutions of administration and police, and theorized in its academies and committees. At the same time, royal administrators sought to regenerate power through knowledge, transforming the irregular and intermittent effects of royal will into the more efficient rule of reason. Thus one might well see in the program of enlightened absolutism at the end of the Old Regime precisely the blueprint for that substitution of surveillance for sovereignty that should have occurred according to the logic of Foucault's analysis. Why, then, did it not occur? Is there a more plausible historical explanation than Foucault's problematic assertion that sovereignty simply continued to be useful as a kind of superstructural justification for the advance of surveillance? And might the French Revolution have anything to do with it?

On the one hand, of course, the Revolution shattered the administrative dream of transforming sovereignty into surveillance under the aegis of the monarchy. On the other, it completely recharged and revivified the ancient notion of sovereignty by identifying it with popular will. In the name of popular sovereignty, as Tocqueville was among the first to point out, power was concentrated, masses were mobilized, and social resources were levied and deployed on a scale unprecedented in the annals of monarchical administration. Foucault might well have found in this phenomenon the proof of his contention that democratized sovereignty served the ends of surveillance precisely by destroying the obstacles hindering the development of disciplinary society.[33] He would certainly have pointed to the normalization of individuals practiced in the Revolution's schools, armies, hospitals, and asylums as citizens were fabricated for a new – and rational – republic. And with Tocqueville he would have seen the Revolution as laying the ground for the Napoleonic regime, that "point of junction of the monarchical, ritual exercise of sovereignty and the hierarchical, permanent exercise of individual discipline."[34]

But the Revolution, as it amplified the power that sovereignty could achieve through its democratization, also made it infinitely more dangerous. The Terror demonstrated not only the energies unleashed by generalizing the sovereign will but the excesses that could result. And in post-revolutionary discourse the experience of the Terror came, above all, to symbolize the constant threat of sovereign will – that scourge, as Benjamin Constant put it, with which the revolutionaries had afflicted an entire society. In this reaction against the excesses of sovereignty, surveillance – in the form of the rational authority of the disciplines – could find an enhanced legitimacy, as it did (for example) in the manifestos of those great prophets of the disciplinary society, Saint-Simon and Comte. The disciplines, one might argue, derived much of their power in the nineteenth century from the fact that they could be discursively constituted as the very antithesis of power: as a form of authority based on reason rather than will, on scientific knowledge rather than arbitrary contrivance, on a recognition and acceptance of cognitive mandates rather than on the political dynamics of consent and constraint. The greater the power of sovereignty, then, the greater the force that surveillance could assume in contradistinction to it. Thus it might well be that, in raising the power of sovereignty, the French Revolution also extended the reach of the disciplines. It might well be that, among its other historical effects, the Revolution served to fix the relationship between sovereignty and surveillance still obtaining in modern society: a kind of dialectical relationship in which neither form of power serves as superstructural justification for the other, but each draws a supercharge from the institutionalized opposition between them.

11

Governing Poverty: Sources of the Social Question in Nineteenth-Century France

Giovanna Procacci

In a chapter of *Histoire de la folie* Foucault argues that a new poor policy removing the poor from the *hôpital général*[1] played an important role in the spatial segregation of madness and the emergence of psychiatry. Economic crises in eighteenth-century France and England were eroding the efficiency of traditional policies of assistance, which were based on charity and on the incarceration of the poor together with the mad and the sick. "Little by little, poverty was extricated from the old moral confusions . . . indigence became a matter of economics."[2] And, indeed, Turgot's reforms in France as well as Gilbert's Act in England presented confinement as a "dangerous mode of financing," immobilizing wealth in foundations instead of responding to new demands for its circulation.[3] Traditional policy was increasingly criticized. "The eighteenth century discovered that the Poor do not exist, that under this rubric two fundamentally different realities had too long been confounded": poverty on the one hand, population on the other.[4] But, in the view of the economists, population was virtually equivalent to wealth. Valorizing population therefore became a central political task, while supporting poor people was seen in the final analysis only as a tragic waste of resources.

The world of the *hôpital général* was breaking down. For the first time, illness and poverty were distinguished from one another; madness remained isolated within the walls of the *hôpital général*, its placement there reinforced by the authority of medical discourse. In the ruins of this old institution, a new social role for the poor was taking shape: free labor became the key to a new policy of assistance which was to be adopted by the Revolution, though it had been elaborated well before 1789.

At this juncture, traditional forms of assistance started to appear as themselves a cause of poverty because they opposed the absorption of poverty into labor. This recognition in turn made possible a moral rehabilitation of the poor, one that was expected to open the way to their economic and social integration. Was this shift in the conception of poverty only a consequence of economic crises, as Foucault seems to suggest? Or can one credit such a shift with revealing, as madness did, crucial features of more general transformations occurring at that time? Although Foucault did not elaborate on this change in the status of poverty, perhaps because of his own reluctance to deal directly with political economy, his later work on liberalism, mostly in his lectures at the Collège de France, does suggest a richer frame of meaning in which such a new conception of poverty can be situated.

To analyse the effect that the need to contend with poverty had on the making of a liberal society in France requires that we reverse the more ordinary view that links liberalism with its policy of producing wealth. In the late eighteenth and early nineteenth centuries, the conception of poverty changed together with other crucial, longstanding transformations of political rationality. Poverty became an issue for society as a whole: no longer exclusively identified with mendicity and vagrancy, it was designated as the "social question." In the course of the shift from religious charity to secular social policies, the core of the problem of poverty came to be seen less as the blighted destiny of the poor than as the coexistence of poverty with the project of expanding wealth. In fact, the "social question" was to reveal that, contrary to the beliefs of eighteenth-century reformers, liberal individualistic principles were not readily compatible with a concern for the public good.[5]

The new policy toward the social question was aimed at moralizing the poor as well as treating poverty as one of the so-called population problems. As Foucault has shown, population emerged simultaneously as a scientific and a political issue, as the result of biological inquiry and power techniques. It became the concern of a bio-power directed to the life of a collective body, intervening in the matter of how people live, instead of limiting its action to preventing them from dying, as in the juridical, "negative" pattern of power associated with classical liberalism. Arising at the conjunction of a moralizing impulse and a sanitary perspective concerning population, the new poor policy thus introduced concerns about social organization different from the concerns typically brought to bear by liberal theory. It therefore offers an opportunity to test some of the central notions of Foucault's later work on power and liberalism – particularly through a focus on the notion of *government*, which expressed, according to

Foucault, that mixture of procedures of individualization and regulation characteristic of the modern power structure. Ultimately, an analysis of the political impact of poverty on the making of French liberal society can throw new light on the organization of wealth,[6] just as Foucault's analysis of madness threw new light on the construction of the category "reason."

I A NEW POOR POLICY

To claim a discontinuity in society's treatment (both conceptual and practical) of poverty from the mendicant haunting the Old Regime to the modern poor requires that we do not consider poverty as a natural object. The poor, of course, have always existed, yet they have been identified with a constantly changing problem of poverty.

A problem, as Paul Veyne has shown, is for Foucault a matter of *mise en relation*, the effect of a practice inseparable from that problem.[7] Poverty and madness do not in themselves exist. What exists is their relation to society. To bring this relation to light requires looking at what people actually do with poverty or with madness, without presuming any preexisting aim; it requires investigating only the effects of their practice. In the "rarity" or scarcity of historical objects, in the interstices between things and facts, a practice takes place, favored by a malleability enabling unusual combinations.

From this point of view, poverty can only be the "objectivation" of a practice. That poor people exist is not a sufficient warrant for treating poverty as a "social question." Mendicants, widows, journeymen, prostitutes, ragmen, workers: they are not all poor in the same way, nor are they recognized as poor by the same practices. Only when, as within the context of liberalism, poverty is no longer viewed simply as begging and vagrancy and is connected to the organization of a free labor market do all these individuals become "poor." Poverty as a "social question" is an effect of a liberal practice of wealth, of rights, and of population. Public hygiene, universal manhood suffrage, labor discipline, savings policy, organization of assistance, all become in a liberal society grist for the mill of poverty.

It is not only the perception of poverty, then, that has changed: the problem itself has changed. That problem now consists in analyzing the mass pauperism that accompanies the making of a modern economic system. The object is, then, itself relative, or "relatively unstable," as Jan Goldstein says.[8] Genealogy shakes the assurance we have about historical objects. Poverty has not always meant the same thing, and genealogy takes seriously those shifts in meaning, instead of holding that the "social question" is ultimately reducible to the general question of poverty. The object and its signification are in fact fused in a genealogical analysis. Together they delimit the problem, under specific conditions. The eruption of a "social question" responded to specific circumstances; it was, so to speak, *l'affaire d'un moment*: what a modern industrial society could conceive as poverty. Here, poverty is interpreted in a grid of analysis defined less by religion than by economic, political, and social categories. Such categories impose on those who accept them the duty to investigate the causes of and solutions to poverty, but the duty in question is less one of religious piety than of a policy designed to foster social stability.

This grid of analysis is, though, not a matter of "ideas" about poverty in Gertrude Himmelfarb's sense,[9] as the *arrière-pensées* one can guess behind the facts, or the essentially intellectual materials introduced by analysts of poverty. There are, of course, people involved in the analysis of poverty, and they do intervene in one way or another in its transformation. Still, problematizing poverty implies focusing less on these active subjects than on the field of political, social, and intellectual interactions that define the process well beyond the intentions and will of any actor. If poverty is the objectivation of a practice, at stake in its definition as a social question is liberalism's "mode of operation"[10] with respect to it.

In the compulsion to define the *agency* that is so diffuse nowadays in social science, there is a tendency to dismiss the fact that all elements of a historical transformation do not perfectly coincide: actors, discourses, practices, intended and unintended effects, can go their separate ways, as Albert Hirschman has shown.[11] "Ça ne se passe jamais comme c'était prévu," says Foucault.[12] The very fact that such elements fail to correspond is itself significant. In the gaps between them, one can discover the *conditions of possibility* of a new conception of poverty. The problem of poverty is historically defined as a "social question" only "under the positive conditions of a complex group of relations."[13] Those conditions are a "prediscursive referent": not only discourse, yet indispensable for speaking about the "social question." They are local and make specific forms perceptible,[14] they render the transformation irreducible to individual actions, and precede any group's interest in it.

Conditions of possibility have little to do with abstract reason. Instead of arguing for rationalization of social spheres hitherto untouched by reason, they rather stress a relative, not a value-laden, sense of the term *rationality*.[15] To be rational means only to be adequate to the set of conditions within which it is possible, at a given period, to deal with a problem. This refers not to reason but to strategy: combining different interests, points of view and aims, "cumulating advantages and multiplying benefits."[16] And above all it includes the possibility of a *rationalité de l'abominable* – a rationality governing the horror of madness, poverty, prison, and the like – that Michelle Perrot regarded as one of the most difficult Foucauldian notions for historians.[17]

For an investigator in quest of "conditions of possibility," then, history is needed for the purpose of localization and problematization, and offers no support for arguing a growing rationality of things. The "agency" position stresses the need to specify the actors who are subjectively at work in a historical transformation. By contrast, the "conditions of possibility" position collects all the socially available elements that make the trans-formation conceivable and feasible. Possibility is a crucial concept in Foucault's analytical work on power: specific conditions are rooted in a range of possibilities constituting both their content and their limits. Therefore all practice can only be a strategic choice made against another possible choice, and as such it assumes some sort of indetermination. This is but another aspect of the "relative instability" already mentioned.

The question is, therefore, to look at all the elements that were available to liberalism for acting on poverty in order to restore the frame of political rationality in which poverty could be treated, both conceptually and practically, during the late eighteenth and early nineteenth centuries. Without coinciding, elements of theory, doctrine, and practice all take part in the definition of the "social question." Important among these elements is the link of traditional poverty with the absolute monarchy and the coherence of charitable relief within the framework of political despotism and economic protectionism. Against such coherence, eighteenth-century rationalism invented the concept of *bienfaisance*[18] to express the secular concern about poverty already at work in Turgot's institutional reforms. Assistance to the poor became a "national debt," a duty for society. An ethical faith, then, in the capacity of *labor* to produce a social order against the disorder of despotism made poverty the opposite of labor, which was the uniquely legitimate mode of self-support and, therefore, also of poor relief. In the context of the Revolution, the war, and conscription, the govern-ment's alliance with the poor became indispensable to defeat despotism. Therefore, the contrast of poverty with the new privileges of wealth after the Revolution was all the more striking, and the destruction of feudal privilege proved insufficient actually to transform the poor into free subjects. Furthermore, the new economic and political rules of a liberal society were transforming them into an utterly new kind of subject. Namely, the poor could no longer be submitted to a regime of tutelage (*tutelle*) as pre-revolutionary mendicants had been. Nor could they be ejected from society; they were after all individuals just like everyone else – morally and juridically autonomous, the subjects of fundamental rights. The poor had to be included in a juridical attribution of rights. Beside the continuing concern with public order, a new concern arose about the role the poor might play, or refuse to play, once integrated as *whole citizens*. Such a concern imposed an obligation to intervene in the area of poverty in an organic and concerted way.

Yet the poor were still disappointingly poor. Depopulation of the countryside and de-Christianization were directly affecting their resources, while the Revolution's fiscal measures produced only a very limited redistribution of income.[19] The poor inevitably reintroduced a manifest inequality, whose necessity was supposedly grounded in a society based on equality. It would be too simple to reduce the difficulty into an opposition between a formal level of equality and a factual inequality. The difficulty came less from the inequality the poor so blatantly showed than from their *being equal* to everyone else, despite their destitution. Already at the formal level of equality the impossibility of excluding the poor was contradicting the universal character of liberalism's egalitarian foundations. Moreover, a free labor market proved incapable of actually reabsorbing poverty and hence was no solution. On the one hand, a duty of assistance accomplished through the provision of employment would have called upon the state to intervene in the labor market as an economic agent, contrary to the liberal aversion to any political interference with economic processes. On the other hand, to acknowledge a subjective right to work would have put the state in the position of being considered responsible for the material means of livelihood, reinforcing its political dependence upon popular consent. The link between poverty and labor, self-evident for liberal theory, actually heightened the political intensity of the social question.

The liberal strategy with respect to the social question was thus oriented by an effort to *depoliticize* it by breaking such a link. It became crucial to separate the question of poverty from claims about labor and about subjective rights, and to attempt to conceive of poverty in terms neither economic nor juridical – that is, in terms outside liberal theory. Liberalism's impasse in matters of assistance depended on the impossibility of preferring arbitrary almsgiving to the certainty of legislation, while the liberal creed could not tolerate the state commitment implicit in the latter. The original economic interpretation, based simply on the link between poverty and labor, was thus elaborated in conjunction with other elements: a moral element that had been developed to dissimulate society's political revolt against despotism,[20] and public hygiene, derived from a "medical police" tradition. These additional elements proved to be strategic in diverting the responsibility for poverty from the economic system by establishing that the reform had to be of a moral nature.

The distinction between a natural, uneliminable poverty and pauperism was a moral distinction. Pauperism, an unnatural excess of poverty, consisted not in material but in moral destitution: a set of asocial habits and behaviors, of differences marking a "culture of poverty" that liberalism would replace by a culture of work. It was in everyone's interest that pauperism be eliminated. A large program of socialization, a disciplinary pedagogy, was to socialize the behaviors of poverty through such techniques as association, education, savings, mutualism, and hygiene. Without denying individual interest as the basis of the economic system, philanthropic techniques made pragmatic reference to some kind of collective interest or moral community that was neither economic (related to the market) nor juridical (related to contractualism). The result was an intermediate position between the rigidity of a classical liberal model incapable of any reform, and the need for social reform that industrial pauperism demonstrably required. The principle of *relief* and not of labor was adopted as an assistance policy. A mixed system of centralized supervision and decentralized *assistance à domicile* was the institutional device created for this purpose, ensuring that the state remained in the background while primary responsibility fell to the communal organization.

The moral analysis of poverty, avoiding both the crisis of the classical economic model and the impasses of the juridical system of natural and positive rights and duties, introduced two main outcomes. On the one hand, the moralistic interpretation of poverty acquired new meanings: if poverty was still regarded as in part the "fault of the poor," it began to seem possible to *moralize society as a whole* by means of the techniques inspired by the treatment of poverty. On the other hand, a new demand emerged to probe the *causes of pauperism*. Together, these outcomes led to an analysis of the social question which was the effect of a practice of depoliticizing problems of inequality in a society of equals: that analysis described inequality as a difference in sociability or in the level of socialization.

II   FROM INEQUALITY TO SOCIALIZATION

As Foucault often stressed, studying "procedures of exclusion" can help to bring to light the political and economic advantages of power strategies.[21] Procedures of exclusion are in the end a way of including, not through juridical rules but through social scientific norms. Beyond madness and poverty, one can see a process of normalization. Through an emphasis on moral reform, the inclusion of the poor turned into a disciplinary action aimed at restoring a "normal" relation between wealth and poverty.

As for the general causes of poverty, liberal social theory hardly offered more insight than a general connection with labor: either a person works or has to be morally educated to work. Such a connection, however, was of little political use because it could lead only to individual pedagogy, while society's interest in eliminating poverty could not rely merely on the good will of the poor to work. The analysis of poverty, therefore, was forced to take other paths. The most relevant was "social pathology," which developed under the influence of the Enlightenment conviction that the physical element had a primary influence over the moral and psychological. To have created new physical conditions of production without fostering a corresponding new moral ethos appeared as a grounding for pathological developments.

Pathology enters a consideration of poverty as a social question as soon as poverty is placed among the collective phenomena accompanying the life of a *population* – birth, death, sickness, hygiene, and accidents. Such phenomena only become significant through global estimations, inspiring procedures aimed at influencing the forces that determine the general phenomenon – the causes of mortality instead of death, the causes of pauperism instead of destitution. This shift opened what Foucault called "the era of epidemics,"[22] the medical configuration of a society centered on *security* techniques.

Public hygiene offered the advantage of a longed-for science directly connected to a moralizing perspective. At stake was a medical definition of modern civilization: hygiene did not track down offenders, but rather studied the influence of various circumstances on the state of civilization. The French hygienist Louis-René Villermé described *epidemics* in terms of a "concomitance," an occasion for the same illness to affect a large number of people at the same time.[23] As Foucault noted, the problem of epidemiology was to find the specific process, never the same, that wove a common texture through all the victims of the illness.[24] Epidemics were simultaneously a collective phenomenon and a unique process. The only way to investigate both aspects at once was to inquire into the epidemic's recurrences, its statistical regularities, probability curves, and the causes influencing the infection. "To know the size and features of the population well, including not only the ratio of deaths to births but also the average age and the expected lifespan, is for governments a matter as important as all those on which they ordinarily lavish more attention."[25]

The main concern was the influence of epidemics on population. Villermé did not believe a clinical solution was possible: vaccines might save some people but, without a general improvement in socio-economic conditions, others would die in their place. A family, said Villermé, can be satisfied if its particular members escape death, whereas a victory of this sort "does not matter for a state": the state's problem is not death, but rather the mortality *rate* and all the factors that influence it.[26] Only social factors have a real influence. Epidemics allowed a crucial discovery – that is, they affected the population in different degrees, and affected most acutely those "who take the least part in the advantages brought about by industry."[27] Because of their social selectivity, epidemics brought attention back to the analysis of the poverty question and inspired its first statistical descriptions. In this way, epidemics helped to measure "the medical distance that separated the rich and the poor."[28]

Why are the poor more susceptible to epidemics? Because, said the early nineteenth-century hygienists, they are immoral. Yet the hygienists described this immorality in physical terms: as a germ that the poor carry on their persons and as a space that favors its transmission. Thus immorality itself assumes an epidemic character and becomes a natural carrier of infection. The only effective mode of intervention is on the space where contagion occurs and where conditions for moral improvement can become effective. Through the medium of space, immorality spread out indefinitely: unhealthy conditions, famines, seasonal influences, bad air, and atmospheric heat were all ways in which the physical space was said to become a decisive factor. In the "epidemic era," a modern notion of population is submitted to the action of the natural environment.

Treatment of the "social question" by means of public hygiene follows the epidemic model. As a social danger, poverty is contagious, and the main point is to stop its effects by erecting barriers in the space where it operates. If the pathology of poverty consists in asocial behaviors, the transmission of such behaviors must be limited even before the casual germs of asociability in the poor are eradicated. In fact, the practical aim is not to eradicate poverty, but to regulate its diffusion. In this way it becomes possible to respond to the immorality of the poor by moralizing the whole of society through a network of social obligations.

Population, environment, and all the concerns of a bio-power regulating phenomena which affect the life of a collective body develop the analysis of the social question outside the bounds of liberal theory. Even more, they are likely to conflict with a liberal model of society, difficult to reconcile with individual rights and conducive to excessive government. Foucault regarded liberalism as "a form of critical reflection on governmental practice" from below, oriented against government's excess and, therefore, toward internal limitation.[29]

As Colin Gordon has shown, concern with government is for Foucault tantamount to moving the focus of political theory from institutions to practices.[30] To govern means "to structure the possible field of action of others,"[31] a form of activity aimed at shaping other people's conduct. At the other end of the relation, the individual is not the counterpart of the power governing him or her, but is "one of its prime effects."[32] Thanks to the field of possibilities offered to individual action, there is always something that goes beyond government. In this sense only, one can say that "there is no power without potential refusal or revolt."[33] This means that subjects and their liberty are internal to government; liberty is "a present relation between the governing and the governed," and not a concern reserved to liberal regimes. Yet such a placement of the subject within the govern-mental relationship raises problems from the vantage point of the liberal definition of individual,[34] and even more so from the vantage point of liberal patterns of socialization.

Foucault analyzed the contradictions introduced into liberal society by two different subjects and their modes of socialization, the subject of interests and the subject of rights.[35] The former never cedes his or her interests and socializes through their spontaneous multiplication. The latter associates with others by renouncing his or her rights and accepting submission. Within this framework, the problem of politics was to identify a social space common to both subjects. Foucault proposed to read the notion of *civil society*, originally aimed at limiting state action, as a specific technique of government responding to this problem. As a specific technique of government, civil society ceases to be the opposite of the state, and becomes instead a reference to all techniques attributing socialization neither to interests nor to rights. Civil society regulates non-juridical, non-economic relationships on a localized, communitarian basis more than on a universal, humanitarian one.

The social question was the first field of a political application of this "art of government" oriented toward civil society. Far from applying liberal imperatives, a strategy to govern the social takes shape from a critique of the liberal notions of interest and right. Given the impossibility of facing poverty squarely from inside the narrow range of individual *interests*, the government of the social refers to practices integrating individual interests through a sort of "disinterested interest" oriented towards the collective rather than the individual and disinterested with respect to the latter. Yet it was difficult to define the collective point of view responsible for such an interest. On the other side, responding to the social question in terms of *rights* would lead to a strong state, able to protect its citizens from the consequences of social inequality. Moreover, to introduce inequality into the language of rights would inevitably open questions about "the ability to exercise positive rights," as in the theory of the "right to work" put forth in 1848. Thus the government of the social elaborated a strategy around the notion of *duty*, which was to regulate the limits between interest and disinterest and to replace the notion of right at the basis of social reciprocity. The political answer to the "social question" was thus not an individual right to assistance and labor, but a general "duty of society" to favor labor, a duty to which, as Joseph Garnier noted, "no individual right corresponds."[36] Duty became the regulator of the "social tie," the key to disciplined sociability and to global patterns of socialization, as was confirmed by the authoritative works of social science on "social solidarity" from Auguste Comte onwards.[37] Duty permitted the linkage of *omnes et singulatim*, the character at once totalizing and individualizing of modern political rationality.

In so doing, the government of poverty has played a crucial role in shaping the political landscape of modern societies. It has been at the origin of *the social*, a field of practices, institutions, and knowledge: treating society as a moral and not a contractual community, it has opposed to liberalism non-liberal patterns of sociability. The moral element eventually proved to be a way-station toward a social analysis of poverty. The strategic conjunction of economy, philanthropy, and police could then consolidate in a social science, finally being able to establish methods and rules to build up rigorous models of sociability. Furthermore, the government of the social promoted a transformation of our societies, from democracies founded on the rights of each, into democracies founded on the duties of everyone toward everyone.

III WRITING HISTORY TODAY

Michelle Perrot sees the uneasy relations between Foucault's theoretical work and the work of historians as rooted in the reluctance of historians to replace causality with a "science of effects."[38] Yet effects illustrate Foucault's use of history for a "history of the present," which is exactly what has made history in the Foucauldian mode appealing to non-historians and has given a sense of "youthfulness" to historical research, to use Jacques Léonard's expression.[39] As for poverty, its status as a "social question" today seems increasingly called into doubt – the result of a revival of the individualistic interpretation of the causes of and solution to poverty. Particularly in the United States, the current debate on the crisis of welfare policies often denies the social nature of the problem of poverty. Such a denial enhances the interest of an analysis of the transformation that first made poverty a social question. Effects allow us to move into history from a "diagnosis of the present," as Robert Castel says.[40]

By replacing causality with a consideration of effects, and universals with practices, genealogy makes possible a rational critique of the present, not a rationalization of it, but a pluralism of rationalities.[41] Effects are the localizations that genealogical criticism opposes to global theories, making room for a great deal of neglected knowledge and lost memories. Effects are also what allow problematization, and the rupture of objects only underscores the continuity of problems. One might evoke Foucault's words to define the peculiarity of his own "mode of operation" by contrast to that of historians: "One [that of historians] consists of taking an object and trying to resolve the problems it poses. The other consists of treating a problem and, starting there, determining the domain of objects that must be traversed in order to resolve it."[42] Treating a problem as an effect shows, surprisingly, that historical materials are never better articulated in their meaning than when we are presently involved in them. They have been cut within a range of possibilities, the meaning of which has never been exhausted. This relieves the sense of determinism and enhances possibility, here and now. As Foucault once said, if one tries to "listen to history," one learns that "behind things there is quite a different thing." At the origin, one only finds the dissimilar.[43]

Some of Foucault's work on history has by now been implicitly accepted – above all, the attention he drew to eighteenth-century socio-political inventiveness, traditionally underestimated because of the lure of the Revolution. Historiography, though, seems to have been diverted from the crucial direction that Foucault gave to genealogical research: to bring to light a fundamental relation between truth and life, or, better put, between truth and contingency, error, struggle, all the things that give a shape to life.[44]

In recent years, ideas seem to have regained, in historians' eyes, some sort of independence from practice. They are most often treated as essentially intellectual constructs, related to a "high philosophical debate" where, presumably, only the real substance of a transformation can appear, thus eventually marking all processes with which they are involved as exclusively intellectual. As a result, permanent historical objects are emerging again, no longer "rare" nor relatively unstable, and problematization is losing ground.

This is particularly the case of the history of the French Revolution, an event directly affecting the sources of a strategy toward the social question. According to the French "new historiography" which dominated the bicentennial celebrations of 1789, the political dynamics of the Revolution consist mainly in a series of oppositions: concepts, dates, and actors are opposed to one another rather than interpreted through their interactions within the context of a problem. Such oppositions favor the claim for the exclusively intellectual nature of political events, but they do not account for the development of a social perspective on political conflicts. Let us look at the concepts crucial to this process. The "new historiography" treats equality and inequality as two series of problems entirely separate from one another. Exclusively formal, equality does not need to be transformed into any institutional practice; it belongs to the realm of social imagination. By contrast, all practical political problems are on the side of inequality: here differences must be organized in order to render viable a social order flattened by equality. By choosing to speak of difference instead of inequality, proponents of the new historiography imply that equality is a claim for identity, to be contrasted with differentiation, a process of social organization needing no philosophical foundations and having only the functional connotations it assumes in sociology's creed. Subjectively, this would be experienced as an opposition between the individual and the citizen, since in the context of the Revolution, and especially of the year 1793, the "participation [of the citizen] in the public good turned ferociously against [individual] liberties."[45] Something is missing in this analysis, though – namely what the government of the social has brought to light: in its liberal definition, individual liberty seems in turn to coexist uneasily with participation in the public good, thus interfering with the power of individuals to influence their own destiny.

Separating fraternity, in turn, from equality and liberty, the new historiography describes it as being "open and euphoric," never demanding modification of the theory of rights.[46] In this view, fraternity would have not been a big issue had the Jacobins not transformed it into a vigorous act simultaneously revealing brothers and enemies: fraternity thus became coincident with the coercion exercised by the general over the individual will, "where the reference to the individual has totally disappeared to the advantage of the social whole." A so-called "expansive" fraternity is barely mentioned, only to regret that it merely consisted in relieving the poor. Yet the community of brothers always implies some further distinction, reintroducing separation independently of the Jacobins' intentions. "Everybody who works," as Lindet defines that community:[47] but not everybody is working, and fraternity, as a consequence, becomes contradictory. Relieving the poor, then, is not a narrow view of fraternity. Rather, it goes to the heart of political problems. If everybody is equal, and all are "brothers," how can those who are in fact excluded by the constraints of poverty be integrated into the brotherhood? Political problems of fraternity arise precisely from the ties of that concept with equality and liberty, and fraternity in turn shows the problematic nature of equality and liberty. Of course, the idea of fraternity was not exempt from illusions concerning *l'homme nouveau*. But the problems that it involved most intimately had to do with its identification with the institutional form of the Republic:[48] from this vantage point, the social appears as a strategy to solve fraternity's institutional problems *without* having to modify the theory of rights.

The question of rights is, of course, crucial. Yet simply to oppose natural to positive rights, instead of allowing their interactive tensions, would once again make it impossible to understand the rise of a social government. Natural rights implying universal citizenship would be contrasted to actual society and would prevent the separation of the political apparatus from its social basis.[49] Positive rights, in turn, would drown individual rights in a social law establishing the domination of the collective body.[50] The strategy of the social emerged from the tensions between the two and organized itself through the notion of duty. If the two remain opposed, a solution to the antinomy can only come from outside the political universe of rights, namely, from sociological functionalism, concealing the radical conflicts that brought about the liberal order.

The functionalist interpretation, reducing inequality to differentiation, leads to taking the strategy of the social literally, and thus to depoliticizing problems of inequality. At the same time, it separates the social from its origins in the criticism of liberal individualism. In this way the political transformations that the social has produced, thanks to its anti-liberal nature, would also be concealed. Social solutions to conflicts between natural and positive rights, and between rights and duties, have profoundly modified our societies. Recovering the political character of those transformations allows us to see that equality has never been just formal, nor inequality just functional. Only by means of such a recovery would it again become possible to acknowledge the political role of poverty at the foundation of modern democracies, reclaiming the role of equality, not as a formal requirement, but as expressing an active longing for democracy – a longing possibly needed more today than ever before.

12

Combined Underdevelopment: Discipline and the Law in Imperial and Soviet Russia

Laura Engelstein

As a political activist, Michel Foucault spoke out against oppressive political regimes and allied himself, as in the case of Poland, with people who fought for political liberty and freedom of expression. Having insisted, in essays and interviews, that he appreciated the importance of the institutional context that distinguished so-called totalitarian systems from liberal states, he did not make that distinction the focus of his scholarly work but concentrated instead on the mechanisms of control characteristic of all governments in the modern era.[1] As Sheldon Wolin has written, invoking a contrast the philosopher himself would not have employed, Foucault "was not directly concerned with great tyranny but with smaller ones."[2] In fact, Foucault's theoretical interest was captured not by the problem of postliberal politics but by the origins of liberalism itself, and his condemnation of certain kinds of state systems (communist regimes, in particular) did not fit comfortably with his insistence that constitutional forms and legal structures do not determine the workings of power in the modern world.

Indeed, the thrust of Foucault's critical energy was directed at identifying the "minor" tyrannies brought into being by the bourgeois order that replaced the "major" tyranny of Old Regime states with the promise of civic freedom. He argued that the fundamental social category central to the bourgeois polity – that of the autonomous individual – has not in fact operated as the precondition for liberty and happiness but as a mechanism of domination, the agent and object of discipline exercised by society upon itself. Where monarchies once imposed order by brute force, through the coercive instruments of the state, Foucault observed, liberal capitalist societies exercise control through the gathering and production of information, the surveillance associated with these scientific projects, the imposition of categories derived from such investigation, and by inculcating mechanisms of self-censorship and self-restraint that compel people to police themselves. By exposing the disciplinary function of subjectivity (the vaunted condition of individual freedom), rationality (prized as an instrument of subjective autonomy), and sexuality (in more recent times hailed as the domain of personal liberation), Foucault strove to unmask the ideological nature of bourgeois claims to have improved on the overt compulsions and unabashed hierarchies of the absolutist state.[3]

The "great tyranny" that did interest Foucault was not the modern "police state" of Nazi Germany or Soviet Russia but the monarchical system of early modern Europe, which finally gave way to the deceptive liberties of the modern era. During this transition, the state ceased to display its might in exemplary theatrical spectacles of publicly inflicted bodily pain when punishing crime. Instead, it created institutions for the concealment and regimentation of offenders, who were kept alive and physically intact but out of public sight and under expert supervision. In regulating sex, the state likewise abandoned public rituals of shame or retribution, delegating the exercise of control to the more insidious offices of the trained professions.[4] The "new mechanism of power" that characterized the modern era took the form of "highly specific procedural techniques, completely novel instruments, quite different apparatuses" from those of the Old Regime and "absolutely incompatible with the relations of sovereignty" associated with absolute rule.[5]

The transition from compulsion to discipline, in Foucault's scheme, coincided with the turn from precapitalist to capitalist social organization, from the absolutist to the constitutional state. The contrast is more, however, than a chronological blueprint. It also represents two different (though not mutually exclusive) principles of social order. The Old Regime state, which Foucault sometimes termed "the juridical monarchy," came into being as a unified center of authority, having established its domination over the competing claims of powerful and multiple rivals. The national monarchs thus identified themselves with the reign of lawfulness, the triumph over anarchy. "Western monarchies," Foucault wrote, "were constructed as systems of law, they expressed themselves through theories of law, and they made their mechanisms of power work in the form of law."[6] But they also arrogated to themselves the right to supersede any law, and their critics came increasingly to identify them in their own right with the arbitrary disregard of formal constraints. In Foucault's view, "A tradition dating back to the eighteenth or nineteenth century has accustomed us to place absolute monarchic power on the side of the

unlawful: arbitrariness, abuse, caprice, willfulness, privileges and exceptions, the traditional continuance of accomplished facts."[7]

Insofar as this critique applied the standard of the law against which to
measure the practices of the Old Regime, it used the monarchy's own
ideology against it and failed to represent a new and different concept of
justice. Like the monarchies they replaced, bourgeois liberal regimes also
used the law to legitimate their claims to political authority, but antiliberal
critics went further than their eighteenth-century predecessors in arguing
not merely that bourgeois states violated the legality they claimed to uphold
but that legality itself was deceptive. The law, they said, was not the
antidote to coercion but a covert system of domination in its own right.
Such critics claimed "not only that real power escaped the rules of
jurisprudence, but that the legal system itself was merely a way of exerting
violence, of appropriating that violence for the benefit of the few, and of
exploiting the dissymmetries and injustices of domination under cover of
general law." But this critique, Foucault argued, "is still carried out on the
assumption that, ideally and by nature, power must be exercised in
accordance with a fundamental lawfulness."[8]

What is inadequate about this critique, in Foucault's view, is that law no
longer operates as the organizing principle for the exercise and constitution
of power in modern societies, despite its continuing pretensions to the
contrary. The judicial system, he wrote,

> is utterly incongruous with the new methods of power whose operation is not
> ensured by right but by technique, not by law but by normalization, not by
> punishment but by control, methods that are employed on all levels and in
> forms that go beyond the state and its apparatus. We have been engaged for
> centuries in a type of society in which the juridical is increasingly incapable of
> coding power, of serving as its system of representation. Our historical
> gradient carries us further and further away from a reign of law that had
> already begun to recede into the past at a time when the French Revolution
> and the accompanying age of constitutions and codes seemed to destine it for
> a future that was at hand.

Operating through the power/knowledge nexus, dispersed (in Foucault's
elusive metaphor) throughout the social fabric, the "new mechanisms of
power" do not emanate from the institutions of the state or formally
constituted authorities and are "probably irreducible to the representation
of law."[9]

This paradigm may or may not adequately describe a transition that
occurred in European nations. Even Foucault qualified his claims in ways
that cloud the opposition between the two ideal types of power. In the first

place, he explained, the regulatory mechanisms characteristic of the modern era find their origin in the custodial functions of the monarchical regime, deriving "at least in part, [from] those [mechanisms] that, beginning in the eighteenth century, took charge of men's existence, men as living bodies."[10] Indeed, the absolutist *Polizeistaat* did not merely punish or coerce but also intruded, examined, fostered, and shaped the economic, social, and demographic body politic. One might illustrate this awkward combination with the example of Russia's Catherine the Great, who sanctioned the slitting of criminals' nostrils and the branding of their flesh, while at the same time sponsoring foundling homes and public hospitals. The bourgeois disciplinary regime, as Foucault recognized, did not represent the complete negation of the absolutist state but, rather, perpetuated certain principles of premodern "enlightened" stewardship.[11]

In the second place, while Foucault maintained that the new techniques were "absolutely incompatible with the relations of sovereignty" central to old regimes,[12] or at the very least "probably irreducible to the representation of law" that legitimated state power, he also admitted that many of the juridical forms associated with the absolutist regime "have persisted to the present."[13] Having sometimes argued that discipline virtually replaces law as the effective mechanism of power in the modern period, at others he depicted the liberal regime as an alliance between the two distinctive – and in principle irreconcilable – forms of power. "The system of right, the domain of the law," he wrote at one point, "are permanent agents of these relations of domination, these polymorphous techniques of subjugation" associated with the disciplinary regime.[14] The theory of sovereignty and the formal structures of the law have, he suggested, bolstered the disciplinary mechanisms in two ways (both pejorative): first, they provide ideological cover for the kinds of coercion and subjugation inherent in the dispersed techniques of power that have superseded the strong arm of the absolutist state; and, second, they are the enabling condition for discipline itself, allowing for a "democratization of sovereignty," which has shifted the hub of power in modern times from the centralized state to a public sphere whose operations are "fundamentally determined by and grounded in mechanisms of disciplinary coercion."[15]

Indeed, it would seem, the modern period is characterized not so much by its contrast with the preceding one but by its deployment of old principles to new ends. "The powers of modern society," Foucault wrote, "are exercised through, on the basis of, and by virtue of, this very heterogeneity between a public right of sovereignty and a polymorphous disciplinary mechanism."[16] Yet the alliance is not without conflict. Rather than a clean break with the past, the bourgeois regime constitutes a parasitic encroachment on it: as the techniques and discourses "to which the

disciplines give rise invade the area of right ... the procedures of
normalization come to be ever more constantly engaged in the colonization
of those of law ... [and] come into ever greater conflict with the juridical
systems of sovereignty."[17]

There is some question as to how Foucault himself stood in relation to
the power systems he anatomized.[18] On the one hand, he straddled the two
critical traditions he himself identified: the one that takes the law to task for
violating its own principles (here providing ideological cover for the
operation of normalizing regimes), as well as the one that denounces law in
its own terms as a mask for domination (insofar as law without discipline –
the absolutist regime – provided no better alternative). In the end, Foucault
could not find an uncontaminated standpoint:

> Against these usurpations by the disciplinary mechanisms ... we find that
> there is no solid recourse available to us today ... except that which lies
> precisely in the return to a theory of right organized around sovereignty and
> articulated upon its ancient principle. ... But I believe that we find ourselves
> here in a kind of blind alley: it is not through recourse to sovereignty against
> discipline that the effects of disciplinary power can be limited, because
> sovereignty and disciplinary mechanisms are two absolutely integral constitu-
> ents of the general mechanism of power in our society.

This situation left him with the wistful reflection that what was needed was
"a new form of right, one which must indeed be anti-disciplinarian, but at
the same time liberated from the principle of sovereignty."[19] That is, not
only do principles of legality not provide a way out of the modern dilemma
but the law actually abets the modern polity's violation of the promise of
freedom. It is not therefore true, in Foucault's scheme, whatever its internal
contradictions, that law is the standard from which to judge the derelictions
of the bourgeois disciplinary regime, because, however opposite in
principle, the law is compromised as well.[20]

But, no matter how complicated Foucault ultimately made the picture of
modernity, he retained the distinction between old regimes, in which power
emanated from the state, and the liberal bourgeois society, in which power
operates through "normalizing" mechanisms based on "scientific knowledge" and is implemented through disciplinary practices widely dispersed
in the social body. Moreover, the chronological vector is never entirely lost:
whatever the overlaps and collusions, Western nations have allegedly
proceeded from absolutist monarchies, through *Polizeistaat* enlightened
despotisms, to liberal states that delegate power through social self-
regulation and control their citizens through the operational fiction of
individual autonomy.

To cast an oblique light on Foucault's historical scheme as well as on his implicit (and not so implicit) political judgments, let us take the case of a nation that both contemporaries and historians have considered an example of cultural and political backwardness or, at best, of "combined development."[21] In the Russian empire, the Old Regime survived almost unmodified into the era in which the modern mechanisms of social control and social self-discipline derived from Western practices had already emerged. Here, the "reign of law" had not "already begun to recede," as Foucault said of the European nineteenth century, but had not yet arrived. Rather, the tsar appropriated the institutional appurtenances of a rule-of-law state (legal codes, independent judiciary, trial by jury), while continuing to exercise absolute sovereignty through the mechanisms of a virtually unimpeded administrative state. Indeed, the Russian example represents the superimposition of the three models of power, chronologically separated (however imperfectly) in Foucault's scheme: the so-called juridical monarchy, the *Polizeistaat*, and the modern disciplinary regime. Furthermore, both the defense and the critique of the law, which Foucault identified roughly with the eighteenth and nineteenth centuries – the one holding the monarchy to the standard of its own stated claims and the other attacking the law as intrinsically obfuscatory – also coincided in time in the utterances of tsarism's liberal and radical critics. And both of these positions coexisted with the articulated interests of trained professionals, representing the social authority of science.

The example of Russia is also instructive as a test case for Foucault's discursive hypothesis, which locates the authority and coercive power of the disciplinary mechanisms in the production of knowledge and the implementation of scientifically legitimated norms. Although Western culture penetrated the empire's official and civic elites, and the model of Western institutions to a large extent shaped the contours of state and social organization, the regime of "power/knowledge" never came into its own in the Russian context. Thus the modern discursive mechanisms did not produce the same effects they purportedly did in the West. Nor, for that matter, did the ideology of the law. To quote the legal scholar Bogdan Kistiakovskii, writing in 1909: "No one, single idea of individual freedom, of the rule of law, of the constitutional state, is the same for all nations and all times, just as no social and economic organization, capitalist or otherwise, is identical in all countries. All legal ideas acquire their own peculiar coloration and inflection in the consciousness of each separate people."[22] To examine the Russian case is to remind ourselves not to mistake Foucault's paradigm for a universal model, for some "discursively" disguised reworking of modernization theory. More to the point, it is to question whether Foucault's understanding even of the European case adequately addresses the political issues at sake.

Using the Russian example, I argue that law and discipline are indeed interdependent principles, but not in the pejorative sense Foucault had in mind, and that Foucault's hostility toward order (whether juridical or disciplinary) has dangerous political implications, some of which were played out on the Russian stage. It is the voice of Russian liberalism that most eloquently expresses the difficulty of negotiating the mutual relation between state and society, between law and discipline, and the urgency of that attempt. The case of the Russian empire and its Soviet successor illustrates the civic costs of failing to achieve the invidious bourgeois solution.

In exploring this counter-example of Foucault's historical hypothesis, the present essay will proceed along two lines. First, it will situate Foucault's analysis and critique of law and social order within the nineteenth-century intellectual tradition reflected in Russian discussions of the same theme. Second, it will locate the discontinuity effected by modernity not in the transition from law to discipline (if evident only, in some of Foucault's renditions, in the residual incompatibility of their continued coexistence) but in the transition from administration to law as the context for disciplinary technology. In short, I will argue that the contribution of liberalism is not to displace an intrinsically ideological legality with the normative power of an equally inequitable and unfree disciplinary regime[23] but to replace the administrative state, in which disciplinary functions emanate from a sovereign superior to the law, with a configuration in which law constrains the operation of discipline. In the Russian–Soviet case, by contrast, the absolutist regime was succeeded by an administrative order that rejected legality and harnessed the professional disciplines to its own repressive ends, rather than a disciplinary society limited and controlled by the authority of the law.

It is often remarked that Russian intellectuals produced a critique of capitalism and bourgeois culture before either had a chance to develop on Russian soil. Alexander Herzen's disillusionment with European politics and his hope that Russia might somehow negotiate the transition from traditional exploitation to future utopia without the painful middle passage provide the classic example of such precocious dissatisfaction. The revolutions of 1905 and even 1917 occurred before the theoretically appointed hour, as Marxists were uneasily aware. In relation to the law, Russians likewise generated an anticipatory critique of institutions not yet imbued with the authority of an established order. While independent liberals and government reformers struggled to build and validate a rule-of-law state, radicals and conservatives joined in denigrating a legality that had yet to take root in social psychology or institutional practice.

For all its resemblance to old regimes elsewhere, tsarism did not produce a similar legal tradition. Unlike the monarchs of western Europe, Russian rulers had not come to predominance by resolving the clash of competing particular powers but had from the beginning constituted themselves as the source of all power in the land. They had never assumed an adjudicative but always an administrative function, creating the social hierarchy from on high, as a dependency of the state. The tsarist regime's persistent antipathy to the constraints of law was obvious to contemporaries and is a commonplace of historians. Eager for the attributes of modernity but unwilling to pay the political price, the nineteenth-century tsars played with judicial reform while consistently violating the meaning of lawful rule. The reforms created institutions that in theory, and to a degree in practice, circumscribed the emperor's absolute freedom to act or, at the very least, created new tensions in the system; these reforms reflected the emergence of legal-minded modernizers both within the bureaucracy and in educated society who pressed to transform the monarchy from within.[24]

Even its flirtation with reform displayed the autocracy's quintessential character, the very features that most angered its critics: arbitrariness and self-contradiction. Thus Alexander I employed European experts to reorganize the existing laws into a systematic compendium yet would not accept general principles, conceptual distinctions, or any winnowing of the chaotic body of historic edicts that could challenge the autocrat's untrammeled might.[25] Russian legal commentators complained that the resulting codes were "medieval" in their deliberately fragmentary conception, a jumble of specific cases designed to inhibit the discretion of the courts.[26] During the reign of Nicholas I (who, despite his conservatism, continued to sponsor the project of codification), the bureaucrats taxed with revising the codes necessarily relied on Western precedent but carefully denied the influence of alien models, pretending their work was merely to assemble the national tradition, not inject principled modifications into the existing corpus.[27] Moreover, the tension between tradition and change worked both ways. On the one hand, allegedly progressive tsars, such as Alexander II, who instituted the judicial reforms of 1864, later inhibited the formulation and application of the law. On the other, the vigorously reactionary Alexander III, who showed utter contempt for proper procedure and presided over a reign of "extraordinary legislation," at the same time failed to curtail the ongoing project of legal reform initiated by liberal bureaucrats in his father's time.

The radical intelligentsia was resolutely antilegal, the mirror image of this relentlessly inconsistent autocratic state. The radicals' hostility to legal principles distinguished them from those contemporaries who saw Russia's future in the strengthening of legality, the creation of a rule-of-law state (the *Rechtsstaat*), and the inculcation of respect for the law as a cultural value. It was this conflict within the educated elite that surfaced in a trenchant essay by Bogdan Kistiakovskii included in a famous 1909 volume called *Landmarks* (*Vekhi*). That provocative collection of articles represented a reaction against the 1905 Revolution on the part of thinkers we might now call neoconservatives: former radicals and socially cautious liberals in some cases repudiating their own activist past and distancing themselves from the ideological posture of their cultural kind. In his contribution, Kistiakovskii deplored the intelligentsia's failure to recognize the importance of formal legal guarantees securing personal rights and inviolability as necessary to the maintenance of social discipline (*sotsial'naia distsiplina*). Rather, Kistiakovskii insisted, the protection of individual liberty and integrity was central to a civic order based on the guarantees of the law, indeed, that individual freedom was the defining feature of the rule of law.[28]

Although the absolutist monarchy did not assure such protection, few of the regime's most outspoken enemies included it in their demands. Radicals as well as critical conservatives were skeptical of both the principle of individualism and the value of formal judicial institutions. In the 1840s, the Slavophiles denigrated the Roman law tradition of the West and the individualism of bourgeois societies as related defects of modern social organization that allegedly had disrupted the communal integrity of former times. They saw in the Russian peasant commune the opposite principle of spiritual and collective solidarity, a retroactive utopia (which they sometimes imagined as contemporary) associated with a premodern wholeness, in which individual persons did not conflict with or separate from the group. The later Populists persisted in this distrust of the West, identifying the great social evil with the capitalist form of production and exalting the folk principles of the peasant commune as the basis for a future socialist transcendence. The Marxists, by contrast, celebrated the historic mission of capitalism, disdained agrarian utopianism, and expressed theoretical, though qualified, respect for the contributions of bourgeois political culture. But they, too, Kistiakovskii complained, reviled the law as an instrument of coercion, a tool of class domination. The historic failure of law to realize its promise of universality was no reason, he argued, to dispense with the promise altogether. As a constitutional liberal sympathetic to socialism's moral claims, he granted that law might not guarantee social justice but insisted that social justice could not be achieved without a basis in law.[29]

Kistiakovskii's analysis of the legal consciousness and principle of social order manifested by the radicals in their own political practice is particularly relevant to my concerns. Instead of respecting the law as a system of externally guaranteed but widely internalized norms, Kistiakovskii observed, the Marxists instituted a system of order based on the imposition of rules and regulations. Their rigidly enforced party strictures, in his view, demonstrated the same style of bureaucratic management exemplified in the tsarist administrative state.[30] "We [Russians]," Kistiakovskii wrote, "need external discipline precisely because we lack internal discipline. In this regard, once again, we understand the law not as a matter of legal conviction [*pravovoe ubezhdenie*] but as a form of coercive regulation [*prinuditel'noe pravilo*]. And this conception once again testifies to the low level of our legal consciousness."[31]

It was precisely the regime of the individual subject, enshrined and protected in the law, exalted by the liberal Kistiakovskii, that Russian radicals disdained. The subsumption of the individual within the class, and of class in a future classlessness, made this concept of law seem irrelevant to the revolutionary project. As Lenin was later to declare in *State and Revolution* (1917), the ideal of socialist government was one that merely administered. In a society without class conflict, only the distribution of goods and services and the assignment of tasks would be left to the public authorities, no longer impelled to keep order by coercive means. The law, as Lenin realized (and Foucault often seems to have forgotten), is not only or primarily about repression but also about the resolution or adjudication of conflict. Lenin consistently postulated that a conflict-free society might safely dispense with the law. In the event, the law disappeared and conflict remained. Repression of an administrative character resulted.

Like Russia's nineteenth-century intellectuals, Foucault was all too aware of the defects of the bourgeois regime, its false promises, its covert constraints, and so could not celebrate the advance it represented over the burdens of absolutism. Yet, unlike them, he focused his ire not on the law, a principle of limitation (repression, he called it) that had presumably ceded preeminence on the historical stage, but on the insidious mechanisms of control, functioning as cultural proliferation or incitement, that had displaced it. Foucault was exercised by the very mechanisms that instill the "social discipline" Kistiakovskii thought essential to the maintenance of order, indeed, to the operation of the law itself. Where Foucault emphasized the coming to predominance of "discourse" (power/knowledge) over prohibition as the regulatory principle of modern life, Kistiakovskii emphasized their mutual dependence. Insofar as Foucault, too, recognized a complicity between the two principles of order, it was a negative one, in which the façade of legality concealed the inequities of discipline, rather than discipline enabling the realization of the law.

In the Russian situation, the two groups to defend the principle of legality were, on the one side, certain bureaucrats and official servitors (the authors of judicial reform within the Ministry of Justice or the men who served as justices of the peace after 1864), and, on the other, professionals outside government like Kistiakovskii himself. The professionals outside government were in the position of having to defend both law and discipline at the same time, to insist on the interdependence, rather than the opposition, between institutional and dispersed authority. Insofar as they engaged in the business of social discipline, these professionals were the natural heirs to the autocratic *Polizeistaat* tradition, yet they actively opposed the official incarnation of *Polizeistaat* administrative rule in the interests of a civic autonomy protected by the rule of law (the *Rechtsstaat* principle).

Whereas in Europe the preconditions for and continuing context of disciplinary authority were established by the law-abiding state (in however imperfect a guise), in Russia, both the reign of law and the ascendance of bourgeois discipline remained largely hypothetical. Jealous of its monopoly on tutelage, the autocracy obstructed attempts by the cultural elite to exercise its own kind of influence on the social body. The efforts of pedagogues, engineers, and other members of the professional intelligentsia to educate workers and provide social services were impeded by bureaucratic interference no less than the endeavors of physicians to raise the level of public hygiene.[32] Far from understanding that the delegation of disciplinary authority would have strengthened its own regulatory hand while winning the loyalty of the modern professional class, the tsarist regime was reluctant to evolve in the direction taken by old regimes in the West. It was as unwilling to allow alternative sources of custodial influence as it was jealous of the intrinsic power of the law.

The regime's reluctance to disperse the mechanisms of social discipline weakened, however, in the last years of imperial rule, as the growing complexity of the modern sector and the spread of education and technology strengthened the professional cohort and multiplied the kinds of social problems with which such mechanisms contend. Thus, at the turn of the century, the police entertained an experiment in state-sponsored labor unions, which enlisted the help of liberal professionals, while the Revolution of 1905 netted the long-desired opening of a (restricted) parliamentary arena and the guarantee of minimal civil rights. For their part, the elite also lost some of their defiance. Before 1905, the possibility of popular mobilization, whether desired or feared in educated circles depending on the particular ideological cast, was in all cases less of a certainty than the burden of repression from above. With the revolution, however, this potential became a reality. In response, many moderates (including the *Vekhi* group) who had sympathized with the left lost their enthusiasm for political extremes or articulated long-held but previously muted doubts.

At the same time, trained practitioners began to lose some of their hostility to state intercession and discovered a new enthusiasm for technologies of public intervention. While some populist-minded physicians, for example, continued to oppose bureaucratic strategies for health delivery and public hygiene in the name of independent, localized deployment of professional expertise, many of their colleagues joined hands with the central bureaucracy in the name of efficiency and modern technique. Those who decided that professional authority could be strengthened in league with, rather than opposition to, the state included more than a few Bolsheviks by political conviction.[33] The old *Polizeistaat* principle, which never trafficked in the pretensions of legality but functioned in a crudely regulatory mode often in conflict with the operation of the law, was acquiring a new plausibility in professional circles on the eve of World War I.

This principle seems to have beguiled the Bolshevik professionals who also helped found the post-revolutionary disciplinary regime. For what evolved after October 1917 was an alliance between the old tutelary state and the new disciplinary mechanisms but without the legal protections that Russian liberals had earlier considered essential to the disciplinary project itself and that *Rechtsstaat* reformers had tried to insinuate into the auto-cractic context.[34] The alliance was reinforced during the Stalin years, when a reconstituted technological elite was recruited as the system's social and ideological mainstay.[35] Ultimately, however, the experts were thoroughly subordinated to the interests of the state, and the scientific standards once evoked to legitimate Marxist claims to truth now depended on Marxism for their own legitimation. The absence of a legal context evidently proved fatal to the disciplinary authority inherent in professional expertise.

The pervasive disdain for the law that had permeated the outlook of the radical intelligentsia came into its own as public policy after 1917. At first elevated to an official philosophy, the critique of the law as an instrument of class domination justified the operation of courts in the absence of written rules and the application of principles of "class justice" that violated the basic liberal postulates of lawful rule.[36] As in the tsarist regime, in which juridical status had determined one's relation to the law and one's vulnerability to punishment, so attributes of social position (in this case, socio-economic or ideologically constructed) affected one's susceptibility to repression. When the legal institutions of the new regime achieved a greater degree of institutionalization, after the publication of the first Soviet criminal code in 1922, certain liberal principles of jurisprudence were still ignored. For example, crimes were punishable retroactively and by analogy: a person might be penalized for an act that had not been illegal at the time it occurred, and acts not defined as criminal in the statutes might be prosecuted on the grounds that they resembled others that were. Despite the outward forms of legality (the famous constitution of 1936, the codes and court system), law did not survive in any meaningful sense into the Stalin period but operated as an instrument of administrative rule.[37] As in the tsarist regime, the business of repression was conducted both judicially and extrajudicially, in the courts, as well as by the ordinary and political police.[38] Precisely because of the law's subordination, discipline also lost the relative autonomy (its separation from sovereignty) it manifests in bourgeois regimes.

A nice example of the perils of discipline operating in the absence of the law, taken from the early post-revolutionary years, is the case of a trial of male homosexuals, staged in Petrograd in 1922.[39] The men in question had come to the attention of the authorities when the political police (Cheka) raided an apartment in which they held periodic gatherings. Suspicious that the meetings might have some politically subversive end, the intruders found no counter-revolutionary conspirators but instead a group of men dressed as heterosexual pairs, some in male and others in female attire. The lot were arrested and put on trial for public indecency. No other charge could be brought, in the first place because the participants had not been apprehended in the course of sexual activity and in the second place because there was no criminal law against the act of anal intercourse between consenting adult men (the old definition of sodomy in the abrogated tsarist criminal code),[40] in which they might be presumed to have engaged.

The charge of public indecency was thus an improvised way of bringing the men to criminal account, although it did not suit the circumstances (the men were not comporting themselves in public) and did not conform to any offense in the law. The significance of this charge was different, as the justification reported in the legal press makes clear: the prosecution of these men, it was said, formed part of a campaign to clean up public morals conducted in the interests of the nation's biological welfare. The effort at moral surveillance, which acquired special urgency in the confused early years of the New Economic Policy,[41] smacked of the old *Polizeistaat* rationale for the state's intervention in sexual affairs. It recalled the language and purpose of the tsarist criminal code, framed during the reign of Nicholas I and lasting in substance until 1917, which included the sexual offenses, among them sodomy, under violations of "public morality" (*obshchestvennaia nravstvennost'*) and more generally of "public orderliness and decorum" (*obshchestvennoe blagoustroistvo i blagochinie*). In so doing, the code underscored the analogy between the role of the statutory law in enforcing sexual norms (classed as a matter of public decorum rather than interpersonal conflict) and the function of the police, which maintained standards of propriety through administrative rather than judicial means.

Objecting to the use of judicial institutions to impose the kind of discipline properly left to the police, liberal reformers had fashioned a new criminal code (completed in 1903 but never enacted), which recast sexual offenses as violations of a person's right to physical and psychic integrity. In decriminalizing sodomy, early Soviet lawmakers had taken the reformers' principles further than they themselves had been willing to go. (The 1903 code continued to penalize sodomy, despite objections from within the progressive legal community.) Yet the new regime's hostility to legality itself opened the door to mechanisms of control rooted in the same administrative tradition that Old Regime reformers had opposed. These mechanisms were buttressed, however, by the authority of "bourgeois" science. In the absence not only of particular statutes but of any guarantee of due process, Soviet courts used professional experts to justify repressive measures not specified in laws or decrees. Thus the prosecution in the 1922 trial summoned the eminent psychiatrist Vladimir Bekhterev, a prominent member of the pre-revolutionary professional elite, who willingly pronounced on the social harm attendant on the free practice of homosexual sex and recommended the application of penal sanctions. By dubbing the defendants an organically defective breed, he translated the issue of political control (the policing of public gatherings) into a scientific, medical prophylaxis (the policing of contagious pathologies).[42] Bekhterev provided the expert testimony, quintessentially in the "disciplinary" mode, that helped condemn the men for behavior not included in the criminal code, which is to say, not against the law.

Both the role of the political police and of Bekhterev's public hygiene argument underscore the extent to which sexual regulation continued to fall within the province of the administrative state. It was precisely this third term in the social control equation, the old-style administrative state, that in Russia never evolved into the bourgeois disciplinary order. Rather, it survived the failure of liberalism to serve as the basis of the Soviet regime, updated and fortified by modern technology and a more aggressive ideology of public intrusion. In the early days of the New Economic Policy, the weight of scientific opinion, heir to the disciplinary authority of the bourgeois professions, reinforced the official project of social control and social engineering. Later, as Stalin consolidated his hold on power, science itself fell under the domination of political orthodoxy; then homosexuality became the disease of fascism and counter-revolution, rather than the medical pathology some experts had earlier seen it to be.[43]

The case of abortion again shows how pre-revolutionary professional discourse set the terms of early Soviet practice and, like the case of homosexuality, also demonstrates the social consequences of discipline forming an alliance with the administrative state in the absence of legal protection. In the few years before the outbreak of World War I, jurists and physicians hotly debated the question of abortion law, which under the tsarist code penalized the medical practitioners as well as the pregnant women. The arguments articulated in the debate defined three possible positions on the question. While all agreed that the existing statute needed reform, many insisted that abortion must remain a crime. The majority, however, favored decriminalization. Abortion, they opined, could not be effectively controlled through legal repression (penal sanctions) but should be regulated by professional discretion. Far from being punished for providing abortions, they asserted, physicians should be empowered by the state to allocate and administer them. The third position, held by only a handful of participants, rejected both these policies in favor of the pregnant woman's absolute right of personal self-determination.[44]

In political terms, those taking the first position (for the continued relevance of the criminal law) tended to be stringent liberals, those assuming the second sat further to the left, even though few identified themselves in openly partisan terms. Self-declared feminists could be found in all three camps, while women (the few who entered the debate) clustered around the third pole. The October Revolution institutionalized the second, "disciplinary" model. Abortion was decriminalized in 1920, but absolute prohibition was not replaced with the positive right to abortion. Instead, women were obliged to apply to clinics, where physicians were authorized to decide who would have access to professional care. The test case in the pre-revolutionary debate had been the educated, privileged woman who wished to limit family size, supposedly for reasons of comfort or vanity. Champions of women's sexual self-determination defended the right to abort even for women such as these, while enemies of that principle used this group as a negative symbol of selfish individualism. As it turned out, no woman in the 1920s could argue successfully that she was entitled to the procedure on purely idiosyncratic grounds. Only material need or medical vulnerability qualified an applicant for help.[45] In 1936, Stalin recriminalized abortion, thus returning to the tsarist *status quo ante*. Referring to this change, commissar of justice Nikolai Krylenko remarked, "A basic mistake is made in every case by those women who consider 'freedom of abortion' as one of their civil rights."[46]

What conclusions can be drawn from the Russian–Soviet case that are relevant to evaluating the paradigms supplied by Foucault in deciphering the modalities of power in the modern world? In what sense can he help us understand the "great tyrannies" of our age? I would suggest that it was his own cultural context that caused him to neglect what was most radical about the very regime whose seductive comforts he deplored. For all his iconoclasm, Foucault, it must be remembered, lived not in Russia but in

France, where he had the luxury to denounce the insidious intrusions of the disciplinary professions and the entangling effects of bourgeois liberation. France is a country in which the juridical monarchy did indeed give rise to the rule of law as well as to its critique, in which Old Regime legalism produced the bourgeois legal regime, which buttresses the vaunted subject that the disciplinary project also invokes and deploys.

The liberal state is not perfect. Beginning in the nineteenth century, critics already complained that the operation of the vaunted public sphere, with its attendant freedoms and connection to political authority, depended on a monopoly of access. Marxists and feminists (in their respective varieties) have explained both the principle and the function of these exclusions on different grounds. The existence (indeed origins) of regulated prostitution in western Europe demonstrates, for example, that administrative incursions on legal rights were not unique to absolutism. And it is certainly not the case that the existence of a legal apparatus and a rule-of-law tradition guarantees the realization of civil and political justice. But one cannot conclude from the negative example that their presence is irrelevant to the chances of success. What distinguishes post-liberal repressive regimes from the inequitable but more porous "bourgeois" variety is not the presence or absence of social "self-regulation" (whose mechanisms, moreover, are not everywhere the same) but the nature of the political apparatus, including its legal ethos, and its relation to other forms of control. The importance of these imperfect, but indispensable, institutional guarantees is what Russian professionals, chafing under the constraints of the shamelessly antilegal imperial regime, repeatedly invoked.[47]

Not surprisingly, Russian liberals, no less than their Western counterparts, sometimes hesitated before the full implications of their own ideas: displaying wariness in regard to women's suffrage and a residual paternalism (though it was the Provisional Government that granted women the vote in 1917, along with civil rights for ethnic minorities), moral revulsion at sexual variation, condescension toward non-Russian local cultures, and at times unseemly nationalist zeal. They also demonstrated ambivalences of their own: chronic doubts about the liberal sacred canon and often a sentimental affection for the political left, which had little use for their niceties. Even to the best Russian liberal, individualism was both an ardently desired prize and a threat to cultural values that distinguished their world from the "out there," a place that often seemed better, but also spiritually impoverished; private property and the marketplace (whether in goods or culture) seemed deeply troublesome attainments; and the rigors of bourgeois morality struck them as narrow and vain. They felt themselves blessed or cursed with a social conscience. As the psychiatrist Nikolai Bazhenov remarked in 1906, Russia was both too early and too late for liberalism. "The time for purely political revolutions has long passed," he wrote. "Russia will witness the struggle for land as well for legality [*pravo*], and not for land alone but for the establishment of social and economic justice [*spravedlivost'*]."[48] In the event, it was not only legality that got short shift but also social justice.

In Russia, liberalism ultimately failed, and the custodial state survived by enlisting and absorbing the agencies of social self-formation it inherited in embryonic form. In contrast to the imperfect world of capitalist liberalism, which both extends and violates the promise of rights, the Soviet regime long offered discipline without rights. This was not merely the old *Polizeistaat* under new ideological auspices – the return of Catherine the Terrible – but its refurbishment with new tactics, by which society was enlisted to do its own policing but in which the discursive authority of the professional disciplines, speaking in the name of "science," functioned only as a dependency of the state. The very meaning of "discipline," as invoked by Foucault in the bourgeois context to signify social self-regulation through the dissemination of scientifically validated norms and professional practices, resulting in the politically useful subterfuge of individual sovereignty, loses its sense in the Soviet context, although it is certainly true that control in Soviet society was not merely exercised by state institutions "from the top down." Without the guarantees promised by the law, even if not always successfully provided, authority, it would seem, cannot reside in society. Without a measure of autonomy, without even the appearance of autonomy, as in the Soviet case, there has historically been no tension between subjectivity and submission. The Soviet regime, often used to symbolize the essence of modern tyranny, has, more accurately, provided an example of illusory modernity, an administrative state that mobilizes disciplines not free in either fact or pretense. In the Soviet aftermath, the "deceptive" visions of civic modernity still remain an alluring dream. Russia is a society that has yet to generate the luxury of a Michel Foucault to push it to consider the enticements of paradox.

13

"Problematization" as a Mode of Reading History

Robert Castel

The work of Michel Foucault does not explicitly accord a central place to the notion of problematization. I would like to show nonetheless that one of his essential methodological contributions can be characterized in this fashion. In so doing, I do not consider myself an orthodox "Foucauldian," and my goal is less to indicate the place this notion has in the internal economy of Foucault's work than to discuss a means of utilizing history to account for the present. What use did Foucault make of history, and what use can be made of it in order to "problematize" a current question? Furthermore, I do not intend to sing the praises of problematization but rather to stress that it is a problematic idea, one which exemplifies Foucault's difficult relationship with history and, beyond him, with non-historians, myself included, who give significant weight to history in their research; it is a way of invoking history with which historians themselves may not agree. My goal, then, is to question those who practice the craft of history about the legitimacy of this attempt to formulate a "history of the present" and also to consider its dangers and limitations with respect to the requirements of historical methodology.

I PROBLEMATIZATION: A PROBLEMATIC NOTION

Let us take as our starting point the description – if not a definition – of this notion as proposed by Foucault in an interview shortly before his death: "Problematization is not the representation of a preexisting object, or the creation through discourse of an object that does not exist. It is the totality of discursive and non-discursive practices that brings something into the play of truth and falsehood and sets it up as an object for the mind."[1]

It is the analysis, then, of "domains of objects," or, as Foucault still calls them in *L'Ordre du discours*, "positivities" that neither are given for once and for all nor are pure creations of discourse. These "discursive and non-discursive practices" refer, in other words, to administrative institutions, regulations, or measures; or architectural arrangements as well as scientific, philosophical, or moral propositions. Psychiatry is an apparatus of this type, comprising scientific claims, specific institutions, specialized personnel, a professional mythology, and special laws and regulations. This sort of apparatus is neither true nor false, but at a given moment it becomes part of a debate on truth and falsehood that has incontestably theoretical claims and practical repercussions. It is also a way of affecting others, a type of governing, a way, in other words, of shaping the conduct of others. "My problem," Foucault says elsewhere, "is to know how men govern (themselves and others) by means of the production of truth (I repeat once again that by production of truth I don't mean the production of true statements but the administering of realms in which the practice of the true and the false can be both regulated and relevant). . . . In short, I would like to place the register of the production of truth and falsehood at the heart of historical analysis and political debate."[2]

One essential characteristic of this historical problematization of any apparatus needs to be emphasized. The starting point of the analysis and the orientation that directs it are *the present situation*, the way in which the question is asked today. In the article from the *Magazine littéraire* cited above, in which Foucault presents the notion of problematization, he goes on to say: "I start with a problem in the terms in which it is currently posed and attempt to establish its genealogy; genealogy means that I conduct the analysis starting from the present situation." And, speaking of the prison in *Discipline and Punish*, he mentions "writing the history of the present."[3] To write "the history of the present" is to consider the history of a problem in terms of how it is seen at present. I would like to make a few comments on the merits as well as the pitfalls of this perspective. Its starting point is the conviction, which I share, that the present reflects a conjunction of elements inherited from the past and current innovations. In other words, the present bears a burden, a weight that comes from the past, and the task of the present is to bring this burden up to date in order to understand its current ramifications. Analyzing a contemporary practice means viewing it from the standpoint of the historical basis out of which it emerges; it means grounding our understanding of its current structure on the series of its previous transformations. The past does not repeat itself in the present, but the present is played out, and innovates, utilizing the legacy of the past.

What are the problems raised by this approach in its relationship to "classical" ways of writing history and the demands of the historian's craft? At least five sorts of difficulties come to mind:

1 How can one write a history of the present, which necessitates a reading of history based on a question formulated today, that is not a projection of today's preoccupations onto the past? This kind of projection is sometimes called "presentism," and is a type of ethnocentrism: sticking onto the past a concern that holds true only, or principally, for our time. Examples abound of this sort of distortion of history, and historians have reason to be particularly wary of the temptation to rewrite history on the basis of contemporary interests.

2 To speak of a problematization means that the formation under analysis had a beginning. To reconstruct the history of a question does not mean going further and further into the past, back to the Romans, the Egyptians, or the Flood. A problematization emerges at a given moment. How can this appearance be dated? What gives one the right to interrupt the move toward an undefined past with the assertion that this current question began to be formulated at such and such a moment in the past? (Inversely, there are questions, once of key importance, that have now ceased to matter: for example, the various theological, philosophical, political, scientific, and practical problems concerning the earth's place at the center of Creation were largely forgotten after the Copernican Revolution.)

3 If one accepts that a problematization has appeared in the past, it does not repeat itself. It has been transformed; significant changes have taken place, but they have occurred against a backdrop of continuity that allows one to speak of the same problematization. How can the key transformations in this dialectic of Same and Other be described? In other words, how can one speak of historical "periods"? It is well known that the practice of dividing up the past into relatively homogeneous units (the "Middle Ages," "Renaissance," and so forth) poses considerable problems for the historian. But in the case of problematization the task is even more demanding, since the unifying principle might not be the coexistence of its elements in the past but their relationship to a question being asked today.

4 A problematization is at least partly constructed using historical data or materials. Therefore it leads to the "choice" of significant elements from a past time. But obviously it does not reconstruct the totality of an epoch with all its institutions, its plurality of individuals and groups, its innumerable problems. How is it possible to avoid making an arbitrary or careless selection? The question is all the more pressing in that what is

"chosen" within the framework of a problematization can appear
relatively minor compared to the problems characteristic of a particular
historical period. For example, the techniques of confinement in the
seventeenth century or the rituals of confession in the Christian pastoral
that Foucault stressed were matters that probably did not receive a great
deal of attention at the time they were established.

5 The preceding difficulty takes a more technical form as well: one who
studies a problematization is not a historian, and it may even be that
historians do not work with problematizations.[4] The outsider may appear
naive or self-taught; history is not a craft that one simply picks up. All the
same, this is a qualified objection; Foucault for one was a great reader of
archival material. But the difficulty recurs. Generally a problematization
covers a long span of time. It cannot be completely constructed from
primary sources, unpublished discoveries, or historical "scoops." It is
largely the outgrowth of the work of historians, which, however, it reads
in a different way. A problematization is a historical account that differs
from an account written by a historian even though it is often based on
the same material – material that is sometimes written by historians
themselves. How is it possible to ensure that an account of this nature
does not appear in the eyes of the "real historian" as at best an
approximation and at worst a fiction? How does one justify a different
reading of historical sources, when the rules for handling them are a
matter of historical methodology?

If the approach called problematization is to be rigorous, two apparently
contradictory demands must be reconciled. On the one hand is the need for
humility toward historical work and history as a profession. No one who has
not worked with primary sources and followed the rules of historical
methodology has any right to claim to offer a "better" interpretation of the
materials studied by historians. On the other hand, the interpretation
provided must be *different*. With a potential for duplicating the historian's
work, the line of questioning opened by a problematization – the questions
for the "history of the present" – must display its own intelligibility.
Foucault, for example, did not write a social history of the asylum or prison
but did something else. But if his account differs from that of the historian
– which it does – it obviously must be consistent and rigorous. It is
unrealistic to think that a problematization could lead to the complete
reevaluation of the primary sources. Hence the question must be put in the
strongest terms: by what right may one give a different reading of historical
material (including what is written by historians) if one has not examined
the sources oneself, when one knows "no more" (and generally less) about
a given period than the historian?

These are a few questions – doubtless there are more – raised by problematization and its connection with the demands of scientific history. Are the differences insurmountable? It would be tempting to gloss over them, by saying, for example, that historians themselves are guided in their choice of object by their own contemporary situation; or that historians do not re-create the totality of a past period and choose from among a virtually infinite mass of historical materials and possible sources. This is true. But these banalities, which today almost everyone agrees upon, are not enough to eradicate the difficulties raised by the notion of problematization.

First, concerning the influence of the present on the reading of the past: the formulation of a series of questions cannot be reduced to a statement that a contemporary issue can sensitize the historian and lead him or her to take an interest in this or that aspect of the past. In a problematization, the diagnostic turned upon the present guides the reading of the past and prompts it to decode history along this line of understanding. For example, Foucault presents *Discipline and Punish* as an attempt to understand "the present scientifico-legal complex from which the power to punish derives its bases, justifications and rules, from which it extends its effects and by which it masks its exorbitant singularity."[5] Likewise, in *The History of Sexuality* he inquires into the meaning of the vast amount of talk in today's society about sex and turns to history with this question, which no previous epoch has asked precisely because it is a contemporary question.

Second, a problematization does not consist only in lifting a question out of the context of a past period. It is true that historians sometimes do this, but it is in order to attain an initial understanding of the meaning of the sequence they have selected from a past epoch. Foucault does so in order to seek the forerunners of the question as it is currently formulated. Thus in the above example it is true that confession is already a way of putting sex into words that first emerged in the monastic tradition and became more widespread in the seventeenth century, when it became a requirement for all Christians. As Foucault says, "The Christian pastoral prescribed as a fundamental duty the task of passing everything having to do with sex through the endless mill of speech."[6] But this is no reconstruction of the history of confession, or an evaluation of its importance and functions in the ascetic culture of seventeenth-century society. Instead it offers an understanding of the technologies of confession as important components of the exercise of power today. Monastic confession and its "democratization" in the seventeenth century only figure in the discussion to the extent that these historically dated apparatuses helped to set the mechanisms of the present apparatus in place. Indeed, then, there is a key difference, if not a contradiction, between this "history of the present" and the way historians carry out their craft – even an open and modern history in which the myths of absolute historical objectivity and/or the total re-creation of the past have been abandoned.

The difference in register between history and the approach taken by Foucault is illustrated in a work containing a series of discussions between Foucault and a group of historians that often turns into a conversation among the deaf.[7] For example, it is not relevant to object to Foucault's use of Bentham's Panopticon on the grounds that he accorded scant attention to "real life" in nineteenth-century prisons. Foucault's aim is not to describe this "real life" but to reveal a program for controlling people within an enclosed space; the meaning of this program is not exhausted by merely knowing whether it "worked" or not. On a more general level, the frequent criticisms condemning the "abstract" quality of Foucault's analyses, their distance from what "really happened," miss the mark. As Foucault says, "When I speak of a 'disciplinary society,' it should not be taken as 'disciplined society.' When I speak of the diffusion of disciplinary methods, it is not to state that 'the French are obedient.'"[8]

Nonetheless, to the degree that this approach relies on history for its proofs, it cannot manipulate history for its own ends. After Foucault outlines two rules of historical methodology, which I will leave it to the historians to discuss, namely, the "exhaustive treatment of all the material" and "equal attention to all aspects of the chronological sequence under study," he extricates himself, perhaps a bit too easily, by stating:

> Whoever, on the other hand, wishes to study a *problem* [Foucault's emphasis] that has emerged at a given time must follow other rules: the choice of material as a function of the givens of a problem; the focus of the analysis on those elements likely to resolve it; the establishment of relationships that permit this solution. Hence the indifference to the obligation to say everything, even to satisfy the assembled jury of specialists.[9]

All right, but the question is less that of "saying everything" – which one doubts is truly a requirement for the historian – than of carefully choosing what to keep. In other words, abandoning the requirement or myth of exhaustivity does not spare one from reflecting on the criteria governing one's choice of source materials. This is an extremely difficult task, since these criteria are not those of the historical methodology that as a rule is qualified to serve as their basis.

On the level of a general presentation of methodological orientations, this question remains an abstract one. Let us try to illustrate it by analyzing the way historical material is treated within the particular framework of a problematization. Two examples will serve my purpose: Foucault himself in *L'Histoire de la folie*, and a current project of my own in which I attempt to understand the current rise in factors of social instability (unemployment, the weakening of relational support systems, the risks of exclusion, and so forth) based on the transformations of the unstable condition of the working and the disadvantaged classes over a long period of time.

II HISTORY AND PROBLEMATIZATION IN *HISTOIRE DE LA FOLIE*

(1) *L'Histoire de la folie à l'âge classique* has incontestably made a significant contribution to our knowledge of the history and social functions of psychiatry. Histories of the treatment of mental illness, of considerable interest, have appeared before and after its publication. But generally these works attempt to follow the developments of the discipline, either from an internal perspective (centered on the development of psychiatric knowledge and institutions or the interests of professionals in the field and their clientele) or in relation to external transformations of a moral, social, or political order (such as the famous episode of Pinel removing the chains from the insane in the context of the French Revolution). Foucault's approach marks a break with these tactics, which moreover have their own value (the desire for better treatment was indubitably one of the reasons behind the evolution of medical practices devoted to the treatment of mental disorders). But the history of an apparatus is not only the history of a progression, of the development of knowledge or a body of practices that attain maturity, even through crises. These transformations, marked by stops and starts, retain elements that could be called archaic. Thus, despite a revolution that the professionals have proclaimed three times – in the days of Pinel, in those of Freud, and after World War II, with social psychiatry – when Foucault wrote *L'Histoire de la folie*, the treatment of mental illness was still largely dominated by confinement. This reliance upon segregative practices is not a belated survival of a long-forgotten past. It continues, even in psychiatric services that claim to be modern, to exert an influence on everyday decisions, to block room for initiative, and sometimes to render the most daring innovations impotent. By reactivating the successive strata to which psychiatric institutions have been heir since the time of the leprosaria of the Middle Ages, this type of analysis offers an interpretative grid capable of revealing the mechanisms of contemporary practice. If this is not the only possible history of psychiatry, at least it is a strong antidote to the histories motivated by the need to retrace the steps followed by the mental health field on its way to scientific maturity and practical efficacy. This "epistemological break" is the necessary condition for revealing and

exploring a level of rationality that eludes the point-by-point, or synchronic, analyses of the present. Taking a completely different route, Foucault achieves a displacement homologous to that made by Erving Goffman in *Asylums*.[10] Each of them opens up a line of inquiry that makes it possible to reintegrate institutional practices and professional ideologies centered on the therapeutic goals of the medical treatment of mental illness. Of course, this not a "total" explanation of the theoretico-practical ensemble known as mental illness, but in my view it is a fundamental contribution to objective knowledge of it.

This "history of the present" enables history to take a double look back. It sheds light on how contemporary practices function, showing that they continue to be structured by the effects of their heritage. But it also sheds light on the entire development of the treatment of mental disorders, by showing that the history of this development began before its official birth. While the originators of the asylum clearly took issue with the then dominant conception of confinement (the indignation caused by the fact that the insane were treated like criminals and confined along with them was decisive in the early nineteenth-century recognition of the need to found "special institutions" having a therapeutic aim), they did not abolish this heritage, but retained and reshaped it. "Therapeutic isolation" is justified, as Esquirol said, by the "need to provide a distraction from delirium" by breaking the sick person's attachment to social and familial surroundings.[11] Sequestering those who are ill is no longer arbitrary; it has become a necessary condition for treatment. The confinement established as the framework for the leprosarium, then the *hôpital général*, is at once renewed and transformed. It has been refashioned by new demands posed by philanthropy and emerging medical science. The undifferentiated space of confinement has shattered, giving birth to institutions with different aims: the asylum, the beggars' hostel, and the prison. But each one also retains a segregative aim.

Could this type of analysis been produced by a "pure" historian? To ask such a question is a way of succumbing to academic habits of analysis. What is certain is that Foucault was able to achieve it within the framework of his problematization – that is, on the basis of his sensitivity to the inherent contradictions within contemporary psychiatry – and that this problematization has enriched our knowledge of both the present and the past of the treatment of mental illness.

(2) However, Foucault's treatment of historical material was not above reproach. Here I will limit my considerations to the theme of the "great confinement," whose place in *L'Histoire de la folie* is well known. Foucault took the edict promulgated by Louis XIV in 1657 "concerning the

establishment of the *hôpital général* for the confinement of the poor and beggars of the City and Environs of Paris"[12] and made it into a founding act reviving the powers of the old enclosed space in which lepers were confined during the Middle Ages and which would serve as the matrix for controlling different types of "problem populations" within the framework of what Erving Goffman called the "total institution." Some reservations can be expressed about Foucault's interpretation of the *hôpital général*, regarding the date of its creation, the types of populations it served, and the social tactics it utilized.

First of all, the date: Catherine de Medici founded an institution of this type in 1612; as of 1614 the Hôpital Saint-Laurent opened in Lyon to house "incorrigible beggars"; its rule combined work and obligatory prayer. So much for France. But in England the Bridewell was founded in 1554 in London, followed shortly thereafter by the Rasphuis in Amsterdam, which was soon imitated by over a dozen Dutch towns.[13] All of these were *hôpitaux généraux* before the fact. To be sure, the Parisian establishment of 1657 was the result of a royal edict, which gave it a special cachet, and after 1662 the measure would spread to "all the cities and large towns of the Kingdom." Still, the *hôpital général* was not an exclusive expression of royal power. Indeed, an edict of 1662 ordered cities to establish *hôpitaux généraux* under their own management and using local resources. The Company of the Holy Sacrament, an organization of Catholic activists, would also be especially involved in the establishment of the network of *hôpitaux généraux*, which thus was not simply a creation *ex nihilo* of the power of the state.

This sort of shifting of central power to local powers and "private" jurisdictions was not unique to the *hôpital général*. It was already in operation in the establishment of "municipal policies" in the sixteenth century. The innovations made in public assistance in various French towns during the 1530s were repeated on a national level by the royal ordinance of Moulins in 1566. The same pattern can be seen in Flanders, where the order promulgated by Charles V in 1531 took responsibility for and coordinated the municipal activities of Flemish and Dutch towns.

Thus no clean break occurred between the new strategy for confinement and earlier forms of controlling the "poor and the beggars." In the sixteenth century public assistance was characterized by the development of local initiatives based on the municipality, which attempted to take on the burden of all of its less fortunate subjects, on condition that they were under local communal jurisdiction.[14] Municipal assistance claimed to be protection[15] based on domicile, which attempted to maintain community links with inhabitants that poverty, lack of work, sickness, or disability threatened to dislodge. According to Foucault, in the seventeenth century confinement would have the opposite, segregative, role: beggars and other categories likely to disturb public order were taken away from the community and confined within an enclosed space. They were stripped of their territoriality and excluded.

However, this interpretation is contestable. The inhabitants of the *hôpital général* were not so much severed from their community as displaced, that is, transferred to a specially determined location where it was possible to continue to care for them. In fact, the resocialization of the inhabitants of the *hôpital général* was supposed to take place through educational means, in the form of prayer and forced labor. Hence confinement was viewed as a kind of hiatus between a period of disorderly life during which the community bond had been stretched, but not broken, and a period of recovery where, once the link was restored by prayer and work, the recluse would once again find a place in the community. Thus the strategy of confinement is better understood as a form of continuity rather than rupture with respect to communal policies of maintaining the social bond. It became more difficult to provide protection in a direct way, no doubt because the urban network grew more extensive and complex from the sixteenth to the seventeenth centuries. Confinement was a new, more energetic (and more brutal) episode, but underlying it was the same aim: not to exclude, but as much as possible to include. However, since the at-risk populations had become more threatened by complete desocialization, a more radical form of assistance was required. Thus, confinement was an indirect route back to the community: a temporary break, not an end in itself.

This is borne out by the fact that the population originally targeted for confinement did not include those individuals who were considered to be the least socialized, the least desirable, or the most dangerous – vagrants. At first the only persons confined in the *hôpital général* were able-bodied beggars or domiciled invalids who were still "living members of Jesus Christ," as opposed to "useless members of the State."[16] The rhetoric of the time was saying that one must be considered part of the community to be eligible for the *hôpital général*. The population barred from confinement (not *excluded by* it) represented the paradigm of asociality and danger according to the standards of the time: vagrants with no fixed abode or community ties. Ordered to leave town within three days, they were subject to brutal police measures that were and would continue to be dictated in order to deal with them. They were not "worthy" of confinement, for they were completely outside of the territorial boundaries of the community.[17]

To be sure, the reformers' utopia of confinement would come to nothing (but the same might be said of what we would call social policies in all the societies of the Old Regime). The *hôpital général* soon began to house various categories of undesirables together, a situation vividly portrayed by

Foucault; and the insane, like the vagrants, found themselves there in the company of beggars, the sick and disabled, the nameless destitute, libertines, loose women, prisoners of the state, and so forth. Nonetheless, the original policy of confinement was not segregative. Segregation from the world by means of placement in the *hôpital général* was not maximal exclusion from social life. Beyond it was the situation of vagrants, who had no place anywhere, not even at the *hôpital général*, and who were driven off, banished, condemned to the galleys, and so on. Instead, confinement was protection in the extreme, so extreme that it had become a contradiction of this desire to provide public assistance.

Thus it can be seen that the discussion of the founding date of the *hôpital général* is not merely a question of historical chronology. Foucault makes 1657 into a founding moment because he wishes to mark a shift in the strategies for controlling problem populations. To display this chronology as historical documentation invites one to do is, on the contrary, to find the continuity in these policies. Then the great confinement of the seventeenth century appears within the context of earlier strategies for controlling beggars who lived inside the community. An extreme and particularly repressive version of municipal policy, it does not contradict the civic intention to keep certain, but not all, categories of the population that threaten the social order within the bounds of the community.

Do such details weaken Foucault's argument? No. It is still true that the *hôpital général* quickly became a place in which all sorts of undesirables, including the insane, were kept apart from society. And this was no accident: the crushing weight of the "total institution" turned the practices of resocialization, work, and prayer that were to have taken place inside it into a fiction. It is also true that at the end of the eighteenth century this structure came apart without being abolished, giving rise among other things to the insane asylum, which inherited its exclusionary function. So the asylum reflects a line of continuity with the locus of confinement of the eighteenth century. But one could add that it also inherited the goal of resocialization that lay at the origin of the *hôpital général*, which in this case reflects the continuity of municipal policy. The "therapeutic isolation" mentioned above emerges as the necessary means to carry out two indissoluble operations: the need to confine the sick person in order "to provide a distraction from delirium," and the desire to treat the patient by creating a therapeutic space based on this rupture with the outside world. This "happy coincidence"[18] (in reality, a carefully wrought combination) reconciles the patient's interests with the need to maintain public order in the presence of individuals who are perceived to be dangerous. The fundamental importance of "moral treatment" within and by the asylum, the therapeutic equivalent of the work and prayer of the *hôpital général*, can be understood in this context. Foucault did not emphasize these techniques of inclusion because, in the case of the asylum as well as the *hôpital général*, he was interested in their segregative functions. He was right to do so, given his goal of establishing the radical otherness of madness with respect to the order of reason. From this standpoint, he had to insist on what, in the emerging discipline of psychiatry, led to this otherness – the segregative character of institutions and practices. Nevertheless, he fully laid out only one of the aims of the *hôpital général* and the insane asylum, while the interpretation of the historical data indicates that their segregative goal could not be separated from their integrative intent.

III   THE PERILS OF PROBLEMATIZATION

I offer these comments about *L'Histoire de la folie* for three reasons. First, they illustrate some of the difficulties, which I first stated in abstract terms, of sorting through historical material, dating beginnings, and delineating periods in order to construct a problematization. That Foucault's attempt bears the brunt of some criticism is all the more significant because he is the unequaled master of this domain. I do not have the audacity to claim to correct his work but simply wish to show how difficult it is to carry out his approach.

Second, these adjustments also reflect the degree to which problematization depends on historical data. In this instance, a more exact historical interpretation of the "great confinement" – at least if my own interpretation of it is correct – would have led Foucault to extend his own problematization to give a larger place to the other goal of confinement (but this correction does not undermine the cause or the project of problematization itself or the overall outlines of the treatment Foucault gives it; on the basis of the segregative function of total institutions, he discerned a powerful interpretative grid – even if it is not the only one – that is valid for the history of these institutions as well as for their contemporary structure).

Third – and from a theoretical standpoint this is perhaps the most interesting observation – the comments I make here are themselves the result of my own attempt at problematization. I have not played the part of the historian that I am not with respect to Foucault but have reread this historical material in light of a contemporary issue as well.

I returned to the issue of the populations affected by the "great confinement" because it seemed important to distinguish between the treatments given to two types of indigents. The first, having fixed domiciles, might receive assistance. The second, stigmatized as vagrants, were considered "useless to the world,"[19] and were doubly excluded: from the community and from the order of work. But this distinction does not apply only to the seventeenth century. If one considers the totality of what would now be termed social policies in the pre-industrial society of the Christian West – regulations concerning begging and vagrancy, conditions in hospices and charitable establishments, efforts at forcing indigents to work, and so forth – one quickly notices that they all reveal this opposition between two types of populations. The first raises issues of assistance because of its links with the community, and the second falls under the domain of purely constabulary measures because it contains individuals lacking a fixed abode who were reputed to be resistant to work.

The emergence of this issue can also be dated. It took shape in the middle of the fourteenth century, with the appearance of mobile populations that no longer participated in the traditional workforce. The Statute of Laborers, promulgated in 1349 by Edward III of England, was a response to that situation. It attempted to fix the domiciles of manual laborers in both town and country, and condemned almsgiving to able-bodied indigents. It marked the beginning of the ban on vagrancy, which would continue for several centuries.[20] But the articles in the Statute of Laborers were not unique to England. In the years that followed, France, the kingdoms of Portugal, Castile, Aragon, Bavaria, and many Italian and Flemish towns – a large proportion of the "developed" Europe of the time – instituted policies that based assistance on domicile, attempted to localize the workforce, and condemned as vagrancy the mobility of able-bodied indigents.

Why bring up this historical data and reorganize it along the double axis of public assistance and the obligation to work? Because today western Europe exhibits a profile of populations, such as the long-term unemployed and young people unable to enter the workforce, who occupy a position similar to that of the "useless to the world" in pre-industrial societies. They are "supernumeraries," in the sense that they are unemployable – unable to find an assigned place in the social organization because of current economic and social changes. At the same time they pose a problem to classic systems of social protection: they are ineligible for traditional forms of assistance because they are capable of working; at the same time they are not covered by insurance or other programs linked with employment because they do not work.

The problem is both new and old. It is new, because during the 1960s western European societies thought that the risks inherent in an unstable workforce had basically been eliminated, owing to the widespread solidity of the salaried condition, with its rights and guarantees; and they reserved assistance for those who could not work. But this success relied on continued economic growth and nearly full employment. Today these societies are confronted with a problem that seems totally new to them:

what to do with needy populations who do not work although they are capable of it. For example, should such people receive a minimum subsistence level of aid? Or should new policies be enacted, what in France are termed "policies of insertion," which attempt to invent socially recognized activities outside of the classical circuits for creating employment?

But this problem also pertains to old historical constants. Social instability, the fact of living "from hand to mouth," and a haphazard relationship to work have almost always been the common lot of the "people." Thus today's experience of social instability is paradoxical. In part it is new, because it is seen against the backdrop of social protection, which formed the basis for the powerful social safety nets that have been developed since the nineteenth century. It is a product of the weakening of guarantees that had been progressively strengthened by the development of the welfare state. But today's lack of security is also an echo of earlier structural components of the condition of the disadvantaged classes: fragile ties to employment, the vulnerability that arises from constant uncertainty about the future. Is it possible to articulate what is new in today's social instability and what has been inherited from the past? This instability and the relationships to it have changed. But they have changed within the framework of the same problematization. One can attempt to write a history of this unstable present by reconstructing the principles of historical transformation that have led to the contemporary situation. I have suggested that this history began in the middle of the fourteenth century, or rather at the time when historical documentation detailed enough to make it possible to discern it began to appear. I have also suggested that one approach would be to follow the treatment of indigents who received assistance and vagrants who were excluded. In fact, those receiving assistance, beggars, and vagrants merely represent the extreme cases of the vulnerability of the masses, populations formed by the various fragmentary and unstable forms of the paid workforce in pre-industrial societies, then the lower strata of the working classes at the beginning of industrialization, and now those who have been left aside by industrialization, who have recently been termed the "Fourth World." Instability does not appear continuously like a historical invariable. It is borne by different groups and treated in different ways. But it displays common traits: types that are characterized by relationship to employment or absence of work or variously defined relationships to social assistance or its absence.

If the present is indeed a conjunction of the effects of the past and the effects of innovation, one ought to be able to discern the basis of the "discursive and non-discursive practices" that have formed it. In this instance, it is an attempt to recover the memory that structures today's formulation of the social question, which is based on the recent recognition of how risks of exclusion have multiplied and forms of protection weakened for individuals and groups located at the outer edge of the workforce and on the fringe of socially acknowledged forms of exchange. What sets these situations apart – in other words, what do they have that is the same and what is different – from periods in the past when the condition of the masses was also marked by vulnerability and uncertainty? This is indeed part of the same problematization, if it is true that different answers have been formulated and continue to be formulated on the basis of constants in the haphazard nature of the relationship to employment and difficulty of finding a stable place in the networks of protection.

I have taken the risk of outlining a work in progress.[21] The very least that can occur when discussing a specific element of Foucault's work, despite the admiration I have for him, is that I expose myself to criticism. "The perils of problematization": every problematization carries with it a risk, which now can be detailed more fully. It attempts a rereading of historical material from the standpoint of categories – in this case, social categories such as instability, vulnerability, protection, exclusion, insertion, and so forth – that are not utilized by historians to organize their own corpus. In other words, a problematization constructs *another* account from historical data. But still it must be compatible with the accounts of historians. Thus a problematization must satisfy two demands whose coexistence can itself be a problem.

First, it must contribute something to what has already been achieved by a classical historical approach. This statement may seem to be a tautology: if a problematization achieves the same insights as a historical approach, there would be no reason to make a distinction between the two, or for it to exist. But what are the standards needed to measure this "increase in knowledge"? These criteria are not based on historical rigor alone. If the original aim of writing "the history of the present" is to contribute to our knowledge of a current situation, it must be tested using other approaches to the present. For example, to what degree does Foucault's approach to the study of the treatment of mental illness enrich (or make it possible to criticize or compare) the discoveries made possible today by other approaches, such as empirical sociology, the ethnography of psychiatric practices, or the administrative or professional literature of psychiatry, and so forth? Or, again, in what way does the interpretation suggested here concerning the factors of dissociation affecting contemporary societies add something to explanations that see in it only the effects of the current economic crises, or of the recent weakening of the regulations of the welfare state?

But there is a second criterion, at least as important as the first, for judging the validity of a problematization. What a given problematization contributes to our knowledge of the present – if it contributes anything at all – must not come at the price of our knowledge of the past. In other words, to the extent that it is based on history, a problematization can be refuted if it contradicts historical knowledge; and historians are the only judges of that. The right to choose one's materials and refocus them in light of a current issue, to place them in different categories – sociological categories, for example – is not permission to rewrite history. It is not a right to make historical errors, which here can be understood as statements about history that a historian could refute. So this rereading of history prohibits even the slightest modification of the data generated by historical technique, not because these data are immutable but because altering them belongs exclusively to the procedures of the historian's craft.

The compatibility of these two demands is not self-evident and must be the object of discussion. And my chief intention here has been to introduce a few elements that would serve in opening this debate, which concerns historians as well as those who formulate problematizations.

Translated by Paula Wissing

Notes

All unattributed translations have been done by the relevant contributors or their translators.

INTRODUCTION

1. The proceedings of the conference were published as *Michel Foucault philosophe: Rencontre internationale, Paris, 9, 10, 11 janvier 1988* (Paris: Seuil, 1988).

2. Despite the huge secondary literature on Foucault, the bibliography on this subject is notably short. It includes the fifty-page opening section of *L'Impossible Prison: Recherches sur le système pénitentiaire au XIXe siècle*, ed. Michelle Perrot (Paris: Seuil, 1980), which compares the theses of *Discipline and Punish* with the findings of historians of medicine and of prisons; Jan Goldstein, "Foucault among the Sociologists: The 'Disciplines' and the History of the Professions," *History and Theory*, 23 (1984), pp. 170–92; Allen Megill, "The Reception of Foucault by Historians," *Journal of the History of Ideas*, 48 (1987), pp. 117–41; and Patricia O'Brien, "Michel Foucault's History of Culture," in *The New Cultural History*, ed. Lynn Hunt (Berkeley and Los Angeles: University of California Press, 1989), pp. 25–46. Two anthologies featuring historians' assessments of *Histoire de la folie* have recently appeared: see *Penser la folie: Essais sur Michel Foucault* (Paris: Galilée, 1992) and *Rewriting the History of Madness: Studies in Foucault's Histoire de la folie*, ed. Arthur Still and Irving Velody (London: Routledge, 1992).

3. This is as much true in France as in the United States; as Jacques Revel described the impact of *The Birth of the Clinic* on the French historical scene, "There arose . . . reflection about medicine, about the history of the sick body, about the history of the body *tout court*, that made explicit reference to Foucault and to the *Clinic* book." See "Foucault et les historiens: Entretien avec Jacques Revel," *Magazine littéraire*, 101 (June 1975), p. 10.

4   That larger historiographical picture is rapidly changing and intensely interesting. As at least one commentator has noted, Foucault's relevance and appeal to historians in the United States has increased as the American historical profession has become more divided and cantankerous about the philosophical underpinnings of its collective venture and as the earlier consensus about the positivist ideal of "objectivity" has been progressively eroded. See Peter Novick, *That Noble Dream: The "Objectivity Question" and the American Historical Profession* (Cambridge and New York: Cambridge University Press, 1988), pp. 471, 524, 535–6.

5   Or three classicists, depending upon the criteria used in the tally. Like David Halperin, the one unambiguous classicist in the group, David Cohen and Richard Saller base their work on the study of ancient Greek and Latin texts. But, in terms of their training and intellectual goals, Cohen and Saller both prefer to identify themselves as social historians.

6   George Huppert, "*Divinatio et Eruditio*: Thoughts on Foucault," *History and Theory*, 13 (1974), p. 192.

7   H. C. Erik Midelfort, "Madness and Civilization in Early Modern Europe: A Reappraisal of Michel Foucault," in *After the Reformation: Essays in Honor of J. H. Hexter*, ed. Barbara C. Malament (Philadelphia: University of Pennsylvania Press, 1980), pp. 249, 259.

8   Paul Veyne, "Foucault révolutionne l'histoire," in *Comment on écrit l'histoire* (Paris: Seuil, 1978), pp. 203–4.

9   On Foucault's recognition and exploitation of the double meaning of "discipline," see his *Discipline and Punish: The Birth of the Prison*, tr. Alan Sheridan (New York: Pantheon, 1977), pp. 186, 190.

10   Michel Foucault, "La Poussière et le nuage," in *L'Impossible Prison*, ed. Perrot, p. 39.

11   For the avowal that "not power, but the subject . . . is the general theme of my research," see Michel Foucault, "The Subject and Power," Afterword to Hubert L. Dreyfus and Paul Rabinow, *Michel Foucault: Beyond Structuralism and Hermeneutics* (Chicago: University of Chicago Press, 1982), p. 209.

12   Michel Foucault, *Power/Knowledge: Selected Interviews and Other Writings*, ed. Colin Gordon (New York: Pantheon, 1980).

13   Few of these lectures have been published; nor, according to the terms of Foucault's will, are they likely to be. One of the lectures appears, together with related pieces by Foucault and a group of scholars, in *The Foucault Effect: Studies in Governmentality*, ed. Graham Burchell, Colin Gordon, and Peter Miller (Chicago: University of Chicago Press, 1991).

14   Michel Foucault, *The Archaeology of Knowledge*, tr. A. M. Sheridan Smith (New York: Pantheon, 1972), p. 162; see also the similar pronouncement on p. 157.

15   Michel Foucault, *L'Ordre du discours: Leçon inaugurale au Collège de France prononcée le 2 décembre 1970* (Paris: Gallimard, 1971), p. 24, translated into English as "The Discourse on Language" as an appendix to Foucault, *The Archaeology of Knowledge*, p. 220.

CHAPTER 1   HISTORICIZING THE SUBJECT OF DESIRE

An earlier version of this paper, entitled "Historicizing the Sexual Body: Sexual Preferences and Erotic Identities in the Pseudo-Lucianic *Erôtes*," has been published in *Discourses of Sexuality: From Aristotle to AIDS*, ed. Domna C. Stanton (Ann Arbor: University of Michigan Press, 1992), pp. 236–61. The version published here has benefited substantially from the criticisms and suggestions of David N. Dobrin, Jan Goldstein, Paul Morrison, Ed O'Neill, Ruth Perry, Eve Kosofsky Sedgwick, and Domna C. Stanton.

1   Northrop Frye, *Anatomy of Criticism: Four Essays* (Princeton, NJ: Princeton University Press, 1957), p. 13: "Most critical efforts to handle such generic terms as 'epic' and 'novel' are chiefly interesting as examples of the psychology of rumor."

2   Julia Kristeva, quoted by Laurent Jenny in *French Literary Theory Today*, ed. Tzvetan Todorov (Cambridge: Cambridge University Press, 1981), p. 39.

3   Michel Foucault, *The History of Sexuality*, vol. 1: *An Introduction*, tr. Robert Hurley (New York: Random House, 1978), p. 69. I quote, whenever possible, from the published English translation; all unattributed translations are my own.

4   Michel Foucault, *Histoire de la sexualité*, vol. 1: *La Volonté de savoir* (Paris: Gallimard, 1976), pp. 161–8; *The History of Sexuality*, vol. 1, pp. 122–7.

5   See Gilles Deleuze, "What is a *Dispositif?*" in *Michel Foucault: Philosopher*, ed. and tr. Timothy J. Armstrong (New York: Routledge, 1992), pp. 159–68.

6   Foucault, *History of Sexuality*, vol. 1, pp. 105–6; *La Volonté de savoir*, p. 139.

7   Michel Foucault, *Histoire de la sexualité*, vol. 2: *L'Usage des plaisirs* (Paris: Gallimard, 1984), p. 10.

8   I recapitulate here the argument of my earlier essay, "Two Views of Greek Love: Harald Patzer and Michel Foucault," in my *One Hundred Years of Homosexuality and Other Essays on Greek Love* (New York and London: Routledge, 1990), pp. 54–71, esp. pp. 65–6.

9   Foucault, *History of Sexuality*, vol. 1, p. 105; *La Volonté de savoir*, p. 139.

10   Foucault, *History of Sexuality*, vol. 1, p. 103; *La Volonté de savoir*, p. 136.

11   Foucault, *La Volonté de savoir*, p. 168; I have altered Hurley's translation.

12   Foucault, *History of Sexuality*, vol. 1, p. 152; *La Volonté de savoir*, p. 200.

13   See, generally, Hubert L. Dreyfus and Paul Rabinow, *Michel Foucault: Beyond Structuralism and Hermeneutics*, 2nd edn (Chicago: University of Chicago Press, 1983); Thomas R. Flynn, "Truth and Subjectivation in the Later Foucault," *Journal of Philosophy*, 82 (1985), pp. 531–40; and the essay by Arnold I. Davidson, chapter 3 in this volume.

14   Foucault, *La Volonté de savoir*, pp. 20–1.

15   Foucault, *History of Sexuality*, vol. 1, p. 25; *La Volonté de savoir*, p. 35.

16   Foucault, *History of Sexuality*, vol. 1, p. 157 (translation slightly adapted); cf. *La Volonté de savoir*, p. 207.

17   Foucault, *La Volonté de savoir*, p. 203. See, generally, Foucault, *History of Sexuality*, vol. 1, pp. 152–7; *La Volonté de savoir*, pp. 200–8. See also Foucault's

remarks on this point in *Power/Knowledge: Selected Interviews and Other Writings 1972–77*, ed. Colin Gordon, tr. Colin Gordon, Leo Marshall, John Mepham, and Kate Soper (Brighton, Sussex: Harvester Press, 1980), pp. 190, 210–11.

18 Compare Foucault's remarks to Jean Le Bitoux in the course of an interview conducted on July 10, 1978, published in Dutch in 1982, and finally printed in two installments under the title "Le Gai Savoir" in *Mec Magazine* during the summer of 1988 (no English translation has so far appeared): "ce n'est pas parce que cette notion de sexualité nous a permis de nous battre qu'elle ne comporte pas pour autant un certain nombre de dangers. Il y a tout un biologisme de la sexualité et par conséquent toute une prise possible par les médecins et par les psychologues, bref par les instances de la normalisation. Nous avons au-dessus de nous des médecins, des pédagogues, des législateurs, des adultes, des parents qui parlent de sexualité! . . . Il ne suffit pas de libérer la sexualité, il faut aussi . . . se libérer de la notion même de sexualité." (I wish to thank Diana Fuss for calling to my attention the existence of this interview, and to Michael West for supplying me both with the text and with his own annotated, but as yet unpublished, English translation of it.)

19 On this point, see my remarks in "Bringing Out Michel Foucault," *Salmagundi*, 97 (Winter 1993), pp. 69–93.

20 For an elaboration of this point, see Judith Butler, "Imitation and Gender Insubordination," in *Inside/Out: Lesbian Theories, Gay Theories*, ed. Diana Fuss (New York: Routledge, 1991), pp. 13–31; see, generally, Judith Butler, "Contingent Foundations: Feminism and the Question of 'Postmodernism,'" in *Feminists Theorize the Political*, ed. Judith Butler and Joan W. Scott (New York: Routledge, 1992), pp. 3–21, esp. pp. 12–15, for a brilliant account of the place of "agency" in Foucauldian subject theory.

21 For an early appreciation of the political usefulness of Foucault, see the characterstically prescient remarks by Gayle Rubin, "Thinking Sex: Notes for a Radical Theory of the Politics of Sexuality," in *Pleasure and Danger: Exploring Female Sexuality*, ed. Carole S. Vance (Boston, MA: Routledge, 1984), pp. 267–319, esp. pp. 276–8, 284–8. Of particular relevance to my argument here are the insightful and incisive discussions by Ed Cohen, "Foucauldian Necrologies: 'Gay' 'Politics'? Politically Gay?," *Textual Practice*, 2, 1 (Spring 1988), pp. 87–101, and "Who Are 'We'? Gay 'Identity' as Political (E)motion (A Theoretical Rumination)," in *Inside/Out*, pp. 71–92.

22 Cf. Teresa de Lauretis, "Eccentric Subjects: Feminist Theory and Historical Consciousness," *Feminist Studies*, 16, 1 (Spring 1990), pp. 115–50.

23 I expand further on this point in an essay on "The Queer Politics of Michel Foucault," which will appear in my collection, *Plato's Locker* (New York: Oxford University Press, forthcoming).

24 *Lucian VIII*, tr. M. D. Macleod, Loeb Classical Library (Cambridge, MA: Harvard University Press, 1967), p. 147. Félix Buffière, *Eros adolescent: la pédérastie dans la Grèce antique* (Paris: Belles Lettres, 1980), p. 481, prefers a date in the second century CE.

25 Notably, Robert Bloch, *De pseudo-Luciani Amoribus* (Strasbourg: Dissertationes philologicae Argentoratenses selectae, 1907).

26 Michel Foucault, *Histoire de la sexualité*, vol. 3: *Le Souci de soi* (Paris: Gallimard, 1984), pp. 243–61.

27 Ibid., p. 261. See, especially, *Erôtes*, 23–4, 35, 48–9, 51, 53 (where Diotima's "steps" of love in Plato's *Symposium*, 211c3, are impertinently transformed into a "ladder of pleasure"), and 54.

28 See, for example, Plutarch, *Moralia*, 751a, 752a; Lucian, *Dialogues of the Courtesans*, 10; Alciphron, 4.7; Athenaeus, 13.572b.

29 Plutarch, *Moralia*, 748f–771e, and Achilles Tatius, 2.33–8: commentary by Friedrich Wilhelm, "Zu Achilles Tatius," *Rheinisches Museum für Philologie*, 57 (1902), pp. 55–75.

30 On the "Debate between Ganymede and Helen," and other such texts see John Boswell, *Christianity, Social Tolerance, and Homosexuality: Gay People in Western Europe from the Beginning of the Christian Era to the Fourteenth Century* (Chicago: University of Chicago Press, 1980), pp. 255–65.

Similarly, al-Samau'al ibn Yahyâ, a Jewish convert to Islam who died in 1180, composed a treatise entitled *Book of Conversations with Friends on the Intimate Relations Between Lovers in the Domain of the Science of Sexuality*, which is largely given over to "a long and highly technical comparison between the anal sphincter and the muscles of the uterus"; the author, who includes in his discussion a striking account of sexual relations between women, invokes the authority of the Prophet to establish the superiority of women as sexual partners for men: see Danielle Jacquart and Claude Thomasset, *Sexuality and Medicine in the Middle Ages*, tr. Matthew Adamson (Princeton, NJ: Princeton University Press, 1988), pp. 124–5. A more classical instance, "The Man's Dispute with the Learned Woman Concerning the Relative Excellence of Male and Female," can be found in the 419th Night of *The Book of the Thousand Nights and a Night*, tr. Richard F. Burton (London, ca. 1886), vol. V, pp. 154–63 (I wish to thank Joe Boone, of the University of Southern California, for helping me verify this reference); this corresponds to tales 390–3 in the J. C. Mardrus-Powys Mathers version of *The Book of the Thousand Nights and One Night* (London, 1972), vol. II, pp. 409–15: Boswell, *Christianity, Social Tolerance, and Homosexuality*, p. 257n.

31 See *Bian er chai* ("Wearing a Haircap but also Hairpins"), dated to the first half of the seventeenth century, with discussion by Keith McMahon, *Causality and Containment in Seventeenth-Century Chinese Fiction*, T'oung-pao Monograph, 15 (Leiden: Brill, 1988); cf. Charlotte Furth, "Androgynous Males and Deficient Females: Biology and Gender Boundaries in Sixteenth- and Seventeenth-Century China," *Late Imperial China*, 9, 2 (December 1988), pp. 1–31. See also the first chapter of *Pinhua baojian* ("Precious Mirror for Judging Flowers"), published in 1849 by Chen Sen: commentary by Bret Hinsch, *Passions of the Cut Sleeve: The Male Homosexual Tradition in China* (Berkeley: University of California Press, 1990), pp. 156–61. (I wish to thank Maram Epstein, of the University of Michigan, and Gregory M. Pflugfelder, of Stanford University, for kindly supplying me with these references.)

32   On the *danjo yûretsu ron* – which is a modern Japanese designation for the
      largely seventeenth-century genre of erotic debate over the relative merits of
      women and boys as sexual partners for adult men – see the translator's
      introduction to Ihara Saikaku, *The Great Mirror of Male Love*, tr. Paul Gordon
      Schalow (Stanford, CA: Stanford University Press, 1990), p. 7.

33   I use "boy" here, when speaking about Greek sexual practices, in something of
      a technical sense: the term "boy" translates the Greek word *pais*, which refers
      by convention in Greek sexual discourse to the junior partner in a pederastic
      relationship, or to one who plays that role, regardless of his actual age; youths
      are customarily supposed to be desirable between the onset of puberty and the
      arrival of the beard: see K. J. Dover, *Greek Homosexuality* (London: Duckworth,
      1978), pp. 16, 85–7; Buffière, *Eros adolescent*, pp. 605–14. "Boy" refers, then,
      not to male children categorically but to adolescents or teenagers, or to young
      men more generally in their capacity as objects of male erotic desire.

34   Halperin, *One Hundred Years of Homosexuality*, p. 34.

35   All translations of the *Erôtes* included in this paper follow closely the text and
      translation of Macleod, though I have freely altered the translation where
      necessary. The vehemence of Charicles and Callicratidas, the participants in
      the discussion about the relative sexual merits of women and boys that occupies
      the body of the text, is balanced by the disengagement of Lycinus and
      Theomnestus, the speakers in the framing dialogue, who are either indifferent
      to both women and boys (in the case of Lycinus: 4) or equally attracted to each
      (in the case of Theomnestus: 3, 4). See Foucault, *Le Souci de soi*, p. 243.

36   *Lucian VIII*, tr. Macleod, p. 147.

37   For a recent example of the inability to conceive sexual preference in terms
      other than those of sexual orientation, and of the abuse to which such a rigid
      approach subjects the Kinsey scale (which Kinsey hmself designed specifically
      in order to categorize sexual behavior without reference to the concepts of
      hetero- and homosexual identity), see John Boswell, "Categories, Experience
      and Sexuality," in *Forms of Desire: Sexual Orientation and the Social Construction-
      ist Controversy*, ed. Edward Stein, Garland Gay and Lesbian Studies, 1 (New
      York: Garland, 1990), pp. 133–73; the abridged version of this essay, which
      appears in *differences*, 2, 1 (Spring 1990), pp. 67–87, under the title, "Concepts,
      Experience, and Sexuality," omits any mention of the Kinsey scale. For some
      current meditations of the use and abuse of the Kinsey scale, see *Homosexuality/
      Heterosexuality: Concepts of Sexual Orientation*, ed. David P. McWhirter,
      Stephanie A. Sanders, and June Machover Reinisch, Kinsey Institute Series
      (New York: Oxford University Press, 1990).

38   See, now, Judith P. Hallett, "Female Homoeroticism and the Denial of Roman
      Reality in Latin Literature," *Yale Journal of Criticism*, 3, 1 (Fall 1989), pp. 209–
      27, and compare George Chauncey, Jr, "From Sexual Inversion to Homo-
      sexuality: The Changing Medical Conceptualization of Female Deviance," in
      Passion and Power: Sexuality in History, ed. Kathy Peiss and Christina Simmons
      (Philadelphia: Temple Universeity Press, 1989), pp. 87–117, esp. p. 99 and
      p. 113, n. 50. Further references to compilations of ancient evidence for the

"tribad" can be found in Halperin, *One Hundred Years of Homosexuality*, p. 166, n. 83, p. 180, n. 2; and in Bernadette J. Brooten, *Early Christian Responses to Female Homoeroticism and Their Historical Context*, forthcoming.

[39] The point seems to be that for a man to keep a boyfriend who is approaching the age of manhood is to cast doubt on his own masculinity – that is, on his identity as sexually "active," or insertive, as opposed to sexually "passive," or receptive; for a similar reproach, cf. Dio Cassius, 62.6.4.

[40] Cf. Saikaku, *The Great Mirror*, 1:4 (p. 69): "It is said that, 'Cherry blossoms forever bloom the same, but people change with every passing year.' This is especially true of a boy in the bloom of youth. . . . When at last he comes of age, his blossom of youth falls cruelly to the ground. All told, loving a boy can be likened to a dream that we are not given time to have."

[41] The first phrase translates *anima muliebris virili corpore inclusa*, the notorious self-description of Karl Heinrich Ulrichs, the mid-nineteenth-century founder of the German movement for homosexual emancipation: see Hubert C. Kennedy, "The 'Third Sex' Theory of Karl Heinrich Ulrichs," in *Historical Perspectives on Homosexuality*, ed. Salvatore J. Licata and Robert P. Petersen, *Journal of Homosexuality*, 6, 1–2 (1980–1), pp. 103–11; Hubert C. Kennedy, *Ulrichs: The Life and Works of Karl Heinrich Ulrichs, Pioneer of the Modern Gay Movement* (Boston, MA, 1988), pp. 43–53. The second phrase refers to the theories of Magnus Hirschfeld and Edward Carpenter, two early writers and activists: Hirschfeld's journal (which began publication at the turn of the century) was entitled *Jahrbuch für sexuelle Zwischenstufen*; compare Carpenter, *The Intermediate Sex: A Study of Some Transitional Types of Men and Women*, 2nd edn (London: Sonnenschein, 1909). For the best general account of the inversion model, see Chauncey, "From Sexual Inversion to Homosexuality"; for the classic literary representation of male inversion, see Marcel Proust, *Sodom and Gomorrah* ("Cities of the Plain"), Part 1.

[42] This is what Eve Kosofsky Sedgwick, *Epistemology of the Closet* (Berkeley: University of California Press, 1990), pp. 87–90, terms the "gender separatist" model – which, as she notes, is still with us today, coexisting with the inversion model.

[43] See, e.g., *Homeric Hymn to Aphrodite*, 225–36; Aristophanes, *Ecclesiazusae*, 720; Dio Chrysostom, 7.117; Pausanias, 7.23.1–2; Lucian, *Dialogues of the Court- esans*, 7.2–3.

[44] Cf. Dio Cassius, 62.6.3, who makes Boudicca, the female leader of the Britons, remark that "Nero is a man in name but he is a woman in deed" (the implication being that he plays a "feminine" or "passive" role in sexual relations) – and one "sign" (*sêmeion*) of that is his use of cosmetics (*kallôpizetai*). (I owe this citation to a paper by Amy Richlin, "Barbarian Queens," delivered at the 1992 meeting of the Philological Association of the Pacific Coast.) Plutarch, *Pericles*, 12, similarly associates cosmetics (*kallôpizein*) with women.

[45] See Chariton, *Chaereas and Callirhoe*, 1.4, where a man who wishes to be mistaken for an adulterer makes a similarly lavish use of cosmetics: "his hair was gleaming and heavily scented; his eyes were made up; he had a soft cloak

and fine shoes; heavy rings gleamed on his fingers" (tr. B. P. Reardon, in *Collected Ancient Greek Novels*, ed. B. P. Reardon (Berkeley: University of California Press, 1989), p. 27). Similarly, Artemidorus observes that men who dream that they wear facial make-up, jewelry, or unguents will suffer disgrace (i.e. will be exposed) as adulterers: see pp. 81.15–17, 106.16–107.2, and 269.11–13 Pack, cited with discussion by Suzanne MacAlister, "Gender as Sign and Symbolism in Artemidoros' *Oneirokritika*: Social Aspirations and Anxieties," *Helios*, 19, 1–2 (1992), pp. 140–60, esp. pp. 149–50. Compare the representations of Agathon in Old Comedy: commentary by Froma I. Zeitlin, "Travesties of Gender and Genre in Aristophanes' *Thesmophorizusae*," in *Reflections of Women in Antiquity*, ed. Helene P. Foley (New York: Gordon & Breach, 1981), pp. 169–217; Frances Muecke, "A Portrait of the Artist as a Young Woman," *Classical Quarterly*, 32 (1982), pp. 41–55.

[46]   Rosemary Daniell, *Sleeping with Soldiers: In Search of the Macho Man* (New York, 1984), p. 71. In the *Erôtes*, Lycinus' description of the erotically ambidexterous Theomnestus, whose life is given over to wrestling schools, fancy clothes, and elaborate hairstyles (3), similarly combines elements traditionally associated with the love of boys (outdoor physical exercise) and the love of women (personal adornment).

[47]   Foucault, *History of Sexuality*, vol. 1, p. 43.

[48]   See, e.g., Achilles Tatius, 2.38.2.

[49]   Could this phrase, *hôs hêdys ho gelôs*, be the source of Rilke's "Sonst ... im leisen Drehen / Der Lenden könnte nicht ein Lächeln gehen / Zu jener Mitte, die die Zeugung trug," in his famous sonnet (in the second part of the *Neue Gedichte*) on an "Archaic Torso of Apollo"?

[50]   Discussion by David Freedberg, *The Power of Images: Studies in the History and Theory of Response* (Chicago: University of Chicago Press, 1989), pp. 331–2, with notes.

[51]   I wish to thank Kevin Lee, Professor of Classics at the University of Sydney, for this attractive interpretation of the comparative force of the Greek adverb.

[52]   A reply to the argument about the relative durability of women and boys as objects of male sexual enjoyment is provided by a character in Achilles Tatius, 2.36: "Kleitophon, you don't know the principal fact about pleasure: to be unsatisfied is always a desirable state. Constant recourse to anything makes satisfaction shrivel into satiation. What can only be snatched is always fresh and blooming – its pleasure never grows old. And as much as beauty's span is diminished in time, so is it intensified in desire. The rose for this reason is lovelier than other plants: its beauty soon is gone" (tr. John J. Winkler, in *Collected Ancient Greek Novels*, pp. 205–6).

[53]   W. H. Auden, *Collected Poems*, ed. Edward Mendelson (New York: Random House, 1976), p. 129.

[54]   See Foucault, *Le Souci de soi*, pp. 246–59, for a detailed elaboration of this point. Compare Saikaku, *The Great Mirror*, 5:2, in which a boy is held back momentarily from having sex with a beautiful girl who offers herself to him – not by his own lack of desire for her but by his personal commitments,

specifically by his hitherto unswerving devotion to the way of boy-love (pp. 200–1).

55 "Julian and Maddalo," vv. 39–42.

56 Saikaku, *The Great Mirror*, pp. 53, 56. Paul Gordon Schalow, the translator, explains in his introduction that "In the first case, Saikaku is describing the age when boys and girls first become aware of themselves sexually. The girl fusses over her outward appearance in a mirror, whereas the boy is concerned about the less noticeable but in some ways more important cleanliness of his teeth. The preference implicit here is for the boy's more innocent and perhaps less calculating concern with hygiene than with superficial appearances. In the second case, neither situation with courtesan or actor allows sexual intercourse for the paying patron, but the 'intimate conversation' possible with the kabuki boy provides a recompense of sorts, suggesting a nonsexual satisfaction found in having an affair with an actor that is lacking with a courtesan. The third example juxtaposes two financially draining situations, supporting a sick wife versus supporting a spendthrift boy. Again the implication is that the sick wife represents a hopeless situation, whereas the boy, in spite of his spending habits, offers some pleasurable compensations" (p. 12). I wonder if a similarly earnest account could be given of the fourth example. For further arguments, see my review of Schalow's translation in the *Journal of Japanese Studies*, 17 (1991), pp. 398–403.

In the *Erôtes*, similarly, Callicratidas juxtaposes the image of a girl with a mirror and a comb to that of a boy with a book and a lyre (44).

57 For a fuller documentation, see Dover, *Greek Homosexuality*; John J. Winkler, *The Constraints of Desire: The Anthropology of Sex and Gender in Ancient Greece* (New York: Routledge, 1990); Halperin, *One Hundred Years of Homosexuality*; *Before Sexuality: The Construction of Erotic Experience in the Ancient Greek World*, ed. D. Halperin, J. Winkler, and Froma I. Zeitlin (Princeton, NJ: Princeton University Press, 1990); and the various studies cited in those works.

58 Cf. Paul Gordon Schalow, "Male Love in Early Modern Japan: A Literary Depiction of the 'Youth,' " in *Hidden from History: Reclaiming the Gay and Lesbian Past*, ed. Martin Bauml Duberman, Martha Vicinus, and George Chauncey, Jr (New York: New American Library, 1989), pp. 118–28, 506–9, esp. p. 120: "Those who pursued sexual relations exclusively with women or exclusively with youths were in a minority and were considered mildly eccentric for limiting their pleasurable options."

59 For more elaborate philosophical arguments to this effect, see my essays, "Platonic *Erôs* and What Men Call Love," *Ancient Philosophy*, 5 (1985), pp. 161–204, esp. pp. 182–7, and "Plato and the Metaphysics of Desire," *Proceedings of the Boston Area Colloquium in Ancient Philosophy, 5 (1989)*, ed. John J. Cleary and Daniel C. Shartin (Lanham, MD: University Press of America, 1991), pp. 27–52, esp. pp. 29–36.

60 D. A. Miller, "The Late Jane Austen," *Raritan*, 10, 1 (Summer 1990), pp. 55–79 (quotation on p. 57, with my italics). Much of the remainder of Miller's essay is taken up with adumbrating that fundamental insight.

CHAPTER 2 FOUCAULT ON SEXUALITY IN
GRECO-ROMAN ANTIQUITY

1   Other critics have pointed to Foucault's selection of texts and his lack of interest in women, but in view of the influence of *The History of Sexuality* we believe it important to offer a detailed analysis. Whether Foucault would have found the following critique relevant – a concern of some reviewers such as Averil Cameron, *Journal of Roman Studies*, 76 (1986), p. 267 – is irrelevant to us, as readers decide for themselves how Foucault's partiality affects his claims.

2   Michel Foucault *The Use of Pleasure*, tr. R. Hurley (New York: Vintage, 1986), p. 4.

3   Ibid., p. 6.

4   Ibid., pp. 10–11.

5   Ibid., pp. 30–1. This denial is quite explicit in a 1983 interview (*Foucault Reader*, ed. Paul Rabinow (New York: Pantheon, 1984), p. 343): "ethics is not related to any social- or at least legal-institutional system." Foucault bases this view upon the failure of Greek philosophers and moralits to problematize the "great interdictions" like incest. Although it is not clear why one would have expected Plato or Aristotle to problematize incest and other "great interdictions," Greek literature certainly did. Foucault claims that incest was not a matter of real concern, yet plays and myths around Oedipus and Electra explore such themes. Likewise the *Oresteia* revolves around matricide and the murder of Agamemnon by his wife, *Medea* focuses on male infidelity which is avenged through Medea's killing of her own children, and *Hippolytus* centers upon the love of a stepmother for her stepson, which leads his father to cause his death. Foucault ignores such texts, though the claims for Sophocles and Euripides to be counted as moralists are certainly at least as weighty for Xenophon and Plutarch. Foucault's claim that "Greek thought" does not problematize its central prohibitions thus does not bear scrutiny.

6   This claim is particularly puzzling for Rome, which, apart from the supervision of morals through institutions like the censor, developed the most comprehensive set of juridicial institutions known in the West until the modern period.

7   See, e.g., Foucault, *The Use of Pleasure*, pp. 250–3.

8   *Foucault Reader*, ed. Rabinow, p. 356.

9   See the detailed discussion of this point in D. Cohen, *Law, Sexuality, and Society: The Enforcement of Morals in Classical Athens* (Cambridge: Cambridge University Press, 1991), ch. 9.

10   Foucault, *The Use of Pleasure*, p. 54.

11   Aristotle, *Rhetoric*, 1368b.

12   Aristotle, *Rhetoric*, 1366b.

13   The same problem often arises in the orators, as in Aeschines' *Against Timarchus*.

14   See also the *Erotic Essay*, attributed to Demosthenes, 17–20, and Cohen, *Law*,

Sexuality and Society, chs 4 and 7, and K. J. Dover, *Greek Homosexuality* (Cambridge, MA: Harvard University Press, 1978), chs 1 and 2.

[15] These are catalogued at length, for example, by Aristotle in the *Rhetoric* and *Nicomachean Ethics*. As Aristotle's *Rhetoric* would lead one to expect, the Athenian forensic orations largely revolve around such judgments. Strikingly, Foucault nowhere discusses the pervasive Athenian antimony of public and private, though this dichotomization of social life is surely relevant to his theme. See Cohen, *Law, Sexuality, and Society*, ch. 4.

[16] Pausanias, in Plato's *Symposium*, claims that some Greek cities prohibit pederasty outright, others explicitly permit it, and yet in others, like Athens and Sparta, its status is ambiguous and complicated.

[17] Foucault, *The Use of Pleasure*, p. 190.

[18] Ibid., p. 196.

[19] Ibid., p. 192. Foucault resolutely maintains, however, that even where the Greeks do recognize sexual norms these norms have nothing in common with later Christian regulations concerning prohibited acts, positions, and so on. Surprisingly, while Foucault draws so heavily upon Dover's general interpretation, he completely ignores Dover's analysis of the portrayal of homoerotic activity in Attic vase painting. Reading the vase paintings together with the literary evidence, Dover and others have argued that there do seem to be norms concerning positions and acts: no anal intercourse or oral intercourse; intercrural intercourse permitted in an upright position facing one another; no assuming the sexual postures appropriate for a woman, slave, prostitute, etc. For a discussion of the problems with such conclusions see Cohen, *Law, Sexuality, and Society*, ch. 7.

[20] Foucault, *The Use of Pleasure*, p. 210.

[21] Ibid., p. 220. See also p. 221: "[I]t is not unusual to find the assertion that relations between men, or more generally, between two individuals of the same sex, is *para physin*, beside [against] nature."

[22] Xenophon, *Memorabilia*, 2.1.30.

[23] See *Foucault Reader*, ed. Rabinow, pp. 344–5.

[24] Foucault, *The Use of Pleasure*, p. 192.

[25] Ibid., p. 196. See also p. 209: Courtship "did not 'go without saying': it had to be accompanied by conventions, rules of conduct, ways of going about it."

[26] Ibid., p. 44.

[27] Xenophon, *Agesilaus*, 5. 4–7.

[28] Indeed, his execution, like the literary portrayal of Athenian perceptions of "intellectuals" in Aristophanes' *Clouds*, provides ample testimony to the limits of personal choice at Athens. On the question of intolerance in ancient societies, see the fundamental contributions of P. Garnsey, "Religious Toleration in Classical Antiquity," in *Persecution and Toleration*, ed. W. J. Shields, Studies in Church History, 21 (1984), pp. 1–21, and K. Dover, "The Freedom of the Intellectual in Greek Society," *Talanta* (1976), pp. 25–54.

[29] See, e.g., Foucault, *The Use of Pleasure*, p. 77, where Foucault describes self-

mastery (*askesis*) as the "practical training" indispensable "in classical Greek thought," "for an individual to form himself as a moral subject."

30   Ibid., p. 77.
31   Michel Foucault, *The Care of the Self*, tr. R. Hurley (New York: Random House, 1986), p. 36.
32   Ibid., pp. 72, 74.
33   Ibid., p. 74.
34   Ibid., pp. 148–9.
35   Ibid., pp. 150–9.
36   Ibid., p. 179.
37   Ibid., p. 164.
38   Paul Veyne, "La Famille et l'amour sous le Haut-Empire romain," *Annales, ESC*, 33 (1978), pp. 35–63, quoted in Foucault, *Care of the Self*, p. 74.
39   Cicero, *De officiis*, 1.12, *De finibus*, 4.17; on slaves, Cato, *De agricultura*, 143.1, and Varro, *De re rustica*, 1.17.5. On the confusion between legal marriage and *de facto* marriage in historical accounts of the European family, see R. Saller, "European Family History and Roman Law," *Continuity and Change*, 6 (1991), pp. 335–46.
40   S. Dixon, "The Marriage Alliance in the Roman Elite," *Journal of Family History*, 10 (1985), pp. 353–78.
41   Tacitus, *Agricola*, 6.
42   R. Saller, "Slavery and the Roman Family," in *Classical Slavery*, ed. M. I. Finley (London: Frank Cass, 1987), pp. 71–6.
43   Columella, 12, preface, 8–10.
44   Plutarch, *Cato*, 20.2.
45   A. Gellius, *Attic Nights*, 1.6.
46   Athenaus, *Deipnosophists*, 13.556ff.
47   Juvenal, *Sixth Satire*, 434–51.
48   Averil Cameron, "Redrawing the Map: Early Christian Territory after Foucault," *Journal of Roman Studies*, 76 (1986), p. 267; it may be, as Cameron suggests, that Foucault felt no qualms about selectivity because he was "conducting a discourse about discourse," yet the interpretation of any element of the ancient discourse depends in part on how the author was situated within the wider discourse.
49   Pliny, *Letters*, 1.14.
50   Pliny, *Letters*, 6.26.
51   Susan Treggiari, *Roman Marriage: Iusti Coniuges from the Time of Cicero to the Time of Ulpian* (Oxford: Clarendon Press, 1991), ch. 3, shows how constant and conventional the criteria for choice of spouses remained throughout the republic and early empire.
52   Musonius Rufus, frag. 7.
53   Plutarch, *Moralia*, 142d.
54   Plutarch, *Moralia*, 754a–d.
55   Foucault, *Care of the Self*, p. 160 (my italics).

56 A. N. Sherwin-White, *Letters of Pliny* (Oxford: Oxford University Press, 1966). See Pliny, *Letters*, 4.19.
57 Musonius Rufus, frag. 3.
58 Ibid.
59 Diogenes Laertius, 6.96.
60 Musonius, frag. 3.
61 Musonius, frag. 4.
62 Plutarch, *Moralia*, 145b–c.
63 Plutarch, *Moralia*, 142d.
64 Plutarch, *Moralia*, 142f.
65 Plutarch, *Moralia*, 139d–f.
66 Plutarch, *Moralia*, 139d, 140d.
67 Plutarch, *Moralia*, 143b–c.
68 Plutarch, *Moralia*, 140e.
69 Plutarch, *Moralia*, 142e.
70 When R. Flacelière, "La Pensée de Plutarque dans les 'Vies'," *Bulletin de l'Association Guillaume Budé* (1979), pp. 264–75, nominated Plutarch, who applauded the Alcestis exemplum, to be patron of the Mouvement de Libération de la Femme, he revealed more about his own attitudes than about those of Plutarch.
71 Foucault, *Care of the Self*, p. 173.
72 Plutarch, *Moralia*, 140b.
73 Plutarch, *Moralia*, 768a.
74 Foucault, *The Use of Pleasure*, p. 162.
75 Plutarch, *Moralia*, 140c.
76 Xenophon, *Oeconomicus*, 10.4.
77 Foucault, *Care of the Self*, p. 74.
78 F. Bartkowski, "Epistemic Drift in Foucault," in *Feminism and Foucault: Reflections on Resistance*, ed. Irene Diamond and Lee Quinby (Boston, MA: Northeastern University Press, 1988), p. 45; it is not only that Foucault "gives no voice to its 'other half'," but that he is uninterested in his authors' own representations of the "other half." Amy Richlin, *Helios* (1991), pp. 160–80, makes this point in a general argument about Foucault's neglect of women and feminist scholarship.
79 *Foucault Live*, ed. S. Lotringer, tr. J. Johnston (New York: Semiotext(e), 1989), p. 2.
80 Ibid., p. 9.
81 Though, as pointed out above, the examination is highly selective.
82 Ibid., p. 59.
83 Ibid., p. 148.
84 Ibid., p. 149.
85 Michel Foucault, *Power/Knowledge: Selected Interviews and Other Writings*, ed. Colin Gordon (Brighton, Sussex: Harvester, 1980), pp. 183–4, tr. Colin Gordon. See also p. 187: "For me the whole point of the project [*History of Sexuality*] lies in a re-elaboration of the theory of power."

[86] *Foucault Live*, ed. Lotringer, p. 320.

[87] Ibid., p. 295. The interview took place in spring 1984.

[88] Ibid., p. 304.

[89] One might even question what room had been left for the subject after the earlier projects. See, for example, *Foucault Live*, ed. Lotringer, p. 329: Question: "The question of the subject is, you say, what deflected your study in a new direction. Yet your preceding books appear to ruin the sovereignty of the subject." Answer: "It was a matter therefore of reintroducing the problem of the subject that I had more or less left aside in my first studies and trying to follow the progress and difficulties through its whole history. Perhaps there is some guile in saying things this way, but in fact what I really wanted to do was to show how the problem of the subject has not ceased to exist throughout this question of sexuality."

[90] Ibid., pp. 309–10.

[91] "Men," because Foucault specifically excludes women from this development.

[92] *Foucault Live*, ed. Lotringer, p. 311. In the same interview he denies that there is a universal form of subjectivity, and claims instead that the subject is formed either through practices of subjection or "through practices of liberation, of freedom, as in Antiquity." See also the interview in *Foucault Reader*, ed. Rabinow, p. 355, on the "self-reforming activity."

[93] *Foucault Reader*, ed. Rabinow, p. 340.

[94] *Foucault Live*, ed. Lotringer, p. 320. The references to the "chief of state" and "chief of the army" are rather puzzling in the classical Greek context.

[95] On the linear model of change, see, for example, the interview (*Foucault Reader*, ed. Rabinow, p. 340), where Foucault traces the gradual shift from concern about food to concern about sex in Western thought from the Greeks to the seventeenth century.

[96] Foucault, *The Care of the Self*, p. 74.

CHAPTER 3   ETHICS AS ASCETICS

I am indebted to Diane Brentari, Stanley Cavell, Jim Conant, Jan Goldstein, Pierre Hadot, and David Halperin for comments on and discussions of earlier versions of this chapter.

[1] My understanding of these unpublished volumes is derived both from remarks made by Foucault in volume 1 of *The History of Sexuality* and from conversations with him in 1976 just after the publication of that volume.

[2] Arnold I. Davidson, "Archaeology, Genealogy, Ethics," in *Foucault: A Critical Reader*, ed. David Couzens Hoy (Oxford: Basil Blackwell, 1986).

[3] Michel Foucault, *The Use of Pleasure* (New York: Pantheon, 1985), pp. 26–32. See also "On the Genealogy of Ethics: An Overview of Work in Progress," in *The Foucault Reader*, ed. Paul Rabinow (New York: Pantheon, 1984).

[4] Michel Foucault, "Subjectivité et verité, 1980–81," in *Résumé des cours, 1970–1982* (Paris: Julliard, 1989), pp. 134–5.

5 Ibid., pp. 135–6.

6 Ibid., p. 134.

7 Paul Veyne, "The Final Foucault and His Ethics," *Critical Inquiry*, 20, 1 (Autumn 1993), p. 7.

8 Michel Foucault, *The Care of the Self* (New York: Pantheon, 1986), p. 41.

9 Ibid., p. 64.

10 Ibid., p. 66.

11 Ibid., pp. 66–7. The quotation from Seneca is from "Epistle XXIII" of Seneca, *The Epistles of Seneca* (Cambridge, MA: Harvard University Press, 1917).

12 Foucault, *The Care of the Self*, p. 66. Pierre Hadot, "Réflexions sur la notion de 'culture de soi,' " in *Michel Foucault philosophe* (Paris: Seuil, 1989), p. 262.

13 Hadot, "Réflexions," p. 262.

14 Ibid., p. 263, and Pierre Hadot, *Exercices spirituels et philosophie antique*; 2nd rev. edn (Paris: Etudes Augustiniennes, 1987), pp. 218–19, 231.

15 Hadot, "Réflexions," p. 263. See also Pierre Hadot, "Le Sage et le monde," in *Le Temps de la réflexion*, vol. X (Paris: Gallimard, 1989), pp. 176–7.

16 Hadot, "Réflexions," p. 267.

17 Hadot, *Exercices spirituels*, p. 232.

18 Michel Foucault, "L'Herméneutique du sujet, 1981–82," in *Résumé des cours, 1970–1982*, pp. 145–9.

19 On the notion of the dilation of the self, see Hadot, *Exercices spirituels*, p. 231.

20 Hadot, "Réflexions," p. 267. See also Hadot, "Le Sage et le monde," p. 176.

21 Hadot, "Réflexions," p. 267.

22 For Foucault's discussion of Baudelaire and dandyism, see "What is Enlightenment?", in *The Foucault Reader*, ed. Rabinow, pp. 39–42.

23 I do think that Hadot's interpretation of these ancient texts is the historically accurate interpretation. Foucault's interpretations are, I believe, motivated, at least in part, by his specific interest in the history of the present, by, for example, his interest in the notion of homosexual *askesis* (that I discuss later in this essay) and by his insistence, in discussing dandyism in "What is Enlightenment?" (pp. 41–42), on linking the ascetic and the aesthetic. For Hadot the relation between beauty and moral value, or the good, is quite different (see *Excercices spirituel*, p. 231). As Hadot recognizes, what it ultimately at stake is not just differences of interpretation, but basic philosophical choices ("Réflexions," p. 261).

24 Arnold I. Davidson, "Spiritual Exercises and Ancient Philosophy: An Introduction to Pierre Hadot," *Critical Inquiry*, 16, 3 (Spring 1990).

25 Hadot, *Exercices spirituels*, p. 218. For more discussion, see Davidson, "Spiritual Exercises."

26 Foucault, *The Use of Pleasure*, p. 9.

27 Ibid.

28 In what follows, I say nothing about the Wittgensteinian idea (which is distinct from that of a way of life and a style of life) of forms of life. My understanding of the latter idea follows Stanley Cavell, *This New Yet Unapproachable America* (Albuquerque, New Mexico: Living Batch Press, 1989), pp. 40–52.

29 Pierre Hadot, "Forms of Life and Forms of Discourse in Ancient Philosophy," *Critical Inquiry*, 16, 3 (Spring 1990), pp. 491–2.

30 Hadot, *Exercices spirituels*, ch. 2.

31 Ibid., pp. 51–2, 57, 225. For more discussion of this point, see Davidson, "Spiritual Exercises," pp. 477–8.

32 Hadot, "Forms of Life and Forms of Discourse in Ancient Philosophy," p. 495.

33 Foucault, "L'Herméneutique du sujet," pp. 148–9.

34 Michel Foucault, "The Concern for Truth," in *Foucault Live (Interviews, 1966–84)*, ed. S. Lotringer, tr. J. Johnston (New York: Semiotext(e), 1989), p. 302.

35 Michel Foucault, "Friendship as a Way of Life," in *Foucault Live*, ed. Lotringer, p. 206.

36 Ibid., pp. 206–7.

37 Foucault, *The Use of Pleasure*, p. 50.

38 Foucault, "Friendship as a Way of Life," pp. 205–7; Michel Foucault, "Sexual Choice, Sexual Act," in *Foucault Live*, ed. Lotringer, p. 228; and "Michel Foucault: An Interview: Sex, Power and the Politics of Identity," in *Advocate*, August 7, 1984.

39 Michel Foucault, "Michel Foucault: Le Gai-Savoir," in *Mec Magazine* (June 1988), p. 34. See also "Michel Foucault: An Interview: Sex, Power and the Politics of Identity," p. 27.

40 Foucault, "Michel Foucault: An Interview: Sex, Power and the Politics of Identity," p. 27.

41 Foucault, "Sexual Choice, Sexual Act," p. 228.

42 Discussions with Pierre Hadot have made it clear to me that my claims here depend on the view, which I believe was Foucault's view, that homosexuality, as he wanted to understand it, could involve a style of life in the sense of a philosophical ethics. It is such an understanding that allows one to link ancient philosophical *askesis* and contemporary homosexual *askesis*.

43 The notion of the history of the present appears at the end of chapter 1 of Michel Foucault, *Discipline and Punish: The Birth of the Person* (New York: Vintage Books, 1979).

44 Jean-Pierre Vernant, "The Individual within the City-State," in *Mortals and Immortals: Collected Essays*, ed. Froma I. Zeitlin (Princeton, NJ: Princeton University Press, 1991), p. 321.

45 Ibid.

46 Ibid.

47 Ibid.

48 Ibid., p. 322. See Arnaldo Momigliano, "Marcel Mauss e il problema della persona nella biografia greca," in *Ottavo contributo alla storia degli studi classici e del mondo antico* (Roma: Edizioni di storia e letteratura, 1987). For related issues, see Paul Veyne, *Roman Erotic Elegy* (Chicago: University of Chicago Press, 1988).

49 Jean-Pierre Vernant, "Psuche: Simulacrum of the Body or Image of the Divine," in *Mortals and Immortals*. The quotation is from p. 190.

50 Vernant, "The Individual within the City-State," p. 330.

51 Ibid.

52 Ibid., pp. 328–9, 332.

53 The first quotation is from Foucault, *The Care of the Self*, p. 42. The second quotation is from Vernant, "Psuche: Simulacrum of the Body or Image of the Divine," p. 192.

54 Pierre Hadot, *Titres et Travaux de Pierre Hadot*, privately printed by the Collège de France, p. 28.

55 Pierre Hadot, "Le Figure du sage dans l'Antiquité gréco-latine" in *Les Sagesses du monde*, ed. Gilbert Gadoffre (Paris: Editions Universitaires, 1991), p. 13.

56 Paul Veyne, "La Médication interminable," in Seneca, *De la tranquillité de l'âme* (Paris: Editions Rivages, 1988), p. 56.

57 Cited by Hadot, in "La Figure de sage," p. 13.

58 Ibid., p. 11.

59 Ibid., pp. 18, 22.

60 I shall not take up here the complicated question of the precise relation between the ideas of the *daimón* and the sage. Each of them corresponds, in a certain way, to a transcendent norm. But the *daimón*, which derives from religious psychology, is perceived as an active presence in the soul, while the sage is conceived of as an almost inaccessible ideal that orients and guides one's life. I am indebted to Pierre Hadot for discussion on this point. See Hadot, *Exercices spirituels*, pp. 102–3, 105–6; *La Citadelle intérieure: Introduction aux "Pensées" de Marc Aurèle* (Paris: Fayard, 1992), pp. 92–3, 139–41, 176–7; and "La Figure du sage," especially p. 20.

61 See also Seneca, "Epistle XLI" and "Epistle CXXIV," *The Epistles of Seneca*.

62 Seneca, "Epistle LIX," *The Epistles of Seneca*, p. 417.

63 The first quotation is from "Epistle XXIII," *The Epistles of Seneca*, p. 161; the second quotation is from "Epistle LIX," *The Epistles of Seneca*, p. 417. See also "Epistle XLI," *The Epistles of Seneca*.

64 Hadot, "La Figure du sage," p. 20.

65 See Pierre Hadot, "La Terre vue d'en haut et le voyage cosmique: Le point du vue du poète, du philosophe et de l'historien," in *Frontiers and Space Conquest*, ed. J. Schneider and M. Léger-Orine (Dordrecht: Kluwer Academic Publishers, 1988); "Histoire de la pensée hellénistique et romaine: La physique comme exercice spirituel et le regard d'en haut," in *Annuaire du Collège de France, 1987–1988: Résumé des cours et travaux* (Paris: Collège de France, 1988); and *La Citadelle intérieure*, pp. 188–93.

66 Pierre Hadot, *Exercices spirituels*, pp. 48–9, 46–7. The revelant text of Plotinus is *Ennead*, I.6.9. I discuss this passage and Hadot's interpretation of it at length in my introduction to Pierre Hadot, *Plotinus or the Simplicity of Vision* (Chicago: University of Chicago Press, 1993). See also Jean-Pierre Vernant, "Psuche: Simulacrum of the Body or Image of the Divine," p. 192.

67 Hadot, *Exercices spirituels*, p. 231.

68 Plotinus, *Enneads*, tr. A. H. Armstrong (Cambridge, MA: Harvard University Press, 1966). *Ennead*, I.6.9, p. 259.

69 Plotinus, *Enneads. Ennead*, I.6.6, p. 251.

70   Hadot, "La Figure du sage," pp. 19–20.

71   Ibid., p. 19. See also Pierre Hadot, "Histoire de la pensée hellénistique et romaine: Intériorité et liberté chez Marc Aurèle," in *Annuaire du Collège de France, 1989–90; Résumé des cours et travaux* (Paris: Collège de France, 1990).

72   See, for example, Epictetus, *Manual*, 5, and Marcus Aurelius, *Meditations*, XI.16.

73   Hadot, "La Figure du sage," pp. 19–20.

74   Cited in Hadot, "Le Sage et le monde," p. 181.

75   Stanley Cavell, "Thinking of Emerson," in *The Senses of Walden* (San Francisco: North Point Press, 1981), p. 134.

76   Cavell, *This New Yet Unapproachable America*, p. 37.

77   Foucault, *The Use of Pleasure*, pp. 28–32; Hadot, *Exercices spirituels*, pp. 13–14, 59–60. I bring together Cavell's and Hadot's work in "La Découverte de Thoreau et d'Emerson par Stanley Cavell ou les exercices spirituels de la philosophie," in *Lire Cavell*, ed. Sandra Laugier (Paris: Editions de l'éclat, forthcoming).

78   Stanley Cavell, *Conditions Handsome and Unhandsome: The Constitution of Emersonian Perfectionism* (Chicago: University of Chicago Press, 1990), pp. 8–10.

79   Veyne, "La Médication interminable," p. 27.

80   Hadot, *Exercices spirituels*, pp. 37–47; "Forms of Life and Forms of Discourse in Ancient Philosophy," pp. 494–5.

81   Foucault, "L'Herméneutique du sujet," pp. 160–6.

82   Ibid., p. 164.

83   Friedrich Nietzsche, *The Gay Science* (New York: Vintage Books, 1974), pp. 273–4. I am indebted to Jim Conant for discussion of this point.

84   Seneca, "Epistle LIX," *The Epistles of Seneca*, p. 419.

85   Foucault's seminar at the University of California, Berkeley, 1983, was on the theme of *parrhésia*. His 1984 lectures at the Collège de France were also on this theme. In my characterization here, I follow Foucault's lecture of February 15, 1984, Collège de France.

86   Georges Dumézil, "Divertissement sur les dernières paroles de Socrate," in ". . . *Le Moyne noir en gris dedans Varennes*" (Paris: Gallimard, 1984); Foucault, lecture of February 15, 1984, Collège de France. See also Eliane Allo's conversation with Dumézil, "Entretien avec Georges Dumézil à propos de l'interprétation de Michel Foucault, juin 1985," in *Actes de la recherche en sciences sociales*, 61 (March 1986). The text from Plato's *Phaedo* occurs at 118.

87   For a brief statement of Dumézil's interpretation, see Eliane Allo, "Entretien avec Georges Dumézil," p. 87. Foucault discusses the relevant texts at length in his lectures of February 15, February 22, and February 29, 1984, Collège de France.

88   This remark occurs at the end of Foucault's lecture, February 15, 1984, Collège de France.

89   On this topic, see Hadot, *Exercices spirituels*, ch. 3.

90   Foucault, "L'Herméneutique du sujet," p. 145. On the history of the theme

"Know thyself," see Pierre Courcelle, *Connais-toi toi-même; de Socrate à saint Bernard* (Paris: Etudes Augustiniennes, 1974–5).

91 Among the Old Testament texts I have in mind is Deuteronomy 4: 9.

CHAPTER 4   KANT, FOUCAULT, AND *THREE WOMEN*

1 This essay was first presented at the conference "Foucault and the Writing of History Today," at the University of Chicago in October 1991. I would like to thank the participants of that conference and especially Jan Goldstein and Patricia O'Brien. I am also grateful to the members of the editorial board of *Representations* for their helpful comments and criticism.

2 Some key theoretical landmarks in the development of this historiographic trend are: Natalie Z. Davis, " 'Women's History' in Transition: The European Case," *Feminist Studies*, 3 (Spring/Summer 1976), pp. 83–103; Biddy Martin, "Feminism, Criticism and Foucault," *New German Critique*, 27 (1982), reprinted in *Feminism and Foucault*, ed. Irene Diamond and Lee Quinby (Boston, MA: Northeastern University Press, 1988); Ann Snitow et al., *Powers of Desire: The Politics of Sexuality* (New York: Monthly Review Press, 1983); Joan W. Scott, "Gender: A Useful Category of Historical Analysis," *American Historical Review*, 19, 5 (December 1985), pp. 1053–75; Cécile Dauphin, Arlette Farge, Geneviève Fraisse et al., "Histoire des femmes: culture et pouvoir des femmes, essai d'historiographie," *Annales ESC*, 2 (March/April 1986), pp. 271–93; and Denise Riley, *"Am I that Name?": Feminism and the Category of Women in History* (Minneapolis: University of Minnesota Press, 1988).

3 Volume 3 of the recently published *Histoire des femmes* (general editors Georges Duby and Michelle Perrot) embodies in its very organizational structure each of the three stages in the recent historiography of women that I have outlined here: Part I, "Les Travaux et les jours," treats the social experience of women; Part II, "D'elle, il est tant parlé," examines discourses on women and gender; and Part III, "Dissidences," explores transgressions and challenges to gender norms: *Histoire des femmes*, vol. 3: *XVIe–XVIIIe siècles*, ed. Natalie Zemon Davis and Arlette Farge (Paris: Plon, 1991). The editors of volume 4 of the same series, Michelle Perrot and Geneviève Fraisse, however, call into question the viability of the notion of "women's history" altogether, and prefer instead a "history of sexual difference." For the editors of this volume, all gender experience is both relationally and discursively constructed: *Histoire des femmes*, vol. 4: *Le XIXe siècle*, ed. Geneviève Fraisse and Michelle Perrot (Paris: Plon, 1991). For a more fully developed theoretical discussion of the uses and abuses of the notion of prediscursive "social experience" in contemporary social theory and history, see Joan W. Scott, "Experience," in *Feminists Theorize the Political*, ed. Judith Butler and Joan W. Scott (New York: Routledge, 1992), pp. 22–40. A very interesting example of recent feminist historiography significantly revises this dominant historiographic trend by interpreting the development of normative gender discourses within the modern disciplines as a response as

much to the needs of middle-class male self-constitution and self-discipline as to the need to regulate women or workers: see Laura Engelstein, *The Keys to Happiness: Sex and the Search for Modernity in Fin-de-Siècle Russia* (Ithaca, NY: Cornell University Press, 1992).

4 For some of his most explicit exchanges with feminists concerning the history of subjectivity, see the "Entretien avec Michel Foucault," in the special issue of *Cahiers du Grif: Le Genre de l'histoire*, 37/38 (Spring 1988), pp. 9–19.

5 Michel Foucault, "What is Enlightenment?," in *The Foucault Reader*, ed. Paul Rabinow (New York: Pantheon, 1984); see especially p. 49.

6 Ibid., pp. 32–3.

7 Ibid. On the limits of Kant's conception of "the public," and the contrasting French conception of "public opinion" at the end of the Old Regime, see Roger Chartier, *The Cultural Origins of the French Revolution*, tr. Lydia Cochrane (Durham, NC: Duke University Press, 1991), pp. 23–30.

8 Foucault, "What is Enlightenment?," pp. 34 and 39–41.

9 Ibid., pp. 45–6.

10 Immanuel Kant, "On the Proverb: That May be True in Theory But is of No Practical Use," in *Perpetual Peace and Other Essays*, ed. and tr. Ted Humphrey (Indianapolis: Hackett, 1983), pp. 61–92 (original edition: 1793). Isabelle de Charrière's novel *Trois femmes* first appeared under the pseudonym of the Abbé de la Tour in a German translation by Louis-Ferdinand Huber, *Drei Weiber* (Leipzig: Pet. Phil. Wolfischen Buchhandlung, 1795). The first (mutilated) French edition was published in London in 1796. A second French edition appeared in Lausanne in 1797, and the first definitive illustrated edition, *Trois Femmes: Nouvelle de l'Abbé de la Tour*, appeared in "Leipsic [*sic*] [actually Zurich], chez Pierre Philippe Wolf" in 1798. The essential details of the publishing history of the novel are to be found in the editors' introduction to the superb critical edition of *Trois Femmes*, in Isabelle de Charrière Belle de Zuylen, *Oeuvres complètes*, 10 vols, ed. Jean-Daniel Candaux, C. P. Courtney, Pierre H. Dubois, Simone Dubois-De Bruyn, Patrice Thompson, Jeroom Vercruysse, and Dennis M. Wood (Geneva: Slatkine, 1981), vol. 9, pp. 38–125. All further references are to this edition.

11 For recent literary scholarship, see in particular: Béatrice Didier, *L'Ecriture-femme* (Paris: Presses Universitaires de France, 1981), pp. 93–110; Elizabeth J. MacArthur,"Devious Narratives: Refusal of Closure in Two Eighteenth-Century Epistolary Novels," *Eighteenth-Century Studies*, 2, 1 (Fall 1987), pp. 1–20; and *Isabelle de Charrière Belle van Zuylen*, ed. Beatrice Fink, a special issue of *Eighteenth-Century Life*, 13, n.s., 1 (February 1989). Two feminist critics, Susan S. Lanser and Elizabeth J. MacArthur, have recently suggested that the privileging of *Caliste* for critical attention over Charrière's more explicitly feminist works may not be entirely coincidence: see Susan S. Lanser, "Courting Death: *Roman, romantisme*, and *Mistress Henley*'s Narrative Practices," in *Isabelle de Charrière Belle van Zuylen*, pp. 49–59 and esp. p. 57.

12 See, in particular, Philippe Godet, *Madame de Charrière et ses amis (1740–1805)*, 2 vols (Geneva: Julien, 1906), vol. 2, pp. 225; B. Munteano, "Episodes kantiens

en Suisse et en France sous le Directoire," *Revue de littérature comparée*, 4, 3, (July–September 1935), esp. p. 421 and pp. 432–3. Similar views are expressed by the editors of the definitive edition of *Trois femmes*: see Charrière Belle de Zuylen, *Oeuvres complètes*, vol. 9, p. 26; Cecil Patrick Courtney, "Belle Van Zuylen and the Enlightenment," *Documentatieblad Werksroep* (Nijmesen, Netherlands), 27–9 (June 1975), pp. 171–86, esp. pp. 182–4; and Ernst Behler, "Kant vu par le groupe de Coppet: la formation de l'image staëlienne de Kant," *Le Groupe de Coppet: Actes et documents du deuxième Colloque de Coppet*, ed. Simone Balayé and Jean-Daniel Candaux (Geneva: Slatkine; Paris: Champion, 1977), pp. 135–67. F. Picavet makes no mention of Charrière in his "Philosophie de Kant en France de 1773 à 1814," preface to Immanuel Kant, *Critique de la raison pratique*, tr. F. Picavet (Paris: Alcan, 1888), pp. i–xxxvii; nor does M. Vallois, *La Formation de l'influence kantienne en France* (Paris: Alcan, n.d. [1924]). More recently, François Azouvi and Dominique Bourel find Charrière worthy of only passing mention in their *De Königsberg à Paris: la réception de Kant en France (1788–1804)* (Paris: Vrin, 1991), pp. 69–70 and 96. For the most recent example of the complete omission of Charrière's role in the French reception of Kant, see Bernard Bourgeois, "Kant en France," in *Philosophie Politique 2: Kant* (Paris: Presses Universitaires de France, 1992), pp. 17–38, esp. pp. 19–21.

13 Bibliothèque Nationale, Nouv. acq. fr. 1836, fols 27–9, report from Villebrune to the Committee of Public Safety concerning the state of the book trade, 12 ventôse, an II (March 2, 1794), forwarded to the Committee of Public Instruction on 24 ventôse, an II (March 14, 1794); and Archives Nationales F17 1009C, doss. 2216, report from Villebrune to the Committee of Public Instruction: "Considérations sur le commerce de la librairie française," s.d., received by the Committee on 29 ventôse, an II (March 19, 1794). This second report has been reproduced in *Procès-verbaux du Comité d'instruction publique de la Convention nationale*, ed, M. J. Guillaume, 7 vols (Paris: Imprimerie Nationale, 1891), vol. 3; pp. 612–18. For a more complete discussion of the perceived crisis in letters and consequent reorientation of French government cultural policies after 1794, see Carla Hesse, *Publishing and Cultural Politics in Revolutionary Paris (1789–1810)* (Berkeley, CA: University of California Press, 1991), ch. 4.

14 Henri Grégoire, *Rapport sur les encouragements, récompenses et pensions à accorder aux savants, aux gens de lettres et aux artistes* (Paris: Imprimerie Nationale, an III [1794–5]). See also *Procès-verbaux du Comité d'instruction publique de la Convention nationale*, ed. Guillaume, vol 4; pp. 758 and 766–7.

15 George Boas, *French Philosophies of the Romantic Period* (Baltimore: John Hopkins University Press, 1925), p. 154.

16 I have made a complete survey of the appeals made by women writers to the Committee of Public Instruction for government grants, pensions, and subsidies during the period of the Directory (1795–9). Of the dozen women who petitioned, only one received patronage: see *Procès-verbaux du Comité d'instruction publique de la Convention nationale*, ed. Guillaume. The one woman author

to receive a government subsidy was the citizeness Boosère whose political pamphlet *Le Triomphe de la saine philosophie ou la vraie politique des femmes* was purchased and distributed by the Committee. For a more complete analysis of government literary patronage after Thermidor, see Hesse, *Publishing and Cultural Politics*, chs 4 and 5.

[17] Letter from Müller to Grégoire, October 27, 1794, cited in Azouvi and Bourel, *De Königsberg à Paris*, p. 68; and in Boas, *French Philosophies*, p. 168.

[18] For Huber's correspondence with Schiller and Grégoire in the spring of 1795, see Picavet, "Philosophie de Kant en France," p. xxxv; Munteano, "Episodes kantiens en Suisse," p. 410; and Azouvi and Bourel, *De Königsberg à Paris*, p. 70.

[19] Azouvi and Bourel, *De Königsberg à Paris*, p. 71.

[20] See ibid., p. 68; and Boas, *French Philosophies*, p. 167.

[21] See Azouvi and Bourel, *De Königsberg à Paris*, p. 69; and Hesse, *Publishing and Cultural Politics*, p. 192.

[22] See Munteano, "Episodes kantiens en Suisse," pp. 407–8.

[23] See Azouvi and Bourel, *De Königsberg à Paris*, pp. 69–70; and Charrière's letters of December 16–20, 1974, and December 18, 1794, in Charrière, *Oeuvres complètes*, vol. 4, pp. 670 and 673.

[24] Charrière began writing *Trois femmes* in November or December 1794. It was completed by early April 1795. See Godet, *Madame de Charrière et ses amis*, vol. 2, pp. 215, 217, and 232. See also Charrière, *Oeuvres complètes*, vol. 9, pp. 26–30.

[25] Charrière, *Trois Femmes*, in *Oeuvres complètes*, vol. 9, p. 106 (my translation). See also ibid., pp. 100–5. She was to develop this criticism of the modern author-cult more fully in a later essay entitled "De l'auteur," which unfortunately was inadvertently omitted from the recent edition of her complete works and consequently remains unpublished: see Jeroom Vercruysse, "The Publication of the *Oeuvres complètes*: Navigating the Risky Waters of the Unforeseeable," in *Isabelle de Charrière Belle van Zuylen*, pp. 69–78.

[26] See the editor's introduction to *Trois femmes*, in Charrière, *Oeuvres complètes*, vol. 9, p. 23.

[27] See Godet, *Madame de Charrière et ses amis*, vol. 2, pp. 216–18; and Charrière, *Oeuvres complètes*, vol. 5, p. 44.

[28] Kant, "On the Proverb," pp. 61–92. The two relevant consequentialist critics in this context are Charles Garves and Benjamin Constant: on Garves's critique, see Kant, "On the Proverb," pp. 63–71; and, on Constant's critique, see Behler, "Kant vu par le groupe de Coppet," pp. 137–140; Azouvi and Bourel, *De Königsberg à Paris*, pp. 95–101; and Munteano, "Episodes kantiens en Suisse," pp. 407 and 444–5.

[29] Kant, "On the Proverb," pp. 61–92. Kant's "Three Maxims" are: (1) act only on a maxim that you can at the same time will to become a universal law; (2) act so as to treat humanity in oneself and others only as an end in itself, and never merely as a means; (3) act so that your will can at the same time regard itself as giving in its maxims universal laws: see Warner Wick, Introduction to Immanuel

Kant, *Ethical Philosophy: Grounding for the Metaphysics of Morals...*, tr. James W. Ellington (Indianapolis: Hackett, 1982), pp. xvii–xx.

[30] Kant, "On the Proverb," p. 76. There is now a great deal of feminist scholarship concerning Kant's attitudes toward women and gender. Much of this work has focused on his anthropological writings, where he offers his most fully developed reflections upon these questions. For the current discussion of women and gender in the anthropological writings, see Olga Lucia Valbuena, "The 'Charming Distinction': *Ur-teil* as the En-gendering of Reason in Kant's Thought," *Genders*, 4 (March 1989), pp. 87–102. The feminist discussion of Kant's ethical writings has, for the most part, followed in the path of other materialist critiques. For a very suggestive article that moves beyond this general trend, see Beverely Brown, " 'I read the Metaphysics of Morals and the Categorical Imperative and it Doesn't Help Me a Bit,' Maria von Herbert to Immanuel Kant, August 1791," *Oxford Literary Review* (special issue on "Sexual Difference"), 8, 1–2 (1986), pp. 155–63. Although I only became aware of this essay after having written my own, strikingly, Brown's analysis of the correspondence between Maria von Herbert and Kant leads her to argue along lines similar to those presented here, that the problem of self-representation is as fundamental as that of self-constitution to the successful formation of the Kantian moral subject itself. I am grateful to Dan Rosenberg for bringing this reference to my attention.

[31] Let me be clear here that I do not necessarily mean law in the juridicial sense, but rather in the normative sense, of universal and equal. Kant makes clear that all notions of moral duty and virtue can only exist in relation to a notion of legislation. He writes, "The notion of duty can only contain self-constraint (by the idea of the law itself)": cited in Kant, *Ethical Philosophy*, pp. xlii–xlv.

[32] Charrière, *Trois femmes*, in *Oeuvres complètes*, vol. 9, p. 46.

[33] Charrière, *Oeuvres complètes*, vol. 5, p. 9.

[34] On the question of marriage and female citizenship status in the eighteenth century, see Isadore Alauzet, *De la qualité de français et de la naturalisation* (Paris: Cosse-Marchel, 1867), pp. 17 and 20; see also Carla Hesse, "Reading Signatures: Female Authorship and Revolutionary Law in France, 1750–1850," *Eighteenth-Century Studies*, 22, 3 (Spring 1989), pp. 469–87.

[35] Charrière, *Trois femmes*, in *Oeuvres complètes*, vol. 9, pp. 63–5; Constance's story is, at one level, an explicit rewriting of the example Kant employs in his response to Garves, but from the female point of view. Both stories examine the moral dilemmas of transmitting an inheritance under circumstances in which a lineage has been disrupted: see Kant, "On the Proverb," p. 69.

[36] While there are many important studies of the dramatic changes in European family law during the era of the French Revolution, to my knowledge there is as yet no substantial study of the complex legal question of female inheritance, and of the legal status of widowed women in particular, that might offer a definitive resolution to the tangled legal question of the civil status of a woman in Constance's circumstances with regard to either her citizenship or her inheritance rights. In France these were matters of continuous debate and reform

from 1789 until the promulgation of the Civil Code in 1804. For current literature that most directly addresses the questions her situation raises, see J.-F. Chassaing. "Les Successions et les donations à la fin de l'Ancien Régime et sous la Révolution," *Droits et cultures* (1982), pp. 85–111; A. Dejace, *Les Règles de la dévolution successorale sous la Révolution (1789–1794)* (Brussels and Liège: Bruylant, 1957); M. Garaud et R. Szamkiewicz, *La Rèvolution française et la famille* (Paris: Presses Universitaires de France, 1978); James Traer, *Marriage and the Family in Eighteenth-Century France* (Ithaca, NY: Cornell University Press, 1980); and Elizabeth Darrow, *Revolution in the Household* (Princeton, NJ: Princeton University Press, 1989).

37   Benjamin Constant warned Charrière that the novel would be considered scandalous. And indeed it generated considerable private and public controversy concerning its morality both during and after its publication. The first French edition was heavily censored on religious, political, and moral grounds by the London agent, the Catholic-royalist émigré Lally-Tollendal, before its publication (1796). Both the German edition (1795) and the first complete French edition (1798) met with harsh moral criticism in the press for immorality, and particularly because of Charrière's indulgent view of Josephine's sexual appetites. For a more complete discussion of the reception of the novel in the French, Swiss, and German press, see the editor's introduction to *Trois femmes*, in Charrière, *Oeuvres complètes*, vol. 9, pp. 30–3; for censorship of the first French edition, see Denise Hermann, "La Première Edition des *Trois femmes* de Mme de Charrière, *Etudes de Lettres*, 33 (1938), pp. 76–89; and Jean-Daniel Candaux, "Notes sur deux éditions mutilées de Mme de Charrière," *Revue des sciences humaines*, 137 (January–March 1970), pp. 87–92.

38   Charrière, *Trois femmes*, in *Oeuvres complètes*, vol. 9, p. 85.

39   Ibid., p. 115.

40   Kant, "On the Proverb," p. 76.

41   Charrière, *Trois femmes*, in *Oeuvres complètes*, vol. 9, p. 116.

42   Ibid., pp. 94, 112, 116–17, 122–3.

43   Ibid., p. 124.

44   See Elizabeth J. MacArthur, "Devious Narratives: Refusal of Closure in Two Eighteenth-Century Epistolary Novels," *Eighteenth-Century Studies*, 2, 1 (Fall, 1987), pp. 1–20.

45   Charrière, *Trois femmes*, in *Oeuvres complètes*, vol. 9, p. 110.

CHAPTER 5   FOUCAULT AND THE POST-REVOLUTIONARY SELF

1   Michel Foucault, *Résumé des cours, 1970–1982* (Paris: Julliard, 1989), pp. 133–4.

2   "Observations des maîtres-gantiers," Bibliothèque Nationale, Collection Joly de Fleury 596, fol. 114. The original reads: "chaque particulier n'a d'existence que celle du corps, auquel il est attaché."

3   For examples of the sensationalist rhetoric employed by the organizers of the

revolutionary festivals, see Mona Ozouf, *La Fête révolutionnaire, 1789–1799* (Paris: Gallimard, 1976), pp. 241–5. For similar rhetoric in the justification of the revolutionary calendar, see the report of Philippe Fabre d'Eglantine, October 24, 1793, in *Procès-verbaux du Comité d'instruction publique de la Convention nationale*, ed. M. J. Guillaume, 7 vols (Paris: Imprimerie Nationale, 1891–1959), vol. 2, pp. 697–706, esp. p. 699. For its use in the renaming of Paris streets, see the report by the Abbé Henri Grégoire, *Système de dénominations topographiques pour les places, rues, quais, etc. de toutes les communes de la République* (Paris, 1794), p. 10.

4   For the vestibule metaphor, see Victor Cousin, *Introduction à l'histoire de la philosophie* (Paris: Pichon & Didier, 1828), lesson 13, p. 14. Each of the lessons is separately paginated in this edition.

5   Sorbonne MS 1907, p. 5; the manuscript is a bound notebook of notes taken on Cousin's course of December 11, 1819 to March 18, 1820, by the student Louis de Raynal.

6   On the curriculum of the central schools, see L. Pearce Williams, "Science, Education and the French Revolution," *Isis*, 44 (1953), pp. 311–30, esp. 314–18; and, for an account which stresses the realities rather than the ideals, R. R. Palmer, "The Central Schools of the First French Republic: A Statistical Survey," in *The Making of Frenchmen: Current Directions in the History of Education in France*, ed. Donald N. Baker and Patrick J. Harrigan (Waterloo, Ontario: Historical Refelctions Press, 1980), pp. 223–47.

7   A.-Pierre Béraud, *De la phrénologie humaine appliquée à la philosophie, aux moeurs et au socialisme* (Paris: Durand, 1848), p. ii.

8   See R. R. Bolgar, "Victor Cousin and Nineteenth-Century Education," *Cambridge Journal*, 2 (1949), pp. 357–68, esp. pp. 358–9; and Doris S. Goldstein, " 'Official Philosophies' in Modern France: The Example of Victor Cousin," *Journal of Social History* (Spring 1968), pp. 259–79, esp. pp. 272–4.

9   See Archives Nationales, F17*1795, "Procès-verbaux des délibérations du Conseil royal de l'instruction publique" (July–September 1832), Session of September 28, fols 434–6.

10 See A.-F. Gatien-Arnoult, *Cours de lectures philosophiques, ou dissertations et fragmens sur les principales questions de philosophie élémentaire* (Paris and Toulouse: J. B. Paya, 1838), p. 81, n. 1.

11 "Procès-verbaux du Conseil royal de l'instruction publique" (my italics).

12 A.-Jacques Matter, "Moi," in *Dictionnaire de la conversation et de la lecture*, 52 vols (Paris: Belin-Mondar, 1832–9), vol. 38, pp. 259–61, esp. p. 259.

13 For this assessment of the nineteenth-century *classe de philosophie*, see Jean-Louis Fabiani, *Les Philosophes de la république* (Paris: Minuit, 1988), p. 10. For a similar assessment by a contemporary, see the Duc de Broglie, speech before the Chamber of Peers, April 12, 1844, in *Moniteur universel*, April 13, 1844, p. 926: "En France, la dernière année des classes [of secondary instruction] a toujours porté, par excellence, le nom de classe de philosophie."

14 In both *Discipline and Punish* and the first volume of *The History of Sexuality*, Foucault challenged the exclusively repressive, juridical concept of power

prevalent in our culture and insisted that the productive capacities of power be recognized. See, e.g., Michel Foucault, *Discipline and Punish: The Birth of the Prison*, tr. Alan Sheridan (New York: Pantheon, 1977), p. 194; and *The History of Sexuality*, vol. 1 *An Introduction*, tr. Robert Hurley (New York: Vintage, 1980), p. 85.

15   See Cousin's lectures on that subject, first delivered in 1817, which, under the title *Du vrai, du beau et du bien*, became an official textbook for much of the nineteenth century. Theodore Zeldin comments that "schoolboys studied [this textbook] on a par with Plato and Descartes. It enjoyed its vogue because it was a true epitome and justification of middle-class common sense"; see *France 1848–1945*, 2 vols (Oxford: Oxford University Press, 1973–7) vol. 2, p. 409.

16   Cousin, *Introduction à l'histoire de philosophie*, lesson 5, pp. 39–40.

17   Ibid., lesson 5. As Cousin puts it, "C'est sur ce fond commun que le temps dessine toutes les différences qui distinguent l'homme de l'homme" (p. 39) and "Toute la différence possible de l'homme à l'homme est là" (p. 40).

18   I have discussed the issue of Cousinian psychology and gender in "Saying 'I': Victor Cousin, Caroline Angebert, and the Politics of Selfhood in Nineteenth-Century France," in *Rediscovering History: Essays in Honor of Carl E. Schorske*, ed. Michael S. Roth (Stanford, CA: Stanford University Press, forthcoming). The virtual exclusion of psychology was part of the generally attenuated nature of philosophy instruction in the girls' lycées. On the curtailment of philosophy instruction, see Françoise Mayeur, *L'Enseignement secondaire des jeunes filles sous la Troisième République* (Paris: Presses de la Fondation Nationale des Sciences Politiques, 1977), p. 33; for the psychology taught to girls, see the text of the 1882 philosophy *programme* in *Lycées et collèges de jeunes filles: Documents, rapports et discours*, ed. C. Sée, (Paris: L. Cerf, 1884), pp. 488–9. On the retention of Cousinian psychology in the reformed, republican philosophy curriculum for boys, see Henri Marion, "Le Nouveau Programme de philosophie," *Revue philosophique*, 10 (1880), esp. p. 427.

19   See the unsigned article "Moi" in *Dictionnaire des sciences philosophiques*, ed. Adolphe Franck, 2nd edn (Paris: Hachette, 1875), p. 1122. The *Dictionnaire*, first published 1844–55, was the compendium of orthodox Cousinian views on things philosophical. For more on the relationship between Cousinianism and Cartesianism, see ibid., articles "Cartésianisme," pp. 242–6, and "Descartes," pp. 362–8, and François Azouvi, "Descartes," in *Les Lieux de mémoire*, ed. Pierre Nora, Pt 3, vol. 3 (Paris: Gallimard, 1992), pp. 735–83, esp. 756–9; Azouvi discusses how Descartes became recognized as a symbol of Frenchness and progenitor of a "French philosophy."

20   Duc de Broglie, Speech before the Chamber of Peers, in *Moniteur universel*, April 13, 1844, p. 926 (my italics).

21   See, in addition to the sources cited in note 19 above, Cousin, *Lectures on the True, the Beautiful, and the Good*, tr. O. W. Wight (New York: D. Appleton, 1867), "Discourse Pronounced at the Opening of the Course, December 4, 1817," p. 27.

22   Abel-François Villemain to the Chamber of Peers, April 30, 1844, in *Moniteur universel*, May 1, 1844, p. 1167.

23   Villemain, Session of May 3, 1844, in ibid., May 4, 1844, p. 1202. As a member of the Chamber of Peers, Victor Cousin was himself present at the debates and made several lengthy interventions; the latter were published as Victor Cousin, *Défense de l'Université et de la philosophie* (Paris: Joubert, 1844).

24   Michel Foucault, *The Archaeology of Knowledge*, tr. A. M. Sheridan Smith (New York: Pantheon, 1972), p. 17.

25   Michel Foucault, *The Use of Pleasure*, tr. Robert Hurley (New York: Vintage, 1986), p. 8.

26   Hubert L. Dreyfus and Paul Rabinow, *Michel Foucault: Beyond Structuralism and Hermeneutics* (Chicago: University of Chicago Press, 1982), p. 126 and titles of ch 7 and 8. The authors take pains to note here that "Foucault has never presented his work in quite this form." But they later go on to assert that *Discipline and Punish* treats the emergence of "objectifying social sciences," that *The History of Sexuality* treats a parallel emergence of "interpretive sciences," and that the "aims and techniques of the two kinds of sciences are quite distinct"; ibid., p. 178.

27   Foucault, *Discipline and Punish*, pp. 190–1, (my italics).

28   Foucault, *The History of Sexuality*, vol. 1, p. 60 (my italics).

29   Foucault, *Discipline and Punish*, p. 192 (my italics).

30   Foucault, *The History of Sexuality*, vol. 1, p. 112.

31   See, e.g., the reference to the "pedagogization of children's sex"; Foucault, *The History of Sexuality*, vol. 1, p. 104.

32   See, e.g., *Discipline and Punish*, pp. 29–30.

33   Ibid., p. 218.

34   Michel Foucault, "The Subject and Power," printed as an Afterword in Dreyfus and Rabinow, *Michel Foucault*, pp. 208–26, esp. p. 208.

35   As he said in an interview with Dreyfus and Rabinow in April 1983, after noting that he had in recent years placed the problem of technologies of the self at the top of his intellectual agenda, "sex is boring." See Michel Foucault, "On the Genealogy of Ethics: An Overview of Work in Progress," in *The Foucault Reader*, ed. Paul Rabinow (New York: Pantheon, 1984), pp. 340–72, esp. p. 340.

36   Foucault, *The Use of Pleasure*, pp. 4–6.

37   Nor, I might add, does Arnold Davidson in his superb and otherwise illuminating article devoted to it; see "Archaeology, Genealogy, Ethics," in *Foucault: A Critical Reader*, ed. David Couzens Hoy (Oxford: Blackwell, 1986), pp. 221–33. Equating the first axis with archaeology, the second with genealogy, and the third with ethics, Davidson writes (p. 230), "Ethics neither displaces genealogy and archaeology nor makes them irrelevant, but it does alter the final methodological implications of both." He never elaborates upon the second half of that sentence.

38   Foucault, *The Use of Pleasure*, p. 27.

39   Ibid., p. 32.

40 Foucault, "On the Genealogy of Ethics," p. 350: "I think we have to get rid of this idea of an analytical or necessary link between ethics [Foucault's term for the domain of the subject's relation to itself] and other social or economic or political structures."

41 See Foucault, *The Use of Pleasure*, p. 11n.; and Stephen Greenblatt, *Renaissance Self-Fashioning: From More to Shakespeare* (Chicago: University of Chicago Press, 1980), pp. 1–2.

42 Foucault, *The Use of Pleasure*, p. 29.

43 Foucault, *The History of Sexuality*, vol. 1, pp. 126–7.

44 Cousin, *Introduction à l'histoire de philosophie*, lesson 2, April 24, 1828, p. 6.

45 Ibid., lesson 5, May 21, 1828, p. 35.

46 Foucault himself avoided the Anglo-American sociological language of professionalization. For a discussion of this point, see Jan Goldstein, "Foucault among the Sociologists: The 'Disciplines' and the History of the Professions," *History and Theory*, 23 (1984), pp. 170–92.

47 Foucault, *Discipline and Punish*, p. 16.

48 Ibid., p. 24.

49 Ibid., pp. 29–30 (my italics).

50 Foucault, *The History of Sexuality*, vol. 1, p. 64 (my italics).

51 I discuss this in "Foucault among the Sociologists," pp. 174, 182–3.

52 These biographical details are given in Didier Eribon, *Michel Foucault* (Paris: Flammarion, 1989), pp. 125–6.

CHAPTER 6   FOUCAULT AND THE FREUDIAN SUBJECT

1 In one of his last interviews (Spring 1984) Foucault designated Heidegger and Nietzsche as his "essential" philosophers, those who had become "instruments of thought" for him. See the "The Return of Morality," an interview with Gilles Barbadette and André Scala, in Michel Foucault, *Politics, Philosophy, Culture, Interviews and Other Writings 1977–1984*, ed. Lawrence D. Kritzman (New York: Routledge, 1988), p. 250.

2 Michel Foucault, "Why Study Power: The Question of the Subject" (1983), in Hubert L. Dreyfus and Paul Rabinow, *Michel Foucault: Beyond Structuralism and Hermeneutics*, 2nd edn (Chicago: University of Chicago Press, 1983), p. 208.

3 In *The History of Sexuality*, vol. 1: *An Introduction* (New York: Random House, 1978, [French original 1976]), Foucault himself stated: "The history of the deployment of sexuality, as it has evolved since the classical age, can serve as an archaeology of psychoanalysis." (p. 130). The enormous literature on Foucault, however, contains very little on his relation to psychoanalysis or his conception of psychoanalysis, despite occasional recognitions of its importance. See, for example, Jeffrey Weeks's comment: "Much of his work, from the early *Madness and Civilization* to the recent *Introduction* to *The History of Sexuality* can be seen as a history (or to use his own term, an 'archaeology') of the emergence of psychoanalysis as a discipline. But it is the conditions of this emergence (in, for example, the religious 'confessional' mode, in the categorical separation of

madness and reason, in the use of sexological investigations), and the effects of the resulting psychoanalytic institution, *not* the truth or otherwise of the theory of the unconscious which preoccupies Foucault." Jeffrey Weeks, "Foucault for Historians," *History Workshop*, 14 (August 1982), p. 108. This distinction between the historicity of psychoanalysis and its "truth" is hardly acceptable in Foucauldian terms. It is precisely the historicity of the "truth" of psychoanalysis that concerns Foucault. See also the two articles by James Bernauer which highlight the importance of psychoanalysis as a dialogical other in Foucault's career: "Michel Foucault's Ecstatic Thinking," in *The Final Foucault*, ed. James Bernauer and David Rasmussen (Cambridge, MA: MIT Press, 1988), pp. 45–82, and "Oedipus, Freud, Foucault: Fragments of an Archaeology of Psychoanalysis," in *Pathologies of the Modern Self: Postmodern Studies on Narcissism, Schizophrenia and Depression*, ed. David Michael Levin (New York: New York University Press, 1987), pp. 349–62.

4   The quotations which follow are from pp. 35–42 and 51 of the English translation of Foucault's introduction by Forrest Williams, published as "Dream Imagination and Existence" in Michel Foucault and Ludwig Binswanger, *Dream and Existence: A Special Issue of the Review of Existential Psychology and Psychiatry*, ed. Keith Hoeller (Seattle, 1986), pp. 31–78.

5   Michel Foucault, *Mental Illness and Psychology*, tr. Alan Sheridan, foreword by Hubert Dreyfus (Berkeley, CA: University of California Press, 1987), p. 56. This is a translation of the 1962 revision of *Maladie mentale et personnalité*, whose title Foucault changed to *Maladie mentale et psychologie*. The first part of the work, which contained the critique of psychoanalysis from a Heideggerian perspective, remained relatively unchanged in the two editions. Many of the formulations from the Binswanger essay are repeated in this section, from which the quotation in the text is taken. The second part, which had contained a Marxian analysis of the etiology of the self-alienating structures represented in psychoanalytic categories, was replaced in the second edition by a synopsis of Foucault's recently completed *Folie et deraison*. I have not seen the original 1954 edition and have taken my information about its Marxian component from Hubert Dreyfus's introductory essay to the 1987 edition.

6   Michel Foucault, *Madness and Civilization: A History of Insanity in the Age of Reason*, tr. Richard Howard (New York: Mentor Books, 1967), pp. x–xi; *Folie et deraison: Histoire de la folie à l'age classique* (Paris: Plon, 1961), pp. ii–iii. Both terms were used to indicate a need to move from a horizontal and immanent history of culture to an analysis of the "otherness" that defined a culture's structure against what it was not. "Archaeology" referred to the analysis of the "silence" that made the language of reason possible; "constant verticality" pointed to the realm where "what is in question is the limits rather than the identity of a culture."

7   Foucault, *Madness and Civilization*, p. 199: "The asylum no longer punished the madman's guilt, it is true, but it did more, it organized that guilt; it organized it for the madman as a consciousness of himself, and as a non-reciprocal relation to the keeper; it organized it for the Man of Reason as an awareness of the

Other, a therapeutic intervention in the madman's existence. In other words, by this guilt the madman became an object of punishment always vulnerable to himself and to the Other, and from the acknowledgement of his status as object, from the awareness of his guilt, the madman was to return to his awareness of himself as a free and responsible subject."

[8]   The conception of the division between Occident and Orient as a construction and control of otherness, which is enunciated in the original French preface of *Folie et déraison* (p. iv), was of course later developed at great length by Edward Said in his *Orientalism* (New York: Random House, 1978).

[9]   Foucault, *Madness and Civilization*, p. 222.

[10] Ibid., p. 204.

[11] Ibid., p. 203.

[12] "The Father's 'No' " (1962), in Michel Foucault, *Language, Counter-Memory, Practice: Selected Essays and Interviews*, ed. Donald Brouchard (Ithaca, NY: Cornell University Press, 1977), pp.81–2. In this essay "psychoanalysis" is clearly identified with the work of Lacan and the perspective of Jean Laplanche, the author of the book on Hölderlin under review. In an interesting reversal, Foucault tries to show that the psychoanalytic perspective used by Laplanche to grasp Hölderlin must itself be situated within the cultural context of the death of God and liberation of language from the signifier represented by Hölderlin's "madness."

[13] Foucault, *Madness and Civilization*, p. 223.

[14] In the early 1960s "desire" or "sexuality" also still claimed the authority of transgressive, "ecstatic" experience. It was, Foucault claimed, "tied to the death of God and to the ontological void which his death fixed at the limit of our thought, it is also tied to the still silent and groping apparition of a form of thought in which the interrogation of the limit replaces the search for totality and the act of transgression replaces the movement of contradictions": "Preface to Transgression" (1963), in Foucault, *Language, Counter-Memory, Practice*, p. 50.

[15] Michel Foucault, *The Birth of the Clinic: An Archaeology of Medical Perception*, tr. A. M. Sheridan Smith (New York: Random House, 1975 [French original 1963]), pp. 144, 197–9.

[16] Michel Foucault, *The Order of Things: An Archaeology of the Human Sciences* (New York: Random House, 1971 [French original 1966]), p. 361.

[17] Ibid., pp. 374–6.

[18] Michel Foucault, "Nietzsche, Freud, Marx," (1964, 1967), in *Critical Texts: A Review of Theory and Criticism*, 3, 2 (Winter 1986), pp. 1–5.

[19] Ibid., and "What is an Author?" (1969), in Foucault, *Language, Counter-Memory, Practice*, p. 131.

[20] This might be seen as Foucault's version of the common view that Freud translated the "poetic" vision of Nietzsche and others into the prose of scientific truth.

[21] Michel Foucault, "What is Enlightenment?" (1984) in *The Foucault Reader*, ed. Paul Rabinow (New York: Pantheon, 1984), p. 46.

22 Michel Foucault, *Discipline and Punish: The Birth of the Prison*, tr. Alan Sheridan (New York: Pantheon, 1977 [French original 1975]), p. 27–30, 193–4, 305.

23 This may be due to the unfinished character of Foucault's last project. He did indicate that the role of psychoanalysis in the apparatus of sexuality did not encompass all of the elements in psychoanalytic discourse, i.e. that it dealt more with the Freud of libido theory than with the Freud who initiated a new type of hermeneutic discourse in *The Interpretation of Dreams*. See "The Confession of the Flesh," conversation with Gosrichard et al. (1977) in Michel Foucault, *Power/Knowledge: Selected Interviews and Other Writings, 1972–77*, ed. Colin Gordon (New York: Pantheon, 1980), pp. 212–13. This conversation with French psychoanalysts was originally published in *Ornicar?* (July 10, 1977).

24 Foucault, *The History of Sexuality*, vol. 1, p. 159.

25 Ibid., pp. 53ff.

26 Ibid., pp. 109–10.

27 Ibid., p. 113.

28 Ibid., p. 150.

29 Foucault, "Truth and Power," in *Power/Knowledge*, ed. Gordon, p.191–2.

30 Foucault, "What is Enlightenment?," p. 47.

31 There is a fairly large body of scholarship devoted to situating Freud's texts within the context of the intellectual traditions and discourses in which they were produced or received. But most of this work remains solidly within the conventional forms of the history of ideas, with a focus on demonstrating influences and analogies related to specific ideas or attitudes rather than structures or systems of representation. See, for example, Henri Ellenberger, *The Discovery of the Unconscious* (New York: Basic Books, 1970); Frank Sulloway, *Freud, Biologist of the Mind* (New York: Basic Books, 1979); Hannah Decker, *Freud in Germany* (New York: International Universities Press, 1977). An overview of the current state of scholarship regarding contextual interpretations of the formation of psychoanalysis can be found in John E. Toews, "Historicizing Psychoanalysis: Freud in His Time and for Our Time," *Journal of Modern History*, 63 (September 1991), pp. 504–45.

32 Attempts to interpret Freudian theory as a response to the threatened collapse of the concept of self-identity (the autonomous rational ego) informing the culture of liberal-bourgeois society, a response which was fueled by his experience as a culturally assimilated and socially excluded Jew, have provided the liveliest component of the history of psychoanalysis in recent decades. William McGrath's *Freud's Discovery of Psychoanalysis: The Politics of Hysteria* (Ithaca, NY: Cornell University Press, 1986) provides an astute recent application of this perspective to an account of the formation of psychoanalysis in the 1890s. However, Foucault's analysis operates more obviously on the generalizing plane of earlier studies like Herbert Marcuse, *Eros and Civilization* (Boston, MA: Beacon Press, 1955); Norman O. Brown, *Life Against Death* (Middletown, CT: Wesleyan University Press, 1959); Fred Weinstein and Gerald Platt, *The Wish to be Free* (Berkeley, CA: University of California Press, 1969); and Philip Rieff, *The Triumph of the Therapeutic* (New York: Harper &

Row, 1966), in which the Freudian concept of man as a desiring subject is placed in the context of the historical fate of modern Western culture and society.

33 Michel Foucault, *The Use of Pleasure*, tr. Robert Hurley (New York: Vintage, 1986), p. 9.

34 "Polemics, Politics and Problemizations: An Interview with Michel Foucault," in *The Foucault Reader*, ed. Rabinow, p. 388.

CHAPTER 7 THE HISTORY OF MEDICINE ACCORDING TO FOUCAULT

1 Cf. Coakley Lettson, *Histoire de l'origine de la médecine* (French translation Paris: Hérissant et Barrois, 1787), pp. 7, 9–10; P.-A.-O. Mahon, *Histoire de la médecine clinique depuis son origine jusqu'à nos jours* (Paris: Bouisson, Year XII/ 1804), pp. 323–4; J.-E. Dezeimeris, *Dictionnaire historique de la médecine ancienne et moderne*, 4 vols (Paris: Béchet jeune, 1828–39), vol. 1, article "Clinique," pp. 830–7.

2 "Epistemological history" is a term frequently employed by historians of science in France; it refers to the position elaborated in the work of Georges Canguilhem, who maintained that "epistemology has always been historical." See Canguilhem, *Ideology and Rationality in the History of the Life Sciences* (French edn 1977), tr. Arthur Goldhammer, (Cambridge, MA, and London: MIT Press, 1988), p. 10.

3 Michel Foucault, *Naissance de la clinique* (1963), 2nd rev. edn (Paris, Presses Universitaires de France, 1972), pp. 53–4 (Eng. edn, pp. 54–5). All English translations from *Naissance de la clinique* were done specially for this paper by Arthur Goldhammer. The location of the passage in question in Foucault, *The Birth of the Clinic* tr. A. M. Sheridan Smith (New York: Vintage 1973), is given in parentheses, prefaced by "Eng. edn."

4 Ibid., p. xi. (Eng. edn, p. xv).

5 Cf. Jacques Léonard, *La médecine entre les savoirs et les pouvoirs: Histoire intellectuelle et politique de la médecine française au XIXe siècle* (Paris: Aubier-Montaigne, 1981), p. 34; J.-C. Sournia, *La Médecine révolutionnaire, 1789–1799* (Paris, 1989), p. 157.

6 Cf. Sournia *La Médecine révolutionnaire*, p. 260; Erwin H. Ackerknecht, *La médecine hospitalière à Paris, 1794–1848* (French translation Paris: Payot, 1986), pp. 9–14.

7 Foucault, *Naissance de la clinique*, p. 63 (Eng. edn, p. 64). Compare with Ackerknecht, *La Médecine hospitalière*, p. 40; Léonard, *La Médecine entre les savoirs et les pouvoirs*, pp. 23–4; H. Ey, *Naissance de la médecine* (Paris, Payot, 1981), p. 213.

8 Erwin H. Ackerknecht, *Medicine at the Paris Hospital, 1794–1848* (Baltimore, MD: Johns Hopkins University Press, 1967), p. 7.

9 See Foucault, *Naissance de la clinique*, ch. 3, esp. pp. 38–43. (Eng. edn, pp. 39–44).

10   See Georges Canguilhem, "Bacteriology and the End of Nineteenth-Century 'Medical Theory,' " in his *Ideology and Rationality*, pp. 51–77, esp. pp. 57–8.

11   Foucault, *Naissance de la clinique*, p. xi (Eng. edn, p. xv).

12   Ibid., p. 197. (Eng. edn, p. 192).

13   Canguilhem, *Ideology and Rationality*, pp. 51ff.

14   Foucault, *Naissance de la clinique*, p. xi (Eng. edn, p. xv).

15   See Gaston Bachelard, *Le Rationalisme appliqué* (Paris: Presses Universitaires de France, 1949) and *Le matérialisme rationnel* (Paris: Presses Universitaires de France, 1953).

16   Foucault, *Naissance de la clinique*, p. 199 (Eng. edn, p. 195).

17   Ibid., pp. 147–8. (Eng. edn, p. 145).

18   See Foucault, *Naissance de la clinique*, p. 133 (Eng. edn, p. 131): "On passait d'une perception analytique à la perception des analyses réelles" – or, in other words, from the method of Condillac (which refers to signs) to the method of Bichat.

19   Ibid., p. 88 (Eng. edn, p. 89).

20   P. Veyne, "Foucault révolutionne l'histoire," in *Comment on écrit l'histoire* (Paris: Seuil, 1978), p. 385.

21   Ackerkhecht, *La Médecine hospitalière*, p. 252.

22   Friedrich Nietzsche, *The Gay Science* (New York: Vintage, 1974), p. 194.

CHAPTER 8   LOVE AND REPRODUCTIVE BIOLOGY IN *FIN-DE-SIÈCLE* FRANCE

1   Michel Foucault, *The History of Sexuality*, vol. 1: *An Introduction*, tr. Robert Hurley (New York: Vintage, 1980), pp. 54–5.

2   For the former view, see Hubert Dreyfus and Paul Rabinow, *Michel Foucault: Beyond Structuralism and Hermeneutics* (Chicago: University of Chicago Press, 1983), pp. 76, 116–17; and Gary Gutting, *Michel Foucault's Archaeology of Scientific Reason* (Cambridge: Cambridge University Press, 1989), pp. 53, 255. For the latter view, see Richard Rorty, "Foucault and Epistemology," in *Foucault: A Critical Reader*, ed. David Couzens Hoy (Oxford: Basil Blackwell, 1986), pp. 41–9; and Allan Megill, *Prophets of Extremity: Nietzsche, Heidegger, Foucault, Derrida* (Berkeley: University of California Press, 1985), pp. 249–50.

3   Rux Martin, "Truth, Power, Self: An Interview with Michel Foucault," in *Technologies of the Self: A Seminar with Michel Foucault*, ed. Luther H. Martin, Huck Gutman, and Patrick H. Hutton, (Amherst, MA: University of Massachusetts Press, 1988), pp. 11–12. For a similar distinction between the "exact" and "human" sciences, see Foucault 's comments in *Michel Foucault: Politics, Philosophy, Culture: Interviews and Other Writings, 1877–1984*, ed. Lawrence D. Kritzman, tr. Alan Sheridan and others (New York: Routledge, 1988), p. 106.

4   Michel Foucault, *Power/Knowledge: Selected Interviews and Other Writings, 1972–1977*, ed. Colin Gordon, (New York: Pantheon, 1980), p. 118. See also Michel

Foucault *The History of Sexuality*, vol. 2: *The Use of Pleasure*, tr. Robert Hurley (New York: Vintage, 1990), pp. 6–7.

5 On Foucault's debt to Canguilhem (and Bachelard), see Gutting, *Michel Foucault's Archaeology of Scientific Reason*, pp. 32–54; and Foucault's own essay on Canguilhem, "La Vie: l'expérience et la science," *Revue de métaphysique et de morale*, 85 (January–March 1985), pp. 3–14.

6 Foucault, "Truth and Power," in *Power/Knowledge*, ed. Gordon, pp. 111–12.

7 For this view, see Mark Cousins and Athar Hussain, *Michel Foucault* (New York: St Martin's Press, 1984), pp. 57–9.

8 Foucault, "The Politics of Health in the Eighteenth Century," in *Power/Knowledge*, ed. Gordon, p. 171.

9 See, for this view, Gutting, *Michel Foucault's Archaeology*, p. 259.

10 On the work done at various marine stations in this era, see Harry Paul, *From Knowledge to Power: The Rise of the French Empire in Science, 1860–1939* (Cambridge: Cambridge University Press, 1985), pp. 93–133.

11 André Armengaud, *La Population française au XIXe siècle* (Paris: Presses Universitaires de France, 1971), pp. 47–51. See also Jean-Pierre Bardet and Hervé Le Bras, "La Chute de la fécondité," *Histoire de la population française*, vol. 3 (Paris: Presses Universitaires de France, 1988), pp. 351–402.

12 On pronatalism, see William Schneider, *Quality and Quantity: Eugenics and the Biological Regeneration of Twentieth-Century France* (Cambridge: Cambridge University Press, 1991); Marie-Monique Huss, "Pronatalism in the Inter-War Period in France," *Journal of Contemporary History*, 25 (1990) pp. 39–68; Richard Tomlinson, "The Disappearance of France, 1896–1940: French Politics and the Birth Rate," *The Historical Journal*, 28, 2 (1985), pp. 407–11.

13 Karen Offen, "Depopulation, Nationalism, and Feminism in Fin-de-siècle France," *American Historical Review*, 89 (June 1984), pp. 648–76.

14 See Robert A. Nye, "Sex Difference and Male Homosexuality in Nineteenth-Century French Medicine," *Bulletin of the History of Medicine*, 63 (1989), pp. 32–51.

15 See, in connection with this set of beliefs, Anson Rabinbach, *The Human Motor: Energy, Fatigue and the Origins of Modernity* (New York, Basic Books, 1990).

16 On the first stages of success of this development, see John Farley, *Gametes and Spores: Ideas about Sexual Reproduction, 1750–1914* (Baltimore: Johns Hopkins University Press, 1982), pp. 185–188. On France, see Denis Buican, "La Génétique classique en France devant le néo-Lamarckisme tardif," *Revue de synthèse*, 95–6 (1979), pp. 301–24, and, in general, *Histoire de la génétique et de l'évolutionnisme en France* (Paris: Presses Universitaires de France, 1984), esp. pp. 17–226.

17 Sabatier was professor at the Collège de France. See his statement of these issues in *Essai sur la vie et la mort* (Paris: V. Babé, 1892), esp. pp. 161–4, 235–76. For the continuation of the ideas of internal equilibria in physiology see Henri Beaunis, *Les Sensations internes* (Paris: Alcan, 1889), and Eugène Gley, *Etudes de psychologie physiologique et pathologique* (Paris: Alcan, 1903). A clear popularization of these ideas may be found in Alfred Fouillée, "Le Tempéra-

ment physique et moral d'après la biologie contemporaine," *Revue des deux mondes* 118 (July 15, 1893), esp. pp. 285–304.

[18] Sabatier, *Essai sur la vie et la mort*, p. 161.

[19] Maurice Caullery, France's most eminent early twentieth-century embryologist, summed up French objections to Weismannian notions of heredity by noting that organisms are ruled by an "indivisible" equilibrium, not the artificial distinction between germ and soma: *Les Problèmes de la sexualité* (Paris: Alcan, 1913), pp. 130–2.

[20] On this experimental tradition and its relation to international developments, see J.-L. Fischer, "Yves Delage (1854–1920): L'Epigénèse néo-Lamarckienne contre la prédétermination Weismanienne," *Revue de synthèse*, 95–6 (1979), pp. 443–61; Camille Limoges, "Natural Selection, Phagocytosis and Preadaptation: Lucien Cuenot, 1886–1902," *Journal of the History of Medicine*, 31 (1976), pp. 178–84; Jane Maienschein, "What Determines Sex? A Study of Convergent Research Approaches, 1880–1916," *Isis*, 75 (September 1984), pp. 457–80.

[21] Joseph Spengler, *France Faces Depopulation* (Durham, NC: Duke University Press, 1938), pp. 138–40. I have discussed this matter in *Crime, Madness, and Politics in Modern France: The Medical Concept of National Decline* (Princeton, NJ: Princeton University Press, 1984), pp. 141–4.

[22] See J.-C. Bénard, "Fille ou garçon à volonté: Un aspect du discours médical au 19e siècle," *Ethnologie française*, 11 (1981), pp. 63–76; also Laure Adler, *Secrets d'alcôve. Histoire du couple de 1830 à 1930*, pp. 80–90, 103–6.

[23] E. Maurel, "Etude sur la masculinité," *Revue scientifique*, 12 (March 21, 1903), pp. 353–60; Arsène Dumont, "Natalité et masculinité," *Revue scientifique*, 24, 4th ser. (June 16, 1894), pp. 752–6; René Worms, *La Sexualité dans les naissances françaises* (Paris: Giard et Brière, 1912).

[24] For this view, see Charles Robin, "Fécondation," *Dictionnaire encyclopédique des sciences médicales*, 1, 4th ser. (1877), pp. 464–5; Dr Armand Sabatier, *Recueil des mémoires sur la morphologie des éléments sexuels et sur la nature de la sexualité* (Montpellier, 1886), pp. 202–3; Dr A. Cleisz, *Recherches des lois qui président à la création des sexes* (Paris: Rougier, 1889), pp. 24–8; J. C. Houzeau, *Etudes sur les facultés mentales des animaux comparées à celles de l'homme*, 2 vols (Paris: Hector Manceau, 1872), vol. 2, pp. 409–10. As John Farley points out in *Gametes and Spores*, the French scientist J.-B. Dumas was the first to articulate this view in the 1820s, as part of his argument that the sperm contributed directly to the fertilization of the egg: pp. 39–43.

[25] On this point, see Farley, *Gametes and Spores*, pp. 125–7.

[26] Léonce Manouvrier, "Sexe," *Dictionnaire des sciences anthropologiques* (Paris: Doin, 1884), pp. 993–7; Charles Letourneau, "Hérédité," *Dictionnaire encyclopédique des sciences médicales*, 4th ser., 13 (1888), pp. 592–3; Houzeau, *Etudes sur les facultés mentales*, vol. 2, pp. 410–13; Dumont, "Natalité et masculinité," p. 753; Dr Serge-Paul, *Physiologie de la vie sexuelles chez l'homme et chez la femme, suivie d'une étude sur la procréation des sexes à volonté* (Paris: Bibliothèque populaire des sciences médicales, 1910), pp. 233–9. Dr A. Corivaud, *Le*

Lendemain du mariage 2nd edn (Paris: Baillière, 1889), pp. 61–70; Worms, *La Sexualité dans les naissances françaises*, pp. 174–212.

27 See, on the period around mid-century, Frederick Churchill, "Sex and the Single Organism: Biological Theories of Sexuality in the Mid-Nineteenth Century," *Studies in the History of Biology*, 3 (1979), pp. 139–78.

28 Farley, *Gametes and Spores*, pp. 160–8.

29 Henri Milne-Edwards, *Elements de zoölogie* (Paris, 1834); *Leçons sur la physiologie et l'anatomie comparée de l'homme et des animaux*, vol. 8 (Paris, 1863).

30 Sabatier, *Recueil des mémoires*, pp. 163–4.

31 Alfred Fouillée, "La Psychologie des sexes et ses fondements physiologiques," *Revue des deux mondes*, 119 (September 1893), pp. 400 (my emphasis).

32 J. L. de Lanessan, preface to L. Tillier, *L'Instinct sexuel chez l'homme et chez les animaux* (Paris: Doin, 1889), pp. ix–xi; see also ibid., 2–11. An excellent summary of the argument may be found in Dr R. Koehler, "Pourquoi ressemblons-nous à nos parents? Essai sur la fécondation, sa nature et son origine," *Revue philosophique*, 35 (April 1893), pp. 267–70. For a more cautious view about the evolutionary *order* of forms of reproduction, see Caullery, *Les Problèmes de la sexualité*, pp. 57–62.

33 Tillier, *L'Instinct sexuel*, pp. 51–70.

34 Fouillée, "La Psychologie des sexes," p. 401. See Patrick Geddes and J. A. Thomson, *The Evolution of Sex* (London, 1889).

35 Fouillée, "La Psychologie des sexes," p. 401.

36 Ibid., pp. 405–6. One of the most innovative French cytologists, G. Balbiani, wrote of "selection" and "struggle" between spermatozoa: "it is the most agile ones which arrive first at the egg and are able to complete its fertilization. Selection does not content itself with individuals alone, but works as well through the sexual elements." in *Leçons sur la génération des vertébrés* (Paris: Doin, 1879), p. 160.

37 Sabatier, *Recueil des mémoires*, pp. 183–7; Beaunis, *Les Sensations internes*, p. 52; André Cresson, *L'Espèce et son serviteur (sexualité, moralité)* (Paris: Alcan, 1913), pp. 39–41; Koehler, "Pourquoi ressemblons-nous à nos parents?," pp. 359–60; Rémy de Gourmont, *Physique de l'amour: Essai sur l'instinct sexuel* (Paris: Société du Mercure de France, 1903), pp. 107–8.

38 A good instance of this is the treatment of the evidence of craniology. See Elizabeth Fee, "Nineteenth-Century Craniology: The Study of the Female Skull," *Bulletin of the History of Medicine*, 53 (1979), pp. 415–33.

39 This is not to say that women were not still in some sense "sick" from childbearing and from the trauma of the menstrual cycle. See the collection of articles in Jeffrey Moussaieff Masson, *A Dark Science: Women, Sexuality and Psychiatry in the Nineteenth Century*, tr. Jeffrey Masson and Marianne Loring (New York: Farrar, Straus & Giroux, 1986); Yvonne Kniebiehler and Catherine Fouquet, *La Femme et les médecins* (Paris: Hachette, 1983), pp. 203–98; Ann-Louise Shapiro, "Disordered Bodies/Disorderly Acts: Medical Discourse and the Female Criminal in Nineteenth-Century Paris," *Genders*, 4 (Spring 1989), pp. 68–85. On Michelet, see Jean Borie, "Une Gynécologie passionnée," in *La*

Femme du XIXe siècle, ed J.-P. Aron (Paris: Editions complexe, 1980), pp. 153–90); Ludmilla Jordanova, *Sexual Visions* (Madison: University of Wisconsin Press, 1989), pp. 66–86.

40 On sexual selection, see Cynthia Eagle Russett, *Sexual Science: The Victorian Construction of Womanhood* (Cambridge, MA: Harvard University Press, 1989), pp. 78–89; Robert J. Richards, *Darwin and the Emergence of Evolutionary Theories of Mind and Behavior* (Chicago: University of Chicago Press, 1987), pp. 187–93.

41 Tillier, *L'Instinct sexuel*, pp. 87–155; Alfred Espinas, *Des Sociétés animales*, 2nd edn (Paris: Baillière, 1878), pp. 321–5; Gourmont, *Physique de l'amour*, pp. 165–170.

42 For other criticism of sexual selection, see Russett, *Sexual Science*, pp. 89–94.

43 Fouillée, "La Psychologie des sexes," p. 404.

44 Caullery, *Les Problèmes de la sexualité*, p. 322.

45 See Schneider, *Quality and Quantity*, passim.

46 Pierre Machery, "Pour une histoire naturelle des normes," *Michel Foucault philosophe* (Paris: Seuil, 1989), p. 203.

47 Dr Henri Thulié, *La Femme: Essai de sociologie physiologique* (Paris: Delahaye, 1885), pp. iv, 161–3.

48 Thulié, *La Femme*, pp. 238–41.

49 Ibid., pp. 510, 516. Free choice will allow the fulfillment of the "social contract" which the republican social theorist Renouvier wrote marriage should be, *and* ensure the proper relation of tradition and "progress" in the biological perfection of the race.

50 Ibid., p. 247.

51 François Maupas, "Recherches expérimentales sur la multiplication des infusoires ciliés," *Archives zoölogiques expérimentales générales*, 6 (1888), p. 261. On this experiment and its subsequent history, see Farley, *Gametes and Spores*, pp. 204–6. Much earlier, another French microscopist, G. Balbiani, was the first to alert scientists to the "sexual" reproduction of infusoria, which he described as an "intimate adherence": *Recherches sur les phénomènes sexuels des infusoires* (Paris: Masson, 1861), p. 58. On the experimental history of this research, see Graham Bell, *Sex and Death in Protozoa: The History of an Obsession* (New York: Cambridge University Press, 1989).

52 Alfred Binet, "La Vie psychique des micro-organisms," *Revue philosophique*, 24 (December 1887), p. 585. This quotation should be compared with the entry on "sexe" in the *Grande encyclopédie*, vol. 29, written around 1914 by the anthropologist Zaborowski, who described the evolution of sexual reproduction as having brought about the present state of sexual dimorphism in men and women. "one must understand that it is inevitable that a civilization that procures for women such complete security and leisure, also develops her sexual characteristics, her grace, the roundness of her forms, and even favors a mental differentiation through her exclusive cultivation of sentiment, her great attention to coquetry, her search for whatever it is that charms or seduces, all of which relieves her intelligence of the efforts that are necessary to maintain its vigor."

53 Sabatier, *Recueil des mémoires*, pp. 163–93, 232–5.
54 Balbiani, *Leçons sur la génération des vertébrés*, pp. 159–60.
55 Beaunis, *Les Sensations internes*, p. 52. See also Binet, "La Vie psychique," pp. 592–3. On the tendency of contemporary science to continue this anthropomorphizing of intrauterine courtship, see Emily Martin, "The Egg and the Sperm: How Science has Constructed a Romance Based on Stereotypical Male–Female Roles," *Signs: Journal of Women in Culture and Society*, 16, 3 (1991), pp. 485–501; Nancy Tuana, "The Weaker Seed: The Secret Bias of Reproductive Theory," in *Feminism and Science*, ed. Nancy Tuana (Bloomington, IN: Indiana University Press, 1989), pp. 147–191. See also Natalie Angier, "In Sperm, a Prenatal Male Advantage," *New York Times*, October 30, 1990.
56 Koehler, "Pourquoi ressemblons-nous à nos parents?," p. 378.
57 Sabatier, *Recueil des mémoires*, p. 172.
58 Alfred Espinas, *Les Sociétés animales* (Paris, 1887), pp. 314–15.
59 Jacques Delboeuf, "Pourquoi mourrons-nous?" *Revue philosophique*, 31 (March 1891), p. 257 (my emphasis).
60 See the feminist tract of Jean Finot, *Préjugé et problèmes des sexes*, 3rd edn (Paris: Alcan, 1913). A feminist work expressing similar sentiments is Pierre Bonnier, *Sexualisme* (Paris: Giard, 1914). Antifeminist positions are expressed in Jacques Lourbet, *Le Problème des sexes* (Paris: Giard, 1900); Dr Jules Roger, *Etude psycho-physiologique sur l'amour* (Paris: Baillière, 1899), pp. 13–14.
61 Roger, *Etude psycho-physiologique*, p. 30; Lourbet, *Le Problème des sexes*, p. 287.
62 Gaston Danville, "L'Amour, est-il un état pathologique?," *Revue philosophique*, 35 (March 1893), pp. 261–83.
63 The most important works in this genre are Paul Bourget, *Physiologie de l'amour moderne: Fragments posthumes d'un ouvrage de Claude Larcher* (Paris: Lemerre, 1891); Gourmont, *Physique de l'amour*; Léon Blum, *Du mariage* (Paris: Ollendorf, 1907); Jules Soury, "La Psychologie physiologique des protozoaires," *Revue philosophique*, 31 (January 1891), pp. 1–44.
64 Blum, *Du mariage*, pp. 37–8.
65 Ibid., pp. 88–9, 158–67, 179.
66 Ibid., pp. 307–11.
67 Jean Finot, "Les Femmes et le Darwinisme," *Revue des revues*, 8 (May 1894), p. 328. See also his *Préjugé et problèmes*, pp. 424–92, for his discussion that dimorphism will prevail and a feminist "equality in difference" will triumph. Alfred Fouillée also believed that for the good of the "race" it behooved women not to upset their "grace" and their natural complementarity with men by working or engaging to any greater extent in the "struggle for life." It is necessary, he wrote, "that her energies be employed in a manner that conforms to the interests and to the natural relations of the two sexes, as well as to the interests of children and the race": "La Psychologie des sexes," pp. 426–8.
68 Gourmont, *Physique de l'amour*, p. 68.
69 This is the argument of Dr Sicard de Plauzolles, *La Fonction sexuelle au point de vue de l'éthique et de l'hygiène social* (Paris: Giard, 1908), pp. 36–7. See also Dr

Edouard Toulouse, *La Question sexuelle et la femme* (Paris: Charpentier, 1918), p. 242.

70 Toulouse, *La Question sexuelle et la femme*, p. 271. For similar, pre-war views contrasting coquettish and sprightly French women with languorous and submissive German women, see André Sanson, *L'Hérédité normale et pathologique* (Paris: Asselin et Houzeau, 1893), p. 417.

71 For instance, Espinas says men must measure up to the "power" of women's collective representations of them: *Les Sociétés animales*, p. 285; Fouillée argues that women are naturally attracted to the "intellectual and corporeal power" of men: "La Psychologie des sexes," p. 412; also E. Dally, "Femmes," *Dictionnaire des sciences médicales*, 4th ser., 1 (1877), pp. 427–38; Charles Letourneau, "Femmes," *Dictionnaire des sciences anthropologiques*, pp. 476–78. On the role of the family in this effort, Dr Armand Marie wrote in 1910 that "In the social order, the progress, the fluctuations, and the regressions of human groups are in a cause-and-effect relation with the modifications in the status of the family; marriage, birth rate, depopulation, and the variable preponderance of numbers depend on the variations in the essential social element that constitutes the conjugal relationship": preface to Dr Anton Nystrom, *La Vie sexuelle et ses lois* (Paris: Vigot, 1910), p. vi.

72 Fouillée, "La Psychologie des sexes," p. 429 (my emphasis).

CHAPTER 9   THE CHIMERA OF THE ORIGIN

1 Michel Foucault, "Qu'est-ce qu'un auteur?," *Bulletin de la Société française de Philosophie* (July–September 1969), pp. 73–104, repr. in *Littoral*, 9 (1983), pp. 3–23, available in English (without the debate following the lecture) as "What is an Author?," in Foucault, *Language, Counter-Memory, Practice: Selected Essays and Interviews*, ed. Donald F. Bouchard, tr. Donald F. Bouchard and Sherry Simon (Ithaca, NY: Cornell University Press, 1977), pp. 113–38; Foucault, *L'Ordre du discours: Leçon inaugurale au Collège de France prononcée le 2 décembre 1970* (Paris: Gallimard, 1971), available in English as "The Discourse on Language," tr. Rupert Swyer, in *The Archaeology of Knowledge and the Discourse on Language*, tr. A. M. Sheridan Smith (New York: Pantheon, 1972).

2 Foucault, "Discourse on Language," p. 222.

3 Michel de Certeau, "Le Rire de Michel Foucault," *Revue de la Bibliothèque Nationale*, 14 (1984), pp. 10–16, repr. in a modified form in Michel de Certeau, *Histoire et psychanalyse entre science et fiction* (Paris: Gallimard, 1987), pp. 51–64.

4 Michel Foucault, "Nietzsche, la généalogie, l'histoire," in *Hommage à Jean Hyppolite* (Paris: Presses Universitaires de France, 1971), pp. 145–72, available in English as "Nietzsche, Genealogy, History," in Foucault, *Language, Counter-Memory, Practice*. The quotations from this article in the following two paragraphs can be found on pp. 160–1 of the French version and pp. 153–5 of the English version.

5 Michel Foucault, "Réponse au Cercle d'épistémologie," *Cahiers pour l'analyse*, 9

(Summer 1968), pp. 9–40, quotation pp. 11–12. For a similar statement, see *Archaeology of Knowledge*, p. 12.

6   Foucault, *L'Ordre du discours*, p. 58; "Discourse on Language," p. 230.

7   Foucault, *L'Ordre du discours*, p. 59; "Discourse on Language," p. 230.

8   Michel Foucault, *L'Archéologie du savoir* (Paris: Gallimard, 1969), p. 86; *Archaeology of Knowledge*, pp. 31–9.

9   Foucault, "Réponse au Cercle d'épistémologie," p. 29.

10   Foucault, *L'Archéologie du savoir*, p. 86; *Archaeology of Knowledge*, p. 65.

11   Foucault, *L'Archéologie du savoir*, p. 212; *Archaeology of Knowledge*, pp. 164, 162.

12   Keith Michael Baker, *Inventing the French Revolution: Essays on French Political Culture in the Eighteenth Century* (Cambridge: Cambridge University Press, 1990), p. 5.

13   Michel Foucault, "La Poussière et le nuage," in his *L'Impossible Prison: Recherches sur le système pénitentiaire au XIXe siècle*, ed. Michelle Perrot (Paris: Seuil, 1980), pp. 34–5.

14   Michel Foucault, "Table Ronde du 20 mai 1978," in *L'Impossible Prison*, ed. Perrot, p. 49.

15   Foucault, "La Poussière et le nuage," p. 35.

16   Ibid., p. 36.

17   Foucault, "Postface," in *L'Impossible Prison*, ed. Perrot, pp. 317–18.

18   Foucault, *L'Archéologie du savoir*, pp. 288, 231; *Archaeology of Knowledge*, pp. 175, 177.

19   Baker, *Inventing the French Revolution*, p. 7.

20   Michel Foucault, *Surveiller et punir: Naissance de la prison* (Paris: Gallimard, 1975), p. 134, quoted from *Discipline and Punish: The Birth of the Prison*, tr. Alan Sheridan (New York: Pantheon, 1977), p. 131.

21   Foucault, *Surveiller et punir*, pp. 223–4, quoted from *Discipline and Punish*, p. 222.

22   See "L'Oeil du pouvoir: Entretien avec Michel Foucault," in Jeremy Bentham, *Le Panoptique* (Paris: Pierre Belfond, 1977), p. 20; repr. as "The Eye of Power," in Michel Foucault, *Power/Knowledge: Selected Interviews and Other Writings, 1972–1977*, ed. Colin Gordon (New York: Pantheon, 1980).

23   Alphonse Dupront, *Les Lettres, les sciences, la religion et les arts dans la société française de la deuxième moitié du XVIIIe siècle* (Paris: Centre de Documentation Universitaire, 1963), p. 21.

24   Dupront, *Les Lettres, les sciences, la religion*, p. 11.

25   Michel Foucault, "Un Cours inédit," *Magazine littéraire*, 207 (May 1984), pp. 35–9. For a very different version of this text published in English, see "What is Enlightenment?," in *The Foucault Reader*, ed. Paul Rabinow, tr. Catherine Porter (New York: Pantheon, 1984), pp. 32–50.

26   Immanuel Kant, *Der Streit der Facultäten in drey Abschnitten* (Königsberg: F. Nicolovius, 1798), consulted in French as *Le Conflit des facultés en trois sections. 1798*, tr. Jean Gibelin (Paris: Vrin, 1988), quotations from pp. 100–8, and quoted here from *The Conflict of the Faculties*, tr. and intro. Mary J. Gregor (New York: Abaris Books, 1979), pp. 152–71.

27 Foucault, "Un Cours inédit," p. 35.

28 Michel Foucault, *Naissance de la clinique* (Paris: Presses Universitaires de France, 1963; repr. 1990), p. 212, quoted from *The Birth of the Clinic: An Archaeology of Medical Perception* (New York: Pantheon, 1973), pp. 199.

29 Foucault, "La Poussière et le nuage," p. 35.

30 Foucault, "L'Oeil du pouvoir," pp. 29, 30; quoted from "The Eye of Power," pp. 163–4.

31 Foucault, *Surveiller et punir*, p. 315; *Discipline and Punish*, p. 308. The next-to-last sentence in this work reads in full: "In this central and centralized humanity, the effect and instrument of complex power relations, bodies and forces subjected by multiple mechanisms of 'incarceration,' objects for discourses that are in themselves elements for this strategy, we must hear the distant roar of battle."

32 Foucault, "La Poussière et le nuage," p. 37.

33 Roger Chartier, "Figures de l'auteur," ch 2 of his *L'Ordre des livres: Lecteurs, auteurs, bibliothèques en Europe entre XIVe et XVIIIe siècle* (Aix-en-Provence: Alinea, 1992), pp. 35–67, in English as "Figures of the Author," in Roger Chartier, *The Order of Books: Readers, Authors, and Libraries in Europe Between the Fourteenth and Eighteenth Centuries*, tr. Lydia G. Cochrane, (Cambridge: Polity Press, forthcoming).

34 Foucault, Discussion following "Qu'est-ce qu'un auteur?," *Littoral*, 9 (1983), pp. 28–9.

35 Michel de Certeau, "Microtechniques et discours panoptique: un quiproquo," in his *Histoire et psychanalyse entre science et fiction*, pp. 37–50, available in English as "Micro-Techniques and Panoptic Discourse: A Quid Pro Quo," in *Humanities in Society*, 5, 3–4 (1982), pp. 257–65.

36 See a series of articles published in the *American Historical Review* (*AHR*): John E. Toews, "Intellectual History after the Linguistic Turn: The Autonomy of Meaning and the Irreducibility of Experience," *AHR*, 92 (October 1987), pp. 879–907; David Harlan, "Intellectual History and the Return of Literature," *AHR*, 94 (June 1989), pp. 581–609; David A. Hollinger, "The Return of the Prodigal: The Persistence of Historical Knowing," *AHR*, 94 (June 1989), pp. 610–21; Joyce Appleby, "One Good Turn Deserves Another: Moving Beyond the Linguistic; A Response to David Harlan," *AHR*, 94 (December 1989), pp. 1326–32.

37 This rejection is expressed, for example, in the discussion following Foucault's lecture, "Qu'est-ce qu'un auteur?," *Littoral*, 9 (1983), p. 28; and in "Discourse on Language," p. 234.

38 Marcel Gauchet, "Changement de paradigme en sciences sociales?," *Le Débat*, 50 (May–August 1988), pp. 165–70.

39 Paul Veyne, "Foucault révolutionne l'histoire," in Veyne, *Comment on écrit l'histoire* (Paris: Seuil, 1978), p. 236.

40 Ibid., p. 217.

41 Ibid. pp. 231–2.

42 Certeau, "Microtechniques et discours panoptique," p. 44.

43 Ibid., p. 49.
44 Michel Foucault, *Histoire de la sexualité* (Paris: Gallimard, 1984), vol. 2: *L'Usage des plaisirs*, p. 19, available in English as *The History of Sexuality*, tr. Robert Hurley (New York: Vintage/Random House, 1980), vol. 2: *The Use of Pleasure*, p. 13.

CHAPTER 10   A FOUCAULDIAN REVOLUTION?

In addition to the initial Chicago conference, earlier versions of this paper were presented to the Center for Comparative Research in History, Society and Culture, University of California, Davis, and to a joint session of the Bay Area Eighteenth-Century Studies Group and the Stanford University Seminar on Enlightenment and Revolution. I wish to thank the participants in each of these discussions for their criticism and advice.

1   Michel Foucault, *The Archaeology of Knowledge*, tr. A. M. Sheridan Smith (New York: Pantheon, 1972), p. 177.
2   Ibid., 176–7.
3   The relationship between power and discourse was already emphasized by Foucault in *The Archaeology of Knowledge*, p. 120. Discourse, he argues there, needs to be understood "as an asset – finite, limited, desirable, useful – that has its own rules of appearance, but also its own conditions of appropriation and operation; an asset that consequently, from the moment of its existence (and not only in its 'practical applications'), poses the question of power; an asset that is, by nature, the object of a struggle, a political struggle."
4   See, especially, François Furet, *Interpreting the French Revolution*, tr. Elborg Forster (Cambridge: Cambridge University Press, 1981); Mona Ozouf, *Festivals and the French Revolution*, tr. Alan Sheridan (Cambridge, MA: Harvard University Press, 1988); Lynn Hunt, *Politics, Culture, and Class in the French Revolution* (Berkeley: University of California Press, 1984).
5   Lynn Hunt has also used the term "dedifferentiation" in her book, *The Family Romance of the French Revolution* (Berkeley and Los Angeles: University of California Press, 1992).
6   Robespierre, "Report on the Principles of Political Morality" (February 5, 1794), in *The Old Regime and the French Revolution*, ed. Keith Michael Baker (Chicago: University of Chicago Press, 1987), 379.
7   Ibid., 372.
8   Foucault, "Questions of Method," in *The Foucault Effect: Studies in Governmentality*, ed. Graham Burchell, Colin Gordon, and Peter Miller (Chicago: University of Chicago Press, 1991), pp. 76–8. This is a translation of an interview published in *L'Impossible Prison: Recherches sur le système pénitentiaire au XIXe siècle*, ed. Michelle Perrot (Paris: Seuil, 1980).
9   Furet, *Interpreting the French Revolution*, p. 19.
10 Foucault, "Questions of Method," p. 85.
11 Michel Foucault, *Résumé des cours, 1970–1982* (Paris: Julliard, 1989), p. 113.

12 Michel Foucault, *Power/Knowledge: Selected Interviews and Other Writings, 1972–1977*, ed. Colin Gordon (New York: Pantheon, 1980), p. 55.

13 The effort to distinguish between these two forms of power runs throughout the essays and interviews published in *Power/Knowledge*.

14 On this theme, see especially *The History of Sexuality*, vol. 1: *An Introduction*, tr. Robert Hurley (New York: Random House, 1978), pp. 88–102.

15 Foucault, "Two Lectures," *Power/Knowledge*, pp. 104–5.

16 Ibid., p. 105.

17 Marcel Gauchet, "De l'avènement de l'individu à la découverte de la société," *Annales, ESC*, 34 (1979), pp. 451–63; *Le Désenchantement du monde: une histoire politique de la religion* (Paris: Gallimard, 1985); Brian C. Singer, *Society, Theory and the French Revolution: Studies in the Revolutionary Imaginary* (New York: St Martin's Press, 1986).

18 The arguments are well summarized in Laurence Dickey, "Pride, Hypocrisy and Civility in Mandeville's Social and Historical Theory," *Critical Review* (Summer 1990), pp. 387–431.

19 I have explored this issue somewhat more fully in "Enlightenment and the Institution of Society: Notes for a Conceptual History," in *Main Trends in Cultural History*, ed. W. F. B. Melching and W. R. E. Velema (Amsterdam and Atlanta: Rodopi, forthcoming).

20 Foucault, "Governmentality," in *The Foucault Effect*, 87–104.

21 Ibid., p. 104.

22 Ibid.

23 Ibid.

24 On this theme, see my *Inventing the French Revolution* (Cambridge: Cambridge University Press, 1990). My own efforts to distinguish between discourses of "justice," "will," and "reason" turn out to have been quite close to Foucault's tripartite distinction of modes of government in this lecture.

25 Ibid., pp. 167–99.

26 On this theme, see Jacques Guilhaumou, "Fragments of a Discourse of Denunciation (1789–1794)," in *The French Revolution and the Creation of Modern Political Culture*, vol. 4: *The Terror*, ed. Keith Michael Baker (Oxford: Pergamon Press, forthcoming).

27 See Chantal Thomas, *La Reine scélérate: Marie-Antoinette dans les pamphlets* (Paris: Seuil, 1989); Sarah Maza, "The Diamond Necklace Affair Revisited (1785–1786): The Case of the Missing Queen," in *Eroticism and the Body Politic*, ed. Lynn Hunt (Baltimore: Johns Hopkins University Press, 1990), pp. 63–89; Lynn Hunt, "The Many Bodies of Marie-Antoinette: Political Pornography and the Problem of the Feminine in the French Revolution," in *Eroticism and the Body Politic*, pp. 108–30; Jacques Revel, "Marie-Antoinette in Her Fictions: The Staging of Hatred," in *Fictions of the French Revolution*, ed. Bernadette Fort (Evanston, IL: Northwestern University Press, 1991), pp. 111–29.

28 Shanti Singham, "The *Correspondance secrète*: Forging Patriotic Public Opinion during the Maupeou Years," in *The Maupeou Revolution: The Transformation of French Politics at the End of the Old Regime*, ed. Keith Michael

Baker, *Historical Reflections/Réflexions Historiques*, 18, 2 (Summer 1992), pp. 86–8.

29 Hans-Jürgen Lüsebrink and Rolf Reichardt, "La 'Bastille' dans l'imaginaire social de la France à la fin du XVIIIe siècle (1774–1799)," *Revue d'histoire moderne et contemporaine*, 30 (1983), pp. 196–234; and *Die "Bastille": Zur Symbolgeschichte von Herrschaft und Freiheit* (Frankfurt am Main: Fischer, 1990).

30 Sarah Maza, "Le Tribunal de la nation: les mémoires judiciaires et l'opinion publique à la fin de l'Ancien Régime," *Annales, ESC*, 42 (1987), pp. 73–90; "The Rose-Girl of Salency: Representations of Virtue in Prerevolutionary France," *Eighteenth-Century Studies*, 22, 3 (Spring 1989), pp. 395–412; "The Véron-Morangiès Affair, 1771–1773: The Social Imagery of Political Crisis," in *The Maupeou Revolution*, pp. 101–35.

31 David Avrom Bell, "Lawyers into Demagogues: Chancellor Maupeou and the Transformation of Legal Practice in France, 1771–1789," *Past and Present*, 130 (February 1991), pp. 107–41; "Lawyers and Politics in Eighteenth-Century Paris (1700–1790)" (PhD dissertation, Princeton University, 1991).

32 Michel Foucault, *Discipline and Punish: The Birth of the Prison*, tr. Alan Sheridan (New York: Pantheon, 1977), pp. 220, 224. I would like to thank Paul Friedland for comments that helped clarify this part of my argument.

33 See above, text to note 16.

34 Foucault, *Discipline and Punish*, p. 217.

CHAPTER 11   GOVERNING POVERTY

1 The *Hôpital Général* was created by Louis XIV in 1657 to house the poor and mendicants of Paris; by 1662 it had been extended to all cities of the realm.

2 Michel Foucault, *Histoire de la folie à l'âge classique* (1961), 2nd edn (Paris: Gallimard, 1972), pp. 427–8.

3 Ibid., p. 431.

4 Ibid., p. 429.

5 Henri Gouhier, *La Jeunesse d'Auguste Comte et la formation du positivisme*, 3 vols (Paris: Vrin, 1941).

6 Many of the issues raised in this paper are discussed in greater detail in Giovanna Procacci, *Gouverner la misère: La question sociale en France, 1789–1848* (Paris: Seuil, 1993).

7 Paul Veyne, "Foucault révolutionne l'histoire," in *Comment on écrit l'histoire*, 2nd edn (Paris: Seuil, 1978).

8 Jan Goldstein, "Foucault among the Sociologists: the 'Disciplines' and the History of Professions," *History and Theory*, 2 (1984).

9 Gertrude Himmelfarb, *The Idea of Poverty: England in the Early Industrial Age*, 2nd edn (New York: Vintage, 1985).

10 Michel Foucault, *Résumé des cours au Collège de France, 1970–1982* (Paris: Julliard, 1989), p. 110.

11 Albert O. Hirschman, *The Passions and the Interests* (Princeton, NJ: Princeton University Press, 1977).

12 Michel Foucault, *L'Impossible Prison*, ed. Michelle Perrot (Paris: Seuil, 1980), p. 49.

13 Michel Foucault, *L'Archéologie du savoir* (Paris: Gallimard, 1969), p. 45.

14 Specific *émergences*, as Foucault says in the interview introducing Bentham's *Panopticon*, in *Le Panoptique*, ed. Michelle Perrot (Paris: Belfond, 1977), p. 24.

15 Michel Foucault, "Débat avec M. Foucault," *L'Impossible Prison*, ed. Perrot, p. 47.

16 Ibid., p. 37.

17 Michelle Perrot, "La Leçon des ténèbres," in *L'effetto Foucault*, ed. P. A. Rovatti (Milan: Feltrinelli, 1986), p. 162.

18 Camille Bloch, *L'Assistance et l'Etat en France à la veille de la Révolution* (Paris: Picard, 1908), p. 146.

19 Alan Forrest, *The French Revolution and the Poor* (Oxford: Basil Blackwell, 1981).

20 Reinhart Koselleck, *Kritik und Krise: Ein Beitrag zur Pathogene des Welt* (Freiburg: Verlag Karl Alber, 1959); English translation, *Critique and Crisis* (Cambridge, MA: MIT Press, 1988).

21 Michel Foucault, *Difendere la società*, Lectures at the Collège de France of 1976, ed. M. Bertani and A. Fontana (Florence: Ponte alle Grazie, 1990), p. 35.

22 Michel Foucault, *De la gouvernementalité: Leçons d'introduction aux cours des années 1978 et 1979* (Paris: Seuil, 1989).

23 L.-R. Villermé, "Des épidémies sous les rapports de l'hygiène publique, de la statistique médicale et de l'économie politique," *Annales d'hygiène publique et de médecine légale*, 9 (1833), pp. 5–58.

24 Michel Foucault, *La Naissance de la clinique* (Paris: Presses Universitaires de France, 1963), pp. 24–5.

25 L.-R. Villermé, "Sur la distribution de la population française par sexe et par état civil, et sur la nécessité de perfectionner nos tableaux de population et de mortalité," *Annales d'hygiène publique*, 17 (1837), pp. 245–80.

26 Villermé, "Des épidémies," p. 39.

27 L.-R. Villermé, "Note sur les ravages du choléra-morbus dans les maisons garnies de Paris, depuis le 29 mars jusqu'au 1 août 1832," *Annales d'hygiène publique*, 11 (1834), pp. 385–409.

28 William H. Coleman, *Death is a Social Disease: Public Health and Political Economy in Early Industrial France* (Madison: University of Wisconsin Press, 1982), p. 304.

29 Foucault, *Résumé des cours au Collège de France*, p. 116.

30 Colin Gordon, "Governmental Rationality: An Introduction," in *The Foucault Effect: Studies in Governmentality*, ed. G. Bruchell, C. Gordon, P. Miller (London: Harvester, 1991), p. 4.

31 Michel Foucault, "The Subject and Power," in *Michel Foucault: Beyond Structuralism and Hermeneutics*, ed. H. Dreyfus and P. Rabinow, 2nd edn (Chicago: University of Chicago Press, 1983), p. 221.

32 Michel Foucault, *Power/Knowledge*, ed. C. Gordon (London: Harvester, 1980), p. 98.

33 Michel Foucault, "Omnes et Singulatim: Toward a Criticism of Political

Reason," *The Tanner Lecture on Human Values*, II (New York: Cambridge University Press, 1981), p. 253.

[34] Alessandro Pizzorno, "Foucault et la conception libérale de l'individu," in *Michel Foucault philosophe* (Paris: Seuil, 1988).

[35] Colin Gordon, "Foucault en Angleterre," *Critique*, 42, 471–2 (1986), pp. 826–39, esp. p. 830.

[36] Giovanna Procacci, "Sociology and its Poor," *Politics and Society*, 17, 2 (1989), pp. 163–87.

[37] Auguste Comte, *Physique sociale: Cours de philosophie positive* (1830–42; repr. Paris: Hermann, 1975).

[38] Michelle Perrot, "La Leçon des ténèbres," *Effeto Foucault*, p. 162.

[39] Jacques Léonard, "L'Historien et le philosophe," *L'Impossible Prison*, ed. Perrot, pp. 9–28.

[40] See chapter 13 in this volume.

[41] Dominique Séglard, "Foucault et le problème du gouvernement," in *La Raison d'état: politique et rationalité*, ed. C. Lazzeri and D. Reynié (Paris: Presses Universitaires de France, 1992).

[42] Foucault, *L'Impossible Prison*, ed. Perrot, p. 32.

[43] Michel Foucault, "Nietzsche, la généalogie, l'histoire," in *Hommage à Hyppolite* (Paris: Presses Universitaires de France, 1971), p. 148.

[44] Michel Foucault, Introduction to Gerges Canguilhem, *On the Normal and the Pathological* (Boston, MA: Reidel, 1978).

[45] Pierre Rosanvallon, *Le Moment Guizot* (Paris: Gallimard, 1986), pp. 13–14.

[46] Mona Ozouf, "La Révolution française et l'idée de fraternité," in *L'Homme régénéré: Essais sur la Révolution française* (Paris: Gallimard, 1989), pp. 158–82, esp. p. 169.

[47] Ibid., p. 178. Robert Lindet was a member of the Committee of Public Safety under the Convention, and eventually became involved in the Babeuvist Conspiracy of Equals that was defeated by the Directory in 1796.

[48] Wolfgang Schieder, "Brüderlichkeit," in *Geschichtliche Grundbegriffe: historisches Lexikon zur politisch-sozialen Sprache in Deutschland*, ed. O. Bruner, W. Conze, R. Koselleck (Stuttgart: Klett-Cotta, 1979–88), 5 vols.

[49] François Furet, Introduction to *L'Héritage de la Révolution française*, ed. F. Furet (Paris: Hachette, 1989), p. 11.

[50] Blandine Barret-Kriegel, *L'Etat et les esclaves*, 2nd edn (Paris: Calman-Lévy, 1989), pp. 202–3.

CHAPTER 12   COMBINED UNDERDEVELOPMENT

I would like to thank Jan Goldstein for inviting me to participate in the Chicago conference and the readers whose comments have helped me sharpen my ideas: Carla Hesse, Joan Wallach Scott, Richard Wortman, and Reginald Zelnik. The present essay is a slightly amended version of the following texts: Laura Engelstein, "Combined Underdevelopment: Discipline and the Law in Imperial and Soviet Russia" and "Reply," *American Historical Review*, 98, 2 (1993), pp. 338–53; 376–81.

1   Michel Foucault, *Remarks on Marx: Conversations with Duccio Trombadori*, tr. R. James Goldstein and James Cascaito (New York: Semiotext(e), 1991), pp. 167–72. On the nature of modern government, see Michel Foucault, "Governmentality," in *The Foucault Effect: Studies in Governmentality*, ed. Graham Burchell, Colin Gordon, and Peter Miller (Chicago: University of Chicago Press, 1991), pp. 87–104. On Foucault's life and political involvements, see Didier Eribon, *Michel Foucault*, tr. Betsy Wing (Cambridge, MA: Harvard University Press, 1991).

2   Sheldon S. Wolin, "On the Theory and Practice of Power," in *After Foucault: Humanistic Knowledge, Postmodern Challenges*, ed. Jonathan Arac (New Brunswick, NJ: Rutgers University Press, 1988), pp. 190–1. For a similar complaint, see Michael Walzer, "The Politics of Michel Foucault," in *Foucault: A Critical Reader*, ed. David Couzens Hoy (Oxford: Blackwell, 1986), p. 63.

3   For helpful characterizations of this transition, see Walzer, "Politics of Michel Foucault," pp. 54, 59; Hubert L. Dreyfus and Paul Rabinow, *Michel Foucault: Beyond Structuralism and Hermeneutics*, 2nd edn (Chicago: University of Chicago Press, 1983), ch. 6; Nancy Fraser, *Unruly Practices: Power, Discourse, and Gender in Contemporary Social Theory* (Minneapolis, MN: University of Minnesota Press, 1989), ch. 1.

4   Leading ideas of Michel Foucault found in *Discipline and Punish: The Birth of the Prison*, tr. Alan Sheridan (New York: Pantheon, 1977); and Foucault, *The History of Sexuality*, vol. 1: *An Introduction*, tr. Robert Hurley (New York: Random House, 1978).

5   "Two Lectures," in Michel Foucault, *Power/Knowledge: Selected Interviews and Other Writings, 1972–1977*, ed. Colin Gordon (New York: Pantheon, 1980), p. 104.

6   Foucault, *History of Sexuality*, vol. 1, p. 87; see also Foucault, "Two Lectures," p. 94.

7   Foucault, *History of Sexuality*, vol. 1, p. 87.

8   Ibid., p. 88.

9   Ibid., p. 89.

10   Ibid.

11   For more on the continuity between absolutist "police" and modern disdpline, see Foucault, "Governmentality," pp. 96, 101, 104. For a historical analysis of the *Polizeistaat*, see Marc Raeff, *The Well-Ordered Police State: Social and Institutional Change through Law in the Germanies and Russia, 1600–1800* (New Haven: Yale University Press, 1983).

12   Foucault, "Two Lectures," p. 104.

13   Foucault, *History of Sexuality*, vol. 1, p. 89.

14   Foucault, "Two Lectures," p. 96.

15   Ibid., p. 105. More along these lines in Foucault, "Governmentality."

16   Foucault, "Two Lectures," p. 106.

17   Ibid., p. 107.

18   On Foucault's contradictory critique of liberal politics and the question of his own value system, see Fraser, *Unruly Practices*, chs 1–3.

[19] Foucault, "Two Lectures," pp. 107–8.

[20] To complicate matters further, Foucault on occasion spoke as though power could be "limited" and liberty protected (though of course not guaranteed) only within the framework of the law; see passages from "Inutile de se soulever?," *Le Monde* (May 11, 1979), quoted in Colin Gordon, "Governmental Rationality: An Introduction," *The Foucault Effect*, pp. 47–8.

[21] This is Leon Trotsky's term to describe how "backward" countries might skip over stages traversed by advanced nations in order to arrive at the socialist goal without enduring the requisite intervening development. It implies the coexistence of elements associated with separate time periods in the Western sequence.

[22] B. Kistiakovskii, "V zashchitu prava (Intelligentsiia i pravosoznanie)," in *Vekhi: Sbornik statei o russkoi intelligentsii*, 2nd edn (Moscow, 1909), p. 130.

[23] Fraser, *Unruly Practices*, argues that Foucault's judgment against both law and discipline ultimately relies on the humanistic (indeed, liberal) values of autonomy, dignity, and rights that he professed to reject as elements of the power regime he criticized. If one accepts her view, then my argument is closer to Foucault's position (or at least to some elements in his often contradictory exposition) than I have been suggesting.

[24] On the judicial reforms of 1864, see Richard S. Wortman, *The Development of a Russian Legal Consciousness* (Chicago: University of Chicago Press, 1976); on the impact of the new institutions and the strength of the post-Reform legal ethos, see Jörg Baberowski, "Das Justizwesen im späten Zarenreich 1864–1914: Zum Problem von Rechtsstaatlichkeit, politischer Justiz und Rückständigkeit in Russland," *Zeitschrift für neuere Rechtsgeschichte*, 3–4 (1991), pp. 156–72 (my thanks to Richard Wortman for this reference); on the liberalism of legal reformers, see William G. Wagner, "The Trojan Mare: Women's Rights and Civil Rights in Late Imperial Russia," in *Civil Rights in Imperial Russia*, ed. Olga Crisp and Linda Edmondson (Oxford: Oxford University Press, 1989). On the pro-law intellectual tradition among Russian liberals, see Andrzej Walicki, *Legal Philosophies of Russian Liberalism* (Oxford: Oxford University Press, 1987).

[25] See complaints in the introduction to Ludwig Heinrich von Jakob, *Entwuff eines Criminal-Gesetzbuches für das russische Reich: Mit Anmerkungen über die bestehenden russischen Criminalgesetze; Nebst einem Anhange, welcher enthält: kritische Bemerkungen über den von der Gesetzgebungs-Commission zu St Petersburg herausgegebenen Criminal-Codex* (Halle, 1818).

[26] V. D. Spasovich, quoted in N. S. Tagantsev, *Russkoe ugolovnoe pravo: Lektsii*, 2nd edn, rev. (St Petersburg, 1902), p. 222.

[27] See D. N. Bludov, "Obshchaia ob"iasnitel'naia zapiska," in *Proekt ulozheniia o nakazaniiakh ugolovnykh i ispravitel'nykh, vnesennyi v 1844 godu v Gosudarstvennyi Sovet, s podrobnym oznacheniem osnovanii kazhdogo iz vnesennykh v sei proekt postanovlenii* (St Petersburg, 1871), pp. viii, xxx–xxxiv. All eighteenth- and nineteenth-century lawmakers in Russia and the West borrowed from each other's laws. The vector of influence usually pointed from west to east, but the Russian draft criminal code of 1903 was cited by European authorities as a

model of contemporary jurisprudence. See N. S. Timasheff, "The Impact of the Penal Law of Imperial Russia on Soviet Penal Law," *American Slavic and East European Review*, 10 (1953), p. 443.

28 Kistiakovskii, "V zashchitu prava," pp. 125, 132, 135, 137. On Kistiakovskii and *Vekhi*, see Walicki, *Legal Philosophies*, pp. 374–403.

29 Kistiakovskii, "V zashchitu prava," pp. 137, 144. On Marxist attitudes toward legality, see Walicki, *Legal Philosophies*, pp. 82–104.

30 Kistiakovskii, "V zashchitu prava," p. 144.

31 Ibid., p. 148.

32 See Reginald E. Zelnik, "The Russian Working Class in Comparative Perspective, 1870–1914," paper presented at the Conference on Germany and Russia in the Twentieth Century, Philadelphia, September 19–22, 1991; and Nancy Mandelker Frieden, *Russian Physicians in an Era of Reform and Revolution, 1856–1905* (Princeton, NJ: Princeton University Press, 1981).

33 See the argument in John F. Hutchinson, *Politics and Public Health in Revolutionary Russia, 1890–1918* (Baltimore, Md: Johns Hopkins University Press, 1990), and Hutchinson, " 'Who Killed Cock Robin?': An Inquiry into the Death of Zemstvo Medicine," in *Health and Society in Revolutionary Russia*, ed. Susan Gross Solomon and John F. Hutchinson (Bloomington, IN: Indiana University Press, 1990).

34 I take my distance here from two opposing interpretations of the relationship between the tsarist and Soviet regimes. Richard Pipes has argued that the Bolshevik state perpetuated the repressive characteristics of the late autocracy: see, for example, his *Legalised Lawlessness: Soviet Revolutionary Justice* (London: Institute for European Defence and Strategic Studies, 1986) (my thanks to Natalie Zemon Davis for this reference). Jörg Baberowski counters by arguing that tsarism was "well on the way" to a *Rechtsstaat* when the Revolution interrupted this development and eliminated the progressive legal personnel responsible for the change: "Das Justizwesen," pp. 158, 162, 170. While I agree with Pipes that the Soviet system reflected certain institutional and cultural continuities with the tsarist one and that Soviet pretensions to legality were hollow, I see the autocracy as less monolithic than he does, though not as deeply transformed as Baberowski maintains it was.

35 This point emerges in John F. Hutchinson's study of the origins of Soviet medicine. On the Stalinist period, see Kendall E. Bailes, *Technology and Society under Lenin and Stalin: Origins of the Soviet Technical Intelligentsia, 1917–1941* (Princeton, NJ: Princeton University Press, 1978).

36 On the articulated hostility to the law in the 1920s, in preference for technical administration, see Robert Sharlet, "Pashukanis and the Withering Away of the Law in the USSR," in *Cultural Revolution in Russia, 1928–1931*, ed. Sheila Fitzpatrick (Bloomington, IN: Indiana University Press, 1978), pp. 176–80.

37 On the appropriation of law in the service of the new regime, see Eugene Huskey, *Russian Lawyers and the Soviet State: The Origins and Development of the Soviet Bar, 1917–1939* (Princeton, NJ: Princeton University Press, 1986).

38 See Peter H. Solomon, Jr, "Soviet Penal Policy, 1917–1934: A Reinterpre-

tation," *Slavic Review*, 39 (1980), pp. 200–3. Elsewhere, Solomon has argued that the Soviet legal system at first encompassed a range of infractions formerly processed by administrative procedure under tsarist rule and only in 1925, as a response to overloading in the courts, diverted many petty cases to non-judicial institutions; "Criminalization and Decriminalization in Soviet Criminal Policy, 1917–1941," *Law and Society Review*, 16 (1981–2), pp. 10, 13. The operation of the administrative alternative was so arbitrary and ineffective, however, that the relevant (petty) crimes were reassigned to the regular courts in the late 1930s; ibid., pp. 26–7, 35–7. But even before 1925, when all crime was in principle handled by the regular courts, the political police ran its own (administrative) penal system for serious transgressions: Solomon, "Soviet Penal Policy," pp. 197, 200–1. In 1936, the regime reasserted the importance of the law as an instrument of governance, rejecting the prevalent hostility to the formal aspects of the law (see Sharlet, "Pashukanis," p. 187), but this shift did not mean that "bourgeois" notions of legality (due process, equality before the law, fair and consistent punishment) were adopted or that recourse to administrative repression was abandoned.

39 G. R., "Protsessy gomoseksualistov," *Ezhenedel'nik sovetskoi iustitsii*, 33 (1922), pp. 16–17.

40 See Laura Engelstein, *The Keys to Happiness: Sex and the Search for Modernity in Fin-de-Siècle Russia* (Ithaca, NY: Cornell University Press, 1992), ch. 2; also Engelstein, "Soviet Policy Toward Male Homosexuality: Its Origins and Historical Roots," *Journal of Homosexuality* 25, 3–4 (1994).

41 See Eric Naiman, "The Case of Chubarov Alley: Collective Rape, Utopian Desire, and the Mentality of NEP," *Russian History*, 17 (1990), p. 7.

42 Indeed, as reliance on legality weakened, psychiatry assumed a more central role in Soviet legal proceedings; Sharlet, "Pashukanis," p. 179.

43 See Engelstein, "Soviet Policy toward Male Homosexuality."

44 For the issues in the debate, see *Otchet desiatogo obshchego sobraniia russkoi gruppy mezhdunarodnogo soiuza kriminalistov, 13–16 fevralia 1914 g. v Petrograde* (Petrograd, 1916); for further documentation and discussion, see Laura Engelstein, "Abortion and the Civic Order: The Legal and Medical Debates, 1911–1914," in *Russia's Women: Accommodation, Resistance, Transformation*, ed. Barbara Alpern Engel, Barbara Evans Clements, and Christine D. Worobec (Berkeley: University of California Press, 1991).

45 On abortion in the 1920s, see Wendy Goldman, "Women, Abortion, and the State, 1917–36," in *Russia's Women*; also Susan Gross Solomon, "The Demographic Argument in Soviet Debates over the Legalization of Abortion in the 1920s," *Cahiers du monde russe et soviétique*, 33 (1992), pp. 59–82. As in the case of Bekhterev, continuity was provided on a personal as well as ideological level. M. N. Gernet, who articulated the middle, "disciplinary" position in the pre-war debates, survived into the Soviet period as a distinguished legal sociologist.

46 Quoted in Goldman, "Women, Abortion, and the State," p. 265.

47 See Laura Engelstein, "Reply," *American Historical Review*, 98, 2 (1993), p. 380.
48 N. N. Bazhenov, *Psikhologiia i politika* (Moscow, 1906), p. 6.

CHAPTER 13 "PROBLEMATIZATION" AS A MODE OF READING HISTORY

1 Michel Foucault, "Le Souci de la vérité," *Magazine littéraire*, 207 (1984), p. 18.
2 *L'Impossible Prison: Recherches sur le système pénitentiaire au XIXe siècle*, ed. Michelle Perrot (Paris: Seuil, 1980), p. 47.
3 Michel Foucault, *Surveiller et punir: Naissance de la prison* (Paris: Gallimard, 1975), p. 35; quoted from *Discipline and Punish: The Birth of the Prison*, tr. Alan Sheridan (New York: Pantheon, 1977), p. 31.
4 Because historians do not undertake problematizations does not mean that they are content merely to describe and to construct no theories. Great historians in particular, such as Fernand Braudel, have a theory of history and of its meaning in the present, but this is not a problematization. It is possible to write history for the present (and this is perhaps what every historian does) without writing a history of the present.
5 Foucault, *Surveiller et punir*, p. 27; quoted from *Discipline and Punish*, p. 23.
6 Michel Foucault, *Histoire de la sexualité*, vol. 1: *La Volonté de savoir* (Paris: Gallimard, 1976), p. 30; quoted from the *History of Sexuality*, vol. 1: *An Introduction*, tr. Robert Hurley (New York: Vintage, 1980), p. 21.
7 *L'Impossible Prison*, ed. Perrot.
8 Ibid., p. 35.
9 Ibid., p. 32.
10 Erving Goffman, *Asylums: Essays on the Social Situation of Mental Patients and Other Inmates* (New York: Anchor Books, 1961).
11 J.-E.-D. Esquirol, "Mémoire sur l'isolement des aliénés," in *Des maladies mentales considérées sous les rapports médical, hygiénique et médico-légal* (Paris: Baillière, 1838), vol. 2, p. 413.
12 Quoted in the appendix of the first edition of Michel Foucault, *L'Histoire de la folie à l'âge classique* (Paris: Plon, 1961).
13 See Catherina Lis and Hugo Soly, *Poverty and Capitalism in Pre-Industrial Europe* (Hassocks: Harvester Press, 1979).
14 Cf., for example, Bronislaw Geremek, *La Potence ou la pitié*, French trans. (Paris: Gallimard, 1987).
15 [Translator's note: Here "protection" (French *protection rapprochée*) is used to refer to early community-based forms of social assistance, while "social protection" is used to designate the more abstract and centralized programs developed by the modern state.]
16 Preamble to the Royal Edict of 1657, reprinted in the first edition of Foucault, *L'Histoire de la folie*, p. 644.
17 Thus the following edict, in 1662, which orders the creation of an *hôpital général* in "all the cities and large towns of the Kingdom," reiterates the need for the confinement of domiciled beggars, but condemns vagrants to the galleys upon

their first arrest, that is, after they have twice refused the "charitable" offer of confinement in the *hôpital général*; see A.-J.-L. Jourdan, Decrusy, and F. Isambert, *Recueil général des anciennes lois de la France depuis l'an 420 jusqu'à la révolution de 1789*, 29 vols (Paris: Berlin-le-Prieur, 1821–33), vol. 18, p. 18.

[18] The phrase comes from the reporter of the law of 1838 concerning the insane in the Chamber of Peers: "At the same time that the isolation of the insane protects the public from their delinquencies and their excesses, it presents the most powerful means of healing in the eyes of Science. A happy coincidence that combines the patient's advantage with the general good in the application of rigorous measures": Ministère de l'intérieur et des cultes, *Législation sur les aliénés et les enfants assistés* (Paris, 1880), vol. 2, p. 316.

[19] To cite the condemnation of a vagrant in the fifteenth century quoted by Bronislaw Geremek, "He deserved to die as one useless to the world, that is, to be hung like a thief"; see *Les Marginaux Parisiens aux XIVe et XVe siècles* (Paris: Flammarion, 1976), p. 310.

[20] The text from the order of Edward III is cited in C. J. Ribton-Turner, *History of Vagrants and Vagrancy, and Beggars and Begging* (1887; repr. Montclair, NJ: Patterson Smith, 1972), pp. 43–4.

[21] Robert Castel, *Les Metamorphoses de la question sociale* (forthcoming). The metaphor of metamorphosis is intended to translate this relationship between same and different, between past and novelty, which characterizes a problematization. The "social question" is the group of situations through which a society experiences the risk of its fragmentation and attempts to deny it – hence the question of vagrancy in pre-industrial societies, that of destitution in the early days of industrialization, or today's thematics of exclusion.

Index